THE MITTERRAND YEARS

First published in Great Britain 1998 by
MACMILLAN PRESS LTD
Houndmills, Basingstoke, Hampshire RG21 6XS and London
Companies and representatives throughout the world

A catalogue record for this book is available from the British Library.

ISBN 0–333–67167–8

 First published in the United States of America 1998 by
ST. MARTIN'S PRESS, INC.,
Scholarly and Reference Division,
175 Fifth Avenue, New York, N.Y. 10010

ISBN 0–312–21082–5

Library of Congress Cataloging-in-Publication Data
The Mitterrand years : legacy and evaluation / edited by Mairi
Maclean.
p.   cm.
"Origins of this volume lie in the 1996 Annual Conference of the
Association for the Study of Modern and Contemporary France ... held
at Royal Holloway, University of London, in September 1996"—Ack.
Includes bibliographical references and index.
ISBN 0–312–21082–5 (cloth)
1. Mitterrand, François, 1916–   —Influence—Congresses.
2. France—Politics and government—1981–1995—Congresses.
3. France—Cultural policy—Congresses.   4. Twenty first century–
–Forecasts—Congresses.   I. Maclean, Mairi, 1959–   .
II. Association for the Study of Modern and Contemporary France
(Great Britain). Conference (1996 : University of London)
DC423.M578 1997
944.083'9'092—dc21   97–13392
                                                              CIP

This book is printed on paper suitable for recycling and made from fully managed and
sustained forest sources.

10   9   8   7   6   5   4   3   2
07   06   05   04   03   02   01   00   99

Printed and bound in Great Britain by
Antony Rowe Ltd, Chippenham, Wiltshire

Contents

List of Tables

Acknowledgements

The origins of this volume lie in the 1996 Annual Conference of the Association for the Study of Modern and Contemporary France (ASMCF) on 'The Mitterrand Era in Perspective', held at Royal Holloway, University of London, in September 1996. I am grateful to all those who attended and contributed to the conference and helped to make it such a success – first and foremost our guest speakers from France, Serge Berstein, Elie Cohen, Eric Duhamel and Dominique David; and also Douglas Johnson, Honorary Vice-President of ASMCF, who opened and concluded the conference in his inimitable style. I would like to thank the Institut Français, especially René Lacombe, for supporting the conference by funding the travel of two of our guest speakers. British Airways kindly sponsored wine and sherry receptions at the conference. ASMCF provided a welcome subsidy towards the cost of translating the four chapters by our visiting French speakers. I am grateful to the Research Committee of the Royal Holloway School of Management for financing the remainder. The translation was carried out most elegantly by Janet Fraser of the University of Westminster, and I would like to thank her for working so speedily. Thanks are due to the ASMCF Committee, especially Alec Hargreaves, for their many useful suggestions. Eric Cahm helped to design the jacket cover. Staff at the School of Management are also deserving of thanks, in particular Marianne Bowyer, for her unstinting efforts before and during the conference; June Bottomley made a sterling job of running the Book Display; and Denise Elliott organized nursing care for the late Brian Darling, who gallantly attended the conference despite illness. (The poignant moment, when our late friend and colleague Peter Morris held the microphone for Brian, ASMCF secretary over 15 years, so that he might make a toast to France, will stay in the mind of ASMCF members and conference delegates for many years to come. Both are sadly missed.) Thanks are due to Tim Farmiloe of Macmillan for his kind assistance in the production of this volume. I wish also to thank my husband Charles Harvey, Director of the School of Management, for all his help during the conference, and my children Emily and Alex for their good humour and patience. Finally, a special word is reserved for Rebecca, who, at eight months, attended part of the conference as its youngest delegate.

MAIRI MACLEAN

List of Abbreviations

CNPG	Centre National des Prisonniers de Guerre
CEA	Centres d'Entr'aide [aux Prisonniers de Guerre]
CERES	Centre d'Etudes et de Recherches Socialistes
CES	Contrats Emploi-Solidarité
CFDT	Confédération Française Démocratique du Travail
CFE	Confédération Française de l'Encadrement
CFTC	Confédération Française des Travailleurs Chrétiens
CGC	Confédération Générale des Cadres
CGT	Confédération Générale du Travail
CIR	Convention des Institutions Républicaines
CNCL	Commission Nationale de la Communication et des Libertés
CNPF	Conseil National du Patronat Français
CNR	Conseil National de la Résistance
COREPER	Committee of Permanent Representatives
CSA	Conseil Supérieur de l'Audiovisuel
CSCE	Conference on Security and Co-operation in Europe
CSG	Contribution Sociale Généralisée
ECB	European Central Bank
EC	European Community
ECOFIN	Council of Economic and Finance Ministers
ECU	European Currency Unit
EMS	European Monetary System
EMU	European Monetary Union
ENA	Ecole Nationale d'Administration
ERM	Exchange Rate Mechanism
ESPRIT	European Strategic Programme for Research and Development in Information Technology
ESSEC	Ecole Supérieure des Sciences Economiques et Commerciales
EU	European Union
EUREKA	European Research Co-ordinating Agency
FACEA	Fédération Autonome des Centres d'Entre'aide
FAR	Forces d'Action Rapide
FEN	Fédération de l'Education Nationale

FNSEA	Fédération National des Syndicats des Exploitants Agricoles
FO	Force Ouvrière
GATT	General Agreement on Tariffs and Trade
GPALS	Global Protection Against Limited Strikes
GRECE	Groupe de Recherche et d'Etude pour la Civilisation Européenne
HEC	Ecole des Hautes Etudes Commerciales
IGC	Intergovernmental Conference
IMF	International Monetary Fund
INF	Intermediate Nuclear Forces
ISF	Impôt de Solidarité sur la Fortune
JALB	Jeunes Arabes de Lyon et sa Banlieue
LICRA	Ligue Internationale contre le Racisme et l'Anti-Sémitisme
MNPGD	Mouvement National des Prisonniers de Guerre et Déportés
MRAP	Mouvement contre le Racisme et l'Anti-Sémitisme et pour l'Amitié entre les Peuples
MRPGD	Mouvement de Résistance des Prisonniers de Guerre et Déportés
MUR	Mouvements Unis de la Résistance
NATO	North Atlantic Treaty Organization
NRJ	Nouvelle Radio Jeune
OECD	Organization for Economic Co-operation and Development
ORA	Organisation de la Résistance de l'Armée
ORTF	Organisation de Radiodiffusion-Télévision Française
OUA	Organisation de l'Unité Africaine
PCF	Parti Communiste Français
PLO	Palestinian Liberation Organization
PME	Petites et Moyennes Entreprises
PS	Parti Socialiste
PSU	Parti Socialiste Unifié
RAI	Radiotelevisione Italiana
RGR	Rassemblement des Gauches Républicaines
RMI	Revenu Minimum d'Insertion
RNPG	Rassemblement National des Prisonniers de Guerre
RPF	Rassemblement du Peuple Français
RPR	Rassemblement pour la République
SDI	Strategic Defence Initiative

SEA	Single European Act
SFIO	Section Française de l'Internationale Ouvrière
SGCI	Secrétariat Général du Comité Interministériel
SME	Small and Medium Enterprise
SMIC	Salaire Minimum Interprofessionnel de Croissance
SNCF	Société Nationale des Chemins de Fer
TDF1	Télédiffusion de France 1
TEU	Treaty on European Union
TUC	Travaux d'Utilité Collective
UDF	Union Démocratique Française
UDSR	Union Démocratique et Socialiste de la Résistance
UN	United Nations
WEU	Western European Union

Notes on the Contributors

Guy Austin is Lecturer in French at the University of Sheffield, where he specializes in French film. His book *Contemporary French Cinema: an Introduction* has recently been published by MUP.

David Bell is Head of the Department of Politics at the University of Leeds and is author of numerous articles and commentaries on French politics, including (with Byron Criddle) *The French Socialist Party* (Oxford: OUP, 1994), the third edition of which is to be published in 1998.

Serge Berstein is Professor at the Institut d'Etudes Politiques in Paris. His many books on political parties, political culture and ideas include *Le Modèle républicain* (PUF, 1992) and *La France de l'expansion* in two volumes (Seuil, 1989, 1994), the first of which has been translated into English (by Peter Morris) as *The Republic of de Gaulle 1958–1969* (CUP/Maison des Sciences de l'Homme, 1993).

Eric Cahm has been Lecturer in Contemporary History at the University of Tours since 1991, having previously been Head of the School of Languages and Area Studies and Professor of French Studies at the then Portsmouth Polytechnic and Visiting Professor at Tours. He is Executive Editor of the journal *Modern and Contemporary France*. His publications include *The Dreyfus Affair in French Society and Politics* (Longman, 1996).

Elie Cohen is Director of Research at the Centre National de Recherche Scientifique (CNRS) in Paris, and author of *La Tentation hexagonale: la souveraineté à l'épreuve de la mondialisation* (Fayard, 1996).

Alistair Cole is in the European Studies Department at the University of Bradford. Recent publications include a second edition of *François Mitterrand: a Study in Political Leadership* (Routledge, 1997) and *French Politics and Society* (Prentice Hall, 1997).

Martyn Cornick is Senior Lecturer in the Department of French Studies at Birmingham University, and is an Editor of *Modern and Contemporary France*. He has published widely on French intellectual history and aspects of Franco-British perceptions.

Dominique David is Special Advisor to the Director of the Institut Français des Relations Internationales (IFRI) in Paris. He is Professor at the Ecole Spéciale Militaire de Saint-Cyr and Lecturer at the Sorbonne. His publications include various books, in particular *Conflits, puissances et stratégies en Europe* (1992).

Marion Demossier is Lecturer in French in the School of European Studies and Modern Languages at the University of Bath. She is the author of *L'Homme et le vin, une anthropologie du vignoble bourguignon* (Presses Universitaires de Dijon, 1997).

Eric Duhamel is Lecturer in Contemporary French History at the Université de Paris X – Nanterre and at the Institut des Etudes Politiques in Paris. His various publications, notably on the Union Démocratique et Sociale de la Résistance, include (with G. Le Béguec) *La Reconstruction du Parti radical, 1944–1948* (L'Harmattan, 1993).

Kenneth Dyson is Professor of European Studies at the University of Bradford and co-director of the European Briefing Unit. His most recent publications include *Elusive Union: The Process of Economic and Monetary Union in Europe* (Longman, 1994) and (with W. Homolka) *Culture First: Promoting Standards in the Age of New Media* (Cassell, 1996).

Kevin Featherstone is Professor of European Political Studies at the University of Bradford and Jean Monnet chair holder. His most recent publications include (with R. Ginsberg) *The United States and the European Union in the 1990s* (Macmillan, 1994) and (with K. Ifantis), *Greece in a Changing Europe* (MUP, 1996).

Peter Fysh is Senior Lecturer in French, Nottingham Trent University. His publications include chapters and articles on French politics and political thought and he is currently working on a major study of the politics of racism in France.

Jack Hayward is the Director of the Centre for European Politics, Economics and Society and Professorial Fellow of St. Antony's College Oxford. Recent edited works include *Industrial Enterprise and European Integration* (OUP, 1995) and *Elitism, Populism and European Politics* (OUP, 1996).

Raymond Kuhn is Senior Lecturer in the Department of Political Studies and Dean of the Faculty of Arts at Queen Mary and Westfield College, University of London. He is author of various publications on the French media, including *The Media in France* (Routledge, 1995).

Mairi Maclean is Senior Lecturer in European Business at Royal Holloway, University of London. She has published widely in the field of French business. Publications include (with J. Howorth) *Europeans on Europe: Transnational Visions of a New Continent* (Macmillan, 1992). She is currently preparing a book entitled *France and National Competitiveness*.

Susan Milner is Senior Lecturer in European Studies at the University of Bath. She has published widely on French trade unions and industrial relations. Recent publications include (with R. Mouriaux), 'The politics of radical unemployment policies in France', in H. Compston (ed.), *The New Politics of Unemployment in Europe* (Routledge, 1996).

Siân Reynolds is Professor of French at the University of Stirling. She is also President of the Association for the Study of Modern and Contemporary France. Her most recent book is *France between the Wars: Gender and Politics* (Routledge, 1996).

Joseph Szarka is Senior Lecturer in French Studies at the University of Bath. His research interests are in economic and environmental policy-making, and electoral politics in France. His publications include *Business in France* (Pitman, 1992), and 'The winning of the 1995 French presidential election', *West European Politics*, Vol. 19, No. 1, January 1996.

Henrik Uterwedde is Deputy Director of the Deutsch-Französisches Institut in Ludwigsburg, and co-editor of the *Frankreich-Jahrbuch*. His many books on French economic and social policy include (with R. Lasserre & J. Schild) *Frankreich. Politik, Wirkschaft, Gesellshaft* (Leske & Budrich, 1997).

Introduction: The Mitterrand Era in Perspective

Mairi Maclean

'There is not a Frenchman whom I have not touched'. (Napoléon)

'Nothing can be done without great men, and great men are great for having wanted to be so'.   (de Gaulle)

A MAN OF HIS TIME AND THE END OF AN ERA

When, on 17 May 1995, François Maurice-Marie Mitterrand ceded his presidential mandate to his long-standing political opponent and one-time prime minister, Jacques Chirac, it marked the end of an era: one which had emerged as significantly different from that which had been originally envisaged on 10 May 1981, the date of Mitterrand's election to the presidency and the symbolic triumph of the left, consolidated at the legislative elections held in June.

The longest-serving French president of the Fifth Republic, with two presidential victories to his name and fourteen years at the helm, Mitterrand ranks only with de Gaulle, and possibly Clémenceau, as one of the greatest French statesmen of the twentieth century. But while de Gaulle and Clémenceau had war to bring them to glory, Mitterrand had to battle to distinguish himself against the much more humdrum backdrop of peace: an altogether more hazardous experience for a national leader, as the example of Churchill illustrates, honoured as a war hero but defeated at the ballot box once peace was restored.

Nor for Mitterrand the political rewards of continuous economic prosperity, such as had graced de Gaulle and Pompidou during the 'Thirty Glorious Years' following the end of war. If, throughout his two terms as president, France's economy continued to grow stronger, aided by full-scale modernization in almost all domains – business and industry, the stock exchange, the media, and Europe in particular –

public perceptions, distorted perhaps by all-too-high expectations
fostered by France's post-war economic success, were nevertheless
dominated by recession, and its unwanted companions, restructuring
and rising unemployment.

Yet perhaps the more fitting date to mark the end of the Mitterrand
era is not in fact 17 May 1995 but rather 8 January 1996, when the
former president passed away in his Paris apartment. For the life of
Mitterrand, like a tree whose rings bear the stamp of the passing of
the years (Mitterrand's experience as a soldier in the Second World
War left him quite literally with shrapnel lodged in his shoulder),
embraces and epitomizes the history of contemporary France in all
its singularity, its convolutions and complexities, in a way subsequent
presidents of France are unlikely to be able to emulate. Born in 1916,
when France and Europe were in the throes of the First World War,
Mitterrand was called up to fight in the Second in 1939, was wounded
and taken prisoner in 1940, and escaped in 1941 on his third attempt.
He experienced at first hand not only the highs of the Resistance and
the Liberation but also the lows of Vichy and the Occupation
(although Mitterrand never condemned his own Vichy past). He not
only met de Gaulle in December 1943, but claims to have told the
General that he was *mortel*,[1] and in 1965, to the latter's indignation,
was to take him to an unexpected second round in the first
presidential elections by universal suffrage. He personally witnessed
the grisly revelations of the concentration camps, being present (on de
Gaulle's invitation) at the liberation of Dachau and Landsberg.[2] As
many as eleven times in as many years he served as a minister in the
Fourth Republic (1946–1958), remembered for its weakness and
corruption under governments of both right and left. His portfolios
included that of minister of overseas territories (1950–1951), minister
of the interior (1954–1955) and minister of justice (1956–1957). As the
winds of change brought a thaw to the Europe of the Cold War,
which had been artificially riven asunder and kept on ice since Yalta,
Mitterand became a privileged observer, and participant, in the
collapse of communism in the late 1980s. Having endured the horrors
of a Europe torn apart by war – as a soldier, prisoner-of-war, escapee
and Resistance fighter – he was to go a long way towards realizing his
vision of a strong, united (but never, he claimed, federal) European
Community, at the centre of which was an ever closer union between
France and Germany. During the Mitterrand presidency, the
Community grew from an essentially economic to an increasingly
political entity, galvanized both by the single market project and the

Treaty on European Union (TEU), each bearing the stamp of Mitterrand upon it.

It is extraordinary that one man should have had so many encounters with History. Some may say that this was due to Mitterrand's regular re-invention of himself – in stark contrast to de Gaulle, characterized by an unswerving constancy and very much a nineteenth-century man.[3] In the eyes of many, Mitterrand's ambition was master of his identity, which was constantly fashioned anew as the need arose, earning him the reputation of a sly old fox, an artful manoeuvrer: 'the Florentine'. His various reinventions of himself included that of the student with right-wing, even nationalist tendencies; the Vichyist and Pétainist; the Resistance figure who launched his political career in the Union Démocratique et Socialiste de la Résistance (UDSR); the defender of French Algeria; the unifier of the left and heir to the inheritance of Jaurès and Blum; the President of all the French, above the mêlée of party politics, wise and serene; and the architect of European union – each of these personae, according to Régis Debray, being surrounded by its own support cast: an 'unholy alliance' of 'Croix-de-Feu, Pétainists, Giraudists, Gaullists, third force, anti-communists, authoritarian anti-capitalists, indulgent liberals and Europhiles'.[4] Mitterrand offers as an explanation for his frequent brushes with destiny the fact that he was, by temperament, never a follower: 'History [. . .] is confrontation and the affirmation of self'[5] – doubtless a valid point, but one which goes only part of the way towards explaining the scale and scope of his achievements.

It is also said that Mitterrand's ambition determined his convictions, seemingly perpetually unstable and able to shift pragmatically as necessity demanded: 'In politics it is the event which commands', he claimed.[6] But in one conviction he did not falter, abolishing as a first presidential act the death penalty to which he had long been opposed, thus ending France's bloody relationship with the guillotine which had endured almost two hundred years.

A kinder judgement, albeit open to the charge of special pleading, might be to suggest that, very much a man of his century, Mitterrand incarnated, in particular, the manifold complexity of that century; that a purist, black-and-white response is inappropriate in a world now more than ever dominated, as Mitterrand himself maintained, by ambiguity, requiring the flexibility to compromise and adapt rather than the intransigence to block and deny. There are times when Mitterrand's flexibility of perspective seemed to embrace a greater understanding (and forgiveness) of humanity. Thus, at Dachau,

witness to the execution of German soldiers, greeted with an understandable jubilation on the part of surviving inmates, Mitterrand
could not resist thinking that 'at the same time, somewhere in Germany, someone who loved them was praying and hoping'.[7] Just as
there are times when what the world exacts is, precisely, a black-and-
white response. Mitterrand's final official engagement in Berlin on the
occasion of the fiftieth anniversary of the end of the Second World
War is a case in point: his praise for the bravery of German soldiers
elicited tears from Chancellor Kohl – but a public outcry in France.[8]

Ultimately, Mitterrand's forte, and perhaps the reason for his political survival often against all the odds, was that he was not a catalyst
for change, nor a visionary, nor, principally, an initiator, but rather a
midwife and companion to far-reaching and relentless change. Mitterrand's strong sense of personal destiny doubtless contributed to his
success at a time of enormous upheaval. At the same time, the French,
perhaps, accepted contradictions in President Mitterrand because
these were their own contradictions. Mitterrand held up a mirror to
France, reflecting its tension between wartime collaboration and
resistance, its need for greatness and prestige on the one hand and
sheer survival on the other, its double standards and *non-dit*, its
tolerance of petty corruption amongst its elites – and said, like Gus-
tave Flaubert of Madame Bovary, 'I am you'.

By the end, Mitterrand's life had turned in many respects full circle.
From Jarnac to Jarnac. From defeat by the Germans to reconciliation
with the Germans: with Helmut Kohl in particular he forged a special
tie. From Catholicism through agnosticism to a professed belief in
'spiritual forces'.[9] From provincial conservatism in his youth to idealistic socialism in opposition to the altogether different and more
realistic socialism-in-power (or Mitterrandism) from 1983. The last
two years of Mitterrand's life were marked by a personal, almost
Proustian coming-to-terms with the past, including its most difficult
aspects. These were now publicly acknowledged: his youthful flirtation with right-wing nationalism; his admiration for Pétain (shared by
many French prisoners-of-war and their families) and participation in
the Vichy regime as a minor official, for which he earned the regime's
highest award, the *francisque*; his friendship with Vichy's chief-of-
police René Bousquet, despite the latter's undisputed involvement in
the Vélodrome d'Hiver deportations; his longstanding mistress and
his illegitimate daughter, Mazarine, who joined Mitterrand's family at
his funeral, united before death and the world. The introduction of
Mazarine, an attractive young student, sparked a fascination on the

part of public and paparazzi to which France, with its tolerance of adultery and its acceptance of the demarcation of public and private life, was unused. One year after her father's death, media interest in Mazarine had not abated, her relationship with Danielle Mitterrand arousing especial interest.[10]

Having scorned in opposition the institutions of the Fifth Republic as created by de Gaulle, decried as a permanent *coup d'Etat*, Mitterrand came to appreciate these in his turn at the Elysée. The promised reduction of the presidential mandate and power never materialized; on the contrary, Mitterrand visibly enjoyed the trappings of his quasi-monarchical role to the full. The simplicity of Mitterrand's funeral in his birthplace of Jarnac in south-west France, with only family and close friends present while world leaders gathered at Notre Dame, is again evocative of the burial of de Gaulle at Colombey-les-Deux-Eglises, bereft of pomp and ceremony, and conducted in total silence.

It is a neat irony that for the man who spent many years cultivating the image of the 'anti-de Gaulle', there should ultimately be no other real point of comparison. Pompidou and Giscard are bypassed; Mitterrand is de Gaulle's real successor. His memory is likely to prove as lasting as the General's, albeit for different reasons. Above all, Mitterrand will be remembered for modernizing France (whose entry into the twentieth century did not pre-date the end of the Second World War) in preparation for the new millennium.

The purpose of this book is not to write another biography of Mitterrand,[11] however tempting this might be in the wake of Mitterrand's death and the re-evaluation of his life which followed the 'revelations' of September 1994 in particular. Rather, it seeks to take a considered look at the Mitterrand presidency as a whole, its place in French history, and the trends for the twenty-first century emerging under Chirac. The fourteen years during which François Mitterrand was at the helm were profoundly formative, ushering in fundamental change in many different domains, as France faced up to new givens in an increasingly interdependent and uncertain world in which full employment was confined to history, and the boundaries of Eastern Europe disintegrated. Given this widespread change – given, too, Mitterrand's distinction as the longest-serving French president – it is appropriate to describe these years as an 'era'.[12] This study aims to evaluate the impact and legacy of the Mitterrand years in the following key areas: the state; socialism; Europe and foreign affairs; business, the economy, and industrial relations; French society, looking both at women in public life and anti-racism on the part of immigrant-origin French citizens; and culture, examining the *grands projets*, cinema, the media, and intellectualism.

If the essence of a man may be gleaned through his actions, through the 'monuments', tangible and intangible, the metaphorical *grands travaux* he leaves behind him, then it may be possible to apprehend something of Mitterrand the man circuitously by exploring the impact of his presidency on the areas listed above. This is not, however, our primary purpose; but we do make a nostalgic foray down that particular road in the section on History and Biography. Eric Duhamel analyses the psychodrama of the 'revelations' of September 1994, which turned the spotlight on Mitterrand's past under the Vichy regime, throwing into sharp relief the paradox of Mitterrand as both the first socialist president to be elected by universal suffrage and a diehard supporter of Pétain, as depicted on the front cover of Pierre Péan's explosive book, *Une Jeunesse française: François Mitterrand 1934–1947*.[13] Marion Demossier explores the central role of a personal fief in Mitterrand's political career. The Nièvre, or more precisely the region of the Morvan in south-west France, served at once as a launching-pad for his career in the capital and as an invaluable sounding-board for a wide range of official speeches and political writings pertaining to the essential France of the provinces. The last of our biographical chapters focuses on Mitterrand as political leader, as Alistair Cole assesses the Mitterrand heritage. Cole puts forward the view that Mitterrand is unlikely to be remembered as a great socialist hero, akin to Jaurès or Blum, at whose tombs he laid a symbolic rose on the day of his inauguration as president, despite being significantly more successful than either. The memory of shared victories and a particular type of party organization apart, the Mitterrand heritage is ultimately a more *general* one, being legated to left and right simultaneously.

Yet there is an obvious sense in which the two aspects – the man and his achievements – cannot but be inextricably linked. Study of the latter is therefore also, if not first and foremost, a legitimate route to apprehend the former.

Finally, this book is intended as a 'landmark' to commemorate what can justly be seen as the passing of an era. At the same time, it provides a summation of the France Mitterrand leaves behind, focusing on the trends emerging in the above areas as the twenty-first century beckons.

SOCIALISM AND THE STATE

'De Gaulle is France, Mitterrand is the Republic', wrote Alain Duhamel to Mitterrand's delight, honoured to be viewed in this way.[14] A paradoxical association, since it was not always so: the institutions of the Fifth Republic were vitriolized by Mitterrand in 1964 in his short treatise *Le Coup d'Etat permanent*.[15] The Constitution of 1958, he wrote, was tantamount to dictatorship, and tolled the knell of democracy: 'the representative regime is dead and gone, a dictatorship is born, to be passed on to an heir elected by universal suffrage'.[16] Pompidou was later accused of cultivating the same 'regime of personal power' as de Gaulle; he retaliated by charging Mitterrand in his turn with being 'fundamentally loyal to the conception of the Fourth Republic'.[17] Mitterrand admittedly modified his stance in 1969, when he claimed to have voted against the Constitution of 1958 more because of its *context* (the return of de Gaulle amid the Algerian crisis) than because of its *text*.[18] But it is nevertheless the case that the text which formed the basis of Mitterrand's electoral programme in 1981, the '110 proposals', included the reduction of the presidential mandate (to five years, renewable once, or seven years, non renewable), a pledge which Mitterrand, over fourteen years, singularly failed to deliver. His oft-cited formula, 'The institutions of the Fifth Republic were dangerous before my tenure of office, and will be so again when I have gone',[19] contains an implicit acceptance of existing institutions as they are, an admission that significant reform is off the agenda, together with the depiction of himself as a safe pair of hands, impervious to the creeping corruption of absolute power to which his successors are deemed susceptible. Altogether, the institutions of the Fifth Republic suited their 'anti-Gaullist' heir very nicely. Love of office undoubtedly played its part in this reversal of policy.

And yet some significant institutional change did occur, ushered in by the processes of decentralization on the one hand and European integration on the other. Their combined effect was to dilute the power of the centre, much of it flowing to Brussels, some of it filtering to the regions. The 1982 Defferre decentralization reforms remain one of the major reforms of the Mitterrand years, striking at the heart of the deep-rooted problem of 'Paris and the desert of the provinces', devolving resources and responsibilities away from the capital to the local authorities. Their impact was less than it might have been, since they did not seek to upset the domination of the politico-administrative system by traditional elites, inviting local elites instead to associate themselves consensually with the established administration.[20] Nevertheless, at a time when Britain was seeing the power of its local government structures severely curtailed by the Thatcher assault on local authorities, France was pursuing the opposite path, instilling an element of much-needed legitimacy and democracy into local politics.

Cohabitation, first with Jacques Chirac from 1986 to 1988, then with Edouard Balladur from 1993 to 1995, clipped the President's wings, fundamentally altering the balance of power between the Elysée and Matignon, despite Mitterrand's undeniable success at carving out for himself a 'reserved domain' of defence and foreign affairs. The President's regal style remained; but he was no longer able to impose his will as in the early days of his presidency. In 1981, Mitterrand was able to insist on a 39–hour working week, without consultation with the ministers concerned; in 1986, his refusal to approve the privatization bill (symbolically, on Bastille Day) delayed its passage by a mere three weeks. However, the need to fight his presidential corner in the power battle with Chirac in particular (his relations with Balladur being more cordial) prompted Mitterrand to hold fire on the reforms which he had once deemed imperative. To increase the authority of parliament at the expense of the Elysée at a time when parliament was hostile to him was not an error of judgement Mitterrand was likely to make.

In our opening section, 'Socialism and the State', Jack Hayward explores the relationship between *moins d'Etat* (reduced state intervention) and its oft-cited corollary, *mieux d'Etat* (improved efficiency and effectiveness). He suggests that the French responded to the neo-liberal challenge by a redefinition of the public sphere rather than a retreat from state intervention, the withdrawal from certain areas regarded as the more natural preserve of private interest being accompanied by a corresponding re-regulation of others, such as competition. Hayward points to the erosion of the belief in the indivisible public interest, separate from and superior to vying private interests. Following a plethora of scandal which erupted in the late 1980s and early 1990s, in which many key government figures were implicated, legitimacy came to be perceived as residing increasingly in private interest, while what was public fell under suspicion. (Mitterrand himself was not untainted by perceptions of the venality of public figures, despite his professed abhorrence of money: one of his closest friends, Patrice Pelat, was implicated in the 1988 Pechiney insider-dealing affair – Mitterrand was never to see him again – while the scandal sparked by his introduction of Mazarine was also fuelled by the fact that she and her mother had been furnished with protection and an appartment at state expense.) Hayward concludes that if the attempt to use the state as the spearhead of socio-economic policy was renounced during the Socialists' first term of office (1981–1986), it was above all the two periods of cohabitation which sealed its fate. The problem remains, however, that whereas the old statist norms, institutions and practices have been substantially discredited, new liberal alternatives have yet to acquire proper definition and acceptance in their stead.

In a complementary chapter, Elie Cohen considers whether the crucial turning-point of 1983 might not be viewed, in retrospect, not only as a break with the 'policy of rupture' of 1981, but more importantly, as a departure from the centralized economic model which had prevailed in France since just after the end of the Second World War. The deindexation of pay, the new focus on the firm, and the deregulation of the economy might all suggest this. But the opportunity, Cohen argues, was not taken. The left failed to negotiate economic, institutional and social change with other social actors, or even to put it to the test of political debate,[21] choosing instead to draw on the traditional sources of its power to implement an authoritarian modernization. The refusal of the Socialist government to debate change and implement it incrementally, thus promoting the transfer of power from the centre to the margins, meant that the rupture with Colbertism did not take place. On the contrary, the Socialist governments of the Mitterrand presidency conformed exactly to the model of authoritarian modernizing government which, intermittently with do-nothing governments, France has experienced since 1945. It is this which, in Cohen's eyes, explains the paradox of the left's achievements in power: its overriding success in pursuing liberal policies against a background of high unemployment, and its undeniable failure to achieve reform through the negotiation of compromise.

In the course of the Mitterrand presidency, the French political landscape nevertheless underwent significant change. The turning of the political kaleidoscope in 1983 was to change the left, in particular, almost beyond recognition.[22] Mitterrand's own Parti Socialiste (PS), finally in power, shed its Communist partner without which it would not have been elected, and assumed the colours of the right. As the star of the Parti Communiste Français (PCF) was largely – although not entirely – eclipsed, that of the Front National (FN) was firmly in the ascendant: circumstances to which Mitterrand himself contributed through the introduction of proportional representation. Decimated in the legislative elections of March 1993, routed still further in the European elections of June 1994, torn apart by corruption, scandal, factional rivalries and errors of judgement, the future of the Socialist Party now hangs in the balance. Is there life after Mitterrand? In 1995 a resurrection seemed to be in the offing under Lionel Jospin, following his 'victorious defeat' in the presidential elections. On 1 June 1997 the incredible occurred, with the victory of the left wing alliance in the legislative elections, resulting in the appointment of Lionel Jospin as prime minister.

Our primary concern here is the left of the political divide, which Mitterrand had united in order to accede to office. An examination of the changing fortunes of all parties under Mitterrand is, admittedly, appealing. The right was not unaffected by Mitterrand's tenure of office. Many of Mitterrand's actions – first and foremost the 1992 Maastricht referendum – were specifically designed to divide the right. The Union Démocratique Française (UDF) receded into the background during his presidency, the rug pulled from under its feet as the left encroached on territory normally the preserve of the centre-right. Following the near wipe-out of the PS at the polls in March 1993, the Rassemblement pour la République (RPR) seemed to offer a stable anchor against tumultuous political waters. Yet it too has been riven by scandal, corruption and fratricide: Balladur stood against his long-standing 'friend' Chirac in the 1995 presidential elections, despite an earlier promise that he would not, thus splitting RPR loyalties – a laceration which has yet to heal fully. But such an analysis would be, of necessity, a separate study. Our purpose here is to examinate the evolution of the left, and the socialist left in particular, the unification of which was a necessary pre-condition of Mitterrand's victory in 1981, and to explore its potential for renewal in the post-Mitterrand era.

Serge Berstein suggests that the key to the regeneration of the left may lie in the renaissance of the Republican model. Focusing on the left's experiment with government, Berstein argues that its 1981 manifesto, based as it was on untested political aspirations, produced government failure and led in turn to a far-reaching crisis, without however throwing up any new political ideas. The resulting disarray has brought about a retreat of the socialist left into Republican values. The Republican model certainly draws on a strong historical tradition – but one which is founded on a number of consensus principles, blurring the distinction between left and right in an ambiguous Republic of the centre rather than offering a real form of identity for the left. Berstein therefore questions whether this withdrawal into the political culture of Republicanism – even that more militant view of Republican culture which affirms its faith in mankind, its support for non-denominationalism, its belief in social solidarity and state control over the economy – represents a valid identity for the French left in the closing years of the twentieth century. Ultimately, the Republican model is a useful palliative, but not a real identity such as the left will have to forge if it is to keep pace with the world of the twenty-first century.

This theme of the identity of the socialist left is taken up by David Bell, who argues that the legacy of the Mitterrand years for the PS is not entirely negative. Significant progress was achieved in many domains: in increased investment, the expansion and modernization of the economy, improved competitiveness, and the subjugation of inflation – all of this despite a difficult international context. Above all, Mitterrand gave the left *time*, a luxury it had not previously enjoyed despite several brief flirtations with power (recounted by Serge Berstein). Mitterrand also accustomed the French public to the alternating of government and opposition, and, somewhat paradoxically, brought about an acceptance by the left of the institutions of the Fifth Republic. The main problem of the left in government, however, was that it had stoked up exorbitant expectations in opposition (particularly at the Congress of Epinay) which it could not satisfy in power, whilst failing to establish viable reform projects which might nevertheless have been accomplished, with the result that by 1995 the French Socialists had little to show for fourteen years of tenure at the Elysée and had yet to achieve modernization. The unexpected success of Lionel Jospin in the 1995 presidential elections and 1997 legislative elections clearly marks him out as the legitimate leader of the PS and the left. But he faces an awesome task: the need to reach out to the floating vote in both the centre and, simultaneously, the extreme ideological left. It is noteworthy that Jospin's presidential electoral programme, based on helping business to create jobs and reduce unemployment, differed only slightly in form and content from the programmes of his rival candidates on the right.

There is nothing in politics which guarantees the Parti Socialiste a future. A galvanizing and credible project is required if it is to hold its ground and avoid electoral wipe-out. Otherwise – and perhaps this is the most likely scenario – the PS may simply become one of the major parties alternating in government, but lacking any real identity.

EUROPE AND FOREIGN AFFAIRS

Of the issues close to Mitterrand's heart, perhaps Europe was the closest. His commitment to Europe was firm and long-standing; indeed, he often referred to his presence at the Hague Conference in 1946. The Mitterrand era was a momentous time for Europe, embracing the single market programe, the end of the Cold War, German reunification, the two intergovernmental conferences (IGCs) on monetary and political union, and the Maastricht Treaty resulting in the European Union. Much of this was directly due to Mitterrand himself. Haunted by the spectre of European fragmentation, he acted as a facilitator for change, confirming France's leading role as co-driver of the European engine with Germany. By the end of Mitterrand's first term of office, it was generally accepted that French power and interests were best served by a strong and prosperous Community: if many of the goals sought by French leaders, including welfare, prosperity, security and independence, could no longer be realized at the level of the nation (the turning-point of 1983 had thrown this into bold relief), they might still be reached at the level of Europe.[23] But the Maastricht referendum in September 1992 was to paint a very different picture, revealing France not as united over Europe but as deeply divided: if the middle ground was broadly supportive of the Treaty on European Union the far left and right were opposed. By the end of the Mitterrand era, suffering the worst recession of the postwar period, France was beginning to strike a much more nationalist pose. What precisely was the nature of her apparently ambiguous commitment to Economic and Monetary Union? While the Juppé government continued to specify EMU as a top priority in the countdown to 1999, grassroots opposition to the welfare cuts and tax increases necessary for economic convergence with Germany sparked a rash of strikes which frequently resulted in a government climbdown, jeopardizing budgetary rigour. The election of a left-wing government in June 1997 made it clear that the public had had enough of austerity.

Kenneth Dyson and Kevin Featherstone explore Mitterrand's relationship with EMU. This was generally perceived as advantageous to France, given that it seemed to promise both the convergence of French economic performance with that of Germany, thereby ensuring French leadership in the Community, and the harnessing of German economic and monetary might to European objectives. France was to be 'rescued' from the 'D-Mark' zone, and the Bundesbank disempowered into the bargain. Yet paradoxically, while Mitterrand exerted strong political leadership in agenda setting on EMU, intervening at key moments, nevertheless French negotiators were ultimately compelled to adopt German institutional arrangements and policy instruments. Germany was indeed asked to cede power; but it legated its own institutional design and policy beliefs in the process, thus guaranteeing German hegemony in the future. Dyson and Featherstone conclude that whereas the Banque de France benefited from these new arrangements through its increased autonomy – as to a lesser extent did the Trésor and the technocrats (benefiting from an inbuilt information advantage but becoming something of a scapegoat in the process) – strong presidential leadership by Mitterrand did not, however, lead to French control over the contents of the policy.

Dominique David casts a critical eye over Mitterrand's record in defence and foreign affairs, comparing and contrasting his two terms in office. The various components of his foreign and defence policy are surveyed and their evolution traced: Mitterrand's implicit attachment to the Alliance tradition coupled with his lack of interest in Franco-Soviet policy; the *rapprochement* with Germany and the quintessential importance of the Paris-Bonn axis as the keystone of European unity; the new emphasis on development aid; the repositioning of France as a credible negotiating partner in the Near East; the continuity of Gaullist logic despite an anti-nuclear background, centring on the concept of deterrence. In Europe, Mitterrand strengthened the integration of Eastern Europe, feeling his way towards a European security apparatus, and sought a redefinition of the Atlantic Alliance within the new, post-communist Europe. Mitterrand may not have been a 'ferryman' from the old world order to the new. But, David concludes, he was at least one of those who best assessed the risks and opportunities of the changes taking shape. As Mitterrand said, 'Il faut donner du temps au temps' – time requires time; the debates around the final part of his foreign and defence policy have not yet stilled, and history will take some time for its judgement on these issues to crystallize.

ECONOMY AND SOCIETY

During the Mitterrand years, France moved from a position of national independence, epitomised by the 1981–1982 go-it-alone reflation of the economy and by the 1982 nationalization programme in particular, to the recognition of economic interdependence with France's trading partners in Europe. At the same time, the ruling Socialist Party replaced outworn ideology with a new pragmatic focus on the firm, helping to bring about the long-overdue conversion of the French to the market economy. The pivotal year of 1983 marked the birth of a new consensus on the primacy of business enterprise. France's large companies, once famous for their ostrich-like insularity, their dual dependence on the state and the home market, found new wings. Many public-sector firms were privatized. Some became global players. Foreign direct investment by French firms increased dramatically in the late 1980s, especially in the US, the UK and Germany. Inflation, once so rife that it was branded 'stagflation', was brought under control, falling from 14 per cent in 1981 to 3 per cent at the end of the 1980s. A key role in the subjugation of inflation was played by the new policy of the 'franc fort': keeping a strong franc pegged to the mark within the Exchange Rate Mechanism (ERM) of the European Monetary System (EMS). The strong franc quickly came to symbolize financial orthodoxy. In Mitterrand's first term of office, France overtook Britain to become the world's fourth largest exporter; in his second, a sharp recovery in the trade figures confirmed the improved competitiveness of the economy.

But, if everything was so right, why then did things appear to be so wrong? Both Joseph Szarka and Henrik Uterwedde, in their respective chapters on the modernization of French business and the evolution of economic and social policy during the Mitterrand years, grapple with this question, one of the most perplexing of this *fin de siècle*. For the society which Mitterrand left behind him in 1995 was not the one – more equal and more tolerant – which he had set out to build in 1981. Mitterrand had been elected on an employment ticket; but he left behind him a nation burdened by an unemployment rate of 12 per cent. By its sheer scale and persistence, even in times of economic growth, unemployment in France had revealed itself as *structural*, not cyclical. The gap between rich and poor had not narrowed but widened. Despite the positive nature of most economic indicators, as many as five million individuals were deemed to be socially excluded, living outside the social system. The French business class, accustomed to being blamed for France's misfortunes,[24] was again in the dock, this time charged with being exclusively preoccupied with productivity, competitiveness and profitability to the detriment of wider social considerations, with the result that in the industrial sector, employment had consistently declined as efficiency gains were achieved.[25] Often presented as 'le capitalisme sans capital', French business was now parodied as 'le capitalisme sans salariés', capitalism without a workforce. The remedy, in the eyes of the incoming president, Jacques Chirac, lay in the creation of *l'entreprise-citoyenne*: a corporate sector exercising civic responsibility, playing an active role in the battle against unemployment, thereby helping to correct the effective exclusion of many of the labour force from the prospect of real work. But with such an intractable and multifaceted problem, so-called 'solutions' appeared premature. The search for a new economic model combining competitiveness with social cohesion is still ongoing: it will doubtless be one of the great battlegrounds of the twenty-first century – but this in itself signals something of a defeat for the Mitterrand presidency. As Susan Milner highlights in her examination of industrial relations during the Mitterrand era, the former president's rallying-cry for a 'new social contract' in his final New Year's address to the nation in December 1994 reflects rather ill on his industrial relations record for the preceding fourteen years. Admittedly, as Milner concedes, cultural shifts take decades, and the process of change for trade unions has clearly begun. Bolstered by societal pressures, the industrial relations system in France is unlikely to collapse completely; but its limited reform over two terms of office on the part of a Socialist president, together with the failure of trade unions to reach out to new types of worker, does not augur well for the future.

Gender-based inequality is the subject of Siân Reynolds' discussion – more particularly, the successes and failures of women politicians during the Mitterrand years. It is a further paradox of the Mitterrand era that while François Mitterrand actively went out of his way to promote women as ministers, the percentage of women parliamentarians hardly improved. Taking as her starting-point 'the family romance' (which Lynn Hunt applies to the French Revolution), Reynolds explores the hypothesis that the Republican ideal of brotherhood – the band of brothers who resist a tyrannical father (or uncle), or a manipulative (step-)mother – gives rise to a symbolic order which contains no obvious place for sisters. Viewed in this light, the promotion of individual women appears as the wrong response to the right question. For what most commentators do not wish to consider is that citizenship may have a gendered content, and that the Fifth Republic may be quintessentially male rather than neutral, designed to serve the interests of French*men*, which do not necessarily coincide with those of French women.

We conclude our section on society with a grassroots study by Peter Fysh of anti-racism in France during the Mitterrand presidency. While the Front National gathered momentum following its initial success in the local government elections of March 1983 – it achieved a surprising 10.95 per cent of the vote in the European elections of June 1984, while Le Pen himself attracted a prodigious 14 per cent of votes cast in the presidential elections four years later – anti-racists nevertheless failed to construct a movement fit to challenge the Far Right's apparently inexorable rise. Fysh explains that this failure was essentially three-fold. First, the *beur* generation failed to produce an independent national anti-racist movement; second, *beur* and main-stream forces of the French left tended to neutralize one another rather than act in concert; and third, they failed jointly to defend in a clear and anti-racist manner the right to be different (largely because this was a right the FN had always maintained). Even SOS Racisme, the most successful of the anti-racist movements of the time, capturing the public imagination with its well-known slogan *touche pas à mon pote*, ultimately subscribed to the melting-pot vision of a non-racist society in which all cultures were equal but where the cultural melting-pot would finally erase all difference. The outlook for the future remains bleak: unless the mainstream left and the *beurs* can begin to work in tandem, Fysh predicts that anti-racism in France will continue to lurch from defeat to defeat.

THE PRESIDENT OF CULTURE

'As the presidential mandate nears its end and work is done, and as, with age, death approaches, the need may often be felt to gather one's scattered thoughts and confine to writing the task of making sense of one's life'.[26] Man cannot live by politics alone, or at least François Mitterrand could not. Culture in its broadest sense, and literature above other art forms, were food for the soul. Mitterrand was a habitual visitor to the bookstalls which line the Seine. Contemporary authors whose work he admired became habitués of the Elysée.[27] Whilst dying of cancer, and in the knowledge that time was running out, Mitterrand again turned to writing – with Nobel prizewinner Elie Wiesel in their joint *Mémoire à deux voix*, and in his own unfinished memoirs. But it was not in literature that the 'President of culture' made his mark. The Mitterrand era will be remembered, on the contrary, as a something of a latter-day 'golden age' of architecture, which Mitterrand saw as an ideal means of affirming French prestige. Not, of course, on the scale of Haussmann or Louis XIV; but, with his *grands projets*, Mitterrand, who as death approached became increasingly obsessed with his own mortality, nevertheless left an indelible mark on the Paris skyline with the sometimes controversial additions of the Grande Arche, the Bastille Opera House, the glazed Pyramids of the Cour Napoléon at the Louvre, the Finance Ministry at Bercy, the Institute of the Arab World, and the four glass bookstack towers of the Bibliothèque François Mitterrand – new and striking architecture in pure geometrical forms to complement the classical and traditional. Eric Cahm sheds light on the genesis of these projects and Mitterrand's personal involvement in them, assesses their symbolic value and examines the nature of their contribution to French architecture. In particular, do they represent monuments to an age, to socialism, or to Mitterrand himself?

Alone among European countries, France boasts a thriving film industry. French success is supported by state-backed initiatives designed to make Paris the centre of a global non-American cinema, a viable alternative to Hollywood, as exemplified by the uncompromising French stance over the so-called 'cultural exception' in the 1986–1993 Uruguay Round of GATT negotiations (General Agreement on Tariffs and Trade). Guy Austin surveys French cinema during the Mitterrand years, focusing in particular on Jack Lang's promotion of the 'heritage film' as its dominant genre, intended to preserve and democratize the literary heritage of the nation while simultaneously transcending the cultural-commercial divide. Despite its heavy reliance on state funding, the socialist heritage film, epitomised by *Germinal* (1993), ultimately proved to be no match at the box office for a classic low-budget French comedy, such as *Les Visiteurs*.

Meanwhile, during the Mitterrand years, the relationship between the state and the broadcasting media underwent significant change, as the state chose to liberalize, deregulate and privatize, relinquishing its former monopoly of ownership. Raymond Kuhn meticulously documents the withdrawal of the state from its previous all-powerful role. However, as the European Union of the 1990s has come to realize, the corollary of deregulation is not the anticipated liberalization but, on the contrary, a paradoxical re-regulation, and in the French broadcasting sector this too proved to be the case. In the first place, the French state continued to exercise a pivotal role in the transition from a monopoly to a mixed system of ownership, and in the second, the resulting policy-making environment proved to be too complex and tension-ridden to be left to its own devices, necessitating the close involvement of the state as regulator.

We conclude our section on French culture with a chapter on the left-wing intelligentsia in the Mitterrand years and its (unspoken) hostility to the president. France, and Paris in particular, is well known as a breeding-ground of intellectuals, virtually institutionalized as purveyors of new ideas. But in Mitterrand's France they fell noticeably silent, betrayed perhaps by the sobering experience of socialism in government, which from 1983 onwards bore little resemblance to the ideological exuberance of the 1970s, and which, now no longer in opposition and electorally victorious, thanks to the active support of the PCF, refused to condemn Communist dictators such as Jaruzelski. Martyn Cornick analyses the debate which climaxed in the summer of 1983 and argues that this silence is at once a symptom and a prognosis of the subsequent crisis of socialism. It is suggested that calls for new ideas (whether by intellectuals such as Max Gallo or indeed political scientists, such as Berstein and Bell) are likely to fall on deaf ears, since, ultimately, the ideas they seek to elicit belong to a past era.

The chapters which follow are conceived as 'Janus-faced': that is to say, while they look resolutely to the past, aiming to shed light on the impact of the Mitterrand years on the above-mentioned critical areas, they also seek to point the way (albeit tentatively) to the future, to the France of the twenty-first century, now only just around the corner.

NOTES

1. See Mitterrand's posthumous work *Mémoires interrompus* (Paris: Odile Jacob, 1996), p. 190.
2. Mitterrand's participation at the liberation of the concentration camps on 29 April 1945 is discussed in *Mémoires interrompus*, op. cit., p. 155.
3. Mitterrand describes de Gaulle as such in *Mémoires interrompus*, op. cit., p. 226.
4. 'An egotist who shared with compatriots a lifelong fascination with himself ', *The Guardian*, 9 January 1996, p. 9.
5. *Mémoires interrompus*, op. cit., p. 154.
6. Cited in Serge July, 'Mitterrand: une histoire française', *Libération*, 9 January 1996.
7. 8 May 1995, Berlin.

8. *Mémoires interrompus*, op. cit., pp. 155–156.

9. F. Mitterrand, New Year address to the nation, 31 December 1994.

10. I owe this observation to Eric Cahm.

11. See, for example, A. Cole, *François Mitterrand: a Study in Political Leadership* (London: Routledge, 1994); W. Northcutt, *Mitterrand: a Political Biography* (New York: Holmes and Meier, 1992).

12. Cf. A. Daley (ed.), *The Mitterrand Era: Policy Alternatives and Political Mobilization in France* (London: Macmillan, 1996).

13. P. Péan, *Une Jeunesse française: François Mitterrand 1934–1947* (Paris: Fayard, 1994).

14. Mitterrand cites this quotation in *Mémoires interrompus*, op. cit., p. 227.

15. F. Mitterrand, *Le Coup d'Etat permanent* (Paris: Plon, 1964).

16. Quoted in 'La monarchie républicaine dénoncée et perpétuée', *Le Monde*, 9 January 1996.

17. Ibid.

18. F. Mitterrand, *Ma Part de vérité* (Paris: Fayard, 1969).

19. *Mémoires interrompus*, op. cit., p. 224.

20. See, for example, S. Mazey, 'Power outside Paris', in P.A. Hall, J. Hayward and H. Machin (eds), *Developments in French Politics* (London: Macmillan, 1990), pp. 152–167.

21. This proved a point of contention at the 1996 Annual ASMCF Conference held at Royal Holloway, University of London, in September 1996: Serge Berstein insisted that there had indeed been a debate.

22. It is accepted here that the real turning-point was in fact earlier, in June 1982, as maintained by Jacques Delors. The date of spring 1983 is used here because it was at that moment that the turning-point, which had occurred in a rather clandestine manner, became fully public.

23. S. Hoffman, 'France and Europe: the dichotomy of autonomy and co-operation', in J. Howorth and G. Ross, *Contemporary France: a Review of Interdisciplinary Studies* (London: Pinter, 1987), pp. 49–50.

24. The classic example of this was de Gaulle's celebrated rebuke, 'Where were you, Sirs?', following allegations of collaboration by French business leaders during the Nazi Occupation.

25. See for example J. Chirac, *Une Nouvelle France: réflexions 1* (Paris: Nil Editions, 1994), p. 24, and J. Chirac, *La France pour tous* (Paris: Nil Editions, 1994), p. 92. Jean Gandois, president of the Conseil National du Patronat Français (CNPF) since December 1994, played a major role in promoting this idea of *l'entreprise-citoyenne*.

26. Foreword by F. Mitterrand, in F. Mitterrand and E. Wiesel, *Mémoire à deux voix* (Paris: Odile Jacob, 1995).

27. While paying a visit to the contemporary novelist Michel Tournier in August 1983, I recall being shown a personal invitation to the Elysée, of which Tournier was immensely proud.

Part 1
Socialism and the State

1 *Moins d'Etat* or *Mieux d'Etat*: The French Response to the Neo-Liberal Challenge

Jack Hayward

Despite ritual assertions by governments of their intentions to act in ways that demonstrate their wish to make policy rather than merely respond to external constraints, their will and capacity to do so has, for the last quarter of a century, appeared increasingly dubious. Although this has been a general phenomenon, its impact upon the conception of the function and scope of state intervention has been especially dramatic in those countries that have traditionally had an imperious, state-centred style of politics, in terms of the norms, institutions and practices of their political systems. If one excludes the states that have emerged from the collapse of Communism in the former Soviet Union and in Eastern Europe, as well as those such as Spain and Portugal which had experienced prolonged periods of dictatorship, France has probably faced the most searching self-doubt about its model of state-economy relations. Far from being able to present itself as an example to others, it now seems ill-adapted to serve the domestic public purposes for whose attainment it had been regarded as the prime instrument. While the resulting demoralization of many guardians of the old state-centred model and their discredit in public opinion may have been exaggerated, nevertheless the neo-liberal challenges to that model have gone some way to displacing it, producing a confusing situation in which old statist norms, institutions and practices have reduced legitimacy without liberal alternatives being fully accepted or adopted in their place.

THE INTELLECTUAL AND EXPERIENTIAL CHALLENGE

Of the various French expositions of the neo-liberal challenge, it is appropriate to select as exemplary that of Michel Crozier, who in *The*

Bureaucratic Phenomenon had presented an influential analysis of the state-centred model.[1] However, whereas in 1963 there was a disposition to resignation in the face of what in a subsequent book he called *The Stalemate Society* (1970) and its incapacity to change, by 1987 – when he published *Etat Modeste, Etat Moderne, stratégie pour un autre changement* – he adopted the posture of exponent and would-be agent of change. Eschewing the more simplistic ultra-liberal economism of a Guy Sorman, Crozier deliberately set out to 'desacralize' the French state. Far from the state being an effective architect of the modernization of society, it was too sluggish, authoritarian and arrogant to fulfil this function. 'It is not France and the French who are out of date but their technocrats, the official political world and this French-style state interventionism, well-intentioned and *bien-pensant* but always out of step in its reactions, claiming to command 'change' which it is unable to master or – more seriously – even to understand.'[2] Far from *society* being in stalemate, it was over-regulated by a *state* devoted to stability in a rapidly changing world, seeking to subordinate private interests as well as local and regional public interests. Crozier regretted the failure of Jacques Chaban-Delmas's 'new society' reformism and (by anticipation) that of Michel Rocard to loosen the stifling grip of the state technocrats.[3]

Rejecting as a model the American 'laboratory of modernity',[4] France had changed from a centralized administrative state to a centralized technocratic state devoted to industrialization and modernization. 'Technocrats cannot conceive of regulation without a regulator, and the only neutral regulator in their eyes is the state.'[5] In an increasingly complex world, old-style regulation would be ineffective – so, instead of devoting itself to industrial redevelopment, the French government should concentrate upon redeploying its own activities. Proclaiming that 'we are all individualists', Crozier asserted that people and groups were able to make their own decisions and that the problem was not to attack the elites but to make them change their behaviour.[6] The fundamental contradiction he faced was that 'society cannot be changed without changing the role of the state and its officials, but like any constituted body, they are hostile to change.'[7] Crozier therefore advocated shifting unavoidably arbitrary power from technocrats to businessmen. It was not enough to rehabilitate the firm, as the Socialists under Mitterrand had done in the mid-1980s. Whereas higher civil servants had colonized big business through *pantouflage*, it was now time for leadership to pass directly to businessmen preoccupied with clients and profit rather than the public service ethic.[8] While Crozier was not invited to play a direct role as actor in bringing about the process of change he advocated, his onslaught did reflect a change of the climate of elite opinion and a disposition to reduce the role of the state in a context in which external pressures and foreign nostrums were to play a much more important role than Crozier accorded them.

Ironically, it was during the Mitterrand presidency that the conversion of the French techno-bureaucratic elite's conception of modernization took place. Instead of predicating this process upon state intervention (of which they had been ardent protagonists), they now saw market competition as the prime means of achieving public purposes. The notion that 'There is no alternative' (TINA) came to France later and less completely than in Britain, but the change in the normative framework of public policy and in the predilections of the politico-administrative insiders, whether governments of the left or right were in office, was in the same direction. The run on the French franc in 1982–1983 and three successive devaluations prompted panic that the Mauroy Government would be subjected to the same humiliation of coming under the supervision of the IMF (International Monetary Fund) in monetary policy as befell the British Labour Government in the mid-1970s. The need to defend the currency parity led to a new consensus that France should pursue a 'strong franc' policy, aligned on the German mark and supported by an economic strategy of competitive disinflation. As Elie Cohen has bluntly put it: 'The policy of competitive disinflation is the result of an improbable marriage between a finance administration seeking the means of making automatic adjustments and a governmental Left unable to make its choices explicit'.[9] The reversal of economic strategy was more painful and took longer under the presidency of Mitterrand than it did in 1995 under Chirac, but in both cases the pre-electoral claim that the French state could impose its will upon recalcitrant economic forces quite rapidly proved illusory. A sharp lesson in state modesty was administered to both Socialist and post-Gaullist interventionists by impersonal market forces. The permissive inflationary consensus was displaced by a rigorous disinflationary consensus.

The ideological shift from Keynesianism to monetarism was not as dramatic in France as it had been in Britain, because 'counter-cyclical action, based upon the assumption that state intervention was subsidiary to the operations of the market, was not typical of French interventionism which in the post-war period was concerned with rapid and sustained growth rather than with stabilization.'[10] In

France it was a matter of substituting sustained disinflation for sustained inflation. Chirac, as prime minister in 1974–1976, had tried to inflate out of recession following the massive oil price rise. It took the Mitterrand victory of 1981 to turn the French right in a resolutely neo-liberal direction, although Raymond Barre when prime minister had (as became an orthodox economist) already shifted policy in a more market-compatible direction. The requirements of adversary politics in a bipolarized political system impelled the French right in a neo-liberal direction once it went into opposition, whereas the French left was pressured into going in the same direction by the requirements of the crisis management of capitalism. Instead of the promised 'logic of rupture with capitalism', the Mauroy government was forced into a rupture with socialism by what Michel Rocard had recognized by September 1982 as not a short-term crisis but a comprehensive change.[11] In the wake of this change, the retreat from the commitment to full employment, nationalization and a state-led industrial policy was covered by the mantle of European integration. Having chosen not to withdraw from the European Monetary System (EMS), monetary integration was put forward as the chosen instrument of rather than the constraint on future progress.

The French state having demonstrated its incapacity to act alone, the European Community (EC) became the context in which, collectively – and particularly with Germany – the external economic constraints were to be mastered. Unfortunately, the German Government did not take the same view as France of economic and monetary policy, and instead a market and competition-orientated policy, was followed at the EC level. The move by Jacques Delors from being finance minister in the Mauroy government to President of the European Commission personified the new strategy and helped legitimize it. Regulatory action that was ceasing to be possible at the national level would now be attempted at the European Community level, even if the efforts to achieve a European industrial policy or concerted action to achieve a reduction in unemployment were to be blocked. This has principally involved reducing the ambitions of regulatory intervention to improving economic efficiency rather than the wider developmental and redistributive objectives pursued previously. When combined with privatization – pursued actively by the right once Mitterrand's *ni ni* holding operation during his second presidential term was abandoned – this has resulted potentially in a redefinition rather than a retreat from public intervention. 'What is observed in practice is a redrawing of the borders of the public sphere in a way that excludes certain fields better left to private activity, while at the same time strengthening and even expanding the state's regulatory capacity in other fields like competition or environmental and consumer protection.'[12]

President Mitterrand acknowledged his inability to prevent the policy of privatization followed by the Chirac and Balladur governments in 1986–1987 and 1993–1995. As finance minister in the Chirac government and later as prime minister himself, Balladur devised a privatization programme calculated to ensure maximum protection from foreign takeovers through the establishment of interlocking directorates of carefully selected consortia of shareholding firms. Despite EC attempts to make it more difficult for member states to follow traditional *dirigiste* provision of public subsidies to slow down the decline of lame-duck industries and ensure their survival in competitive international markets, French governments have continued to maintain a micro-economic role as state-protectors even when they have ceased to act as state-shareholders.[13] However, they are less inclined to follow a systematic policy of tolerating overmanning for socio-political purposes, accepting that the survival of firms depends upon their competitive efficiency. Attempts to emulate German-style links between banks and firms led to some notable financial fiascos (like that of the Crédit Lyonnais) with the result that the Anglo-American model appears less unattractive than it used to be.[14] Neo-liberalism, at least in homeopathic doses, seems unavoidable.

RESPONSES TO THE NEO-LIBERAL CHALLENGE

If these are some of the challenges the French state faced by the time the Mitterrand presidency had come to an end, what has been the response within the state apparatus, in public enterprises and among extra-state business and trade union organizations? Before one explores the answers to that question, it is important to make the point that the public-private separation, based upon the view that the indivisible public interest was clearly distinct from the various private interests, has become blurred. The public interest alone used to be deemed legitimate and the private interests were not. The impact of neo-liberal values has not only been to challenge the public-private dichotomy but – to the extent that the distinction persists – even to reverse the order of priority. What is private is identified as respectable, efficient and virtuous, while what is public is regarded as suspect, inefficient and all too often corrupt. The delegitimation of state service has meant that money rather than power now overtly enjoys the highest esteem. It is ironic that whereas Mitterrand frequently and perhaps sincerely expressed his contempt for a money-motivated society, he presided over a dramatic change in official morality in which his own entourage played a conspicuous part but which reflected a much more pervasive social and cultural phenomenon.

Jobert and Théret make a useful distinction between doctrinaire and managerial neo-liberalism, emphasising that whereas the ideological debate was strong on rhetoric, it was its managerial variant that directly came to dominate the minds of public policy makers and the policies pursued.[15] To personalize matters, it was through the influence from the late 1970s of public officials such as Simon Nora, rather than the subsequent speeches of politicians like Alain Madelin, that the new orthodoxy took hold where it counted. On the left, while Jean-Pierre Chevènement and his CERES (Centre d'Etudes et de Recherches Socialistes) faction in the Socialist Party were allowed to make the rhetorical and programmatic running, when the moment of choice came in 1983 their views were rejected in favour of the option of competitiveness and European integration. Bérégovoy, the future Socialist finance minister and prime minister, who changed standpoint in 1983 and came to personify the policy of the strong franc, reflected the tendency of political leaders, provisionally in charge of the state's government, to be persuaded of the need to adopt the policies favoured by the state's permanent officials. Jean-Claude Trichet, former *directeur du Trésor* and currently governor of the Bank of France, exemplifies the new style in the way that François Bloch-Lainé exemplified the old style senior state official.

Lacking the support of President Mitterrand and without a reliable majority in the National Assembly, Michel Rocard as prime minister was not able to press his reformist approach. He sought to achieve a more effective state rather than a minimalist state, although to increase its effectiveness meant a modification in its role. However, the report of the 'Horizon 2000' group (a characteristic way of floating ideas for change) in 1990 explored how a state, on the defensive against external and internal challenges, should react to 'an intellectual climate propitious to the Anglo-Saxon tradition, long disdained in France.'[16] Taking up Crozier's idea of a 'more modest state', the report argued that while 'world market constraints had been used as an argument to restrict the demands of society and render it governable, henceforth it was no longer a matter of using the market to instil fear but to participate in it.'[17] Rather than extending the *dirigiste* practice of paternalist state intervention, the French state 'has attempted to organize its own decline as master of economic affairs by handing over to larger, multinational organizations of French origin the defence of part of its national economic interests.'[18]

Expressing wishful thinking rather than describing what had already happened, the report claimed that the French state's role should be very different from the past, 'renouncing the illusion of mastery and centrality, henceforth acting as one amongst others in matters that have their own laws which no one decides alone.'[19] While arguing that French elites identified decreasingly with the state and the norms of 'public service', handing over to business firms the task of teaching the need for moderation in incomes and to competition the safeguarding of consumer interests, they had not tackled the issue directly, relying upon market globalization and European Community regulation to achieve this purpose indirectly.[20] Such was the new normative framework – shared by the administrative elite and many economists – which led successive governments to seek to restrain public expenditure, end wage indexation, encouraging the 'downsizing' (that increased unemployment) and the opening up of financial markets. The consequence has been an increase in the power of a rehabilitated business sector and a further decline in an already debilitated trade union movement – a paradoxical result, given that it favoured the socialists' political enemies and weakened their political friends.

Public enterprises in France have played a pivotal role in the *pantouflage* process, linking the higher civil service and the banking and industrial worlds. The interlocking directorate that constitutes the state in action was not significantly changed by the politically controversial transfer of ownership that occurred with the 1982 nationalizations and the subsequent privatizations. However, because the 1980s were characterized by a recognition of the need to allow more managerial autonomy in order to adapt flexibly to market competition, the ability of government to use firms for public purposes – which was always problematic – had diminished. The popularity and legitimacy of nationalization had been due primarily to the belief, based upon past experience, that it was identified with security of employment. However, in practice there was massive demanning in many of the enterprises taken over – hence the lack of much public opposition to privatization when it came. Loss-making firms, having been made viable thanks to lowered costs and increased investment, became fit to face the new neo-liberal environment. In retrospect, the nationalization interlude can be seen as state intervention to 'modernize' parts of the private sector that had been unable or unwilling to adapt to an unprotected economic environment. It did so with variable success.

Private business and its main representative organization, the Conseil National du Patronat Français (CNPF), accompanied rather than prompted the neo-liberal change of direction. Their leaders, notably the CNPF's President Yvon Gattaz, made unrealizable promises to create hundreds of thousands of jobs in return for the fiscal favours they were accorded. Many prominent firms turned increasingly to foreign alliances – American as well as European – and took advantage of the political parties' financial needs to spread a system of domestic corruption that embraced the left as well as the right. The close contacts that existed between the higher reaches of politics, administration and business ensured that the old-style collusion was put to more venal use – both personal enrichment and partisan support in return for political favours. Just as the Stock Exchange, private profit and the entrepreneur were being lionized in a country that had hitherto been allergic to capitalism for Catholic as well as socialist reasons, the behaviour of prominent businessmen was revealed as disreputable, more deserving of imprisonment than praise. Mitterrand turned a blind eye to many of these practices.

Because French trade unions have always been able to recruit most strongly in the public sector – civil servants (especially schoolteachers) and employees of nationalized industries – the dramatic fall in their membership during the Mitterrand years cannot be disassociated from the problems in that sector. This 'desyndicalization', which appears to have gone faster and further in France than in any other major industrial country, has meant that in terms of a proportion of French active wage-earners, less than ten per cent, it is estimated to be at its lowest point since the end of the First World War.[21] The fall particularly hit the Confédération Générale du Travail (CGT), due to its close association with the Communist Party, but all the unions suffered. In occupational elections, the vote for non-trade unionists rose sharply, while the number of abstentions also increased. The Confédération Française Démocratique du Travail (CFDT), which under the leadership of Edmond Maire had become increasingly linked to the Socialist Party (especially its Rocardian wing) and in 1981 contributed generously to the *cabinets ministériels* in the Mauroy government, quickly became disenchanted with this overt politicization after 1984 (when the old CFDTiste Delors prepared to depart for Brussels) and by 1985 decided not to advise its members how to vote in future (the strategy called *recentrage*). Over the next decade, the failure of the 'second left' to influence the PS (exemplified by Mitterrand's marginalization of Rocard, even when he was prime minister) meant that the CFDT chose to displace Force Ouvrière (FO) as the main interlocutor of business and the government, even when the latter was represented by a Balladur or a Juppé. This policy has been most explicitly identified with Nicole Notat, who took control of the CFDT in October 1992.

Relying upon playing a role in industrial relations and vis-à-vis the government when they were losing their credibility because of their membership haemorrhage, the 'reformist' unions – notably the CFDT – have tried to make up in occupational expertise what they lack in representativeness. Gone are the dreams of self-management. Without the voluntary commitment of ideologically-motivated activists, unions like the CFDT have had to become like the CGT and FO, relying upon full-time officials paid for indirectly by state subsidies rather than from their shrinking membership subscriptions. So France is relying upon trade unions with few members, just as it has been renowned for its 'capitalism without capital' – or, more accurately, with modest amounts of capital. The battle among trade unions for control of the social security institutions, with its implications for their reform aimed at reducing public expenditure, is partly to be explained by this need to acquire from above the status and resources they cannot secure from below. The CNPF is left to arbitrate the battle, throwing in 1996 behind the CFDT the weight which it had previously used to favour FO. It is in this parlous situation that the French trade unions find themselves at the end of the Mitterrand years, so that spectacular strike action, when it comes – as it did in the autumn of 1995 – takes the unions as well as everyone else by surprise.

RETREATING IN DISORDER

The changes we have traced have not been made as the result of public pre-electoral debate, assumed to be the basis of legitimate decisions in a liberal democracy. The French have been accustomed to being told by the contending candidates that they are confronted with a *choix de société* at each national election, only to realize afterwards that they were facing not a drama but a melodrama. When the major turning-points do come, they do so between elections, unobtrusively and incrementally. It is only after the event that they are understood to have been *faits accomplis*. This is because it is the guardians of the state themselves who bring about the redefinition of the state's role, asserting the self-evident necessity of the new arrangements with the same self-assurance with which they had defended the old order. Modernization now requires *moins d'état* in some of its past interventions – control of prices and incomes, planning and public ownership, for example – so that it can perform its remaining functions more effectively and more efficiently, i.e. *mieux d'état*.

The position at the end of the Mitterrand era has been summed up by one of the closest and most perceptive observers of the French techno-bureaucratic elite. Noting that the persistent public demands for state intervention at a time of economic turbulence paradoxically coincided with its discredit, Ezra Suleiman remarks that 'the central state is not or cannot any longer be the organizer of change. It no longer has the necessary legitimacy, having been deprived of it by the success of the neo-liberal arguments. It no longer has either the will or the material or legal possibility to do so. This leads to a management of public affairs not based upon anticipation and foresight but on defensive reaction.'[22] Governments respond to external imperatives by adopting monetarist economic policies and then respond to the internal protest movements provoked by the socio-economic consequences of these austerity financial constraints. The temptation to put the blame for the latter on 'the foreigner' is seldom resisted – with the consequence that a belief in the self-confessed impotence of their own state is instilled in the public, which increases the discredit with which the state elites are regarded.

Can one say that the French state, under Mitterrand, organized an orderly retreat from its *dirigiste* presuppositions? Because there was a pretence that the 1983 fundamental change of direction had not taken place, a pretence dictated by the need not to demoralize Mitterrand's supporters, no clear sense of direction was possible. Michel Rocard encouraged wishful thinking when he declared in January 1992 that 'If the 1980s legitimated the firm, the 1990s will witness the rehabilitation of the state and public service.'[23] Not merely has the abandonment of the ideological underpinnings of such a view left the protagonists of state socialism with both feet firmly planted in mid-air; they are desperately struggling to find practical ways of giving it expression in a period when a neo-liberal orthodoxy has established itself within the sanctum of the state. Those who enter the *grands corps* now see the state service as a means rather than an end, not the service of the public interest but a way of furthering their own career. This was always true to some extent in the past, but it has become more overt and legitimate in terms of hospitable prevailing values. The *pantouflage* into private business of graduates of the Ecole Nationale d'Administration (ENA) has in general accelerated. In the case of the Finance Inspectorate, in particular, this acceleration has been dated from 1982, in anticipation of a context in which the firm has been given priority over the state.[24]

The changed relationship between the state and firms was clearly enunciated by the president and prime minister in 1984. Speaking on television in January 1984, President Mitterrand hammered the point home: 'the French are beginning to understand: it is the firm that creates wealth, it is the firm that creates employment, it is the firm that decides our standard of living and our place in the world hierarchy.' The new prime minister, Fabius, addressing the National Assembly in July 1984, put the other side of the equation even more bluntly: 'the state has met its limits and it should not exceed them.'[25] It only remained to draw the conclusions of these new parameters of public policy.

Mitterrand's mid-September 1985 commitment to reduce the combined burden of tax and social security payments signalled a switch away from the extension of the welfare state to the need to find other sources of revenue in order to sustain the growing financial demands it was making. From there it was a short step to imitating the Thatcherite policy of privatization, which was adopted enthusiastically by the right, eagerly supported by those who hoped to benefit personally from the switch from public to private ownership. So, despite attempts to conceal the retreat and give it a semblance of order, the two periods of cohabitation in the Mitterrand presidency sealed the surrender of the attempt to use the state as the spearhead of French socio-economic policy that had already been conceded when the Socialists held power. French statesmen have surreptitiously conceded the discretionary capacity to achieve a self-directed overall coherence of national economic action, pretexting the multinational monetary disarmament of national governments within a European Economic and Monetary Union that allows them to divest themselves of responsibility for the consequences. They are fleeing forwards from *moins d'état* in the hope of achieving *mieux d'Europe*.

NOTES

1. For an assessment of the development of the ideas that led to this book, see P. Grémion, 'Michel Crozier's Long March: the Making of *The Bureaucratic Phenomenon*', *Political Studies*, Vol. XL, March 1992, pp. 5–20. See also F. Pavé (ed.), *L'Analyse Stratégique. Autour de Michel Crozier* (Paris: Seuil, 1994).
2. M. Crozier, *Etat modeste, Etat moderne* (Paris: Fayard, 1987), p. 46.
3. Ibid, p. 61.
4. Ibid, p. 93. More generally, see M. Crozier, *Le Mal américain* (Paris: Fayard, 1980).
5. Ibid, p.124.
6. Ibid, p. 205; pp. 144–145; p. 219.
7. Ibid, p. 212; p. 209.
8. Ibid, pp. 294–295; pp. 266–267.
9. E. Cohen, 'Contrainte économique et action politique', *Pouvoirs*, No. 68, Jan. 1994, p. 92, cf. p. 100; see also B. Jobert and B. Théret, 'France: la consécration républicaine du néo-libéralisme' in B. Jobert (ed.), *Le Tournant néo-libéral en Europe* (Paris: L'Harmattan, 1994), pp. 36–37.
10. J. Hayward, *The State and the Market Economy* (Brighton: Harvester-Wheatsheaf, 1986), pp. 220–221; cf. p. 234. See also K. Barker et al., 'Macroeconomic policy in France and Britain', *National Institute Economic Review*, Nov. 1984, pp. 73–74.
11. M. Rocard, 'The challenges of the 80s', 8 September 1982, Commissariat du Plan, mimeo, pp. 2–3.
12. G. Majone, 'The Rise of the Regulatory State in Europe', *West European Politics*, Vol. XVII, No. 3, July 1994, p. 80.
13. E. Cohen, *L'Etat brancardier. Politiques du déclin industriel. 1974–84* (Paris: Calmann-Lévy, 1989), and E. Cohen, 'France: National Champions in Search of a Mission' in J. Hayward (ed.), *Industrial Enterprise and European Integration: from National to International Champions in Western Europe* (Oxford: OUP, 1995). For Balladur's discussion of the accelerated switch to neo-liberalism in the first cohabitation period, see his book with the revealing title: *Je crois en l'homme plus qu'en l'Etat* (Paris: Fayard, 1987).
14. M. Albert, *Capitalisme contre capitalisme* (Paris: Seuil, 1991).
15. Jobert and Théret, p. 47.
16. *Entrer dans le XXIe siècle. Essai sur l'avenir de l'identité française*, La Documentation Française, 1990, p. 51, report commissioned by Lionel Stoléru, minister in charge of the Plan, working under Prime Minister Rocard.
17. Ibid, p. 161; cf. p. 162.
18. Ibid, p. 163. See also J. Hayward (ed.), *Industrial Enterprise and European Integration*, op. cit., Introduction, Ch. 1 and Conclusion.
19. *Entrer dans le XXIe siècle*, op. cit., pp. 164–165.
20. Ibid, p. 57; p. 178.

21. D. Labbé and M. Croisat, *La Fin des syndicats?* (Paris: L'Harmattan, 1992), pp. 13–14.
22. E.N. Suleiman, *Les Ressorts cachés de la réussite française* (Paris: Seuil, 1995), p. 23; cf. p. 213, p. 258.
23. Reported in *Le Monde*, 18 January 1992, quoted in Suleiman, ibid., p. 86.
24. M. Bauer & D. Danic, *L'Inspection des Finances: 16 ans de pantouflage, 1974–1989* (Paris: Heidrick and Struggles, 1990), p. 13. See also M. Bauer and B. Bertin-Mouret, *Les Enarques en entreprise de 1960 à 1990: 30 ans de pantouflage* (Boyden Global Executive Search, 1994).
25. Quoted in H. Machin and V. Wright (eds), *Economic Policy-Making under the Mitterrand Presidency, 1981–1984* (London: Pinter, 1985), p. 3.

2 A *Dirigiste* End to *Dirigisme*[1]?
Elie Cohen

With the benefit of hindsight, it might be argued that the key turning-point in Socialist policy in 1983 represented not only a break with the 'policy of rupture' heralded by President Mitterrand in 1981 but also, and more significantly, a departure from the centralized economic model that had been in place since just after the Second World War. After all, 1983 saw a left-wing government de-indexing pay, halting the increase in compulsory levies on employers, making entrepreneurs the key economic players and deregulating the economy. Yet such a major shift in policy was never debated or explained – nor even explicitly adopted by Mitterrand or by the left as a whole, which remained nostalgic for 1981–1982, the early days of the Socialist government.

So how are we to interpret this gulf between ideology and actual policy, between European rhetoric and a strong pull towards national introversion, and between deregulatory policy and the revival of Colbertism? It could be read both as the difficulty the left experienced in putting its ideas into force once in power and, more fundamentally, as France's difficulty in reconciling its place in the world economy with its claims to singularity, summed up by the discussion of France as a 'special case'.

A STRATEGY OF RUPTURE

After a quarter of a century in opposition, the left came to power in France in 1981 with a radical manifesto. Within two years, the much-vaunted 'rupture' had been superseded by accelerated liberalization. Moreover, social unrest, absent as the experiment got under way, was also absent in 1983. As a result, the shift of political power had simply highlighted, rather than transformed, the institutional characteristics of what has been called 'French-style regulation'.[2]

The left's 1981 manifesto was radical in that it combined traditional economic recovery and Keynesian-type redistribution policies with a

36

wide range of structural reforms, covering ownership (through nationalization), workplace power (through the Auroux laws) and social and economic institutions (through decentralization and the strengthening of planning).

This voluntarist manifesto was implemented with determination from the outset of the left's period in office. There was a clear boost to consumer spending, family allowances and retirement pensions, and during the first year public expenditure rose substantially. The statutory minimum wage was also increased by a large amount, while paid holidays were extended and the working week was reduced to 39 hours, without loss of pay. The highest earners were surtaxed, and a wealth tax was introduced.

Besides these Keynesian policies to boost demand, the government also envisaged reform of economic structures, so as to promote a new development model. The three key terms here were nationalization, planning and self-management (*autogestion*), and together they inspired the policies adopted. The French left wanted to use 100 per cent nationalization of major industrial and financial corporations to distinguish its line clearly from previous policies. There were less difficult ways to take control, such as holding a 51 per cent stake or minority control, and France's role in Europe made it impossible for her to nationalize companies under foreign control (such as Roussel Uclaf); moreover, the nationalization of some small banks in financial difficulty involved more disadvantages than advantages. Nevertheless, Mitterrand carried out this part of his first manifesto without compromise.

French indicative economic planning, in continuous decline since the late 1960s, was once again brought to the fore and assigned a new role; it was to be the tool for organizing the forces of French industry around new plans for manufacturing and regaining dominance on the domestic market as well as cornering new foreign markets; and it was to serve as the framework for contractual relations between the state and the *régions* with a view to creating a modern infrastructure. Decentralization had been adopted for reasons other than economic ones, but it too was to play its part in this new voluntarist climate; above all, the *régions* were to stop expecting Paris to do everything for them and were to stimulate the influx of new company locations in their areas as well as reviving their complement of small and medium-sized businesses. However, as the reform was based on the *département* structure, the concentration of funds in towns and *départements* made it very difficult for the *régions* to play their full part in the regional development programme.

The left's most ambitious undertaking was, however, the employment legislation known as the Auroux laws. The aim of this legislation was to establish social democracy by involving citizens in the workplace. There was no point in nationalizing companies or in promoting a new model of economic development based on human creativity, so the argument went, if the workers themselves had no rights to express their opinion in the workplace, to become involved in shaping company policy or to feel part of the company's growth. Ideally, this was a dual democratic process, operating both bottom-up and top-down, and the left's vision was that it would enable 'workplace councils' (*conseils d'atelier*), the boards of nationalized companies and the Commission Specialisée du Plan to revolutionize the business and economic direction of France.

It did not take long for the effects of such a radical policy to be felt. The revival policy not only failed to bring about economic recovery, it also cost dear in political terms: the left had to devalue the franc three times in under two years and the serious economic impact of this caused France to miss out on the global economic upturn in 1984, thereby losing the benefits of a more favourable period in the economic cycle. The same fate met the reduction of working time; this was introduced without loss of pay for workers and as a result it put an abrupt halt to all previous progress in negotiations towards reducing working hours. The austerity policy introduced from March 1983 aimed to claw back some of the workers' gains and triggered a marked increase in unemployment. Above all, however, it set the seal on the clear failure of the Auroux laws' stated aim of increasing social democracy, because when the turning-point came in 1983, the *conseils d'atelier* were not in place to exercise the democratic influence the left had envisaged for them.

This marked the end of French capitalism's experiment with nationalization, planning and voluntarist industrial policy, because once the new government had emerged from its euphoria and faced up to the financial needs of an industrial apparatus weakened by ten years of imposed restructuring, it realized that it had rapidly to allow nationalized companies to re-enter the financial markets. The ambitious manufacturing development plan foundered on France's external trade commitments, the refusal of major public sector corporations to follow the new policy and a severe lack of funds.

After 1983, the left adopted competitive deflation, the quest for profits, European integration, the return to market forces, and involvement of workers at the workplace; the results were higher unemployment, loss of purchasing power and a decline in budgetary control.

The left, defeated in 1986, regained power in 1988 after France's brief flirtation with prototype liberalism. The left had nationalized, it had failed to curb unemployment and it had imposed wage restraint. Even its successes in the areas of inflation, the profitability of nationalized companies and the parity of the franc should have gone against it, given that these were policies traditionally associated with the right. Nevertheless, it regained power in 1988, promising measures to benefit those most on the margins of society, via the RMI (*revenu moyen d'insertion*) or income support plan, rather than measures to reduce wider inequalities. Ultimately, its commitment to Europe sent a clear signal that its priorities were to be globalization, liberalization and deregulation rather than productivity-stimulating voluntarism. This manifesto gained Mitterrand more support in 1988 even than in 1981 – so what had happened in the meantime?

The brief change of parliamentary power in 1986 had been salutary for a country that preferred a tame version of socialism to adventurous liberalism. The government presided over by Michel Rocard between 1988 and 1991 was to remain basically loyal to the 1983 manifesto of liberal solidarity, and its only mistake was to campaign positively for this policy rather than present it as an 'interlude'. Competitive disinflation, European integration and partial privatization were the economic thrust of the policy Rocard implemented, while in the area of the RMI and the CSG (*contribution sociale généralisée*), an additional social security levy in favour of the underprivileged, he sought to create a new form of solidarity, at the same time reforming the social security network. The return of economic growth even enabled Rocard to increase public sector pay, devote substantially more resources to education and cut taxes. A brief fall in unemployment also showed how growth could bring about job creation.

THE END OF A CONTROLLED ECONOMY

An assessment of the left's achievements in power reveals a paradox. It undeniably succeeded in its liberal policies to bring the economy back into shape without exacerbating pay inequalities and against the backdrop of high unemployment. However, its political thrust, achieving reform by negotiating compromises, failed.

In economic policy terms, Giscardism and early (1981–1983) Mitterrandism are just two variations on the theme of the national-rational–equitable state based on inflationary social compromise, the centrally-controlled economy and industrial Colbertism. The 1983 turning-point, however, smacks more of 'revolutionary politics'; the implicit inflationary social compromise of the post-war years had been destroyed, and both unions and employers' organizations had to look to the state for economic and social regulation once pay and benefits started to rise for the former and prices and profitability were guaranteed for the latter by a consumer boom and periodic devaluations. As soon as devaluation lost some of its potency as a weapon, however, the price had to be paid in the real terms of prices, pay and jobs.

One of the main driving forces of post-war growth was centralized economic financing, a mechanism founded on the Treasury and involving cheap finance for companies on the basis of the fruits of 40 years of interventionism. As the cost of capital rose worldwide in the early 1980s and markets became more closely linked as a consequence of financial deregulation, the French state in 1984 pulled out of its central role in company financing, leaving business to find its own money on the markets.

Ultimately, the major Colbertist plans that the left had wanted to implement foundered on three factors: the demise of major regional capital programmes and the subsequent emergence of 'national champions'; European regulation, which excluded national protectionist policies; and the Europeanization of new technology initiatives for financial and market-size reasons.

A *DIRIGISTE* RUPTURE

What explanations can there be for the left's success in unexpected areas and its failure in other areas where its mission was to change the natural order?

Since 1945, France had experienced alternate periods of political impotence and economic decline, as in 1945–1952 and again between 1974 and 1981, and of sweeping authoritarian reform, as in 1959 and again in 1983. For many years, the class struggle carried out through the trade union movement and the employers' struggle to hold on to industry's heritage masked the fundamental weakness of both unions and employers' organizations; hence, resorting to state control was for a long time the ideal solution, enabling the two sides to continue avoidance and guaranteeing the continuation of agreements already reached while at the same time also guaranteeing real scope for intervention, complete with knock-on effects, throughout the huge public sector. The model was able to function well particularly because the state was powerful in macro-economic terms and because the model promised 'ever more' in a positive redistribution policy. This was, however, no longer the case by 1983.

By that time, the state was able to draw on the traditional sources of its power to carry out an authoritarian modernization. In harnessing the forces of the international market and accommodating the constraints of Europe, it had to sacrifice social actors and, particularly, social democratic-type compromises.

The turning point of 1983 was based on the classic model of authoritarian modernization, and the new economic course was charted on the basis of direct confrontation between the people and their leader. External dangers threatening sovereignty, the future role of the *'grande nation'* within Europe and proud affirmations of national genius against the backdrop of a new industrial revolution were all marshalled to justify 'the policy interlude', 'the new phase', and 'a long haul'. Reformist trade unions which had embarked on the huge collective bargaining process and which had often instructed their key activists in reaching consensus suddenly found themselves redundant and ill-equipped to meet the needs of the few private-sector workers who belonged to a union.

Everything the left had wanted to achieve by way of economic, social and institutional change could have been negotiated, put to the test of political debate and implemented by stages. These changes could have been an opportunity to transfer power from the centre to the margins, from the state to other social actors, and from the technocracy to the new local political elites.. The opportunity was not taken, and this is almost certainly the major reason for the left's failure.

An attempt to give an account of this very specific instance of managing reform inevitably means considering France's system of political institutions. The 1983 turning-point was made possible by the conjunction of France's economic policy strategy (private and public Treasury, industry and finance sector 'technostructures') and of a left-wing political elite in search of a big political idea after the failure of 'Keynesianism in one country', in a climate of institutional impotence, both in parliament and in society. The only way to secure an economic system designed to break with automatic inflation, regular devaluation and soaraway pay levels was to have a monetary policy that fell outside the government's power and appeared to be dictated by ineluctable external factors. Yet only Mitterrand, with the unshared authority his institutions gave him, could have imposed a U-turn and continued to claim that he was working for socialism. Ultimately, only a flabby parliament, unions riven by disagreements and a Socialist Party in thrall to the cult of its founding leader could have accepted such a radical change of course without missing a beat.[3]

The combined power of Mitterrand's words and the action of enlightened despots on both the left and the right who had been high-ranking public servants meant that the 'Europe of the Twelve', used from 1985 in a manifesto of liberalization and deregulation, was presented as a staging-post for France, as the tool of continental European Keynesianism and as an advanced social area. At that time, no one understood the full implications of the choices that had been made, but the implementation of the manifesto of liberalization and the dismantling of the centralized economy were to have devastating effects once the Maastricht Treaty was adopted and the long 1990s economic crisis began in France.

FRANCE ORPHANED FROM ITS SOCIO-COLBERTIST STATE

The emergence of this 'alternative policy' in French debate, the deep crisis in the financial sector, the re-emergence of the 'special case of France' in GATT (General Agreement on Tariffs and Trade) negotiations, and the current radicalization of the left's discourse were all evidence of the many difficulties that the elite, public opinion and left-wing activists had in accepting the new economic and social order imposed on France by the left from 1983. While authoritarian reform enabled the country to adapt to the new economic circumstances of the 1980s, it failed to bring about any real change in the reflexes of the elite, in the reactions of public opinion or in the identity of the Socialist Party.

The crisis in the financial sector at the time was as effective as a laboratory experiment in demonstrating the effects of a *dirigiste* end to *dirigisme*. Initially – until 1984 – France's financial system was almost wholly nationalized, protected and centrally controlled. The state was simultaneously regulator, owner and interventionist. The Treasury's control of the Banque de France, the underwriting of loans, the ceilings on deployment of funds, cheap funds, and the specialization of areas of operation formed a world in which the Treasury ruled and in which internationalization and diversification were the only areas in which the managers of the financial institutions had any autonomy at all. From 1984, the government launched a brutal deregulation policy, involving *inter alia* the abolition of cheap funds, disintermediation, despecialization and the opening up of networks, but without challenging the public-sector nature of financial institutions. In 1986, the Balladur government then decided to stop underwriting loans, resulting in a brutal challenge to the status quo and exacerbating competition between networks in the search for new areas of activity. Lending literally exploded and poor risks proliferated. Between 1988 and 1990, the Cooke ratios were adopted, the free movement of capital became a reality and the Banque de France began to become more autonomous. Banks that remained largely nationalized became caught up in this whirlwind and had to start behaving like private companies, but still benefited from the state's ultimate protection and also still escaped being subject to independent professional regulation. The outcome of a system in which banks remained under the protection of the state whilst competing against one another for new custom and building up their own funds included the disasters that hit Crédit Lyonnais, Crédit Foncier, the Comptoir des Entrepreneurs, GAN and the Banque de Phénix, among many others.

The social stumbling-blocks to authoritarian reform are demonstrated by the way the socialists managed the reduction of working time. It is well known that at the beginning of Mitterrand's first presidential term there was already discussion of the conditions under which a staged introduction of the 35-hour week could create jobs. The CFDT, in particular, publicly announced its support for a plan to reduce working hours with only partial compensation for loss of pay, provided it was linked to job-creation. Mitterrand, acting alone and in secret, without any consultation with the ministers concerned, decided to reduce the working week to 39 hours on full pay. This decision was to be a major factor in the discrediting of social bargaining and the idea of compromise negotiated with the trade unions; moreover, it had no effect at all in terms of jobs and it stalled the debate for a further ten years. When redistribution was back on the agenda after a period of rising unemployment and when there seemed to be growth again, in 1988 and 1989, Mitterrand publicly instructed Michel Rocard to increase pay, starting with that of public servants. From mid–1991, unemployment started rising again inexorably.

The social stumbling-blocks to enlightened despotism, on the other hand, are illustrated by the debate on Maastricht and on the 'alternative policy'. Maastricht was the culmination of a process of integration that went on largely outside public debate, and the treaty was the crowning glory of a project designed to deprive politicians of their power to manipulate currencies. Because of the constraints of the national political agenda and the need to relegitimate Mitterrand, France opted for a referendum. However, once again war and peace, a social Europe and national authority were invoked instead of a debate on the economic, commercial and monetary virtues of European integration, prompting the Gaullists to spearhead a debate about sovereignty that confused the issue still further. From then on, mistakes in economic policy (such as the calamitous management of German reunification) and the delays in articulating strategy, which inevitably fuelled speculation, called into lasting question the benefits for France of continuing with its strategy on Europe. However, just as the politicians finally understood the degree of integration that had already been achieved and the potential cost of the decline of Europe, the policy was endorsed, and the incomprehension of the French people grew.

Many more examples could be given of the permanent effects of the hiatus between national rhetoric in favour of special pleading and European policy, always with the same result. In the macro-economic context, initial changes eventually resulted in a policy in line with the status quo of the Franco-German axis, while in the meso-economic and social context (for example, institutional reform and reform of social security, the public sector, etc.), brief flurries of authoritarianism alternated with do-nothing strategies, making the cost of change and harmonization very high.

The only question that remains unanswered is whether this form of failure will last and whether the French are destined to oscillate between do-nothing and authoritarian modernizing governments, or whether the European context might provide a decentralized model for resolving conflicts and negotiating compromise.

NOTES

1. I have been criticized vehemently in my work for using the concept of *dirigisme* to describe the state's economic and social role. In this paper, I use the term in its most commonly-used sense – that is, the existence of institutions whose stated aim was to shape economic development, to finance growth and to provide the country's infrastructures, regardless of the realism or effectiveness of the institutions' action.

2. E. Cohen, 'Représentation de l'adversaire et politique économique: nationalisation, politique industrielle et acte unique européen' in *Revue Française de Science Politique*, Vol. 43, No. 3, October 1993.

3. Cf. G. Grunberg in M. Lazar (ed.), *La Gauche en Europe depuis 1945* (Paris: PUF, 1995).

3 The Crisis of the Left and the Renaissance of the Republican Model, 1981–1995

Serge Berstein

When the French left came to power in 1981 following François Mitterrand's election as president, a crucial stage was reached in the history of the left; thanks to the institutional arrangements of the Fifth Republic, this was the first time it was embarking on an experiment in government in the knowledge of the time it had in which to conduct that experiment. However, this was also the first time that the left had had to match its political aspirations against reality. It was to be a formidable test, and one that would confront the left with having to assess whether or not the ideas on which it had based its very identity were viable in practice. The answer was to be in the negative: the left's manifesto produced governmental failure and led to a far-reaching crisis without throwing up any new political ideas. The fundamental disarray resulting from this explains why there has been a return to support for the Republican model, drawing on a solid· historical tradition but also on a series of consensus principles rather than a real form of identity for the left. The history of the left's experiment with government, and of its failure, have real significance only when seen in the complex context of the ambiguous relationship the left had with power.

THE LEFT AND POWER BEFORE 1981

The Republican Left's Experience of Power

Contrary to a view widely held in France but broadly inaccurate, the left held power on a number of occasions after the foundation of the Third Republic. Two qualifications need to be made to this statement, however. The left in question exercised power in a parliamentary-style regime; majorities comprised coalitions in which the different elements had no hesitation in abandoning unfruitful alliances, with the result that the left frequently exercised power in precarious conditions or conditions in which it governed in only the most ephemeral way. This left was primarily a Republican left, and for a long time the socialists played only a minor, even marginal, role within it.

The moderate Republicans of the years 1879–1902 were the left that defended the Republican regime against the monarchist and Bonapartist conservatives. The radicals who exercised power briefly before 1902 and, more sustainedly, from 1902 to 1911, as well as after the First World War in the left Cartel coalitions between 1924 and 1926 and in the neo-Cartel between 1932 and 1934, were a left opposed to progressive Republicans, anti-Dreyfus moderates, or the right of the national bloc and of nationalist Republicans. This was, however, always a precarious exercise of power, threatened at any moment by the break-up of majority coalitions or by grass-roots political movements. The opportunist Republicans of the early days of the Third Republic governed in a context of instability where ministers went in and out of office as a result of clashes between programmes or personalities within the Republican camp. Radical ministers foundered on the hostility of the moderate groupings who were concerned about their vague social impulses – such as that of Léon Bourgeois in 1896 which was concerned about income tax; alternatively, they foundered on sectarianism that threatened national cohesion, such as in the case of Combes in 1904. The crisis of the franc and the revolt of small savers (*le plébiscite des porteurs de bons*) caused the downfall of the Cartel in 1926 on the stumbling-block of money[1] and the uprising of the leagues on 6 February 1934 put an end to the neo-Cartel.[2] It is therefore true to say that although the left governed, it did so under difficult conditions and the experiments were short-lived.

Moreover, it could be argued that between 1880 and 1902, the left sought, throughout the struggle to consolidate the Republic, the 16 May 1877 crisis, *boulangisme*, and the Dreyfus affair, to create a political model based on five fundamental, interconnected elements, the 'Republican model'.[3] The first of these was the absolute primacy of the individual and of his natural rights by 'reason of state' as a legacy of the Dreyfus affair. Then came, in institutional terms, the unconditional attachment to the institutions of the Third Republic, and especially to a practice that ensured the absolute domination of parliament, representing the sovereign nation. Third, at the level of core values, the 'Republican model' drew inspiration from eighteenth-century philosophers and their nineteenth-century successors, the positivists and neo-Kantians, but also from the historical heritage of the French Revolution. Fourth, the 'Republican model' involved a social project – the promotion of Republicanism which, by focusing on school, work and savings, promised the people the creation of a democracy of small landowners each with the tools of his own trade, an ideal dear to the middle class. Finally, at international level, the Republican ideal linked a desire for peace based on the notion of the need for law to resolve disputes between nations with the desire to defend the nation against aggression; France's grandeur was under-written by the spread of its culture, its technical and economic achievements and colonial expansion. This 'Republican model' gradually became the government's manifesto and was to a large extent achieved when, in the early twentieth century, Marxist socialists took over the baton of the thinking of the left.

Marxist Socialism and Power

Until the early twentieth century, socialism was little more than one marginal element within French political life. Its division into numerous factions did not help it to strengthen its influence, and its most revolutionary wing, that of *guesdisme*, was torn between a doctrinal dogmatism that prompted it to refuse to exercise power within a bourgeois regime it was plotting violently to overthrow and support for the Republican movement that ensured its voice reached the population in general and enabled it to capitalize in electoral terms.[4] This contradiction was acceptable while the socialists had no chance of coming to power, but became untenable once the question arose of taking part in a 'bourgeois' government. This was the situation in 1899 when the socialist Millerand agreed to come into the moderate Waldeck-Rousseau's Republican Defence government at the height of the Dreyfus affair. Matters were clarified under the influence of Jules Guesde by condemning 'ministerialism' and then by bringing the socialist parties together in 1905 under the wing of the Section Fran-çaise de l'Internationale Ouvrière (SFIO), on the basis of support for Marxist revolutionary concepts and rejection of participation in government. This theoretical attitude, endorsed from congress to congress under the influence of the militant base of the SFIO, went hand in hand with the increasing integration of socialism within French polit-ical society, its success in legislative and local elections, and the irresistible attraction of the Republican model to the majority of the French population, including the working class. How, then, was this contradiction to be resolved? Enter Jean Jaurès, who was to disentangle the SFIO's long-term aim of proletarian revolution along Marxist lines from its short-term aim of accepting the socialist and reformist elements of the Republican model as a starting-point for achieving immediate improvements in the daily lives of workers. The SFIO was to operate along these lines for more than fifty years, taking 'Jaurès' synthesis' as a purely rhetorical solution, enabling congress resolutions of impeccable revolutionary purity to go hand in hand with practical reformism in everyday matters. The yawning gulf between theory and practice made the SFIO the locus of a permanent crisis, with the activists constantly accusing those in charge of compromise with the bourgeoisie. Above all, the preservation of doctrinal purity, so essential if socialism were to survive, actually required socialism to stay out of power, since the exercise of power would immediately throw up all the contradictions between principle and reality.[5]

This view of power as a curse to be avoided at all costs was exacerbated immediately after the First World War when the Communist Party attempted to capitalize on the ideological legacy of Marxism, criticizing the electoral alliances the SFIO had agreed to with the radicals. French socialists, accused by their erstwhile brothers of collusion with 'bourgeois parties' and described as 'social traitors' and then 'social fascists', found themselves forced by Communist hyperbole to defend their loyalty to the revolutionary tenets of Marxism. Yet at the same time, their electoral success made them a key element in any left-wing majority and it was difficult for them to canvass votes if they would then have to prevent such a majority from taking power. Léon Blum, the Socialist Party's leading theoretician of the interwar period, tackled the dilemma and it was he who gave the party the key to resolving the clash between doctrine and action. He reserved the notion of 'winning power' for the unlikely scenario in which either the Socialists would have an absolute majority in parliament or a majority was held by one of the 'proletarian parties' – that is Socialists and Communists – and defined a number of other notions. The first of these was 'support without participation', a fragile and transient notion that did not survive the Cartel government of 1924. Then he evoked the 'exercise of power in a capitalist regime', for the situation in which the socialists were the major group within a left-wing majority, and also 'occupation of power' under which the fascists were prevented from taking office after 1934. The 1936 elections represented the SFIO's worst nightmare: it had to take power but exercise it within a capitalist regime. The Popular Front's attempts in 1936–1937 at social (but not socialist) policy ended after a year in disappointing failure, opening deep splits within the Socialist Party that were deepened further by the Second World War.[6]

The events of the Liberation only briefly changed the left's relationship with power. From 1945 to 1947, all left-wing movements were represented within tripartite governments, bringing together Socialists, Radicals and Christian Democrats to implement a socialist-style manifesto based on wide-scale nationalization, economic planning by the state, improvements in the lot of workers, and a bold social security programme. However, the outbreak of the Cold War in 1947 marked the end of what could be described as an interlude. The Christian Democrats shifted to the right, while the Radicals, who represented the independent middle classes opposed to intervention by the state, came to appear as the representatives in France of Soviet imperialism and found themselves isolated in a political ghetto. Meanwhile, under their leader, Guy Mollet, the Socialists institutionalized the traditional contradictions between revolutionary Marxist theory, endorsed by successive congresses, and political practice, rendering them allies of the right against the Communists. As in the pre-war period, this gulf brought about a permanent crisis and required the party to keep out of power so as to avoid splits; this happened in 1950, 1957 and again in 1959.[7] The arrival of the Fifth Republic resolved the matter by putting a unified left in opposition for 23 years.

The French Left in 1981

The recasting of the Socialist Party at the Epinay-sur-Seine Congress in 1971 was the undoubted start of the renaissance of the left and its changed attitude towards power. Socialism seemed to keep its identity although, unlike in 1905, 1921 or 1946, Marxism was no longer the unswerving, dogmatically defended doctrine of the movement. Yet the Socialist Party continued to claim vehemently that it was the party of rupture with the capitalist system, claiming that capitalism prevented democratic reform and hence stood in the way of improvements in workers' conditions. As a revolutionary party in the former SFIO mould, it wanted to achieve gradual 'socialization' of the means of investment, production and trade. The party probably banked on winning elections and using democratic means to achieve these changes, yet it rejected the notion that its final objective was to be reformism. Its declaration of principles is crystal-clear on this point: 'Socialist transformation cannot be the natural product or the sum total of reforms which modify the effects of capitalism. Its aim is not to manage a system but to replace it with another'. Moreover, in repudiating the 'Third Force' alliances of the Fourth Republic, the new party declared its willingness to achieve its aims by means of a union of all left-wing organizations and specifically by means of an alliance with the Communist Party. The signature in 1972 of the 'common programme of government' with the Communists under Georges Marchais and the 'left radical' faction under Robert Fabre was evidence of the new Socialist Party's desire to put forward a social alternative to the capitalism of de Gaulle and Pompidou.

Beyond this apparent continuity, however, the rupture was real. The first break was with the heterogeneous composition of the Socialist Party which belied the statements contained in the declaration of principles. It could be argued that there were four major elements to the 1981 Socialist Party. The first was a Marxist wing, represented by CERES and Jean-Pierre Chevènement, who wanted to keep close links with the Communists and shared their analysis of society but not their choice of democratic centralist policies and conformity with the Soviet model. The second was a movement legated by the former SFIO and comprising reformist administrators, the mayors of major cities such as Pierre Mauroy in Lille or Gaston Defferre in Marseille, heading up 30,000 local councillors who were suspicious of the Communist Party. The third was the Republican left, from which emerged the new First Secretary, François Mitterrand, and a number of those involved with his Convention des Institutions Républicaines (CIR), in the mould of Charles Hernu or Roland Dumas. Finally, after 1974, there was the Assises movement made up of self-managing Socialists who had come from the Parti Socialiste Unifié (PSU), the CFDT or the Christian left and who joined the Socialist Party under Michel Rocard. There was the widest possible gap between the first and last of these elements, as there had been in the past between the right and the left within the SFIO. Like his predecessor, Léon Blum, Mitterrand was going to have to manoeuvre between them.

Yet beyond all the images of restoration, the new Socialist Party had split in three ways from the former SFIO and this put a new slant on the left's difficulties with power. These three areas were all related to Mitterrand's personality.[8] Mitterrand had emerged not from the inner circle of socialism but from the milieu of the right, with its imprint of Catholicism, before aligning himself with the Republican left movement with its base of radicalism, and so he had come to socialism through a distrust of money and the financial world that prompted him to declare the capitalist 'monopoly' as anathema. He was relatively indifferent to theoretical discussions of the mechanisms of the capitalist economy and argued that congress resolutions were of less importance than concrete action; nor did he share the party spirit of the former SFIO members or the hope of one day putting an end to the Tours split. Rather, Mitterrand offered the Socialist Party a different way forward. To him, the Party was not the guardian of doctrine but a means of securing a shift in political power that would bring the left to government, and this was one major split that also implied another, that of acceptance of the institutions of the Fifth Republic against which the left had been railing since 1958. Viewed in this way, the key element in the shift in power was the 1965 presidential election in which Mitterrand first took up the fight against de Gaulle and the one he so nearly won in 1974. His argument was that the institutions, tailor-made to de Gaulle's measurements, were able to give a future left-wing government the means of imposing its views, unlike its position in former experiences of government.

The second split is based on the fact that the First Secretary rejected the idea of the party as guardian to which everything else should be subordinate, and this is why he viewed the party as open to all left-wing trends that recognized his desire to transform society; after all, Mitterrand was determined not to limit his changes to the rapidly dwindling working class in a society with a burgeoning service sector. This also had the effect of making the elector more important than the party activist, and the role of the party was reduced to promoting its leaders' election.

The third split, meanwhile, affected the party's relationship with the Communist Party. Mitterrand had no interest in a reconciliation between the two 'proletarian parties', given that he was convinced that the Communists' culture was radically different from that of the rest of the left. Although he abided by the alliance with the PCF, this was because the Communists had electoral support which was crucial to the victory of the left. In other words, the new logic was subordinated not to a doctrine whose purity could have been jeopardized by power, but to the exercise of power itself; this took precedence over sectarianism and congress resolutions because, as Mitterrand repeatedly argued, the party had 'a vocation of government'.

However, the strategy of the left under Mitterrand did not consist solely in taking power but also in exercising that power in a way that would benefit the people and would break with the discourse of private gain. The proposed manifesto centred on three key issues: combating the crisis that had resulted from the rise in purchasing power and the resulting consumer boom, especially among the poorer sections of the population; structural reform to bring about a socialist economy 'on the basis of private and public sector activity but with the public sector dominating', implying wide-scale nationalization 'dominated by the Plan but respecting market forces'; and major reform of various sectors of civil society to protect the most vulnerable in society and change people's moral thinking to a more humanist line.[9] Although this was a long way from the huge revolutionary plans of the erstwhile Marxist parties, the left's plans as outlined by Mitterrand in 1981 seemed to be a useful starting-point for a government of the left, able to function as a common currency for the three elements within the union of the left even if, both inside and outside the Socialist Party, some considered them as no more than the minimum, while others thought they represented risk within the context of a worldwide economic crisis from which France could not extract itself.

'CHANGING LIFE': THE LEFT'S FAILURE OF POWER, 1981–1993

The Left's Experiment (1981–1983)

Having been out of power for 23 years, by the end of June 1981 the left turned into a political majority ready to implement the major changes it had promised the country.[10] For the first time in its history, it seemed to have the resources to do this. Its leader was ensconced as president with the widest-ranging powers of any head of a major democracy. Its key policy-makers were in a government that included not only four Communists alongside representatives of all Socialist Party wings but also, and above all, individuals close to Mitterrand but without parliamentary seats, while Michel Rocard was marginalized as minister of state for the Plan; this deprived him of any influence over immediate decisions, and bore witness to the president's desire to implement the new policy he had made so much of. After all, the Socialist Party had an overwhelming majority in the

Assemblée Nationale, enabling it to impose its views. And it became clear at the Valence Congress in October 1981 that that was exactly what the PS intended to do, appearing to all intents and purposes like a party ready to cash in on its victory by taking control of all the levers of the economy and of society.

Over the next few months, France became an enormous laboratory in which every aspect of national life came under the microscope and reforms were designed, inspired by the ideological foundations of the Socialist Party even though some of them were aimed at combating the crisis or meeting the very real need to adapt society to new conditions. The nationalization policy, for example, owed as much to crisis management as it did to ideology; its aim was to give the state the levers of command over the economy in the shape of the five top performing companies in French industry, two financial companies (Suez and Paribas), and 36 commercial banks which between them accounted for 95 per cent of national deposits, alongside the energy sector, the transport sector and the savings banks that had been nationalized in 1945. Economic planning, sitting on a back burner since the 1960s because of the economic liberalism of former governments, now headed up the menu under Michel Rocard, who instigated a transitional two-year plan, to cover 1982–1983, to correct the trends inherited from the preceding president. He then went on to lay the foundations of a ninth Plan that would translate the Socialists' manifesto into real action. The desire to play the democratic card by bringing citizens closer to the decision-making process explains the measures on decentralization championed by Gaston Defferre as Minister for the Interior; these were to represent a real split from the Jacobin tradition of the French left.

At the same time as structural change was happening in line with the left's ideology, steps were taken to modernize society and make it fairer, more democratic, more humane and more likely to respect the government's values. The Communist minister for health, Jack Ralite, instituted a new health policy that included modernization of facilities, reform of medical training, abolition of private beds in hospitals and the election of the heads of medical services by the whole staff rather than just by doctors, as before. In the field of justice, Minister Robert Badinter stressed the humanization of penal practice, brought about the abolition of capital punishment and of the state security court, and abolished high security wings in prisons. In social and labour policy, the Auroux laws improved workers' rights within the company, while social security reform increased workers' representation on the bodies overseeing management of the social security schemes. To make the elite political academy, the ENA, accessible to a wider section of the population, a special entry pathway was created for those who had held political or trade union office. To ensure the independence and smoothing running of television and radio, a broadcasting authority was created, appointed – like the Constitutional Council – by the Head of State and the presidents of the two assemblies. The minister for education, Alain Savary, drafted a law on higher education that was adopted in 1983 with the aim of helping universities to adapt to the needs for economic and social development within France, while committees worked on reform in primary and secondary schools and training schemes. More sensitive was the implementation of Mitterrand's electoral pledge to make the whole of the education system into a unified, public and non-denominational service, with private schools operating under a kind of licence, and long, tricky negotiations began on this in 1982. In short, no area of national life escaped the reforming zeal of the new government.

However, the key element was the effectiveness of the action taken by the Socialists to combat the crisis, on which public opinion would judge them. There, too, the split with the line taken by the previous president was total; Raymond Barre's policy had been to allow the mechanisms of market recovery to come into place once inflation and public deficits had been dealt with, on the assumption that unemployment would come down as a result of renewed growth, whereas the left juggled the order of these priorities. Their approach was voluntarist action against unemployment, with economic recovery resulting from a boost to consumption following action to increase the purchasing power of the poorest; the money for this policy was to come from higher taxation on the wealthiest. Social justice thus became the instrument of economic recovery which the experts thought would hasten the end of the world recession. In June 1981, the government began implementing this policy by raising family allowances by 25 per cent, increasing basic pensions by 20 per cent and increasing the minimum wage, the SMIC (*salaire minimum interprofessionnel de croissance*), by above the rate of inflation. At the same time, tax rates were increased for high incomes and a wealth tax was created for assets of over FF3 million. To help the fight against unemployment, all workers were given a fifth week's paid annual leave, the statutory working week was reduced from 40 to 39 hours with promises of further cuts eventually to 35 hours, without loss of pay, and it became possible to retire at 60. The package was an impressive one, yet within a few months it became clear that it had failed.

The Left's Threefold Failure[11]

When, on his election, Mitterrand claimed that 'the government of France is now in line with what a majority of society wants', he was saying that from the viewpoint of converting France to a Marxist policy, the left represented the interests of the majority of the French people. Yet the left was to fail socially, economically and politically.

Society itself put up the first resistance to the new policies. The first wave of reforms had been welcomed by a public opinion desperate for change, and the new government enjoyed a brief honeymoon. However, this was over by the autumn of 1981, for rather contradictory reasons. The activists of the left saw themselves as agents of change and grew frustrated with reforming activity that they saw as being too slow or too cautious; their reaction was to support those within the PS and PCF willing to act as gadflies to the leadership. However, their vehemence, and some of the decisions taken by the government to pacify them, exasperated not only this section of the party but also a section of the electors who had elected the left to get the country out of crisis, but who had not expected it to attack their acquired benefits or interests. The government, caught between the demands of the activists and social resistance to its reforms, initially opted to pacify party activists, unleashing a torrent of disaffection in specific groups that contributed to a level of political agitation throughout the country. For example, the residents of large estates around major towns and cities with high levels of ethnic minorities made a major issue of security; traders and manufacturers complained at the level of employers' social security contributions; farmers demonstrated against Agriculture Minister Edith Cresson's policy of challenging the farming world's sole representation by the French farmers' union, the Fédération Nationale des Syndicats et Exploitants Agricoles (FNSEA); executives complained about the fiscal pressure they had been put under as well as the loss of authority they had suffered due to the Auroux laws; doctors banded together to protest against hospital reforms and changes in medical training; university teachers accused Savary of being controlled by political rather than academic considerations; and in the spring of 1982, mass demonstrations were organized by the champions of private education in an attempt to secure a climbdown from a government they suspected of wanting to abolish all private schools. The majority of these protests probably began in political circles more inclined to vote right than left, but they spilled over into substantial sections of those who had voted left and voted the Socialists into power. In late 1982, the split between the government and a major section of French society was a fact, giving the lie to the old idea that a left-wing government would remain in power for a long time since its policies were aimed at satisfying 'the sociological majority'.

Economic failure was no less rapid nor critical, and its consequences were probably even more serious. The left had based its policy on a worldwide economic recovery in which France would lead the rest of the world, but this proved to be wrong. In the autumn of 1981, consumer recovery was producing higher inflation and exacerbating a situation that had already become serious under the right; inflation reached 14.1 per cent in 1981. Unlike its predecessor under Raymond Barre, the new government did not make the value of its currency a priority, although in October 1981 there was an 'adjustment' to the currencies in the Exchange Rate Mechanism (ERM) which produced an 8.5 per cent devaluation of the franc in relation to the deutschmark. The left was more concerned about unemployment, which topped the two million mark at the end of October 1981. The left was unable to change a policy it had been vaunting for so long without admitting it had been mistaken, and the resulting need to hold the line exacerbated the imbalances in the economy: the growth in consumer spending was concentrated mostly on imported goods, the deficit in the balance of trade widened considerably, inflation produced a second devaluation in June 1982, of 9.5 per cent in relation to the mark, and the increase in public spending led to a higher budget deficit which the state attempted to deal with by increasing its domestic and foreign borrowing. In a radical break with the policy implemented since 1981, the government was to take austerity measures, including budget cuts, a major overhaul of social security funding, a one per cent levy on civil servants' pay to meet the deficit in the unemployment insurance scheme, a freeze on prices and wages until the autumn of 1982.

It is clear that regaining economic balance had become a priority for the government. The left was anxious about a shift that appeared to the trade unions, the Communist Party and a section of the Socialist Party to be a fundamental questioning of all the pre-1981 objectives and yet was being presented by the government as being of only minor significance. However, in March 1983 it had to make the

choices it had ducked in 1982. Despite extensive government borrowing, currency reserves dipped as deficits in the balance of foreign trade
and the balance of payments fuelled speculation against the franc. In
January 1983, currency losses reached a level that made further devaluation and a new austerity plan unavoidable. These drastic measures
were postponed until just after the municipal elections in March 1983,
but then revealed two opposing strategies that questioned the very
identity of the French left. On the one hand were the supporters of
Jean-Pierre Chevènement, who argued that the left's manifesto should
be implemented by making a break with the constraints of the market
economy, taking the franc out of the international monetary system,
putting up protectionist barriers and instituting an economy presided
over and run by the state. On the other hand, there were those who
defended the line of Prime Minister Pierre Mauroy, Economics and
Finance Minister Jacques Delors and Budget Minister Laurent
Fabius: they stressed the danger of stepping out of line with the
other major industrialized nations in the world and of resultant
reduced development, and argued instead for accepting international
and European constraints at the cost of austerity. The left had its back
against the wall. It hesitated for ten days, then the president decided in
favour of the latter policy, paving the way for the crisis of the left.

The decision taken in March 1983 can be explained not only by the
constraints imposed by France's close involvement in the world markets, which had been underestimated by the left, but also by the left's
political failures, which unleashed great disillusionment. Initially
stunned by the extent of its defeat in 1981, then torn between the
supporters of Valéry Giscard d'Estaing and those of Jacques Chirac,
who declined all responsibility for the defeat, the right-wing opposition took advantage of the left's economic failure and the social
dissatisfaction this produced. It had only a small representation in
the Assemblée Nationale but made up for lack of numbers by the
force of its speech-making, the sheer number of ways it found to delay
Socialist-instigated measures and its repeated appeal to the Constitutional Court, which vets all proposed legislation in France. It was
encouraged in these robust tactics by public opinion polls that showed
how disillusioned the French people were with their new government
and by its consistent success in winning by-elections. It managed to
channel discontent to its own advantage, in particular the huge rallies
in defence of private schools, and rapidly reaped electoral dividends.
Local elections, which had become more important following legislation on decentralization, illustrated how the right was gaining in public

support. In March 1982, half of all regional councils came up for re-election and the right did extremely well, gaining control of 59 councils to the left's 36. In municipal elections a year later, in March 1983, the right won a majority of the poll, with 53.6 per cent of votes cast against 44.2 per cent for the left. It took control of the 20 *arrondissements* in Paris but also seized control from the left of 30 towns with over 30,000 inhabitants each. Under these circumstances, the left's defeat in the 1986 legislative elections seemed a formality, and within two years its experiment had failed.

The Left in an Impasse

Despite the government's efforts to deny abandoning its 1981 manifesto, the events of 1983 gave it a problem with the validity of the social solutions it had tried to impose on the crisis. It also had a more general problem with the credibility of its political manifesto. To acknowledge that France's openness to the rest of the world made it impossible to operate a national Keynesian-type policy, running counter to trends elsewhere in the world, was to challenge the entire line of argument that underlay the identity of the French left. If it could not carry out a voluntarist economic policy under the control of the state within a liberal economic regime, which was a precondition for the economic growth that formed a cornerstone of the fairer society the left wanted to achieve, then the left had nothing more to offer the French people. It was obliged to admit that market forces prevailed, without any chance of being mitigated by the government, that profit was the sole force driving the economy, that a balanced budget was the key priority of any government, whatever its political complexion, and that social justice was not a precondition for growth but rather a marginal spin-off from unpredictable growth which could result only from international economic trends that France had to adapt to and which it could not safely overcome by measures that went against the grain of the economic cycle. In other words, the choice of more liberal policies in March 1983 brought with it a series of consequences that the left could not openly acknowledge without renouncing its very essence.

And, indeed, from 1983 the consequences of these choices made themselves known.[12] There were three very clear stages in this abandonment by the government of the dogma of the French left, which was to bring it to a state of impasse. The first was the shift in government policy implemented by the Mauroy government after

March 1983. It was symbolized by the resignation from the government of Jean-Pierre Chevènement, champion of a union of the left just tinged with Marxism, who rejected austerity as a new government policy, and also by the less significant resignation of the unclassifiable Michel Jobert, minister for foreign trade, who rejected the liberal logic implied in the choices that had been taken. Four men came to represent this new market forces-oriented policy: Economics and Finance Minister Jacques Delors, Social Affairs and National Solidarity Minister Pierre Bérégovoy, Industry and Research Minister Laurent Fabius, and Michel Rocard, strait-jacketed in the agriculture portfolio by the president's mistrust of him. While intensifying austerity came to mean restrictions on consumer spending, higher unemployment and renewed fiscal pressure, Fabius took up the baton from the president as chief exponent of the new line, arguing for modernization, innovation, business profits and the use of public funds for investment in industrial equipment rather than bailing out poorly performing industries. As a result, there was a wave of restructuring resulting in high levels of redundancy and even threats to the economic viability of entire regions, such as Lorraine. It is hardly surprising under these circumstances that the left's traditional supporters, workers and trade unions, should have organized strikes and demonstrations to protest against the government's policy and that the Communist Party, as well as CERES within the Socialist Party, should have distanced themselves from the policy and accused the government of betraying the union of the left.

The second stage came in early summer 1984, when more than a million people demonstrated in defence of private education and provoked the resignation of the Mauroy government, leading to the appointment of Fabius as prime minister. The new arrival was the perfect embodiment of the social market economy line the president had been pushing since 1983. His manifesto, to 'modernize France and bring the French people together', clearly involved renouncing the 1981 strategy of breaking away from old practices and policies as well as the major plans for change that had torn society in two. The departure from the government of the Communists is itself significant in illustrating the way the government had shifted to more free-market measures, such as a major drop in inflation, unexpected buoyancy on the stock markets, the gradual deregulation of prices and banking, and a slow-down in increases in government spending. The shift also, however, saw unemployment rising to 2.5 million by 1986, with especially high youth unemployment rates, and the introduction of community work schemes (*travaux d'utilité collective*, TUC) paid at rates below the level of the SMIC; these enabled the statistics to be massaged so as to mask the acceptance by the left of a return to job insecurity, since Socialist views on this issue had had to be sacrificed on the altar of the economy in favour of business which now, in a complete reversal of 1981 priorities, took precedence.

The third stage was marked, after Mitterrand's re-election in 1988, by the installation of a Rocard government typified by a desire to be open and to seek consensus that was out of keeping with the traditions of the socialist left. The make-up of the government, including sympathetic centrists and representatives of civil society, demonstrated its intention to seek consensus and to limit its ambitions to reformist social management of society within a framework of market forces, rejecting any large-scale reform. It was a serious government, intent on solving society's long-term social problems without great self-aggrandisement or ideological pretensions, a 'study in greyness' as the new prime minister was to dub his method.

However, this trend precipitated the crisis of the left. Abandoning the policy of breaking away from capitalism marked the demise of the dream that for so long had made the French left the focus of hope for a new type of society. The trade unions, the political parties of the left and their activists had been traumatized by the events of 1983 and disappointed in Fabius, who seemed to them to have been merely a stopgap to pacify public opinion, and now saw Rocard's consensual policies as a weakening of the aims of socialism, a hesitation in endorsing social priorities and an alignment with the arguments of the right that were submerging the identity of the left in a tidal-wave of management. However, although before 1986 the 'people of the left' found virtually no alternatives to the government of the day, this was not the case in 1988. The barely veiled hostility of the president towards his prime minister made Mitterrand's sphere of influence an internal opposition to the government that had its official champion in Fabius, who played the card of a return to old traditional left-wing values (though he himself had not exactly done this) and openly appealed to activists to call for the return of major ideological debate to political life. The forces gathered along this line included the Communists, now in opposition; the supporters of Jean-Pierre Chevènement, whose membership of the Socialist Party seemed more and more of a facade; an emerging Socialist left, the president's supporters, who sometimes sat with the government on the basis of his sovereign will; and the Fabius movement, including those close to the president – with the result that Mitterrand sometimes appeared to be the leader of the opposition within his own government.

This crisis in the left was marked by the fragmentation of the Communist Party, with both the 'reformers' and the 'revisionists' opposed to the leadership of Georges Marchais, and by the disastrous Rennes Congress in 1990, where movements within the Socialist Party, transformed into presidential stables, were launched into a merciless clash with the party heavyweights, Lionel Jospin and Pierre Mauroy, who were discreetly supported by Rocard and the defeated Fabius, the president's quasi-official candidate for the party leadership. It was an internal row that could be explained by the collapse of the left's ideological certainties; the credibility of the Communist solution, questioned for so long, had definitively come crashing down along with the Berlin Wall and had thus brought an end to any suggestion of a policy of state intervention in the economic and social management of French society (that is, the social-democratic solution); and the left's failure in government had wrecked the experimental 'break with capitalism'. All that was left in the wreckage were liberal policies: market forces, free competition, monetary orthodoxy, a balanced budget without a balance of payments deficit, and an unregulated labour market, *inter alia*. The left had completely lost its identity.

THE RENAISSANCE OF THE REPUBLICAN MODEL

An Ideology of Withdrawal

For the left, the alternatives were stark: either to resign itself to the dominance of the force of money and to the law of unbridled profit and allow the richest and most powerful to grow even richer by abandoning workers to the forces of supply and demand, or to return to the modest Republican solution of limited intervention by the state to correct market forces by means of taxation policy and social security expenditure. By promoting the principle of 'solidarity', the French left chose the latter, finding its inspiration in what the radical Léon Bourgeois, the theoretician of 'solidarity', had advocated a hundred years previously, although no one remembered him or acknowledged his role.

There are many examples of this withdrawal of the Socialist left into Republican values (the Radicals had long since done so). It is worth noting that in the 1981 campaign, Mitterrand was faced with

Giscard, who sought to present himself as a disciple of modernism by deliberately rejecting any reference to history; Mitterrand reacted by stressing Republican culture, even though this had apparently gone out of fashion, rather than the 'break with capitalism' of the Socialist manifesto. With his theme of 'quiet force', and against the backdrop of the countryside steeple depicted on the election posters, Mitterrand implicitly evoked the golden age of rural and Republican France, where each individual could enjoy the fruits of his labour in peace, a million miles away from the model of growth his opponent was propagating. This trend was to be accentuated in the 1988 campaign, during which the slogan 'France united' put forward Republican culture as the basis for national consensus. Pierre Mauroy, who was prime minister between 1981 and 1984, moreover, kept up a permanent Republican discourse in which the France of the lowly individual was contrasted with the France of the châteaux, a discourse which of course resonated with the left. Finally, it was the old solidarity principles of the Radicals that became translated into the policy of 'a social solution to unemployment' or, during the Rocard government, the 'solidarity tax on wealth' that was used to finance the RMI and the social security levy in favour of the under-privileged.

The issue is whether this withdrawal into the political culture of Republicanism has been a valid identity for the French left in the late twentieth century.

An Ambiguous Political Model

While reference to the political culture of Republicanism belongs incontrovertibly to the tradition of the left, it is nevertheless self-evident that from the early part of the twentieth century Republican culture has been changing and that (particularly with the Fifth Republic) it took on a significantly different content from that envisaged by the founders of the regime or the Radicals of the Combes era.[13] Moreover, the history of the Republic itself is too long and complex to result from one single tradition. To simplify matters, let us assume two different views of the political culture of Republicanism.

The first is minimalist, legal and largely consensual and has the support of virtually all groups in contemporary France, with the exception of the extreme right and a few small factions without any real basis of popular support. This is the basic Republican culture which Gaullism recast between 1958 and 1974. It refers back to the very first Republic in its attachment to national sovereignty, equality before the law, and defence of human rights as fundamental principles of social organization. However, it distinguishes itself from this by the fact that there is no longer any specific philosophical theory attached to it, as positivism and neo-Kantianism had pertained to the Third Republic in its beginnings; nor does any particular period of history play the key role of the French Revolution as a turning-point in the history of humanity. Instead, all phases of national history, except Vichy, have their own legitimacy. Above all, this form represents a break with the original Republican model by representing the view that there is no conflict between the sovereignty of the national and a strong executive. Finally, in keeping with Republican solidarity, this form of Republicanism seeks to implement social solidarity to combat the effects of recession. The problem is that this minimalist Republican model is in no way the prerogative of the left. The majority of the French right also claims it, and it is worth noting that President Chirac had, under the aegis of Philippe Séguin, centred most of his electoral campaign on restoration of the 'Republican pact' and on traditional Republican discourse. From then on, reference to the Republic and its principles was the subject of a broad consensus that tended to blur the distinction between left and right in a rather ambiguous 'centre Republic' and could not therefore constitute a real identity for the left.

Yet there is another view of Republican culture, more militant and less anodyne than that in which the Republic is a regime with primarily legal rather than cultural values. It is around this second view that the left seems to be rallying now that it has been disoriented by the collapse of its traditional values. This form affirms its continued faith in the progress of mankind, its attachment to non-denominationalism as a positive doctrine rather than a simple passive neutrality, its rejection of monarchical drift in the shape of the institutions of the Fifth Republic, its desire for social solidarity beyond the struggle against poverty, presupposing state control over the economy which would not be abandoned to market forces, and a vision of international affairs in which ethical principles count for more than *Realpolitik*. It has still, however, to formulate clearly the manifesto implications of this shift so that it becomes evident what new programme would emerge after the government's failure to justify putting the left back in power again.

The left's experience of power under Mitterrand's two presidential terms has been a formidable test for the left. It has emerged shattered in its age-old certainties, and fragmented. The term 'bomb-site', applied by Rocard to the Socialist Party, goes for the whole of the left. Economic trends probably played their part in the failure, since in times of economic crisis governments always lose elections – as evinced by the defeat of the Juppé government and the surprise victory of the left in the 1997 parliamentary elections, after two years of austerity. Nevertheless, there is more to it than that. There is little doubt that, even taking into account the changes since the 1970s, the left's manifesto once it gained power in 1981 was one of Marxist aims tempered by Keynesian principles. Yet the world in which it had to function was now ruled by different theories; greater liberalism and the dominance of monetarism put the left at odds with worldwide trends, and the clash between the left's manifesto and world reality in the late twentieth century led to the collapse of the left. All that the left can now do to save face is to manage the country along liberal economic lines and to shelter behind the rhetoric of a Republican model that has proved useful. It is a palliative, though, not a real identity and the left is going to have to invent a new political culture and a vision of society more in keeping with the world of the twenty-first century.

NOTES

1. J.-N. Jeanneney, *Leçon d'histoire pour une gauche au pouvoir. La faillite du Cartel (1924–1926)*(Paris: Seuil, 1977).
2. S. Berstein, *Le 6 février 1934* (Paris: Gallimard-Julliard, 1975).
3. S. Berstein and O. Rudelle (eds), *Le Modèle républicain* (Paris: PUF, 1992).
4. C. Willard, *Les Guesdistes*, (Paris: Editions sociales, 1966).
5. A. Bergounioux and G. Grunberg, *Le Long Remords du pouvoir* (Paris: Fayard, 1992).
6. Ibid.
7. S. Berstein and P. Milza, *Histoire de la France au XXe siècle* (Brussels: Complexe, 1995).
8. A. Bergounioux and G. Grunberg, op. cit.
9. Ibid.
10. The account of the left's experiences in government is drawn from Berstein and Milza, op. cit.
11. Ibid.
12. Ibid.
13. S. Berstein, 'La Ve République, un nouveau modèle républicain', in S. Berstein and O. Rudelle, op. cit.

4 The *Parti Socialiste* after Mitterrand: A Half-Finished Modernization

David Bell

The legacy of the Mitterrand years for the Parti Socialiste is not one of unrelieved gloom. Although the 1980s was a bad decade in which to come to power, the Socialist governments made significant progress in many areas. Notwithstanding recession and sluggish growth in France's main export markets, investment increased, the economy was expanded and modernized, competitiveness improved, and inflation, like the balance of payments deficit, was brought under control. At the same time the welfare system was markedly expanded. In sum, the French economy was further freed up, but without the excesses of 'Thatchernomics' or the cutback in industrial output suffered in the UK. A difficult international environment of transition from Cold War to American withdrawal was mastered by a vigorous European foreign policy. The 'Mitterrand governments' of 1981–1986 and 1988–1993 were not miracle workers, but they acted on a broad front and in some domains were comparable to the great reforming socialist governments in the rest of Europe. Mitterrand also gave the left time, something it has not had in the past: before 1981, France had known only five years of Socialist-led administration (including Mendès France). To the list of President Mitterrand's achievements could therefore be added the habituation of the French public and political elite to the alternating of government and opposition and the acceptance by the left of the Fifth Republic.

But if things were so good, why were they so bad? Part of the answer lies in the international conjuncture, for which Mitterrand cannot be blamed. The Socialists came to power after the 'Trente glorieuses', and the dash for growth of 1981–1983 did not yield its expected fruits. The result was the U-turn and an acceptance of competitive disinflation: the success which dare not speak its name. The 'failure' of the PS, climaxing in its near meltdown at the polls in 1993, comes not from the balance sheet of government itself (or not exclusively) but from the failure of reformist culture in the PS:[1] a failure by Mitterrand and his entourage to develop a governmental philosophy, a moderate social democratic position, and to bring the party into line with that vocation. The result has been a virtual return to the Parti Socialiste's beginnings after fourteen years of tenure at the Elysée, together with the need to recreate the party on an entirely different foundation. This is the work which Prime Minister Lionel Jospin, the party's 1995 presidential candidate, has begun to undertake and which will have to be pushed to a conclusion if it is to have any realistic future in national government (rather than as a protest party achieving the spasmodic capture of power followed by rapid collapse).

The argument here is one which bears on the Mitterrand years, but also on the future of the French left. Briefly stated, Marxist philosophy – pervasive but inappropriate and misleading – had not merely a rhetorical effect on the PS but also a practical, political one. The party was prevented from modernizing during the Mitterrand years, and then when it did change, it did so on the wrong terms. However, the PS remains to be transformed; and the nature of the task undertaken by Lionel Jospin from 1995 was essentially to deal with its lack of direction and the crisis of 'socialist thought'. The party's takeover by Jospin has led to its shedding much of its Mitterrand heritage – paradoxically, given that Jospin was one of Mitterrand's 'dauphins' and a loyalist against those (notably Rocard) who had wished to make-over the party in the decade before. There are other problems with French socialism, but the view here is that the unadapted political culture was (and is) the main one.

The starting-point for the contemporary folk-memory of the PS is the 1971 Epinay-sur-Seine Congress of unification. Here, Mitterrand joined the party and took it over, supported by the unlikely coalition of the Marxist CERES and the Nord-Bouches-du-Rhône. But the 'party of Epinay' merely rebuilt a rhetorical purity around 'opposition', as had happened before, and with which it tried to dominate the Communists in the continuing fraternal combat. The consequences of this doctrinal rigidity were far-reaching and diverted the PS from its reformist vocation. It never came to terms with the need to establish viable reform projects and was content instead with a Marxist gloss on the rhetorical threat to overthrow 'capitalism'.

Hence the Mitterrand years, like the Popular Front, began with a fierce ideological commitment which stoked up expectations of *les lendemains qui chantent*, but were not backed up by achievement. From this archaic ideology follow the problems of the contemporary party which seeks to find its new course. The change in direction was not as rapid nor as fatal as is often presented, but the 'dash for growth' was ended in 1983 and the shift towards a 'culture of government' (rather than opposition) was well underway by 1986. Nevertheless, the regeneration was aborted and by 1993 the PS was a shambles. The year 1993 was the apotheosis of the Mitterrand era and the end of the 'Epinay' party.[2]

If this interpretation of French socialism is accurate, then what the Mitterrand domination of the party did was to use and reinforce the revolutionary outlook in the Marxist tradition of the SFIO, and to expand the radical rhetoric without providing any substance to this verbal excess. There then followed the cauterization of the 'fabianite', gradual and consensual reformism which would normally have been dominant in a social democratic party like the PS. Of course, the French Socialist Party did not possess the secret remedy for the socialist and 'self-managing' 'Third Way' between Communism and social democracy (a philosopher's stone claimed by a variety of parties at different stages of the Cold War). As the election platforms such as the *110 propositions* show, the radical reformist remit was intact and the PS had a standard Western socialist agenda in the final analysis. But by the same token, the party was unable to fully 'social democratise' after the rout of the PCF at the polls and the collapse of Soviet 'really existing socialism'. It was unable to do this because the Mitterrand heritage had to be repudiated and no movement could have turned on its past with the speed required. Moreover, the factional life of the party, never torpid, had been flailed into further vigorous action in battles between the old-guard Mitterrandists (themselves divided) and Rocard, the party's eternal *'présidentiable'*. Thus both institutional and ideological reasons prevented a modernistic regrounding and rebuilding of the party. This failure can be briefly summarized.

What was the mythical 'party of Epinay' other than a vehicle for the Mitterrand presidential bids of 1974 and 1981? The party had made a Faustian bargain with Mitterrand, the only potential president on the left, and had become the vehicle for a presidential bid (and was gratified to be so). Hence the party has to be understood in this context: the Florentine but unremitting search by Mitterrand for the pole position in the presidential race. The PS's revolutionary origins, however, were evident and worth revisiting, because Mitterrand used what he found. An artful politician who travelled ideologically light, Mitterrand did not create a new political culture of the left.

Moreover, the PS's institutional machinery was set up and run for Mitterrand's purposes; it became steadily more obedient. The Mitterrand 'vanguard' party which drove the movement from 1971 to 1981 spoke of the 'break with capitalism' and the domination of capital through planning and 'self-government'. Behind this attack on the 'contradictions of capitalism' lay the billowy notion of the Socialist 'alternative' in which profit would no longer be the master of humanity and exploitation would end, with 'mass action' potentially playing a determining role.[3] The party derived its ideology from a variety of sources, not the least being '*soixante-huitards*', but the political intent was to cover the gap between the PS and the PCF with a plausible Marxism and to re-emphasize the party's left-wing credentials against the PCF. It also opened up a flank for Rocard to attack the PS leadership for their head-in-the-clouds lack of realism – an elephant trap into which most of the Mitterrand entourage fell (Fabius being a famous example). That the party won in 1981 was a demonstration of the presidential effect, a result of the careful tailoring of the message to different audiences as well as the discounting of the more colourful aspects of the Socialist stances.

The 'break with capitalism' was relentlessly promised in the party's various position papers throughout the 1970s and into 1980. The 1979 Congress of Metz was exemplary in this respect, with the various leadership supporters (and CERES) hammering the internal opposition for this 'deviation' from the narrow path. The break-up of the alliance of the left by the Communists in 1977 meant that the PS was under attack from the PCF for a rightward move, the better to 'betray' the workers. This was the political dynamo which drove the ideological posturing: the PS was prepared to bury any *parler vrai*, to persist in its 'archaism', to persuade a relatively small group of activists. The revolutionary ideological mode, the anti-Americanism and the state-centric nationalism, which it adopted for reasons of political expediency, turned the party towards such fanciful notions as suppressing the market and overcoming the constraints of 'bourgeois' economics. This outlook was light-years away from the practical problems of government. The question to which the party has had to return, and which it successfully evaded while holding power, is how to match up words and deeds, how to give a reasoned explanation of the state of contemporary France without either excessive optimism or excessive 'realistic' pessimism. Mitterrand provided two Molletist (or Blumian) responses – both rejected: the one of rhetorical excess, the other of tactical manoeuvre. The Party took a U-turn in 1983, but this renewal was not carried through to completion.[4]

The Socialist Party, while in government, had to change its ideological thrust, no longer taking the desirable for the possible.[5] The language of the 1970s was ill-adapted to a governing party, especially one competing for the 'floating vote', with the PCF a spent force. The point of pressure came in 1983 with the third crisis of the franc and the end of the 'lyrical phase' of Socialist government. The initial 'Popular Front' interlude had introduced a raft of measures of a populist nature and had been intended to promote rapid growth through redistribution and consumption, and was associated (unfairly) with Prime Minister Pierre Mauroy. The change was endorsed by President Mitterrand in style: he reaffirmed the virtues of the 'mixed economy' and in July 1984 appointed a young prime minister, Laurent Fabius (now representing a new modernism and market discipline). The austerity policy put in place by Mauroy was extended by Fabius, who began to restructure the recently nationalized (and loss-making) industries.

But the Socialists had not come to power in order to 'administer the crisis', and they faced the difficulty of remaining consistent with their previous declarations. Continuity was initially maintained by assertions that *rigueur* was a temporary measure to enable the corner to be turned. Nor was the past entirely repudiated: the victories over inflation remained orphans, never properly adopted by the PS. Nevertheless, the Fabius government managed to develop a certain credibility with the financial markets and the public about its administrative competence. Its commanding theme was 'modernization' (this new line started in 1983 under Mauroy, not in 1984 with Fabius) and the slogan was used to introduce the managerial issues lacking in previous Socialist declarations. The PS was torn by the same forces which wracked the SFIO: electoral opportunism on the one side but flanked by an uncompromising ideological Marxism. Would the party succeed in reconciling the romantic with the real?

The 1985 Congress of Toulouse was ostensibly one of unity and consensus, very different in tone from the triumphalism of 1982. It was characterized by indirect rather than direct debate (it being thought potentially disastrous to indulge in factional squabbles while in government). Fabius's pragmatic approach was both endorsed and contested. The main change was what the PS dropped rather than what it embraced: the party did not resume its commitment to 'break with capitalism' and acknowledged the constraints of the world economy while accepting market disciplines. Yet its pro-gramme – still Marxist in tone – was not redrafted to 'modernize' its appeal (being rewritten only in 1995), and remained wedded to the state as the instrument. Inside the party, the Rocard problem persisted (Rocard had resigned from the government), and any change could look uncomfortably like a retrospective concession to the 'enemy' within. No rediscovery of the meaning of socialism was made and the result of the congress was a 'bran-tub' with something for every-body, as the PS sought to draw the left back behind it and position itself to seek new allies in anticipation of the legislative elections of 1986 and the presidentials of 1988.

The 'cohabitation' between Mitterrand at the Elysée and the neo-Gaullist Chirac at Matignon served to dampen debate still further, as PS leaders strove to give the president a free hand in the battle against the right. Nothing innovative was attempted and, by intention, the 1987 Lille Congress resembled more of an American campaign rally than any preceding Socialist congress. It was left to the presidential candidate's manifesto, 'Propositions pour la France', to introduce a restrained and unspecific reform programme in the most general terms. The sweeping declarations of previous campaigns were replaced with anodyne promises and the commitment to a 'France unie'. The left-wing inflection evident amongst some PS leaders (hop-ing to keep together the *peuple de gauche*) was not echoed in a statement which renounced all calls for nationalizations, planning, self-government and revolutionary change. If it was not registered and codified, the drift was towards a non-sectarian social democracy. This slow evolution eventually led Chevènement's supporters to leave the PS altogether.

However, the party had postponed the overdue re-examination of its basic outlook. Nor was this resumed at the March 1990 Rennes Congress, where factional infighting surged onto centre stage (before a horrified public), despite the president's efforts to prevent a full-scale bust-up at a critical point in the electoral cycle. The Rennes Congress was not an academic seminar on the Socialist future: it was a bruising confrontation of factional (and presidential) ambitions from which no coherent position emerged. The ideological differences remained and, although partially muted, they were untouched by the experience of government, cohabitation, or the collapse of the Soviet bloc. The ensuing composite (*Rassembler la gauche*), which enabled a Carthaginian peace to be established in the leadership, was another fudge, and reconsideration of the future was postponed to a national convention to be held the following year. The renovation of the PS again became caught up in the Mitterrand faction's internal politics, as the main forces (Fabius and his allies) refused to disown the heritage and refused to embrace any social democratic option. With Rocard as prime minister, the implicit deal (leave the party alone and keep Matignon) was broken by the Rocardians, although not openly, and Rocard's practical consensus method in office proved insufficient to dominate the party (though he remained astonishingly popular in the polls).

It was this standstill in programmatic renewal which led Rocard to propose the 'big bang' of the left in February 1993. Rocard noted that the term 'socialism' itself belonged to another epoch, that the movement needed a much wider, more eclectic 'rally' and a discovery of a stage beyond social democracy to succeed. Coming as it did before the elections, the 'big bang' began with the collapse of the Socialist universe, but did not go into expansionary mode. Rocard engineered a coup against First Secretary Fabius in April 1993 and organized an '*Etats généraux*' in Lyons in July 1993. This meeting was a vast consultation process but had the political inconvenience of cutting the party out of the activity (why bother to join or support the PS?) and failing to cut other groups in (they were consulted but not given power). The problem was reinforced at the October 1993 Bourget Congress because the party, reduced to an isolated archipelago of strongholds, hesitated between a return to opposition and the culture of government.[6] This was the position when Rocard was in turn evicted by the Mitterrandist Henri Emmanuelli after the disastrous European elections of June 1994.

This brief review of the Socialist Party in the Mitterrand years illustrates that while its origins and strategic dilemmas are very different from those of the big northern social democratic parties, nevertheless its crisis is much like that in the Western movement as a whole. The make-over of the PS under Jospin is not an exact parallel with Blair's New Labour, but there are points of similarity. Thus any discussion of the position of the post-Mitterrand PS will inevitably sound like a general tour of the current difficulties of social democracy. The French situation illustrates some wider points about the limits of the Social Democratic model without, unfortunately, bringing any clear solutions. All the same, the French Socialists were by 1995 at the starting-point (*année zéro*) with little tangible to show for fourteen years of tenure at the top and the formidable task of modernization yet to be achieved.

The first, most evident problem is the ideological vacuum on the contemporary left. This necessitates in particular the rethinking of the welfare state in a new individualistic climate. Paradoxically, the collapse of Communism did not benefit the socialist parties, which had set their face against the totalitarian version of socialism; on the contrary, it further discredited the idea of the state as an intervening regulator and planner. Socialism after 1990 appeared less as an alternative to *laissez-faire* than as a variant of Communist state socialism. The rejection of the state was not taken as far in France as in the UK, but the right won some notable victories, and the same 'Thatcherite' traits were apparent: privatization, welfare reform, and a squeeze on public spending.

Rocard's famous speech to the 1977 Congress of Nantes stressed the virtues of the market as an institution and set of unimpeded exchanges as against the (Marxist) central direction of civil society. However, by 1990 the problem was less about promoting free markets than about grappling with the 'social deficit'. The positive side of the message goes back to 1983 and the strategy of deflation to keep the franc in line with the mark (and then to fulfil the Maastricht criteria). This *pensée unique* has been widely criticized, but cannot be denounced by a PS which introduced it and implemented it with determination. The social accompaniment to a 'Bérégovoy' economic policy has yet to be developed and the PS's most strident critics are those on the left who come from unrealistic positions. This new relationship has yet to be mapped out, but the PS in government did try the classical remedies of stimulating growth through redistribution. External constraints showed that 'social democracy in one country' will meet balance of payments problems before it can solve the crisis of the 'two nations'.

Unemployment was the *tête de turc* for the 1981 Socialist government and the principal cause of discontent in the French electorate during the 1980s and 1990s. The parties in power in Europe presided over a seemingly inexorable rise in unemployment. The commitment to full employment had been abandoned in the UK by the Labour governments in the 1970s, but the big continental parties took longer to reach that position. In the PS the re-evaluation of the role of the welfare state has yet to begin in earnest. The state's role is still seen as largely positive in most continental countries, but the Mitterrand policies largely bolstered the 'privileges' of those in work without providing for the unemployed. This could be the French version of the 'culture of contentment' (to use Galbraith's term) but the effect of

the Socialist governments was to fail to tackle the growing divide[7] – a
political problem since the increased demand on taxpayers is open to
political exploitation, and since unemployment is the main cause of
inequality in French society. There are also questions about the cost
to employers of the social security system and its effect on job creation. The steady increase in costs to the state of the welfare state (itself
a product of the crisis) has prevented intervention in other areas such
as the estates and suburbs which have become symptomatic of the
lack of resources for the marginalized of French society.[8] What is
needed, and balked at, is a tax reform to facilitate reinforcement of
social solidarity – perhaps on a means-tested selective basis. All of this
touches directly on the left's commitment to 'universal' benefits.

Expectations in 1981 had been high and were further fuelled by
unguarded rhetoric concerning the elimination of the job queues. The
Socialists escaped condign punishment from the voters for this failure
to return to full employment, largely through the manipulative arts of
the president. Jospin has to live with the legacy that the years of
Socialist government failed to make any appreciable impact: his proposals in the 1995 presidentials were realistic but very limited.[9] Jospin
envisaged the rebuilding of the run-down parts of cities and a house-
building programme, an extension of social services and a programme
for the environment. To help the business sector to create jobs, a
series of similarly modest measures was proposed, including the les-
sening of taxes and credit facilities. The other, more controversial,
measure floated by Jospin was the left's touted reduction of the working week, in this case to 37 hours by 1997. This reduction of working
time runs up against the difficulty of the cost to business (which could
be counter-productive) or the resistance of unions to wage cuts (even
in the service of the unemployed). The benefits of the reduced working
week on employment are not unambiguous. Jospin's views were very
similar in form and presentation to the right's proposals: had they
been put into effect, their impact on the dole queues would have been
small. His proposals on unemployment were low-key and restrained;
on this as on other matters, he did not inflame expectations.

The attack on 'collectivism' by the new right was principally economic but it also touched on another aspect of social democracy: its
over-reliance on 'mass' bureaucratic solutions to social demands. The
standard of provision in the welfare state might have been unprecedented, but the uniformity of provision was also a potential political
problem. Political liberty had never been attacked directly by social
democracy (which had enhanced freedom and bolstered parliamentary

regimes in post-war Europe and in Mediterranean Europe after the dictatorships) but the tables were turned by the new right.[10] By widening the dimensions of liberty to include choice, the new right succeeded in appealing to the core constituencies of the socialist parties: the skilled working class and middle class became a target group, because the compromise between them and the welfare state had to be ended.

The tension between welfare provision and individual choice is not new and the philosophical argument about positive and negative liberty itself hardly novel, but the right succeeded in making choice a spearhead of its attack on socialism. One response has been to re-argue the case for social welfare as a contribution to positive liberty: this Rocardian line that social security and liberty were not incompatible was taken by a number of northern social democratic parties, and social solidarity has been stressed as a social value elsewhere. It is not the sole property of social democrats that in order to participate in society one needs certain basic prerequisites: the Christian Democratic centre and the French Republican traditions take a similar view of the value of provision to enable full citizenship.

However, in some societies people have begun to opt out of systems of state provision, reducing further the general support for social democratic welfare regimes. The problem of payment for the 'lavish' welfare regimes of Western Europe began to be raised as an economic issue.[11] In political terms, the society which has moved most has been the UK, which has created a culture of contentment: as long as people do not need welfare or state provision – and most people most of the time do not – why pay for it for other people? The original 'social democratic compromise' brought the middle classes into the welfare system, something which was broadly accepted. This provision was attacked in the 1970s on the grounds that the middle classes did not need it (or could provide for themselves) before it became an issue for the new right. How the constituency which supported the original welfare states and the extension of provision can be reconstituted (in the UK) or kept together (in France and Scandinavia) is a political conundrum which has not yet been solved. The tension between who pays and who receives has been made more acute in Western Europe than at any time since the war. A French response to the liberal challenge has yet to be made.

Meanwhile, the international milieu has been changed out of recognition in the years since the collapse of the Eastern bloc. Perhaps the most crucial contemporary issue here is European integration.[11] The relationship between the social democratic parties and Europe can hardly be said to be simple. At the outset most socialists, despite an avowed internationalist background, a determination to transcend the nation-state, were sceptical or had significant anti-European sentiments. By the 1970s most of the socialist parties had been reconciled to the European enterprise and some were very enthusiastic. The French party had passed through its Dark Night of the Soul in the mid–1970s, when the pressures of the Communist alliance transmitted through CERES occasioned a move towards a less federalist position than the old SFIO.[12] The issue was debated in lurid terms in the mid–1970s, with the anti-Europeans making the running and the pro-Europeans on the defensive. However, Mitterrand's U-turn and the 'decision for Europe' in 1983 (the rejection of the 'Albanian option'), had served to confirm the PS's inherent pro-Europeanism. Its contribution to the construction of Europe was substantial: the southern enlargement, the SEA and the TEU.

Thus in a backhanded but politically awkward way, Mitterrand in the early 1990s was the pacemaker and the originator of moves to reinforce the EU which led to the Maastricht treaty of 1992. However, the commitment to Europe was partly an alibi for the U-turn and the perspective of the new Europe has not been spelt out (other than by neo-liberal supply-siders) so that the left's constituency has not been brought along by these developments or by the federal idea. The Maastricht referendum revealed the extent to which there was a disparity between the left's European project and the voters. The 'oui' and 'non' vote echoed the cleavage between *les deux France*: the centre and periphery, the one Republican and secular, the other Catholic and conservative. The PS has worked against the current of its core support and is vulnerable to the protectionist, nationalist, anti-foreign appeal of the FN and (possibly still) the PCF.[13] The successive Mitterrand governments, which did so much to integrate Europe at an elite level, did not marry the free-market Europe that impacts on ordinary people with the over-arching European ideal. The Maastricht treaty would have included a social chapter to balance the market-oriented thrust of its other aspects had the PS been successful. But the treaty did not reinforce the powers of the parliament which the Socialist parties of Europe, in a federalist mood, had seemed to want at one point in 1991, and if anything reinforced the Council.

One problem with the Socialist Party's European commitment is that Europe has become associated with the rise of unemployment (from 9.4 to 11.2 per cent in France from 1989–1993 and from 8.9 to

11.1 per cent in the Union as a whole) and the decline of job security, leading to growing public disquiet about Europe.[14] Despite the strength of the Socialists in the European Parliament (198 seats out of 567), the socialist parties have not found a way to use the issue or unite on a European programme. The transposition of the national model of social democracy to a European level and the construction of social Europe have barely started, and it is an irony that the Maastricht treaty, which caused such problems for Socialists, was meant to remedy the social protection gap opened up by the SEA. While there has been a recognition of Europe as the forum for social democracy, the European enterprise does challenge some socialist tenets: events are no longer exclusively influenced at national level and national regulations are dismantled without any corresponding EU laws being elaborated. Hence the Socialists' European commitment runs counter to the current trend of Europhobia on the left, and this is especially so in France after the divisive 1992 referendum: (in the elections of 1993) 59 per cent of constituencies with a deputy on the left voted 'no' as against 35 per cent with a deputy of the right,[16] and the party found itself at odds with its working-class and white-collar electorate.

The European policy of the PS stands revealed as a French perspective on Europe's problems rather than a vision of the new Europe or part of a socialist approach (which, in truth, few parties have supplied because the current crisis of socialist ideology has made a coherent approach difficult to develop). The French party set underway, as noted, the process which led to the liberalization of the European social space and presided over the rise of unemployment which characterized the 1980s. It also used the EC as an excuse to ditch the policies on which it was elected in 1981, sold to voters as the sovereign remedy for French unemployment. This has been compounded by the debate on EMU in 1999 and the strictness of the convergence criteria. In France as elsewhere, the decade has therefore witnessed a rise in public worries about Europe. The 1992 Maastricht referendum did nothing to allay these anxieties; on the contrary, it allowed them to be expressed to the detriment of the federalist momentum in the PS, which was curtailed.[17] Thus Mitterrand, using the referendum to divide the right, placed the Council at the centre of European affairs and emphasised 'subsidiarity'. Other Socialist personalities have downplayed the stringency of the conditions for monetary union. In short, the Socialists have no more solved the incipient tension between the state and the European dimension than have other socialist parties, and are poised between a federalism which has become increasingly timid and a national sovereignty which offers tempting demagogic possibilities.

It need hardly be said that if the Socialists have shown good intentions they have not progressed much further than the declaratory stage in practice. The 1994 manifesto of the Party of European Socialists foresaw an introduction of qualified majority voting instead of unanimity and the development of a European army.[18] A common foreign and security policy was launched as a result of Mitterrand's initiative; yet this is still at some distance and kept thus by differing national outlooks. French 'exceptionalism' has steadily been reduced during Mitterrand's tenure and, even though France's defence policy remains distinctive, relations with NATO have improved and the Western European Union (WEU) has been given a European dimension. For the PS, which has a commitment to military intervention and armed action, this is a crucial point and it is difficult to see how Europe itself can progress unless it is resolved in favour of a real European defence policy. If national calculations still weigh heavily in the balance, Europeanism made a definite advance in the Mitterrand presidency.

In France, as throughout Western Europe, party membership has been in decline and the nature of activism has undergone substantial changes with the individual members playing a smaller role. Collective decision-making has been replaced by small teams, the party press has all but disappeared and bureaucracies have grown.[19] This decline in numbers and the mutation in the nature of commitment is evident in left-wing (and extreme left-wing) parties; nor are conservative forces exempt.[20] Where the party membership still plays a role is in the selection of candidates and the increasing trend to vote for leaders: Jospin was made leader by the party members, a form of designation exclusive to the PS.

However, the SFIO was the first mass activist party and the left's originality and self-image stem from this mass support. The socialists were part of tight communities participating in a vast social network of clubs, unions, newspapers, self-help organizations, co-operative societies and the like. The position of the PS is slightly different in that the PCF took over some of this natural 'social democratic' society in the mid–1930s and held its loyalties until recently, leaving the PS correspondingly weak. However, the same traits were evident in the big working-class federations of Nord, Pas de Calais and in the Bouches-du-Rhône, and the PS aspired to the same level of activism.

It was organized as a mass activist party but without the same close links to the unions as in Northern Europe and without the same populist base (still largely Communist, where it survived) even though its middle-class intellectual and professional membership was always large.

The organizational distinctiveness of social democracy is fast diminishing. Individualism has sapped the organizational culture of the PS and put a freer, more 'liberal' party structure in its place, often in the name of internal 'democracy'. At the same time recruitment to the party has become more eclectic. The rigid secularism which once almost defined the SFIO has dissipated in the PS, revealing the effect of the long march of the *'soixante-huitards'* through the party. This has facilitated the break-up of its homogeneity and an increase in factionalism often along highly distinctive ideological lines. The French party needed no lessons in factionalism and in the 1980s it shared these centripetal features with the traditionally more stolid Northern parties. Factional fighting in socialist parties (left-right divisions) was intense in the 1970s; in the French PS it was at its most bitter around the time of the Metz Congress, which saw CERES/ Mitterrand defending a Marxist outlook pitted against the 'American left' led by Rocard. Similar clashes took place elsewhere, but with different outcomes and without the flexibility to resolve the conflict (as the French party did) whilst in government.[21] In many cases the generational conflict was envenomed by the attempt to control wages, thereby making demands on the party's traditional supporters. If these left-wing insurgencies were mostly over by the late 1980s, the factionalism, which Mitterrand used to manipulate the party, was not.

Social democratic parties are in most systems 'natural governing parties'. Having held the Elysée since 1981, the PS also face contemporary challenges of political competition in the electronic media and in the press and like other parties have risen to this by developing an increasingly professional political and public relations elite. The media also magnify the prescience and importance of the new elite. Socialist parties are no longer dependent on the transmission belt of activist supporters getting the message across and the vote out. In most Western European societies they have ceased to depend on activists for fund-raising as well. The springs from which these supporters were drawn have also dried up, as they have for other parties. At the same time, the percentage of manual workers joining the party has declined and the trend for middle-class *cadres* to take over has been accentuated. The French party was appreciably post-modern from 1969 in its low working-class representation (pinched out as you ascend the apparatus) but now resembles most other Western socialist parties in this respect and in its high number of public-service workers.

The PS faces particular difficulties as a result of the presidentialization of the political system and the corresponding concentration on an individual at the top. Leadership is expected from one individual, who has the command of overall strategy in government and opposition. Legitimacy flows from the leader (not the party) and Mitterrand's victory in 1981 reinforced this tendency. Leaders draft personal, not party, manifestos for presidential elections. The PS benefits by being the only party from which a serious challenge to the right can be mounted; therefore any politician ambitious for the presidency must stake a claim within it. But the same logic turns the party into a vehicle for a presidential bid by one or other of its leading figures. It has been fortunate in having a number of politicians of 'presidential timber' but this, too, has its difficulties, animating the already incipient factionalism. Jospin's credibility, deriving first from his showing in the presidentials, then from his victory in the 1997 legislative elctions and subsequent appointment to the premiership in a new cohabitation with Chirac, makes him the legitimate leader of the PS (and the left). He has tried to square the circle by both leading the PS and renouncing the usual presidentialist ambition of organizing a faction. This self-denial may be self-defeating. The lack of organized 'Jospinism' leaves the field open to competitors who can cause the debate to lurch unsteadily in unwanted and unpredictable directions. The surge of the *gauche socialiste* into this vacuum during the March 1996 debate on European policy almost caused the defeat of a carefully crafted platform, and this danger of the argument going by default could lead to the organization of a 'loyalist faction', whether or not endorsed by Jospin.[22] Jospin has less of a problem with coalition-building than did the previous generation of French Socialists, who had to bridge the gap between two very different conceptions of society (Leninist and socialist). The gap remains, but public opinion is becoming less tolerant of the opaque rhetoric which blurred differences in the past, and now expects straight talk. Jospin has gone some way towards solving the problem of renewal within continuity by detaching himself from the Mitterrand years with timely criticisms. But between the need for economic realism and the management of the party lies the link of the presidential aspirant giving leadership and a plan for the future. This is a tall order.

As has been argued at length by Merkel amongst others, there is no evidence in the electoral statistics of a long-term decline of social democratic parties.[23] There are fluctuations, many quite dramatic, but over the decades the Socialists have more or less kept their place.[24] The PS illustrates this proposition: it grew from the marginal SFIO in 1969 to become the dominant electoral force in the 1980s, only to appear to go into virtual meltdown in the early 1990s. The 'victorious defeat' of the Socialist presidential candidate Lionel Jospin in 1995 had all the signs of a regeneration, and the revival of the PS in the polls (and by-elections) was a feature of the early Chirac presidency.

The Socialist Party has also consolidated its domination of the left despite its fluctuations of fortune. Having overtaken the Communists in the 1978 legislative elections, it consolidated this position as the pole for organization on the left and the alternative to the right. However, if in 1981 the electoral map of French Socialism was similar to the old SFIO, with a breakthrough into some Catholic districts, the party of 1994 fell back on its bastions in the industrial north and the mainly rural and Méridional areas. A complication for the PS is that it is still not the only party on the left, and its position is compromised by fragmentation and competition (often acrimonious) within the left: coalition-building cannot be taken for granted. It remains to be seen how the wide-ranging Josphin government – with three PCF ministers, one Green Minister, and Jean-Pierre Chevènement as minister of the interior – will work in practice. The PCF, for its part, remains a presence in Limousin, Périgord, Roussillon and Gard, in the Nord, Seine-Maritime and the Paris suburbs.[25]

Throughout its existence, the PS has been dependent on allies to support it in government. The party has survived the disaster of 1993, but coalition formation and the fragmentation on the left put pressures on its programmes and declarations of intent.[26] The PS faces a variation of the social democratic dilemma, a two-way stretch in which it must reach for the floating vote both in the centre and the extreme ideological left. Moreover, the divisions in the French political arena have changed in significance with the decline of the PCF and the collapse of the Soviet Union: they are now neither so intense nor so dramatic. The 1980s also witnessed a decline in party identification, the development of a more volatile electorate, and the emergence of the radical right (Le Pen's National Front), the radicals of Bernard Tapie, and the ecologists as significant forces, this last-mentioned polling almost 11 per cent in 1993. Ecology can perhaps be regarded as a part of the left, and the mainstream Greens see

themselves as on the left of the PS. The Socialist Party itself is one
factor in the rise of electoral volatility, bringing about a growing
disillusion with the political class; the credibility gap, opened up by
a decade in government, will not easily be closed. The reaction to the
new situation has been a cautious search for allies in the centre of the
political spectrum and a recasting of the political appeal to accommodate new 'individualist' issues and some populist ones – although
these do not sit easily within a socialist framework.

CONCLUSION

The socialist parties in the post-war world succeeded in promoting a
model of society which was widely popular and successful by most
criteria. The 1970s saw the first real challenge to this model in the oil
price hikes and rising inflation. Nevertheless, the French Socialist
governments came to power in 1981 and held power until 1993 (with
the exception of 1986–1988).[28] These years were more challenging
than the 1950s or 1960s, and the PS could not find a convincing
answer to social problems and anxieties about unemployment over
which they (for the most part) presided. Despite these serious reservations, the legacy of the Mitterrand era for the PS is not the archaism
of the Marxist left with which the Socialists came to power, but a
fitful and incomplete modernization. The schizoid personality divided
between romantic revolution and pragmatic grubbing which has characterized French socialism since the beginning, and which found its
justifying theorist in Léon Blum's distinction between the conquest
and exercise of power, was very evident at the outset in 1981 but less
so in 1995.

The Parti Socialiste is far from demoralized – partly due to
the presidential factor which complicates the situation. The despair
in the ranks amongst ordinary activists at the shambles in 1993 led to
the search for a new *présidentiable*. The party which had once seemed
excessively blessed with presidential timber was devoid of a credible
candidate. The distress at the condition of the party and at the
leadership's inability to solve the crisis led to Delors-mania in December 1994, followed by 'Jospinomania' the following February. Too
many expectations were placed on the back of one man, but the
presidential system has encouraged these rising hopes and the party
seems, temporarily perhaps, well satisfied that it has found its way
back to government.

Yet the problems it faces run deep, and it is not up to individual leaders, however accomplished, to solve current dilemmas. These, to recapitulate, arise from the crisis which has hit European society and which has gone hardest with the unemployed and the marginalized. Old communities have been dissolved, and the working-class culture which supported socialist 'communities' has been weakened and in some cases has disappeared. The new industries and workforces which have replaced them are not nearly so cohesive and lack the social institutions (such as unions) which gave collective expression to demands. The Socialists also face competition from the new political movements expressing an anti-establishment line. The PS has, by virtue of its long participation in the political system and in government with the right, become identified with the ruling class. The Socialists are open to attack from across the political spectrum and, if the economic situation gets worse for their supporters, they could be very vulnerable to renewed appeals to old fears. The new leadership has tried to meet this threat by changing the orientation of the party from the Poperen-style (*y'a qu'*) to a more restrained defence of 'socialist values', by which is meant 'solidarity' and the state as the expression of the community and the protection of those left by the wayside in industrial change. This, as has been indicated, will not be enough and the examination of social philosophy is insufficiently radical given the current situation of society (in this it is no different from other 'social democrats').

Moreover, the Socialist 'solution' to the social catastrophe of the 1930s – which in some ways resembles the 1990s – depended on action within a nation state. Moving up from the state level to a more meaningful milieu of action (which can only mean Europe in today's world) is an obvious recourse and one which figures in the PS programme as re-written. However, this Europeanization of social democracy has yet to be implemented and will not happen overnight. It also clashes with the deep convictions of the left's supporters, a contradiction which has yet to be thought through.

The SFIO and PS have long histories; but that does not guarantee them a future. The French Socialist Party almost disappeared on two occasions, and there is nothing in society or politics which will ensure its continued existence. The party put together a series of responses 'on the run', prompted by the need to be a presence in the elections of 1995. These were stopgap measures and, as the leadership realizes, they are a start, not a finish. Similarly, in 1997, the PS was returned to government (albeit without an overall majority) largely due to public discontent over the right-wing Juppé government's austerity programme. The elaboration of a new synthesis and a new 'alternative' to the liberal free-market ideology is what is needed, and what the activists appear to want. This will not be provided by one social philosopher (any more than was the welfare state) and its outlines are not evident. Yet the PS needs a motivating and credible project if it is to survive in anything like its contemporary condition. The other possibility (other than annihilation at the polls) is that it becomes one of the governing parties alternating in power but without any distinct identity – in other words, to go back to where it came into government in the 1920s.

NOTES

1. A. Bergounioux and G. Grunberg, *Le Long Remords du pouvoir* (Paris: Fayard, 1992).
2. E. Morin, *Le Monde*, 11 April 1993.
3. P. Perrineau, 'Adolescence et maturité précoce du PS', *Intervention*, No. 5–6, Sept.-Oct. 1983, pp.28–34.
4. E. Cohen, 'Les socialistes et l'économie', in E. Duporier and G. Grunberg (eds), *Mars 1986* (Paris: PUF, 1986).
5. M. Duverger, *Le Monde*, 8 October 1985.
6. *Le Monde*, 26 October 1993.
7. J. K. Galbraith, *The Culture of Contentment* (London: Sinclair-Stevenson, 1992).
8. Denis Olivennes, 'La société de transferts', *Le Débat*, No. 69, March–April 1992, pp.110–121.
9. L. Jospin *1995–2000. Propositions pour la France* (Paris: Stock, 1995).
10. See I. Hampshire-Monk, 'The individualist premise and political community', in Preston King (ed.), *New Fabian Essays* (London: Cass, 1996), pp. 201–222.
11. P. Rosenvallon, *La Nouvelle Question sociale* (Paris: Seuil, 1995).
12. E. Todd, 'Comment la gauche en est arrivée là ...', *Le Nouvel Observateur*, 1–7 April 1993.
13. G. Lemaire-Prosche, *Le PS et l'Europe* (Paris: Edns Universitaires, 1990).
14. *Le Monde*, 20 March 1996.
15. P. Delwitt, 'La Gauche et l'Europe' in M. Lazar, *Invariants et mutations du socialisme européen* (Paris: PUF, 1996).
16. P. Martin in J. Poperen et al., *Vers quel paysage politique?* (Paris: Nouveau Monde, 1993).
17. Delwitt, op. cit.

18. *Manifeste pour les élections au Parlement européen de juin 1994*, 6 November 1993.
19. S.R. Katz and P. Mair, *How Parties Organise* (London: Sage, 1994).
20. G. Voerman in M. Lazar (ed.), op. cit.
21. A. Bergounioux and G. Grunberg, op. cit.
22. *Le Monde*, 31 March 1996.
23. See, for example, W. Merkel, 'After the Golden Age' in C. Lemke and G. Marks (eds), *The Crisis of Socialism in Europe* (London: Duke University Press, 1992).
24. C. Vandermotten et al., 'Géographie électorale de la gauche en Europe', in M. Lazar, op. cit.
25. P. Perrineau and C. Ysmal (eds), *Le Vote des douze* (Paris: FNSP, 1995).
26. W. Merkel, 'Between Chaos and Catch-all', in W. Merkel (ed.), *Socialist Parties in Europe* (Barcelona: ICPS, 1992).

Part 2
Europe and Foreign Affairs

5 EMU and Presidential Leadership under François Mitterrand

Kenneth Dyson and Kevin Featherstone

The project of economic and monetary union (EMU) emerged by 1985–1986 as a centrepiece of presidential leadership by François Mitterrand. Yet, paradoxically, the negotiation of this project within the EC transformed the French state in ways that would not be readily predicted from the perspective of traditional French Socialist policy beliefs about the appropriate relationship between state and economy.

This paradox throws into bold relief certain key features of the Mitterrand presidency: how Mitterrand's motives came to be inspired by the *étatisme* with which the presidential office clothed him, rather than by party ideology; his preoccupation as incumbent with strengthening the bargaining resources available to his office, involving a fundamentally Realist perspective on power; his recognition after 1983 that EMU was basically about 'rescuing' the French state from the 'D-Mark' zone (better the 'Ecu' zone); finally, in embracing the terms of that rescue (which were essentially German), the Mitterrand presidency was forced to come to terms with a process of transformation and reconstruction of the French state: of its political agenda, the distribution of domestic political power, and the action capacity of the state. That process of transformation embodied in large part the unintended consequences of embracing the EMU project.

Whilst there was an undeniable Realist component to the adoption of the EMU project by 1985–1986, and to its subsequent vigorous pursuit in Franco-German bilaterals, underpinning the definition of French interests and calculation of relative gains for France was a dynamic presidential learning process. That process had two components. In the first place, there was, from 1982–1983, a learning process about structural dependency. Repeated devaluations within the ERM, culminating in the crisis of March 1983, graphically underlined the weak bargaining position of France in Europe. The presidential decision of 1983 to remain within the ERM was made in order to avoid

89

being thrown to the mercy of the International Monetary Fund (IMF) after exit. But it also involved a decision to avoid future humiliations within the ERM by adopting the *franc stable* policy. By 1985–1986 Mitterrand had drawn the lesson that acceptance of the constraints of the ERM must be translated into opening up new opportunities for French influence in Europe by embracing EMS reform and eventual EMU (though he had no clear understanding of its meaning and implications at the time).

A second learning process, commencing in 1984–1985, involved the reactivation of Mitterrand's long-standing but neglected commitment to *construction européenne*.[1] The personal reinvention of Mitterrand accompanied the collective reinvention of the state. For Mitterrand, the lesson of 1982–1983 was that the unity of the Franco-German relationship was the essential precondition for French influence in the EC and beyond. His recommitment to *construction européenne* was also a response to the signal from Helmut Kohl, directly following the latter's election in 1982, that he was likely to be the last Chancellor with whom it would be possible to build Europe. A later political generation would not share Kohl's sense of urgency about building Europe, inspired by his experience and memories of war. In short, he developed a sense of mission: of being a president with an historic window of opportunity unavailable to his successors, and giving him the possibility of leaving a major historical legacy.

The consequent dedication to a belief in Franco-German reconciliation took on a momentum of its own from 1984, inspiring his approach to EMU. Indeed, one of his key contributions was the attempt to provide EMU with an historical legitimation that transcended the elimination of 'asymmetry' between France and Germany in the EMS and the specific exigencies of German unification in 1989–1990 and reached deep back to his identification of common Franco-German cultural roots in Carolingian Europe.

EMU had two profoundly paradoxical effects on the French state. Firstly, the exigencies of external dependency were exchanged for the institutionalization of German hegemony and of financial market imperatives. Secondly, power slipped from presidential and political levels to technocrats in the Finance Ministry and the Banque de France who negotiated the policy content. The bargaining strategy of technocrats on EMU was to use it to strengthen their domestic power to push through 'necessary' policy reform. In turn, their definition of 'necessary' reforms derived from a tradition of conservative liberalism in economic policy (*grands équilibres, rigueur, franc stable*), which was reinvigorated by the new exigencies created by global financial markets and German monetary power. EMU involved, in other words, the differential empowerment of executive actors. These effects illustrate the paradoxical nature of presidential leadership on European policy under Mitterrand: at once reactive in developing policy (notably the learning processes of 1982–1983 and 1989–1990) and yet creative in transforming constraints into opportunities.

EMU AND THE TRANSFORMATION OF THE FRENCH STATE

The process of EMU in Europe, embodied in the Maastricht Treaty, represents arguably the most important qualitative change in the conditions under which EC member state governments act since the Treaty of Rome. In France, as elsewhere, it has served as a catalyst for transforming national policy agendas, structures and processes; for altering the domestic balance of power between different actors; and for reshaping the action capacity of member states.

First, the shift in policy agenda is apparent in the ongoing primacy of budget retrenchment, welfare state reform and privatization implicit in the treaty's tough convergence criteria and in prospective Stability Pact provisions for Stage Three. Abandonment of devaluation as an instrument of economic adjustment places extra weight on wage and price flexibility, particularly on deregulation of labour markets and plant-level wage bargaining.

Second, national policy structures and processes have been altered by central bank independence and by the power of central bankers as a transnational epistemic community.[2] They are united around a normative belief in price stability, a causal belief that credibility is the prime requirement of an effective monetary and fiscal policy, and a shared policy project of their own independence. The consequence has been a shift in the location of political power, favouring central banks at the expense of finance ministries, monetary policy technocrats being the main beneficiary. In effect, a new structural bias has been reinforced in domestic politics: savers are privileged over welfare recipients; and the notion of personal responsibility for planning one's future has gained ground against the idea of the state as responsible for social solidarity.

The action capacity of the state has been strengthened to deal with
inflation and international competitiveness – but weakened with
respect to social solidarity. Concern about the implications of this
rebalancing of the action capacity of the state was registered in the
stress that Jacques Chirac placed on solidarity in his 1995 presidential
election campaign and tensions with the governor of the newly independent Banque de France, Jean-Claude Trichet. But by November
the Juppé government, concerned whether France would be in a
position to meet the fiscal criteria to qualify for EMU in 1999, was
proposing huge cuts in the social security budget, unleashing a wave
of strikes and demonstrations. In effect, this social movement was
testing the limits of the action capacity of the French state to implement disinflation and revealing the extent to which France had shifted
towards a 'stability culture'.

We should also note that the scale of these transformative features
and effects of EMU embraces all policy levels: the way in which
existing policy instruments are used; the introduction of new policy
instruments and elimination of old ones; and, more radically, a shift
of policy goals.[3] Together, these implications of EMU for the French
state raise the question of why this kind of policy project was
embraced under the leadership of a Socialist president. After all, one
would not predict from party control of government the embrace of
such a direction of agenda change, such a shift in the balance of
domestic power or such a change in the action capacity of the French
state. How, then, is French endorsement of the EMU deal at Maastricht to be explained? What were the motives and calculations? From
where did leadership come? Who were the major beneficiaries in terms
of domestic political power?

EMU AND DEPENDENCY: US GLOBAL POWER AND
GERMAN REGIONAL HEGEMONY – THE DOLLAR AND
THE D-MARK

French endorsement of the EMU deal at Maastricht exemplifies a
characteristic solution for its policy-makers to the main problem that
has confronted them in the post-war period: namely, how best to
protect and promote French interests and power in a context of
dependency and to retrieve a leadership role for France. Overwhelmingly, Europe was not adopted by French elites as the frame
of reference for solving this problem out of an idealistic commitment

to the cause of European union. It was a diplomatic necessity that French policy-makers learnt to accept, and then many – like Trichet – to love. 'Realist' calculation of French gains from European integration was overlaid by, and redefined in the context of, an emerging policy belief in Europe as the appropriate frame of reference. The great contribution of the Mitterrand presidency was to initiate and systematically sustain a cognitive learning process within French government and administration that led ministers and officials to redefine their activities in terms of European construction.

In defence, where France was caught in Cold War bipolar politics, the solution to this problem of dependency had been different. It involved a policy of national independence, symbolised by the nuclear *force de frappe* and withdrawal from the military wing of NATO. But, more broadly, French security interests were met by a policy of Franco-German *rapprochement*. This core relationship was seen as a value in its own right and often (notably by Presidents Giscard and Mitterrand) as the motor of European integration. As an innovation of French diplomacy under Robert Schuman, European integration was a novel means of containing German economic power in Europe through sharing in the exercise of sovereignty. Given the greater relative economic (and above all monetary) power of Germany, EMU fitted naturally into this post-war policy response of giving a European frame to French policy problems of dependency.

In economic policy, French interests were defined as based on two requirements. Firstly, Finance Ministry negotiators sought concerted international intervention to protect exchange rates, in the process binding 'unreliable' US power to a strong international regime. By underpinning a *franc stable*, such a regime would provide two key gains for France: a solid external anchor of stability for the domestic economy; and a strengthening of France's international bargaining position. Secondly, French negotiators sought to use the EC in order to secure three gains: first, to build up a stronger and more distinct European identity in order to bargain more effectively with the US and Japan and thereby regain a share in global leadership; second, to promote a convergence of French economic performance with that of Germany, thereby securing French leadership in Europe; and finally, to bind the exercise of German economic and monetary power to European-defined objectives. These motives underpinned the promotion of EMU by Giscard as finance minister in the 1960s, French backing for EMU at the Hague Summit in 1969, and French support for the EMS in 1978–1979.

In achieving these French economic objectives the key problems were twofold: firstly, the 'irresponsible' neglect of exchange rate issues by the US, especially from 1971, and the collapse of the Bretton Woods system; and, secondly, emerging German economic leadership within the EC, which became apparent by the late 1960s and began to fuel tensions between the two countries. The search for a solution to the first problem made G7 a key forum for French economic diplomacy. France played a leadership role in its creation and in the Plaza-Louvre period of agreeing concerted intervention. But, given American intransigence, the EC and Franco-German relations offered alternative, more amenable fora for both exchange rate stabilization (the EMS in 1979, Basle-Nyborg in 1987, and the Franco-German Economic Council of 1988) and, more ambitiously, EMU (the Werner Plan of 1970, the Balladur Memorandum of 1988, the Delors Report of 1989). The EMS was originally seen as a means of securing symmetry in intervention and domestic policy adjustment obligations between France and Germany. When it failed to do so in practice, and reform attempts (eg. Basle-Nyborg) failed to remedy this defect, French initiatives changed in 1987–1988 to the establishment of a Franco-German Economic Council and to putting EMU (tentatively) on the EC agenda. Success in attaining the G7 Plaza and Louvre agreements and the Basle-Nyborg agreement within the EC emboldened French economic diplomacy in Europe, while the January 1987 crisis of the ERM, centred on the franc, motivated that diplomacy to find a new way of avoiding further French humiliations at the hands of the financial markets.

French strategy was concerned with more than managing economic dependency: its objective was to find an escape from the constrictions imposed by that dependency. The continuing weight of these constraints was manifested in the *de facto* operation of the EMS (the burden of adjustment being borne by the currency under pressure). More seriously, that weight mounted with the growing scale, power and complexity of the global financial markets during the 1980s under the impact of a deregulation unleashed by US domestic policy and emulated by Britain. French policy under Mitterrand underwent two dramatic experiences of the implications of increasing dependency for French bargaining strength. Together, they unleashed a domestic learning process about the need to reconsider the whole frame of reference within which French policy was being developed. This new frame of reference involved the Europeanization of economic, financial and monetary policies.

The 'Road to Damascus' was provided by the three devaluations within the ERM of 1981–1983 and by the two devaluations of 1986 and 1987. The March 1983 crisis provided the genesis for the evolution of the 'competitive disinflation' strategy, key components of which were the *franc stable* within the EMS and budgetary *rigueur*. At the same time, President Mitterrand signalled to the administration that projects consistent with a strategy of *relance européenne* would be welcome. Thereafter, French policy was increasingly set within the framework of presidential leadership on European construction and on the *franc stable*. The *franc stable* was conceived as an indispensable instrument for political leadership of *construction européenne* by the president. The 1986 devaluation administered the lesson that the costs of devaluation in terms of lost credibility far exceeded any gains; whilst the 1987 crisis of the franc showed that, without major reform, the global financial markets were too powerful for the existing 'asymmetrical' EMS to contain. In consequence, French policy became committed to the avoidance of devaluation at all costs. Additionally, a new climate for policy innovation permeated and united the presidency, the administration and both government and opposition parties. During the cohabitation it provided Edouard Balladur as finance minister with a context in which he could press ahead with an agenda of G7 and IMF reform; of the Franco-German Economic Council; and of EMS reform.[4]

EMU was a powerful catalyst for the transformative effects outlined above – in effect, it institutionalized them. At the same time it mediated changes that had already been set in process by US global power and German regional hegemony. Financial markets acted as disciplines on fiscal policy, shifted the policy agenda towards price stability and privileged savers, with or without EMU. The strength of the mark privileged German bargaining power and hence the influence of German economic policy ideas over French ideas, with or without EMU. Indeed, the transformative effects that we associate with EMU were apparent before EMU returned to the French and EC agenda in 1987–1988. Raymond Barre's RPR–UDF government of 1976–1981 had put economic stabilization at the centre of macroeconomic strategy, convergent with German economic priorities; 'competitive disinflation' after 1983 under the Socialists represented a return to, and development of, this priority to embrace microeconomic reforms; financial market liberalization post-1984 involved a radical shift from state-administered credit to market-based financing, initiated by the Socialists; whilst privatization was central to the agenda of the RPR–UDF Chirac government of 1986–1988, again before EMU came on the agenda. Before EMU a complex redistribution of domestic power was underway. Thus the Trésor's power was enhanced by 'competitive disinflation': but its traditional prerogatives were eaten away by financial market reform and privatization. Overall, the effect of financial liberalization was to strengthen the state's capacity to finance its deficits efficiently and to improve the competitive capacity of France's financial sector; the effect of 'competitive disinflation' was to lower long-term interest rates, benefiting the management of public debt and industrial financing.

But, of crucial importance, these domestic policy projects were indispensable bases for strengthening France's political capacity to bargain more effectively in international negotiations, and in particular to bargain more credibly on EMU in the late 1980s than had been possible in the early 1970s. France had in effect provided consistent policy signals that it was potentially a credible partner in bargaining on EMU. It took just two extra signals to clinch that credibility in 1988–1989: acceptance of freedom of capital movement in June 1988 (under the single market programme); and acceptance of the principle of independence for a European central bank (ECB), in effect acknowledged by Pierre Bérégovoy as finance minister in August 1989. The former signal meant accepting the financial markets as the final arbiter of French economic and monetary policies; the latter meant acceptance of the hegemony of German economic policy ideas.

Under Mitterrand French policy was bending, with real difficulty, to the harsh realities of dependency in a world of market deregulation and economic liberalism, defined by US global power in terms of markets and German regional hegemony in terms of policy ideas. The keys to strengthening French power and interest and engineering escape from these constraints for a Socialist government were: firstly, co-decision via EMU (an ECB whose decisions reflected European interest was more likely to accommodate France than following the Bundesbank, whose decisions were focused on the needs of the German economy); secondly, giving a French content to EMU (the concept of a *gouvernement économique*, of the political direction of economic policy); and, thirdly, flanking EMU by measures to promote social justice in order to promote a socialist agenda (notably action on an EC social charter and an EC-wide withholding tax on capital income). Together, they involved the adoption of a Europeanized policy paradigm by the French presidency and government.

But it should not be assumed that European policy discourse was simply a light, transparent cover for a nakedly 'Realist' calculation of French relative gains from EMU. This discourse took on a momentum of its own after 1982–1983 as the president carved out a new historical legitimation for EMU, *construction européenne* and Franco-German relations which, in its own right, facilitated a French deal on EMU.[5] Most importantly, consistent presidential signalling about the primacy of *construction européenne*, particularly with Mitterrand's second *septennat*, initiated a cognitive learning process within which perceptions of French interests were redefined.

CONTEST FOR EMPOWERMENT: PRESIDENT, FINANCE MINISTRY AND BANQUE DE FRANCE

For reasons outlined above, EMU enjoyed – in principle – widespread support. It was nested within a high level of diffuse public support for European integration and much more active elite commitment. The prospect of relative gains from EMU was clearest to those who were best informed about the constraints within which French power had to be exercised. Not least, its domestic politics was shaped by three factors: the widespread public support for the *franc stable* policy, a basic pillar of the EMU project, across the political spectrum; the highly technical character of monetary policy which meant that potential domestic opposition lacked information with which to build credible alternatives; and uncertainty about the distributive effects of changes to exchange rate and monetary policy arrangements, which made it difficult to mobilize social groups either strongly pro-EMU or strongly anti-EMU, at least till the stage when specific policy reforms to meet EMU criteria (like the Juppé reforms of November 1995) made the distribution of costs clearer. In consequence, the negotiation of EMU took place in the splendid isolation of the French core executive, involving a small grouping of actors who interacted flexibly.

French Bargaining Strategy for EMU

This 'permissive consensus', allied to the calculation that EMU involved relative gains vis-à-vis Germany, meant that domestic ratification of an EMU agreement was not the central preoccupation of French negotiators.[6] In May 1988, President Mitterrand had won the

presidential election on a platform that prioritized European construction. In this context any attempt by French negotiators to use
the bargaining strategy of claiming that their hands were tied by
domestic difficulties would have enjoyed little credibility. Their bargaining strategy on EMU was, in fact, closer to that of the Belgians,
Italians and Spaniards than to that of the British and the Germans.[7]
The British and the German negotiators sought to strengthen their
hands by focusing on domestic ratification problems: in the first case,
within the governing Conservative Party; in the second, with the
Bundesbank and German public opinion.[8] In effect, in negotiating
EMU they sought to exploit a key paradox of international negotiations: that domestic political weakness can be used as a source of
external bargaining strength. For French negotiators that option was
not really open, given the clear relative gains that France could
achieve via an EMU agreement and the lack of domestic controversy.
To them the attraction of EMU was as a means to empower the
executive to deal more effectively with domestic opposition to a policy
designed to secure long-term economic stability. In short, French
negotiators adopted a bargaining strategy of 'cutting slack' rather
than 'tying hands'. An EMU agreement was a means to discipline
and reshape French political and economic culture. The net beneficiary would be the French executive.[9] Such a strategy was not new to
them, notably in the use of the 'asymmetry' of the ERM as an
instrument of domestic discipline: to promote both macro-economic
reform (*rigueur*) and micro-economic reforms (as in collective bargaining and wage policy).

But the use of EMU as a means of 'cutting slack' and empowering
the French executive left open a crucial question: who precisely within
the French executive would be relative gainers and who relative
losers? Whereas in Italy this question played a subordinate role, the
contest about empowerment between the Elysée, Finance Ministry
and Banque de France was a central feature of the EMU negotiations.

Presidential Leadership

Formally, EMU fell clearly into the 'reserved domain' of the president: both as EC business, not least involving the European Council
in treaty revision, and as a key agenda issue for Franco-German
summits. These twin fora offered a privileged role to the president in
EMU negotiations. Given its centrality to European construction,
Mitterrand intended to provide strong political leadership and contain

technocratic power over EMU. For this purpose he relied on Roland Dumas as Foreign Minister, his most trusted personal adviser, and on Elisabeth Guigou as Elysée technical counsellor, former Trésor official and (after 1990) as European Minister.

The prime minister's possible role and influence was minimized by keeping EMU away from the formal Secrétariat Général du Comité Interministériel (SGCI) machinery for co-ordination of EC business and indeed from any interministerial group that would involve Matignon co-ordination.[10] This issue of the premier's role was made more sensitive whilst Michel Rocard held the office (1988–1991). Edith Cresson was, by contrast, able to play a key role in the process of activating Bérégovoy, then finance minister, to raise the issue of the dates for Stage Three at the very end of the IGC.

Mitterrand's political leadership on EMU was demonstrated in the following ways. First, in June 1988 at the Evian Franco-German summit he conceded freedom of EC capital movement, without an accompanying EC-level withholding tax, despite a reluctant finance minister – to ensure that no obstacle to Helmut Kohl's relaunch of EMU was raised at the Hanover Council. Second, he was determined that the 'committee of wise men' proposed by the German Foreign Minister Hans-Dietrich Genscher should not be chaired by a central banker (the president of the Bundesbank, Karl-Otto Pöhl, had been mentioned) and should not be totally dominated by central bankers. Third, prior to the start of the Delors Committee, he clarified (following persuasion by Jacques de Larosière) that independence of the ECB was not to be seen as a potential French bargaining concession but as a precondition accepted in advance of negotiations, despite the opposition of Rocard as prime minister. He backed Dumas's proposal for a new high-level group to give extra political momentum to EMU after the Delors Report by working on the questions for the future IGC (appointing Guigou as its chair). He preoccupied himself with clarifying dates to give momentum to EMU: the date for the IGC (gained from a reluctant Kohl at the Strasbourg summit in December 1989); the date for Stage Two (where Kohl was put under pressure to resolve his domestic conflicts on this issue); and the fixed dates for Stage Three pushed by Mitterrand and Andreotti at Maastricht in order to ensure that in 1998 there would not be a vote on the principle of EMU, only on which countries qualified (a French bargaining objective was to ensure no veto). He countered those in the government (notably Bérégovoy) who were keen to explore concessions to Britain, as a means of balancing Germany and keeping Britain on board for EMU, by flirting with the parallel currency and the British alternative of an evolutionary approach to EMU via the so-called 'hard ECU' (European Currency Unit) – Mitterrand took a sceptical view of John Major's claims to want to be at the 'heart of Europe'. He ensured that the final decision on the start of Stage Three would be taken in the European Council, not in ECOFIN (European Council of Finance Ministers), in order to ensure continuing political direction. It is difficult to avoid the conclusion that Mitterrand, in his conduct of European policy as a whole, was fundamentally driven by a pessimistic assessment of human nature and the human condition. This pessimism made him a profound exponent of political 'Realism'. He was motivated by a strong sense of French interests; discrete, secretive and enigmatic in his behaviour; by experience, if not nature, suspicious and capable of cynicism; and a cold technician of power and master of political tactics, capable of being different things to different people. But – and this was crucial to his attitudes to European integration and Franco-German relations – Mitterrand saw institutions as essential to civilize people. He saw in the EC and in Franco-German relations a means to escape from malevolent nationalism; to overcome history, as exemplified by his own biography as a member of the war generation. His Carolingian model of Europe was in part an artful literary attempt to legitimate this aim. But it also expressed something deeper in Mitterrand's political make-up.[11]

For Mitterrand, EMU was the key project of his second term, alongside his ambition to use the Franco-German relationship to carve out a European defence identity based around the Euro-corps. Indeed, looking at his presidency as a whole, defence weighed most strongly in his approach to Franco-German relations. From a 'Realist' perspective this emphasis on setting EMU in the framework of defence strengthened France's overall bargaining position vis-à-vis Germany. By focusing Franco-German relations on a policy sector where French leadership was clear, he could make concessions – like a Franco-German Defence Council – to tempt German concessions on EMU (and German agreement to a Franco-German Economic Council). Promoting a defence-economic balance and trade-off in Franco-German relations made 'Realist' political sense.

In addition, Mitterrand saw the *franc stable* and a French economy whose *grands équilibres* were strong as an indispensable basis for his Franco-German diplomacy and for the progress of EMU in particular. His readiness to pay economic and social costs for this objective illustrates that his outlook on economic policy became conditioned above all by the objective of strengthening the bargaining resources available to his presidential office rather than derived from socialist principles.

When it came to defining the content of French bargaining positions on EMU, Mitterrand provided three instructions for French negotiators. First, EMU was to be achieved as quickly as possible, but without breaking up European solidarity. Second, they were to avoid conceding national central bank independence at an early stage, only playing this card as a last resort to extract major concessions. Finally, Mitterrand pushed the concept of *gouvernement économique*. His aim was to stress the continuing need at the European level for a political counterweight to the ECB in order to provide political direction to economic policy. He retained strong reservations about the Bundesbank as a model for the ECB. In addition to legitimating EMU by reference to inherited French beliefs about economic policy, and containing the power of technocrats, Mitterrand sought in this way to empower the presidency by making the European Council the site for *gouvernement économique*. Though the concept was written into the French Draft Treaty on EMU submitted to the IGC, it made no headway against German opposition. *Gouvernement économique* seemed to deny the reality of the independence of the ECB to which the French government had committed itself. Its presence opened up a large negotiating gap with the Germans, and its use was tactically withdrawn. What remained was French insistence on ECOFIN agreeing economic policy guidelines for the EC and on ECOFIN having the final decision on participating in exchange rate regimes with other states. Here the French could claim some success, albeit based on compromise with the Germans. But the location of action on these aspects of *gouvernement économique* was with the EC finance ministers rather than the European Council.

On measures to flank EMU by promoting social justice, Mitterrand was less successful. In response to the technocratic nature of a Delors Report largely penned by EC central bankers, he actively promoted the idea of a 'social Europe' in conjunction with the Spanish presidency at the Madrid Council in June 1989. But, then and later, this policy of improving employment conditions made little progress. The Social Charter was approved (minus Britain, which did not announce its decision to join until 1997, following the election of a Labour government) during the French presidency at the Strasbourg Council in December 1989 – but as a statement of intent. To Mitterrand's great irritation with the Dutch presidency, the attempt to empower the EC's social policy role by treaty provision was limited to the separate protocol and agreement of the 11 (again minus Britain) attached to the Maastricht Treaty. The linkage of acceptance of freedom of capital movement with prospective agreement of an EC-wide withholding tax (the Germans agreed to support this at Evian in June 1988) failed in the face of Luxembourg and British opposition and of German withdrawal of their withholding tax soon after introducing it in 1989. Mitterrand was left with more rapid progress on a technocratically defined EMU than on his flanking social projects and with little progress on *gouvernement économique*.

The two key features of Mitterrand's leadership role on EMU can be summarized as follows. Firstly, he instrumentalized the *franc stable* and EMU for the political purposes of strengthening Franco-German relations and for European construction. His role involved the provision of historical legitimation rather than a concern with the detailed technical contents of EMU as a self-contained project. Secondly, whilst Mitterrand's socialism remained important as a contextual factor, his attitudes and behaviour on the *franc stable* and EMU were more strongly shaped by the nature of his presidential office. As the occupant of that office, Mitterrand's key interest was in strengthening the bargaining resources available to him as the nation's chief negotiator. For this institutional reason the *franc stable* and EMU became indispensable to him.

Empowering the Finance Ministry and Trésor

Mitterrand's determination to provide strong political leadership, and the Mitterrand-Dumas and Mitterrand-Guigou axes, could not translate into the technical expertise to negotiate the technicalities of an EMU agreement. Indeed, the requirement to negotiate a technically viable EMU forced Mitterrand to cede power to the monetary policy technocrats. Faced with his own lack of economic expertise, and by a contest for power over EMU between Dumas and Bérégovoy, Mitterrand opted for the compromise of a team approach to the IGC negotiations. Dumas was to be in overall charge of the Maastricht negotiations; unlike in any other EC state, both Bérégovoy and Dumas were given joint formal ministerial responsibility for the EMU negotiations, but it was accepted that the Finance Ministry would take the lead role in the technical negotiations and after the opening IGC at ministerial level in Rome Dumas did not attend again.

Whatever the formality of a team approach, Bérégovoy was determined to be the centre of domestic power over EMU. He was intent on underlining his credentials as a strong finance minister and Mitterrand loyalist and, in so doing, keeping alive his hopes of becoming prime minister. Hence Bérégovoy sought to carve out a distinctive French and socialist content to his EMU policy, whilst continuing with his historic project of linking socialism to economic stability and his own career to the reputation of being the only finance minister of the Fifth Republic to have avoided a devaluation of the franc. The Trésor too was used to operating in a relatively independent way at EC level on economic and monetary affairs. The SGCI did not play an important role in preparing French bargaining positions within the EC Monetary Committee; its involvement took the form of reports on progress. Moreover, within the Council machinery at EC level, the EC Monetary Committee had significant independence of COREPER (Committee of Permanent Representatives) co-ordination, so that the French Permanent Representation in Brussels was less involved in its work than in other areas. Hence there was a corporate expectation in the Trésor that it would be given substantial freedom of manoeuvre during the IGC negotiations.

Bérégovoy's determination and outlook had led him to accept an independent ECB only with reluctance. In return for conceding this principle after the Delors Report (a personal victory for de Larosière), his preoccupations became twofold: to balance the new EC 'monetary pole' with an 'economic pole' (an idea coined in his cabinet and later christened by the Elysée 'gouvernement économique'); and to avoid granting independence to the Banque de France at the beginning of Stage Two of EMU. Motivating these two key policy positions on EMU was a fusion of motives: to strengthen the role of the finance minister in ensuring the basic political direction of economic policy rather than ceding power to central bankers (consistent with Republican and Socialist traditions); and to stand up for the corporate interests of the Trésor in maintaining its prerogatives within the framework of EMU. For such reasons both Bérégovoy and the Trésor were unhappy with de Larosière's 'one-sided' championing of a new powerful European Reserve Fund of EC central bankers for Stage Two in the Delors Committee, as well as with his concession of independence for the ECB in Stage Three. They took up the idea of avoiding an 'empty' Stage Two by getting the ECB established at its beginning or during its middle. But the 'political' pole was always as important as the 'monetary'.

Bérégovoy and the Trésor also flirted with the idea of a new parallel currency for Stage Two right up until January 1991, though the Banque de France – sensing its technical difficulties and the unbending opposition of the Bundesbank – had dropped it early in the Delors Committee discussions without pressing the case. One of its attractions was in creating a rival strong currency to the mark whilst avoiding the creation of an independent ECB at an early stage. Another tactical benefit of the parallel currency idea for Bérégovoy, as well as of opposing central bank independence in Stage Two, was that it seemed to improve the prospects of Britain joining EMU as a counterweight, with France, to German power. But such calculations were quickly and effectively countered by the Foreign Ministry and the Elysée in January 1991 during the internal debate on the French Draft Treaty on EMU. The Elysée distrusted British motives as 'diversionary' from the final goal of a single currency.

Crucially, the Finance Ministry took firm control of the process of drafting a French Draft Treaty on EMU in December 1990 to January 1991. Bérégovoy was strongly personally involved in this exercise, along with Trichet as director of the Trésor and lead personal negotiator for Bérégovoy in the IGC. Pierre de Boissieu from the Foreign Ministry, as formally joint negotiator for EMU alongside Trichet (as well as solely for European political union), and Guigou as European minister were also important players, particularly on institutional and legal issues and on geostrategic aspects. But overall co-ordination remained with the Finance Ministry. Indeed, unlike in Britain, Germany and Italy, there was no provision for an interministerial working group on EMU to co-ordinate and monitor the IGC negotiations. Such a group would have invited a stronger role for Matignon, an outcome that Bérégovoy was keen to avoid. This procedure of producing an early French Draft Treaty gave Trichet the reassurance of a clear negotiating mandate from the government as a whole on terms basically defined by the Finance Ministry. He, and the Trésor, were less politically exposed, and entered the negotiations in greater comfort about handling potentially difficult relations with the Elysée and the Foreign Ministry.

Both the evolution of the *franc stable* within the framework of the EMS and the rationale behind EMU were strongly consistent with traditional Trésor policy beliefs rooted in conservative liberal ideology – in the *grands équilibres*, budgetary *rigueur* and in securing discipline of the French economy by a strong external anchor.[12] Its intellectual grip on economic policy – weakened in 1981–1982 by the incoming

Socialist government's reflationary programme – had been restrength-
ened in March 1983 (the conversion of Budget Minister Laurent
Fabius by the director of the Trésor to acceptance of the ERM
constraint was a crucial turning-point in the 1983 crisis). But the
Trésor's intellectual ascendancy, policy leadership and obstructiveness
to reform can be exaggerated. Financial market liberalization and
privatization were implemented despite Trésor reluctance. The
Franco-German Economic Council proposal and the Balladur Memorandum on EMS reform came from political levels, not the Trésor.
Later, over EMU, independence of the Banque de France was pushed
through against Trésor reservations. Overall, in fact, the Trésor con-
nived in depriving itself of a range of powers during the 1980s and
1990s.

The attraction of an EMU agreement lay in the potential to institutionalize 'competitive disinflation' by an EC procedure to control
'excessive deficits' and by the abolition of monetary financing of
budget deficits. Hence French Trésor negotiators were willing
participants in discussions about fiscal convergence criteria. They
were under some political pressure from the Foreign Ministry to
find a means of ensuring that Italy and Spain were not excluded by
this means from early membership of Stage Three (to achieve a
political balance against Germany). The French preference in this
respect was to avoid a 'two-speed' Europe (and hence to seek a long
Stage Two). But their inclination was to accept a 3 per cent budget
deficit criterion (seen at that time as rather lax), and – remembering
the painful devaluations of 1982–1983 and 1986 – to be pleased to
adopt an exchange rate criterion. French negotiators sought to gain
political credit from Belgium, Italy, Spain and others by supporting
attention to trend performance in fiscal criteria in making the final
judgement about who qualified for Stage Three, whilst making it clear
to the Germans and Dutch that they stood for *rigueur* and, as a
'stability-oriented' state, would definitely qualify for Stage Three at
the first attempt.

The biggest negotiating difficulties were caused by trying to argue
for a *gouvernement économique* whilst seeking to avoid independence
for the Banque de France as a condition of Stage Two, and by the
contradiction between acceptance of an independent ECB and reluctance to cede independence at home. In these ways French negotiators
opened themselves to claims that their basic disposition remained
dirigiste: to want to give political direction to economic policy. This
claim had some truth: socialist ideology, and memories of 1924 and

1936 when the Socialists and the Banque de France had been in conflict, conspired with Trésor desires to retain established prerogatives. At the end of the negotiations there was little progress on *gouvernement économique*, which had precipitated a sharp conflict – not just with the Germans, who opposed it, but also with Delors who was angered by Bérégovoy's interpretation of it as involving only an executive role for the EC Commission in serving a strengthened ECOFIN and upgraded EC Monetary Committee. But the main political relief came when a tentative agreement on central bank independence at the start of Stage Two was dropped in the face of British resistance and the lack of persistence of the German Finance Minister, Theo Waigel. For Bérégovoy an independent Banque de France was the main political concession that he might have had to make in the Maastricht Treaty.

Overall, the Finance Ministry could gain some satisfaction from the final Treaty provisions. Via the adoption of the broad guidelines of economic policy, multilateral surveillance to monitor economic convergence and consistency with the guidelines, and the excessive deficit procedure, ECOFIN and the EC Monetary Committee had been upgraded. Within Stage Three there was provision for ECOFIN to apply certain sanctions when a decision specifying remedial action on an excessive deficit had not been respected; whilst ECOFIN could conclude exchange rate agreements between the single currency and non-EC currencies or formulate 'general orientations' for exchange rate policy. But on the key question of central bank independence change had been deferred, not prevented. Indeed, the French government had pre-committed itself to reform. Equally seriously from the perspective of giving a distinctive French and Socialist content to EMU, economic policy co-ordination remained underdeveloped and the idea of an EC-level dialogue about the appropriate economic-monetary policy mix unrealized.

Empowering the Banque de France

In international comparisons of central banks and states the Banque de France has typically been located nearer to the 'dependency' end of the spectrum, with monetary power concentrated in the Finance Ministry.[13] In fact, before the IGC negotiations got under way, the functioning and development of the ERM had already promoted a shift of relative power between the Trésor and the Banque de France. Firstly, the ERM gave the Banque more independence by shifting power to those concerned with the operation of foreign exchange markets. This shift was underlined once the *franc stable* policy emerged after March 1983. Secondly, the demise of state-administered credit, consequent on Bérégovoy's financial market liberalization programme of December 1994, took away a key Trésor policy instrument. Thirdly, once the Trésor's priority was no ERM realignment and once exchange controls had been abandoned as a policy instrument, flexible use of interest rates became a more important mechanism of adjustment to markets, making the Banque de France more important. The Banque was able to use comparison with the level of real interest rates in Germany as a means to bring pressure on the Trésor about appropriate short-term rates. Finally, the German Bundesbank was intent on keeping debates about EMU amongst the EC central bankers, not least to avoid dealing with a more 'politicized' French Trésor. This German strategy helped empower the Banque de France.

In the second half of the 1980s the Banque de France went through a huge cultural change as it embraced a new market orientation in the face of fast-changing financial market realities and, in particular, as it became aware of the importance of low long-term interest rates for investment and of the linkage between credibility of the franc and the level of long-term interest rates in the French economy. The credibility argument ('high credibility equals low long-term rates equals stimulus to investment and jobs') came to be used from 1987 onwards, along with a shift of attention to convergence of long-term interest rates with Germany as the indicator of that credibility. Long-term rates became the key market price for the Banque de France; the test for short-term interest rates was whether they promoted low long-term rates. In other words, the Banque developed new intellectual weapons to strengthen its position vis-à-vis the Trésor before the EMU negotiations. By the 1990s it was ready for independence; indeed, when it came with the 1993 law, independence did not in itself prove such a major change.

In this shift of relative power, two factors served as important catalysts. Firstly, the intellect of the new governor, de Larosière, had been formed by his experience at the IMF, notably of the American and Canadian models of central banking. The factor of the personal credibility of de Larosière to German negotiators, particularly the Bundesbank, cannot be exaggerated. His strong role in the management of the 1993 crisis of the franc was an important reassurance to the Germans after the disaster of the French finance minister's attempt to use public pressure on the Bundesbank to cut interest rates. Secondly, work in the Committee of EC Central Bank Governors in preparing for EMU, notably the draft statute, meant greater exposure of Banque officials to Dutch, German and British ideas. De Larosière used his participation in the Delors Committee, and Mitterrand's desire to make progress on an EMU agreement, to persuade the president that acceptance of the principle of independence for the ECB was a precondition for any hope of an agreement with the Germans. But persuasion of the French government to champion independence for the Banque de France proved more difficult. It took the aftermath of the September 1992 ERM crisis to persuade Michel Sapin, the Socialist finance minister, that this policy measure was necessary to reinforce the credibility of the franc. This last-minute Socialist conversion was overtaken by the March 1993 legislative election results. The new finance minister, Edmond Alphandéry, backed by his prime minister, Balladur, made an independent Banque de France the legislative priority.

Just how powerful a transformatory effect is to be ascribed to EMU becomes apparent when one considers that the French Constitutional Council blocked this legislation on the grounds that, under the constitution of the Fifth Republic, government could not delegate responsibility for the conduct of monetary policy to an independent body. Once the Maastricht Treaty had been ratified, or the constitution appropriately amended in some other way, the legislation could come into operation.

CONCLUSION

The way in which EMU has affected France has been intimately shaped by the following factors. First, a permissive consensus around the view that European integration was broadly consistent with French power and interests, albeit challenged on the far right and left. Second, the difficulty of specifying the economic and social distribution of winners and losers from EMU and hence of mobilizing interests on the issue. Third, the sense that France was a clear relative gainer vis-à-vis Germany if an EMU deal disempowering the Bundesbank was struck. Fourth, the high technical content and opacity of the issue area, giving technocrats an inbuilt information advantage. And lastly, the existence of a well-established EC machinery for processing negotiations, focused around ECOFIN, the EC Monetary Committee and the Committee of EC Central Bank Governors.

Together, these factors ensured a high degree of executive insulation in the EMU negotiations; a bargaining strategy that stressed using EMU for domestic empowerment to effect policy reforms rather than the use of domestic constraints on EMU for external empowerment; and the reduction of EMU to a contest over empowerment between the Elysée, the Finance Ministry/Trésor and the Banque de France. The main victor was the Banque de France in securing acceptance of the principle of central bank independence and in changing the criteria by which economic success were judged. The Finance Ministry can claim to be a partial victor. Its greatest achievement was in using EMU to institutionalize 'competitive disinflation'. But, on the other hand, it ceded both powers and status.

With the presidency we come to the paradox of EMU. On EMU Mitterrand exerted strong political leadership, intervening decisively at certain points. During the cohabitation of 1986–1988 Chirac and Balladur had been much more cautious about EMU;[14] whilst Bérégovoy had reservations about proceeding in the absence of an EC-wide withholding tax and about central bank independence as a price to be paid. Mitterrand was important in providing historical legitimation for EMU, not least against the unfolding drama of German unification and its long-term implications for a French leadership role in Europe.[15] In so doing he provided important signals to the government and administration about the direction in which policy positions should be developed. More importantly, Mitterrand injected a frame of reference and set of policy beliefs into the process of negotiating EMU. He was also successful in embodying two of his major preoccupations in the treaty: to create an 'irreversible' process leading to Stage Three; and to maintain political discretion for the European Council over the final decision on who would go into Stage Three on 1 January 1999. But otherwise, notably on social flanking measures and fiscal harmonization, Mitterrand had little success. The substantive content of the EMU agreement was hammered out at technical levels, far removed from the intellectual interests of the president. The political interests of Mitterrand (as now of Chirac) were defined more by the concern to strengthen the bargaining resources available to the presidential office than by party political factors.

The paradox of strength and weakness in presidential leadership on EMU was nested in a more profound paradox: that. in order to escape from the constraints of external monetary dependency on Germany, French negotiators were forced to adopt the policy beliefs and institutional arrangements of the country that was being asked to cede power. The price of a balancing of the relational power between France and Germany via EMU was acceptance of German hegemony in the institutional design and policy instruments of EMU. That price was easiest to pay for the Banque de France and, to a lesser extent, the Trésor. Another profound paradox was that the search via EMU for greater strength vis-à-vis global financial markets involved a new institutionalization of market imperatives: in, for instance, the form of the convergence criteria and of the Waigel Stability Pact proposals for automatic sanctions on tightly defined budget deficits within Stage Three. The combination of institutionalizing market imperatives and German hegemony in EMU privileged certain actors over others and meant that presidential leadership in agenda-setting on EMU and on historical legitimation was not translated into leadership on economic and monetary policy ideas. In short, presidential leadership in providing strong *political direction* on EMU was not synonymous with *power over policy contents*.

NOTES

This paper is based on a research project funded by the British Economic and Social Research Council (ESRC) Grant R000 234793, entitled 'The Dynamics of European Monetary Integration'. The project has included over 260 elite interviews, of which over 50 were conducted in Paris.

1. H. Védrine, *Les Mondes de François Mitterrand: à l'Elysée* (Paris: Fayard, 1996).
2. K. Dyson et al., 'Strapped to the Mast: EC Central Bankers between the Maastricht Treaty and Global Financial Markets', *Journal of European Public Policy*, Vol. 2, No. 3, 1995, pp. 465–487.
3. P. Hall, 'Policy Paradigms, Social Learning and the State', *Comparative Politics*, Vol. 25, No. 3, pp. 275–296.
4. E. Balladur, 'La construction monétaire européenne', Ministry of Finance, Paris, 8 January 1988; K. Dyson, *The Elusive Union: the Process of Economic and Monetary Union in Europe* (London: Longman, 1994).
5. K.-H. Bender, *Mitterrand und die Deutschen* (Bonn: Bouvier, 1995).
6. D. Putnam, 'Diplomacy and Domestic Politics', *International Organization*, No. 42, Summer 1988, pp. 427– 461.
7. K. Dyson and K. Featherstone, 'Italy and EMU as *Vincolo Esterno*', *Southern European Society and Politics*, Vol. 2, No. 3, 1996.
8. K. Dyson and K. Featherstone, 'EMU and Economic Governance in Germany', *German Politics*, Vol. 5, No. 3, 1996.

10.	See, for example, P. Evans et al., *Double-Edged Diplomacy: International Bargaining and Domestic Politics* (Berkeley: University of California Press, 1993).

11.	C. Lequesne, *Paris-Bruxelles* (Paris: Presses de la Fondation Nationale des Sciences Politiques, 1993).

12.	K.-H. Bender, op. cit.

13.	Y. Mamou, *Une Machine de pouvoir: la direction du Trésor* (Paris: La Découverte, 1988).

14.	J. Goodman, *Monetary Sovereignty* (Ithaca: Cornell University Press, 1992).

15.	E. Balladur, op. cit.

16.	F. Mitterrand, *De l'Allemagne, de la France* (Paris: Odile Jacob, 1996).

6 Independence and Interdependence: Foreign Policy over Mitterrand's Two Presidential Terms
Dominique David

Whatever their political sympathies, the French will for a long time see François Mitterrand as a man who wanted to represent them in all their contradictions and contrasts, however attractive or unattractive. In people's political minds, this two-term president will remain a symbol and direct exponent of two particularly French demands: an inconceivable shift of political power within the country and the need to resist external forces and steer a steady course that carried the voice of France into the world. In keeping his own voice, was Mitterrand, as a prominent symbol of the shift from one world to another, the heir of a dying century or the visionary of a nascent one? The debates around the final phase of his foreign and defence policy have not yet ended.

TAKING OVER A FLEXIBLE HERITAGE

It may seem too rigid to divide Mitterrand's time in office into the two seven-year terms, yet this division reflects accurately a parallel shift in world events. As far as foreign policy was concerned, his first term was marked by taking over a policy that was flexible. He had no choice, since the policy was dictated by an East-West block over which France had no control and in which France already occupied a clearly-defined position that had to be defended. The policy was also flexible, however, since within a stable geopolitical context, the new government made major changes.[1]

Euromissiles and the Alliance

The first major shift in policy, which provided both continuity and change, was in France's relationship with the Atlantic Alliance and, indeed, the Atlantic community. Analysts now refer in shorthand to the good relations between the United States and 'left-wing' France, citing the need for France to demonstrate positive goodwill to make up for the unorthodox presence of Communists in the government. This explanation is, however, only part of the story and ignores the fact that Mitterrand's position on Atlantic solidarity in general (and more particularly, on the deployment of Euromissiles) was consistent and pre-dated his election in 1981 by some considerable time.[2] It also omits the fact that this shift in policy towards the Alliance was accompanied throughout the 1980s by a number of clashes between Paris and Washington over such issues as GATT, the limitation of trade with Eastern Europe, the attempt to globalize Western security, the Geneva negotiations and the Strategic Defence Initiative (SDI).

There are a number of explanations for the fact that Mitterrand's 1979 'double-track decision'[3] broke with the neo-Gaullist tradition represented by Giscard and for the fact that he endorsed it before the German Bundestag in 1983, when he supported the deployment of NATO (North Atlantic Treaty Organization) Euromissiles and in so doing, supported the German government against both peace campaigners and the majority of the European left. We should not underestimate Mitterrand's attachment to the Alliance tradition; his roots were undeniably to be found in the Fourth Republic and he was one of the critics of de Gaulle's decisions in 1966 to distance France from the Alliance. His intellectual espousal of traditional reasoning on the balance of forces was a major factor here, and during his first presidential term, it was to return like a *leitmotif*. There was also, however, the German argument, that opposing the Alliance's position and, hence, the German position was to jeopardize German political stability and Germany's commitment to the Alliance – in other words, to encourage Bonn to consider itself outside the Western community.

These arguments certainly explain the position Mitterrand adopted in the 'Euromissile battle' but also justify his constant *rapprochement* with the Alliance, which gradually found support in public opinion and which was to symbolize France's global position, which remained largely unchanged from the Atlantic Council's first meeting under the Fifth Republic in Paris in 1989 to its reiteration in 1996. One further element in Mitterrand's position throughout the 1980s needs to be highlighted, however: opposition to Moscow strong enough to be described as anti-Soviet.

This period, typified by the Euromissile debate, the Afghanistan war and the decline of Brezhnev's power in the Soviet Union, was not one of extrovert policies generally. Nevertheless, the private reticence of a man who seemed to have little understanding of the Soviets and, later, the Russians, and to be removed from their concerns, reasoning and culture, played a major part in shaping policy. Mitterrand kept his distance from Moscow for political reasons that were easily understood in the early 1980s, but he never gave support to a major Franco-Russian policy, even when successive new regimes at the Kremlin gave him many opportunities to do so. In France, as often elsewhere too, it was the right that was communicating with Moscow. An invisible curtain of suspicion seemed to separate the president of France from the decision-makers in Eastern Europe. Mitterrand failed to take advantage of the opportunities offered by Andropov, although it is true that at that time Soviet overtures were muted. For a long time, he ignored the opportunities opening up under Gorbachev; Gorbachev's first foreign tour was to France, yet there were no real benefits from it. Indeed, two years after he took office, France implemented military planning legislation that included a major increase in military expenditure, and France's defence budget continued to rise, although at a slower pace than originally envisaged, until 1991. At the same time, the US had in late 1987 reached agreement with Moscow on a first disarmament treaty. Mitterrand's private friendship with Mikhail Gorbachev, which he eventually acknowledged, never brought the two governments close together. Paris cannot take the entire blame for this; Moscow preferred to deal with Washington, one of the few remnants of its super-power status. Nevertheless, Mitterrand's lack of understanding and his complete lack of interest in Franco-Soviet or Franco-Russian policy no doubt played a key part.[4]

The Paris-Bonn Axis

Mitterrand preferred a Paris-Bonn focus to the traditional axis of French diplomacy, Paris-Moscow. He repeatedly argued that 'without Germany, there is no Europe'. From 1981 and the Euromissile crisis to German reunification, Mitterrand's obsession remained the same: Germany had to remain European and had to continue its links with France, come what may. It was a simple and fair geopolitical vision, since the Franco-German alliance was in many ways the anchor-point for Germany within Europe, but it was also a personal vision, shaped by memories of the two World Wars; the fear of war, often cited when difficulties or crises arose, was particularly relevant here.[5]

This *rapprochement* was not a veneer but gradually created a real shared sensitivity, bringing together structures and people and forming an alliance that would prove robust throughout good times and bad. From 1986, Franco-German agreement enabled the process of European integration, stalled since 1979 over UK demands, to start up again, and from then on, Paris and Bonn acting together set the pace for institutional reform, from the 1987 SEA to the 1992 Maastricht Treaty. Of key significance here is the exceptional private relationship between Helmut Kohl and François Mitterrand, and this accounted in large part for the consistency of the image of the two countries' alliance, even when the going was difficult, such as during German reunification or after ratification of Maastricht.

At the same time as a joint European policy was being formulated as the framework for Community integration (to the discomfiture of the UK, which remained trapped within its own impotent isolation), bilateral relations between the two countries improved dramatically. There were frequent declarations of shared defence concerns, leading to the institution of a major defence commission, a number of summit meetings, the Verdun conference and a whole-hearted revival of defence co-operation. Two decisions are particularly symbolic in this respect. First, the creation within the framework of the first military planning legislation of Mitterrand's first term of the Forces d'Action Rapide (FAR), a grouping of military resources better able than the main body of troops to get quickly to the scene. France's German allies saw this as reassurance that France had the resources to intervene early in a crisis and thus to help Germany rather than having to wait for the approach of Warsaw Pact troops and the deployment of the French army. The second key decision was the signing of the Franco-German Protocol[6] in 1988 which marked the twenty-fifth anniversary of the Elysée Treaty. This set up the Franco-German brigade and a Franco-German Defence Council whose task was to flesh out the defence provisions within the latter treaty that had never come into force. Future events in Europe were to change the rules and thereby marginalize the Council to some extent, but nevertheless, the 1988 decision was a crucial one in terms both of ambition and of symbolism. On 14 July 1994, Mitterrand presided over the final Bastille Day celebrations of his second term at which, with Kohl by his side, he watched the parade of the Franco-German brigade, the first German unit to march down the Champs-Elysées since 1944.

Consistency in the South

Outside Europe and NATO, the reality of Mitterrand's polices was more varied. French Socialists had come to power accused of a 'Third Worldism' and 'anti-imperialism' that was a hangover from the 1970s. However, the newly-elected politicians were responsible for the 'anti-bloc' league for which de Gaulle campaigned and orchestrated French influence within a very specific geographical area. These factors led to both militant discourse on overseas aid and action on development and to a policy that with a few exceptions could be described as relatively traditional. The main hallmarks soon emerged: the Cancun speech in October 1981, the visit to Algeria in December 1981, the appointment of Jean-Pierre Cot to the Ministry of Co-operation (foreign development) with responsibility for relations with the African nations, the arrival of Régis Debray at the Elysée Palace to take on the Third World portfolio and an announcement of increased French development aid.[7] Mitterrand's main idea here was that development determined the political progress of southern nations as well as stability in international relations, and he remained consistent in this theory.

Mitterrand's foreign policy was particularly significant in the Near East. As soon as he took office, he shifted France's position to such an extent that Paris came to be seen as much as a friend of Israel as the friend of the Arabs it had been since de Gaulle's controversial statements in 1967. In 1982, Mitterrand went to Israel and made his (in)famous speech to the Knesset, and in the same year, France intervened in the Lebanon to safeguard Yasser Arafat's Palestine Liberation Organization (PLO) and, hence, its own opportunity to play a part in the peace process in the region. This shift of policy was aimed at making France a respected, even crucial, negotiating partner for all sides. Yasser Arafat's speech in which he declared that the section in the PLO Charter contesting the existence of the state of Israel was null and void was, indeed, made in Paris.

In Africa, concrete choices soon diverged widely from ideological certainties. Mitterrand's policies in Africa were remarkably traditional once Jean-Pierre Cot was no longer on the scene, focusing on the support and defence of existing regimes, direct personal contact with leaders, the continued existence of networks, and defence of France's sphere of influence: in other words, the policy confirmed the existence of special African diplomacy,[8] implemented directly by the president with a few senior members of the Council of State. The confrontation with Libya in Chad symbolised Mitterrand's wish to maintain France's policy across the Mediterranean through familiar channels. The attempts to breathe new life into the continent's collective security structures, that is, the OAU (in French, Organisation de l'Unité Africaine, or OUA), at the beginning of his term of office were then abandoned. Other regions in the world featured prominently but traditionally in official discourse, particularly on development, and there was no attempt to restructure policy, either in Latin America, where early anti-American provocation (such as the sale of arms to Nicaragua) was short-lived, or in Asia, where reinvestment in Indochina was slow and limited. Mitterrand, in short, moved within the traditional strategic geography of France and failed – as his predecessors had done – to break free of the constraints of financing which only partly reflected his own aspirations.

Continuity in Defence

Defence was probably the area of the most noticeable continuity in policy during Mitterrand's first presidential term. He arrived in power with an anti-nuclear background and an image of being ill at ease with defence issues and suspicious of the military. In fact, he did not merely follow the policy of his predecessors; he actually strengthened Gaullist logic. From the first economic plan to the 1994 White Paper on Defence, in which he expressed his views directly, Mitterrand continued to refine and streamline the nuclear concept, removing it from all possibility of use, which was for most of the time linked with the increase in tactical or operational weapons. Politically ('deterrence, *c'est moi*'), doctrinally (the shift to calling tactical nuclear weapons *pre-strategic* weapons) and technically (putting pre-strategic weaponry under one unit under the president's control, then gradually marginalizing it), Mitterrand ensured the survival of a concept of deterrence that affirmed France's power, made war a thing of the past and enabled him directly to control a military machinery that he mistrusted.[9] The debate on the 'neutron bomb' is typical of this policy: Mitterrand authorized research into it (although in a very characteristic way, blowing hot and cold) and then later banned its production and use on the grounds that it could be used like a nuclear weapon. This was a rare example of a decision not to use an available weapons system.

Mitterrand's rejection of the SDI in 1986, reiterated in the GPALS (Global Protection Against Limited Strikes) initiative in 1992,

certainly partly reflected the French distaste for Washington's dominant behaviour but can be attributed largely to defence of the French
nuclear concept which was inevitably complicated by the proliferation
and increasing sophistication of defence systems, at least those that
worked. The key characteristic of the nuclear system was to be reiterated throughout the Mitterrand presidency, as though he intended
to make this heritage a key part of his legacy to his successors.

In the area of conventional defence, Mitterrand created the FAR
(see above), which was a concept aimed politically at strengthening
France's relationship with her German partner but also represented
strategic innovation for an army that had grown used to carrying out
manoeuvres around national borders. The FAR contained the seeds
of the idea of projecting France's strength that was to be so fashionable in the 1990s and indeed, in the late 1980s there was discussion of
whether the *'farisation'* of the ground forces was possible or desirable.
This was, then, clearly a central concept in the military strategy
debate, one that was crucial to the relationship between France and
Germany and one that, indeed, represented and reflected the *rapprochement* with NATO that had begun earlier over Euromissiles and
that had less to do with shared rules of engagement than with patterns
of behaviour and psychological reactions. It should be borne in mind,
finally, that Mitterrand's failure to keep an electoral pledge to reduce
compulsory military service to six months met an astonishing degree
of indifference in public opinion.

It could therefore be argued that Mitterrand's first presidential term
bore both his own hallmark and that of France as a whole. He
adopted, but also changed, policy in a number of key areas, adapting
Yalta rather than rejecting it; he created consensus on France's attitude to the Atlantic Alliance and on a Franco-German alliance; he
safeguarded an independent voice for France in the world; and,
finally, he adopted a defence policy that both ensured the country's
position and secured its power.

THE IRREVERENCE OF HISTORY

However, history is no respecter of persons and at this point, its
verdict on Mitterrand needs to be considered. France has debated at
length Mitterrand's responses to the upheavals in Europe in the late
1980s, and it was probably at this period of uncertainty that Mitterrand's international initiatives best reveal him in all his vision and

reserve, his contradictions, his aspirations and above all his idiosyncratic style.

Mitterrand's strategy on reshaping Europe was developed over time, with small points explained but large areas left undiscussed; it was basically fairly clear, even though the president preferred to muddy its terms. Haunted by the fragmentation of Europe and the possible fragmentation of the Community, Mitterrand tried to implement a political and institutional framework that would restructure Europe and stabilize the process of European integration. Central to his logic was the idea that this would ensure that France would not be marginalized either by history or, perhaps more importantly, by Germany. Mitterrand's strategy took three main directions.

Complexity and Coherence in Europe

The first main direction was to strengthen the integration of Eastern Europe. Following the end of the Cold War, Europe needed a focus for stability, but – the argument went – only a Europe of the Twelve could ensure influence and stability beyond its member states' own borders. It was also important to ensure that German reunification did not take place in isolation from Germany's European partners and on the basis of its own power. The Franco-German agreement on developing Europe from an economic community to political union was to prove crucial. It was as though Mitterrand had looked into the breach so dramatically opened up by history and seen in it his opportunity to accelerate the progress he had so long sought towards political union. This acceleration, of course, required having Germany on board, and in view of its own hasty progress towards reunification, Germany had to approve this acceleration in European integration to reassure not only its allies but also itself.

It has probably been too easy to equate Mitterrand's attitude to German reunification with psychological rejection and political obstacles. The former would be a misjudgement, since there are many historically documented instances of Mitterrand's acceptance of the likelihood of such an event, and Mitterrand was not the only person to have overlooked the possibility of reunification being telescoped into just a few months. Mitterrand's main concern was rather to make reunification – which he knew was unstoppable, even though he had misjudged its form and speed – part of a multilateral process that guaranteed simultaneously German reunification and the structure of Europe, both on a wide scale (hence his discussions with Gorbachev) and on a smaller scale (the Maastricht Treaty). His desire was not, as Margaret Thatcher's was, to slow down the process so much as to influence every part of it.[10] For example, he insisted that changes in Germany should be guaranteed by multilateral negotiations, and that the border with Poland be recognized before the treaty was signed. These demands were in conflict, although fairly discreetly, with Germany's unilateral line, resulting in progress and counter-progress that could be interpreted differently and that were more or less adroit or impenetrable since Mitterrand never intervened directly over the issues and events moved very quickly. The future of co-operation and of the Franco-German agreement was probably enough to demonstrate that these clashes of opinion were less serious than certain commentators claimed.

The second main thrust of Mitterrand's European policy was to seek a pan-European system of negotiation and stability, a collective security apparatus to take over from the alliance system to ensure the peaceful cohabitation of the states of Europe. From the end of the Second World War, the destiny of Europe went far beyond the people of Europe themselves, determined as it was by the superpowers. Yet now Europe faced crisis and fragmentation that neither Moscow and Washington, nor Washington alone, could avert. Readers will recall that at the end of 1989, Mitterrand had launched the idea of a European Federation. The terminology was poor, since what he described was not what a constitutional expert would recognize as a federation, and it was poorly supported, since the concept was never adequately clarified. Moreover, too many other interests opposed it, including the Americans, who were concerned that such a move would marginalize them; France's closest European allies; Central European nations, who wanted direct contact with Washington and would have been prevented from having this by a specifically European grouping; and, finally, Moscow, which preferred to have direct dialogue with the US. The project therefore failed rapidly. However, it contained a real vision for the shaping of Europe, even though its content was debatable. Its failure can be attributed primarily to the inability of Western Europe to rethink its relationship with the former members of the Warsaw Pact in Central Europe, whom they regarded as neither totally outside Europe nor wholly part of Europe. The institutionalization of the Conference on Security and Co-operation in Europe (CSCE) was the preferred method for dealing with this, symbolized by the signature in Paris of a charter for a new Europe. Mitterrand's attempts to shape the continent of Europe with largely unchanged institutions failed, and the federal idea was finally laid to rest in Prague in June 1991. Meanwhile, the CSCE, proceeding cautiously, enjoyed enormous success.[11]

The role of the Atlantic Alliance within the new Europe remained to be redefined. France's political leaders never wanted the Alliance to disappear. Quite simply, by remaining a defence alliance restricted to the political and military issues laid down in the Washington Treaty, the Alliance changed positions within Europe. From being an institution with a monopoly over issues of security in Europe, it changed to being one institution among others (and specifically European institutions) with responsibility for guaranteeing Europe's security. Ultimately, the Alliance became a system used to reassure the people of Europe against increasingly remote eventualities. The calls for reform voiced in Paris in 1989–1990 reflect this shift in NATO's role, although the US and its allies might have preferred the term 'marginalization'. The main difficulty France had in this area was its lack of support from its own allies in Europe, who were seriously alarmed by the possibility of American withdrawal. The US's strategy was simple: it took hold of the idea of reform at an early stage, refused to hold detailed discussions until the machinery had been reformed, and did all it could to secure dialogue aimed at putting the Alliance back at the heart of the debate on security within Europe, only nodding at the idea of a European security identity[12] such as was included in the negotiations that eventually produced the Maastricht Treaty.

Overall, Mitterrand's policy on Europe may seem both coherent and visionary, at least in terms of the reality if not of the appropriateness of the vision. It failed to take more concrete shape, however, with the exception of the Maastricht Treaty, whose implementation in strategic matters was hampered by the failure of the other two policy thrusts. The policy probably had at least two main shortcomings: in terms of form, it was never made explicit in a coherent form and in terms of content, it was too isolated.

The Impact in the South

As the end of the superpower relationship had implications well beyond Europe, the question then arose of how a system of international co-operation could be envisaged that would represent the new common spirit that seemed to exist between former rival powers as well as the apparent alignment of virtually all social models with 'Western'-type values. The United Nations (UN) was both the

symbolic and the real framework for such a large-scale redefinition,
and under Mitterrand France spared no efforts to provide the new
world order with a new foundation. Between 1990 and 1995, French
troops intervened in operations ordered or supported by the UN in
Yugoslavia, the Western Sahara, Haiti, El Salvador, Angola,
Rwanda, Somalia, Cambodia, Turkey (to protect the Iraqi Kurds)
and in Saudi Arabia, over the Kuwait invasion.[13] It is an impressive
list, and indeed, at the time, France was the major contributor of
manpower to UN forces.

Under Mitterrand, France conspicuously lent support to the UN on
the stated grounds that the UN was the key to a new framework of
law for international society: 'the United Nations Organization must
dictate law', the president was to say during the Gulf War, supporting
major conceptual changes in the form of the idea of the law on
humanitarian intervention right at the end of the 1980s and by taking
action and lending financial support (France was one of the few states
to be more or less up to date with its contributions). Mitterrand's
position was clearly stated and can probably be attributed to a number of factors. Mitterrand was a lawyer by profession and had always
cultivated the notion of the crucial pre-eminence of the rule of law.
Moreover, France was a Permanent Member of the UN Security
Council, and any revival in the UN's fortunes would boost its influence. Thus, the UN was a channel for French multilateralism and at
the same time for affirmation of unilateralism or a policy of power.
Yet this tension between what could be seen as either opposing or
complementary extremes is entirely characteristic of Mitterrand's
international philosophy. After all, the fact that the president decided
to be a part of the international coalition opposing Saddam Hussein
was both a multilateralist phenomenon, along the lines of rejection by
the international community of such aggression as threatening its own
existence, and a unilateralist one: France as a major power could not
possibly be absent from the reshaping of the region that would follow
the conflict.

However, on a smaller scale, the shifts in France's policy in the
Mediterranean or in Africa, areas crucial to France's diplomatic
strategy, seemed more tentative and incomplete. In neither area did
Paris's concept of 'regional security' take shape, even though the
French government was giving the idea prominence as crucial to the
future world order.[14] The Mediterranean was subjected to particular
attention towards the end of the 1980s: Paris gave priority to dialogue
with the Western Mediterranean in what was called the '5+5' process

on the CSCE model after the rapid failure of the globalist aspirations of a conference on security and co-operation in the Mediterranean. However, the 5+5 dialogue rapidly foundered on uncertainty over Algeria and the international embargo on Libya, which in the event spelled an end to the concept of the Union of the Arab Maghreb, a crucial partner in dialogue with the South.[15] Because of a lack of real investment or a lack of structural vision for the region, Mitterrand ultimately had virtually no significant Mediterranean or Latin American policy, despite having taken office in 1981 with plans to reorient the EC more towards the south by improving dialogue with Italy and as a result of the accession of Spain and Portugal.

In sub-Saharan Africa, France's support for some democratic conditions on aid came late (at La Baule in 1990) and appeared ill thought out in terms of its political impact. As a result, it was difficult to implement. It was as though Paris was merely following events on the 'dark continent', not anticipating them and still less having any role in producing them. France behaved as though challenges were dangerous for national stability and for stability within the structures or networks of France across the Mediterranean.[16] Future generations of historians will judge whether the repeated elections and changes of political power in Africa from the early 1990s, most of them representing progress towards political democracy, created a lasting situation and whether Africa owes this to France. All that can be said at this, very early, stage is that Africa probably owes little to France and that for a number of years, France had been struggling to find forms of Franco-African dialogue that were appropriate for the changed climate. Mitterrand was probably not the right man to revolutionize affairs: he was content to fill a few gaps (although that in itself was no small achievement), supporting shaky regimes put in place by newly-fledged democracies (such as in Gabon) or intervening on humanitarian grounds, as in Rwanda. The idea of an Inter-African Intervention Force, launched in 1994 in Biarritz, was still-born, even though co-operation between Paris and London should have ensured its implementation.

Unchanging Defence

The high level of activity of French troops concealed for a while what remains a relative political enigma: Mitterrand's resolutely immobile stance on defence during his second term. There may be a number of explanations for this. The traditional importance of the military in defining the power of France was enhanced under the Fifth Republic, which saw French forces being redefined around nuclear weapons against a backdrop of renewed prestige, and this meant that France was very suspicious of any attack on the military symbols of its rank. In more personal terms, however, Mitterrand was suspicious both of the military as an institution and of individuals within it and was probably concerned about any movement to discredit nuclear weapons in favour of traditional tangible weapons when he had identified himself to such an extent with the concept of deterrence and of 'non-war'. The pressure of the threat lobby also played a part: in late 1987, André Giraud, then Minister for Defence, described the INF Treaty as 'the Europeans' Munich', and France generally was slow to respond to overtures from Gorbachev. Finally, political 'cohabitation' was for a while a time of dramatically higher stakes in the run-up to the next set of elections. Hence, between 1986 and 1995 France had a series of surreal economic plans or bills which were never implemented but which, without exception, promised a major increase in defence expenditure. This could be seen as the sole case of chronic short-sightedness among the major Western nations.

Yet, of course, this myopia stopped short of blindness and eventually, France reduced both expenditure and manning levels. However, the reduction in expenditure was very small compared with the wholesale cuts in Germany and Britain or, indeed, the US. Nor did the 'Armées 2000' plan envisage reductions and restructuring on anything like the scale undertaken by France's allies. More importantly, it failed to take account of the requirements of a radically changed military climate. The 1994 White Paper on Defence therefore remained a curious exercise in political tightrope-walking, offering more scope for future debate than current policy.[17]

Parallel to this structural paralysis, France did however shift its position on nuclear disarmament, yet in Mitterrand's typical blow-hot-blow-cold way. The freezing of the Hades short-range missile programme, the reduction of the programme to build nuclear rocket-launching submarines, and the unilateral moratorium on nuclear testing declared in 1992 were all evidence of France's desire to be part of the general trend towards reducing arms. At the same time, Mitterrand defended to the hilt the 'purity' of the nuclear concept against considerable calls for the development of new and more flexible equipment that could, for example, be used against the emerging nuclear powers of the Third World.

All we can do here is report the facts. Mitterrand's lack of familiarity with military apparatus and his instinctive distrust of rapid change prevented him from moving beyond minor changes at a time in his second term when what was needed was radical debate on France's strategies and forces. The French defence system was too inflexible in a world where the role of armies was changing beyond recognition, and where arms exports – a crucial element of French policy since the early days of the Fifth Republic – were collapsing, and that meant that very rapid decisions had to be taken in 1996.

The Trial of Chaos

Reality moves rapidly, and over the past ten years all the existing political scenarios for reshaping Europe, and the world, have been turned on their heads. At a global level, UN-style world policy as pushed by France in the early part of the decade gradually gave way to the resigned acceptance of a new power policy, with the new powers tailoring their efforts and intervention to their own interests. Heavy or weak media pressure also played a key part.

In Europe itself, the events in Yugoslavia symbolized the practical difficulties Mitterrand's logic encountered. It posed a problem of strategic time and space dimensions that ran counter to the Franco-German logic Paris was trying to shape. In terms of the chronology, the Maastricht process was not operative, but nor was the CSCE process, which had become paralysed, nor that of the Alliance which was hampered by American policy. The US failed to produce a common diplomacy because it could not be implemented on the basis of military deployments that were properly European; there simply was no institutional framework for it. The long Maastricht negotiations, with the emergence of diplomacy, then of a defence policy and then of defence structures, and finally fragmentation under the pressure of events, proved this. In spatial terms, Mitterrand's traditional reluctance to give his blessing to new states and to see frontiers being broken up – in other words, his antipathy to the fragmentation of traditional political divisions within Europe and to the possibility of having to go to war to regain or defend such changes – appeared wholly reasonable in the light of events, but was far from being supported by the rest of Europe.[18]

In Yugoslavia, France quite simply lacked the means to implement its hopes. It lacked the means to prevent the Yugoslav Federation from breaking up or to suggest and implement a European political solution on the ground. It lacked the means, too, to solve the conflict solely through humanitarian measures. The Yugoslav question was to be the forum for a major shift in policy which heralded a number of subsequent changes. While the Europe of the Twelve and then of the Fifteen (the Union was enlarged without real consideration of the consequences and with disregard for France's reservations) could not voice a common diplomacy, there was recourse, at least temporarily, to the powers with political and military significance. Hence, the 'contact group' was formed; if the Europeans were incapable of running a joint military policy because they lacked the relevant structures, the argument went, they would have to use existing structures, in this case, those of NATO.

As a result, France became more involved with the Alliance and acknowledged in January 1994 in Brussels that Europe needed Alliance structures and forces to carry out stabilization or peace-keeping operations in Europe, apart from traditional defence operations of the kind laid down in Article 5 of the Treaty. It was entirely in keeping for Paris to authorize institutional *rapprochement* between the hierarchies of the French defence system and those of NATO, on areas referred to as extra-Article 5 operations. Conversely, the US at the same time agreed to recognize the legitimacy and utility of a European security identity and thereby to acknowledge that relative autonomy could be granted to Europe in matters of use of the military resources of the Alliance. This political compromise produced the concept of the Combined Joint Task Force, which made a distinction between different operational modes. NATO troops were to be allowed to be used under American command if all the allies and thus the traditional hierarchy of NATO was concerned; otherwise, they would be under specifically European command.

For Mitterrand, the pragmatic decision-maker, this development was dictated by necessity, but he wanted it to be limited to the absolute minimum necessary since at bottom, it ran counter to his strategy to give the EU autonomy in diplomatic and strategic matters. Mitterrand's reluctance to legitimate the return of the Alliance to a central position in European strategic discussions was clearly demonstrated by the constant brakes he sought to apply to the enthusiasm of top military or political officials in the Ministry of Defence for taking part in the work of various Alliance committees. The policy followed since June 1995 can therefore be seen both as contiguous with and as a departure from Mitterrand's previous policies. The Yugoslav crisis produced a very different Europe from the one Mitterrand had envisaged, and in fact one very similar to what he feared, as a result of a number of failures: the failure of the Europe of Maastricht to respond even partially to the acceleration of events; the CSCE's failure to set up credible procedures for political conflict management; the UN's failure to have any influence beyond pure supervision of forces; and the Alliance's failure to demonstrate that it was anything other than a conduit for American decisions.

Overall, Mitterrand's foreign policy represented France superbly in terms of depicting its grandeur and its weakness, just as Mitterrand as an individual incarnated the French people in all their shades of opinion, roles, certainties and misjudgements. When Mitterrand first came to power, one of the key concerns of the French was to keep a specific, individual French voice. This uncompromising stance was reinforced by a less prominent perception; Mitterrand undoubtedly recognized that he took power at a time when French sovereignty was being redefined by collective institutions that could lend weight and new direction to his action, which had previously been so impotent and isolated. Hence the contradictions of the final period of Mitterrand's time as president, the rapid shifting between individual posturing and collective action. Mitterrand's last message is that the major issue of the time was to balance all the deliberate or imposed trends towards collective international action, whether they were created by Europe or merely experienced by it, against affirmation of individual identities.

This synthesis of individual will and collective action was something Mitterrand found in the process of European integration and in the affirmation of the Franco-German alliance, consistent choices that gave coherence to a long, subtle and sometimes apparently fragmented process. Today, the legacy takes on an appearance that Mitterrand did not care to imagine, in an economic climate where Europe struggles and has no soul. Yet the legacy is probably part of the long-term impetus that will prove to be more significant than the vagaries of economic cycles.

So was François Mitterrand the means of ferrying people from the old world to the new? Probably not: without a prophet to decipher the hidden power lines, there can be no systematic crossing. Yet Mitterrand was undoubtedly one of those who best assessed the risks and the opportunities of the changes taking shape, and who did so with a degree of sophistication that is wholly characteristic. He was lucid, flexible and contradictory, opposed to rapid change, both rational and changeable in an economic climate that was neither. François

Mitterrand represented a consistency of policy of which, given his indirect style, he may well not have been the best champion. However, history will not be rushed in its judgement of that assessment.

NOTES

1. For a summary of Mitterrand's own views on the key issues in his first term as president, see F. Mitterrand, *Réflexions sur la politique extérieure de la France* (Paris: Fayard, 1995).
2. H. Védrine, *Les Mondes de François Mitterrand* (Paris: Fayard, 1996).
3. The 1979 'double-track decision' of announced negotiations with the Soviet Union on withdrawal of the SS20s or, if that failed, the deployment of new medium-range NATO rockets.
4. Védrine (op. cit.) explains this phenomenon by anti-Soviet feeling in French public opinion in the 1980s, but he ignores the fact that the attitude of the political leadership also helped create public opinion. It was, after all, in the preamble to the 1984–1988 Plan that the Soviet Union was identified for the first time as a probable enemy.
5. On the fear of war, see Védrine (op. cit.). On the German question, see F. Mitterrand, *De l'Allemagne, de la France* (Paris: Odile Jacob, 1996).
6. For the official documents of the period, see D. David (ed.), *La Politique de défense de la France: textes et documents* (Paris: FEDN, 1989).
7. On the early days of Mitterrand's term as president, see P. Favier and M. Martin-Roland, *La Décennie Mitterrand*, in three volumes (Paris: Seuil, 1990, 1991, 1996).
8. Védrine pays very little attention to Africa in his charting of diplomacy during Mitterrand's two periods in office, and this reflects the fact that African diplomacy was kept at the highest levels, and thus fell outside the traditional machinery of diplomacy and even the ordinary departments of the Elysée itself.
9. Evidence of his consistency, his last major speech on this topic was on 5 May 1994.
10. For a radically different view, see B. Lecomte, 'François Mitterrand et l'Europe de l'Est: le grand malentendu' in *Commentaire*, No. 75, Autumn 1996.
11. On the CSCE and subsequently the OSCE, see *Arrangements régionaux et sécurité collective* in *Annuaire Arès*, Vol. XV, No. 2 (Grenoble: SDEDSI, 1996).
12. The idea of a European Security Identity was accepted reluctantly by the French authorities at the NATO Council in Rome in 1991. The situation then changed, and there was a more positive inclusion of it in the communiqué of the Brussels Council in January 1994.
13. For complete references to these interventions, see the special issue of *Revue de la Défense Nationale* of 14 July 1996, entitled 'Vers une nouvelle défense'.

14. See the French disarmament plan of 1 June 1991.
15. B. Khader (ed.), *L'Europe et la Méditerrannée, Géopolitique de la Proximité* (Paris: L'Harmattan, 1994).
16. On general overseas development issues, see *Sociétés africaines et développement*, 'Travaux et recherches de l'IFRI' (Paris: Masson, 1992).
17. On the general diagnosis before the reforms carried out by Chirac, see F. Heisbourg, *Les Volontaires de l'An 2000 – pour une nouvelle Politique de Défense* (Paris: Balland, 1995).
18. On France's logic in Yugoslavia, the only source is the chapter in Védrine (op. cit.).

Part 3
Economy and Society

7 Mitterrand's Economic and Social Policy in Perspective

Henrik Uterwedde

Economic and social policy in the Mitterrand era had many faces. The president, not as familiar with economic affairs as his predecessor Giscard, had no clear-cut vision or doctrine on economics himself. Nor was there any continuity. Over fourteen years, Mitterrand worked with seven prime ministers, each of them giving his (or her) personal touch, and was forced into two periods of shared power with a right-wing majority (cohabitation) when his Socialist Party lost parliamentary elections. This produced a pattern of changing and partly contradictory policies over the whole period.

Moreover, the initial ambitions of the left were soon abandoned and replaced by another logic of economic management. Mitterrand had come to power with the ambition to change society, to overcome capitalism, and to find an alternative way out of the economic crisis which had hit the world since the first oil shock in 1974. The irony of history is that he turned out to be the president who adapted French capitalism to the new challenges at the end of the century.

This chapter retraces the main strands of economic management in the Mitterrand years, and seeks to point out the underlying logic in this patchwork of different policies.[1] The first part recounts the main phases of economic and social policy in the Mitterrand era. The second part evaluates successes and failures in key areas of economic policy, while the third part seeks to place the Mitterrand years in the historic perspective of post-war economic development.[2] This chapter argues that the Mitterrand presidency constituted a largely unintended adaptation of French capitalism and a reshaping of the state-economy relationship, thus ending the 'French model' of post-war economic and social modernisation. Furthermore, it can be seen as a transition between the post-war 'Fordist' economic growth model (which had specific characteristics in France) and a 'post-Fordist' model still to be defined, in France as elsewhere.

133

CONTINUITY AND CHANGE, 1981–1995

The Short Period of Socialist Reform, 1981–1982

Coming to power after 23 years in opposition, the left-wing government installed by Mitterrand, including Socialist and Communist ministers, aimed to foster a new type of economic development – social, if not socialist – breaking with that of the Giscard era (1974–1981) which had been a period of painful adaptation to the international economic crisis, to internationalization, and to the emergence of mass unemployment.[3]

The new economic and social policy had three main characteristics. First, it was inspired by redistributive Keynesianism: economic growth was expected to come from domestic demand, fuelled by higher wages and social transfers. The government's programme of 'social growth' thus combined macroeconomic and social targets, aspiring to introduce a new growth cycle, to be reinforced by investments later. Second, a series of structural reforms were set out. As promised by the candidate Mitterrand, 12 main industrial groups, 39 banks and two financial holdings were nationalized in 1982 (see below); the Auroux laws prudently reformed the possibilities for worker participation within firms; an important decentralization process was set up by the Minister of Interior, Gaston Defferre, in 1982. Finally, an ambitious industrial policy was announced, aimed at strengthening national production in order to 'reconquer the domestic market', using the newly nationalized sector and sectoral programmes (such as in the electronics industry) to protect traditional and immature sectors.

This ambitious programme to change the logic of macroeconomic, social and industrial policy with a new political voluntarism soon reached its limits. The growth of domestic demand, far from strenghtening French industry, increased imports, caused the trade balance to deteriorate, and threatened the stability of the franc. Furthermore, it caused domestic instability (inflation, public debt), without reversing the tendency of growing unemployment.

U-turn to 'Rigueur', 1983–1985

Without nothing positive to show on growth and jobs, and faced with growing internal and external difficulties, the government was confronted with a dilemma as early as the summer of 1982. By continuing the policy of 'social growth', France would be forced to abandon its participation in the EMS (the macroeconomic discipline necessary to maintain the franc parity), running the risk of isolating France within the European Community. Staying in the EMS – as was clearly articulated by France's EMS partners, especially Germany – meant a radical change in French economic policy: the abandonment of the Socialist policy set out in 1981 and a realignment to the more classic, stability-oriented policy of France's European neighbours.

Following initial modifications in June 1982, after a long period of oscillation by the president between these two possible policies, Mitterrand finally settled on a drastic U-turn in March 1983, following the advice of Prime Minister Pierre Mauroy and Finance Minister Jacques Delors, and rejecting that of Socialist left-wingers (the Minister of Industry Jean-Pierre Chevènement) and the Communist Party. The government's decision to stay in the EMS earned German consent to revalue the deutschmark. The corollary to this was a new macroeconomic policy, which sought to restrain domestic demand in order to restore domestic stability and the balance of payments. Taming inflation and reducing the public deficit were the new priorities, implying a more restrictive policy on social transfers. Moreover, Jacques Delors began to install a new restrictive prices and incomes policy in order to reduce the inflationary expectations of economic actors.

This new macroeconomic 'rigueur' (austerity) policy soon intruded upon other central areas of the Socialist reform policy. In 1984, the government made another U-turn, in industrial policy. Faced with crisis in many industrial sectors, with nationalized firms making substantial losses, and given the new financial constraints, the government was forced into a more realistic industrial policy, thus abandoning its initial ambitions. The restructuring of crisis-ridden sectors, postponed for years by successive governments, was now boldly proposed. The government accepted the closure of production sites and massive rationalization programmes but accompanied this with new retraining schemes for the several thousands of employees facing redundancy.

The new course of economic management embraced other spheres of the economy. The new prime minister, Laurent Fabius (1984–1986) began a prudent deregulation and liberalization policy, to reduce massive and omnipresent state intervention, especially in the finance sector (new legislation on banking and finance; liberalization of capital markets and movements).[4]

The Return of the Right: Ideological Liberalism, 1986–1988

In a climate marked by political polarization, the defeat of the left in the parliamentary elections of March 1986 and the return to power of a right-wing majority (initiating a period of shared powers, or 'cohabitation', with President Mitterrand) was not without drama. The new government under the neo-Gaullist prime minister, Jacques, Chirac, wanted to end socialism and show 'the way to freedom',[5] relying heavily on the doctrine of economic liberalism (which was new for the traditionally interventionist neo-Gaullist movement). In fact, the government continued the monetary and macroeconomic policy of 1983, and accentuated some deregulation policies begun by their Socialist predecessors. This was partly due to the Single European Act of 1985, instigating a single market in the European Community by tearing down many national regulations.

The most notable contrast to the Socialist period was the massive privatization programme outlined by the Chirac government in 1986–1988, concerning a dozen industrial and banking groups.

Modest Social Reforms, 1988–1991

Mitterrand's re-election in May 1988 put an end to 'cohabitation'. The new, if small, Socialist majority elected in June restored a Socialist government with Michel Rocard as prime minister. But this was not a return to the 1981 scheme: whereas Mitterrand's first mandate had been characterized by stormy political left-right confrontation, the president won his second victory with the consensual slogan 'United France', promising the end of sterile polarization. In terms of economic policy, this meant that pragmatism and continuity prevailed: continuity in monetary and macroeconomic policy and in deregulation, a consequence of the Single Market programme; pragmatism in industrial policy and on the privatization–nationalization agenda.

The government could take advantage of the favourable international and domestic economic environment prevailing since the mid-1980s: growth and employment had returned; the French economy seemed to earn the first dividends of the 'rigueur' policy maintained since 1983. Held back by the small parliamentary majority and by his personal ambitions for a presidential career, promoting a 'Rocard method' of change by consensus, Michel Rocard was rather hesitant to reform. Nevertheless, the Rocard government was innovative in the social field, attacking growing poverty and social exclusion resulting from mass unemployment: the introduction of a universal minimum social income, the RMI, not only aimed to guarantee a minimum standard of existence to the growing number of people excluded from the welfare system, it also included an incentive for beneficiaries to participate in programmes of job retraining and re-entry into the labour market. Another Rocard reform consisted of the launching in 1991 of an innovative parafiscal levy, the CSG, in order to finance the social security system. This turned out to be the first step in a slow but continuing (and still ongoing) reform of the financing of social security which had depended primarily on labour and employers' contributions.

New Challenges and Shadows, 1991–1995

The 1990s put an end to the favorable economic years of 1985–1990. The recession of 1991–1993 led to a sharp rise in unemployment and its social consequences (poverty, social exclusion). This revealed the limits and the damaging effects of the stabilization policy maintained since 1983: the recovery of the economy, trade balance and private enterprise had been attained only at a cost of rising unemployment and growing social disintegration. This revived the debate on macroeconomic policy. The 'rigueur' policy was again seriously questioned by leading politicians on the left and right, as well as in the media.[6]

The new questioning of economic policy was reinforced by the consequences of German unification. The Bundesbank raised interest rates in order to control inflation and public deficits, the consequences of the bad financial management of the transfer costs in favour of East Germany. The EMS mechanisms forced Germany's neighbours to follow the Bundesbank's lead even when the weak economic cycle called for low interest rates and cheap money. This intensified the constraints on domestic economic policy in France and elsewhere.

The debate on the Maastricht Treaty turned out to be highly controversial. The close outcome of the Maastricht referendum in September 1992 could be read as a deep defiance of the population at large towards a European unity whose constraints seemed to tie the hands of national governments, rendering them powerless against unemployment and recession.

When the right won the 1993 parliamentary elections, the new government headed by Edouard Balladur's was seriously split on economic policy. High spokesmen of the neo-Gaullist RPR movement, like Charles Pasqua and Philippe Séguin, proposed an 'alternative' economic policy, loosening the ties to the EMS and again giving priority to economic growth. Nonetheless, the 'British temptation'[7] (to leave the EMS, as the UK government did in the autumn of 1992 in order to gain margins for manoeuvre in domestic economic policy) continued to be ruled out by the government. Like his predecessor, the socialist Pierre Bérégovoy, Balladur maintained a 'franc fort' policy, maintaining the parity of the franc within the EMS.[8] But he remained as lax as Bérégovoy on public budget deficits (government and social security) in order to temper the social consequences of the recession.

SUCCESSES AND FAILURES

There is no doubt today that the U-turn of March 1983 and the adaptation of economic policy which followed constituted a major landmark, not only of the Mitterrand years but also of post-war French economic development. The Mitterrand era may be summarized as the difficult, erratic and contradictory process of changing the post-war logic of economic government since 1983.

Macroeconomic Policy: the Limits of 'Rigueur'

There has been an extraordinary continuity in the management of macroeconomic policy since 1983. The 'rigueur' policy initiated by Jacques Delors (then finance minister) turned the page on the period of inflationary growth which had characterized post-war economic development (accompanied by frequent devaluations of the franc). The government adhered to French membership in the EMS and to the stability of change as a central guideline for its domestic policy. Accordingly, deflation (instead of growth) became the first priority of macroeconomic policy; the external trade balance was prioritized over economic growth: in short, this meant that the French economy could not afford a rhythm of growth higher than its neighbours, fearing an import pull. The constraints of EMS mechanisms restricted the possibility for a national growth stimulation policy.

The objective of the policy of 'competitive desinflation' was to regain stability, which would improve French competitiveness, thus creating (or protecting) jobs. It was accompanied by measures designed to create a more favourable framework for business.

Incomes and fiscal policy, later also social and labour regulations, were gradually changed in favour of companies, helping them to make necessary profits and to find financial resources for investment and modernization.

Table 7.1: Macroeconomic performance, 1976/1980–1996

	76/80	81/85	86/90	1991	1994	1995	1996
GDP growth[1]	3.3	1.2	3.2	0.2	2.7	2.2	1.0
Price inflation[2]	10.5	9.4	2.9	2.6	1.8	1.6	1.8
Unemployment[3]	5.4	8.8	9.8	10.5	12.3	11.5	11.7
Current account balance[4]			–0.3	+0.2	+1.1	+1.6	+1.6

[1]: annual growth, volume, in per cent
[2]: annual, in per cent
[3]: unemployment rate
[4]: as a percentage of GDP

Sources: P. Hall, *Governing the Economy. The Politics of State Intervention in Britain and France* (Cambridge: Polity Press, 1986), p. 223; Eurostat (Europäische Wirtschaft, Beiheft A, Mai 1996).

The results of this policy are ambiguous (see Table 7.1). France managed to suppress inflation and to keep a strong and stable franc within the EMS. The French economy became more international, and its competitiveness improved. The trade balance, in the red for many years, showed a surplus of exports in the 1990s. Moreover, the improved financial situation of public and private companies has allowed them to modernize, to invest abroad and to gain the necessary stature in the global economy.

On the other hand, the initial objective of the 'competitive disinflation' policy has not been reached, since the fundamental amelioration of micro- and macroeconomic conditions has not engendered a new growth and employment cycle. Unemployment has not been mastered and rose to three millon (12 per cent) in 1995. Even in the better years of economic growth (1985–1990), when 800,000 new jobs were created, unemployment fell by only 200,000, whereas in the recession of 1991–1993, 800,000 persons lost their jobs. This obvious failure has nourished repeated questioning about austerity. Moreover, the lax budgetary policy of the 1990s increased the national debt considerably, creating an impediment to meeting the Maastricht criteria for entry into EMU.

One of the consequences of growing mass unemployment has been growing social inequality,[9] the appearance of new poverty, the increase of badly paid, unprotected jobs and of social exclusion: young people leaving school with no chance of entering the labour market; long-term jobless falling out of the social security network, and marginalized persons. The danger of exclusion and of general social disintegration has become a frequent topic in the media as on the political agenda.[10] It has engendered considerable potential for conflict, such as in the suburbs where social deprivation is prevalent and where violent confrontations spread throughout the 1980s; it has consequences on the political plane, too, where signs of a protest vote and voting abstention seem to confirm the thesis of growing alienation between the people and the 'political class'.

Employment Policy: Expensive Social Treatment

Faced with rising unemployment, which doubled during the Mitterrand years (six per cent in 1980, twelve per cent in 1995), and given the limits of macroeconomic policy, a broad variety of specific employment measures have been developed since 1981 (as they had been before, after the first oil shock of 1974). These measures can be divided into two categories.[11] The first includes measures concerning specific 'target' categories of unemployed. Older workers were given incentives to leave the labour market: the retirement age was fixed at 60 for all workers in 1981; different formulae for early retirement were set up. Another target group were young persons under 25. High youth unemployment was, and remains, one of the specific features of the French labour market; the unemployment rate of young persons under 25 is double the average. Job programmes were created for young people leaving school in public services and administration (TUC, and later CES – *contrats emploi-solidarité*); different work experience programmes were launched to help school leavers enter working life and gain qualifications. Specific job-training measures, coupled with regional conversion programmes (*pôles de conversion*), were aimed at the casualties of important restructuring programmes in several industries in 1984: shipbuilding, steel, coal-mining, cars, telephones (*congés de conversion*). When the number of long-term unemployed rose, measures for this group began to multiply, especially as part of social insertion programmes developed with the RMI (see above).

Most of these measures amounted to the social treatment of unemployment, an attempt to ease the pressure on the labour market by reducing the number of job-seekers. Some measures, however, tried to improve the professional qualification of the unemployed, enhancing their future chances on the labour market.

The second category of employment measures follows another approach, to do with job creation. Varying sorts of financial incentives for private firms were introduced, such as the relaxation of labour regulations, direct subsidies for the hiring of young or long-term unemployed or the reduction of employers' social security contributions in specific cases. The latter approach became widespread in the 1990s, as employers' contributions were reduced for all low-wage categories.

This 'economic treatment' has been strongly favoured since the beginning of the 1990s. Its underlying logic – the reduction of indirect labour costs – became the dominant philosophy of economic policy directed at unemployment at the end of the Mitterrand era, currently being reinforced by Chirac.

The results of this policy are ambiguous. The net effect on unemployment figures is estimated at 200,000 to 300,000 jobs preserved from unemployment per annum over the period 1974–1988, and probably less for the 1990s.[12] This must be compared to the overall number of persons affected by the various employment measures (2.4 million in 1994), and to the enormous costs of these measures. Substitution effects and other side-effects considerably diminished the efficiency of employment programmes. The policy seems to have acted primarily on the distribution of unemployment among different social and age groups, but less on actual job creation. Since the late 1980s, governments have tried (inconclusively) to introduce greater coherence and transparency into the jungle of employment measures and to rationalize the various types of programmes.[13] The prevalent judgement is that nearly everything has been tried, and that 'the toolbox is empty'.[14]

Industrial Policy: From 'High-Tech Colbertism' to Structural Adaptation

Industrial policy acting on the coherence of a broad, modern national production system has played an important role in the post-war modernization of the French economy, notably in the Fifth Republic, when sectoral programmes for traditional and nascent sectors were started and when the 'grand projet' policy (the development of new product lines in high-tech industries like nuclear power, aerospace, electronics, high-speed trains, telecommunications) became a trade-mark for Gaullist 'high-tech Colbertism'.[15] Whereas Giscard had proposed a more liberal approach of structural adaptation following the evolution of international markets, Mitterrand and the left tried to renew the Gaullist voluntarism of the 1960s and to re-establish a 'grande politique industrielle'. The precarious French production network, partly damaged by the effects of rapid internationalization and economic crisis since 1974, was to be restored and strengthened. The aim was to consitute integrative productive clusters including all steps of manufacture from raw materials to finished products (the *'filière'* policy, as opposed to the more liberal Giscardian approach of market niches, *'créneaux'*). The state was to play a major role, notably by using the nationalized industrial and banking sectors as a lever to realise its objectives.

However, the macroeconomic U-turn of 1983 heralded the end of this ambitious industrial policy and paved the way for another decisive U-turn in industrial strategy. Faced with multiple sectoral problems and the poor financial situation of the major public industrial groups on the one hand and limited resources on the other, the government opted for an industrial conversion programme in March 1984, accepting harsh rationalizations and structural adaptations (including plant closures and redundancies) in order to modernize three traditional sectors with surplus production capacities (coal mining, steel, shipbuilding) and two modern industries experiencing problems of competitiveness (cars, telecommunications).

This programme was the beginning of a gradual shift towards a liberal industrial policy.[16] The state withdrew from excessive intervention; the central role and responsibility of the firm in the modernization of industry was now acknowledged. The sectoral approch ceded to a micro-economic approach designed to enable firms to develop their strategies. Direct sectoral state intervention was replaced by indirect, 'horizontal' measures concerning the whole of industry and targeting general economic conditions: fiscal policy, innovation policy, labour regulation and the like. Small and medium-sized firms, permanently neglected by the post-war modernization policy centred on big business, now benefited from specific measures and aid programmes. The general deregulation policy carried out in the 1980s in accordance with the Single Market programme reinforced these tendencies. Moreover, the Colbertist nature of French industrial policy, focusing on the coherence of the national productive system, yielded to a more European and international approach. The internationalization of French firms by direct investment, which developed rapidly from the mid–1980s, was actively encouraged.

If the development of a more liberal industrial policy engendered a withdrawal of the state from excessive interventionism, it did not necessarily mean a general withdrawal of state activity but a change in the patterns of state intervention. The state was still engaged in an active research and innovation policy, but concentrated its activities on setting the general framework for the economy. Nor did French governments abandon their visions of a coherent productive system. They sought instead to transfer their industrial policy objectives, no longer operable on a national level, to the European Community, notably in foreign trade and industrial policy. Several government memoranda to EC partners throughout the 1980s proposed repeatedly (and often successfully) a comprehensive industrial strategy for Europe, notably through European programmes in high-tech domains. The ESPRIT (European Strategic Programme for Research and Development in Information Technology) telecommunications and EUREKA (European Research Co-ordinating Agency) high-tech co-operative R&D programmes were French initiatives.[17]

It is difficult to evaluate the results of this industrial policy. Clearly, the shift to a more liberal policy encouraging structural adaptation and change was overdue. Gaullist industrial voluntarism had reached its limits; the perverse effects of the Etatist management of economic modernization had become obvious; a wide range of sectors urgently had to make up for the long postponed but necessary adaptation. French industry has recovered since the early 1980s and has adapted to internationalization and globalization. Severe problems of competitiveness have been partly resolved. The remaining problems of competitiveness concern the structural, qualitative frameworks of industry. Competitiveness, now conceived as 'global competitiveness', requires an overall political approach which goes beyond industrial policy.[18]

Towards the End of Nationalized Industry

The changed role of the nationalized sector similarly exemplifies the radical shift in economic policy under Mitterrand. The important nationalization programme, first conceived in the 1972 Socialist-Communist common programme of government and rapidly realized in 1981–1982 was the heart of the left's philosophy of a non-capitalist economy. The nationalization of 12 major industrial groups, 39 banks

and the important financial holding companies Suez and Paribas
raised the proportion of state-led companies to 16 per cent of the
national workforce and to 36 per cent of investment.[19] While the
1944–1946 nationalizations had included most of the banks, insurance, transport and energy companies but few industrial ones (except
Renault and the chemical sector), the left now concentrated on industry. Public industrial companies were to play a major role in the
ambitious restructuring of the productive system pursued by industrial policy (see above), and the public financial sector was assigned to
assist them.

With a few exceptions (such as the chemical industry), this use of
public companies for industrial policy never really worked. The government had no clear, workable industrial strategy for the public
sector; most of the state-owned industrial companies proved to be in
a precarious financial situation, unprofitable and lacking equity capital. Budget restrictions after the 1983 U-turn considerably narrowed
the government's room for manoeuvre to finance them. Prime Minister Fabius ordered that state-owned companies make profits instead
of losses, and the ambitious plans of industrial strategy were abandoned.

With this '*banalisation*' of the public sector (forcing it to behave
according to the rules of private business), arguments for nationalized
industry weakened. This, too, prepared the way for privatization,
carried out on a massive scale by the right-wing Chirac government
in 1986–1988. Fourteen companies with 500,000 employees were
transferred to the private sector. Since then, the privatization process
has never stopped. Even when the left returned to power in 1988, the
official status quo policy of 'ni-ni' (neither privatization nor re-
nationalization) did not prevent hidden partial privatizations under
various formal procedures. After 1993, the Balladur government continued with privatization proper. At the end of this process, continued
by Mitterrand's successor Chirac, most of the nationalized banks,
insurance groups and industry will be in private hands, leaving only
general network services (energy, transport) and some 'strategic' companies in the armaments industry (see Table 7.2) in the public domain.[20]
It should be noted, however, that following the return of the left to
government in June 1997, the privatization process was put on hold.

The public debate on nationalization and privatization, very passionate in the 1970s and 1980s, has calmed. There is a large consensus
about the limits of state-owned industry. The voluntarist illusion of
1981 is no longer shared by public opinion and the main political

Table 7.2:   Nationalizations and Privatizations of Main Companies

Nationalization before 1945	Nationalization 1945–70	Nationalization 1981–82	Privatization 1986–95
Banks			
	Banque de France 1946		Crédit Lyonnais 1993*
	Crédit Lyonnais 1946		Société générale 1987
	Société générale 1946 BNP 1946		BNP 1993 CCF 1987
		CCF Paribas	Paribas 1987
		Suez	Suez 1987
Insurances			
	AGF 1946		AGF 1996
	GAN 1946		GAN 1993*
	UAP 1946		UAP 1994
Transport, Communication			
	RATP 1945		
	SNCF 1945		
	Air France 1945/48		Air France 1993*
Energy			
	EDF 1946		
	GDF 1946		
	CEA 1946?		
	Charbonnages de France 1946		
		Usinor-Sacilor	Usinor-Sacilor 1995
Industry			
Elf-Aquitaine 1936			Elf-Aquitaine 1936
Aérospatiale 1941			Aérospatiale 1941
	Renault 1946		
	SNECMA 1946		
	CII (1966)		
	SNIAS (1970)		
		Bull Pechiney	Bull 1993*
		Thomson CGE	Pechiney 1995
		Dassault Matra	Thomson 1996
		Rhône-Poulenc	CGE 1987
		Saint-Gobain	
			Matra 1988
			Rhône-Poulenc 1993
			Saint-Gobain 1986

Source: Author
* Privatization decided in 1993 but not carried out yet, and now on hold
(1997)

forces. However, there have been some positive results. The poor financial situation of many companies in 1981, due to the parsimony of the then private shareholders, has been largely improved by the state's financial transfers of new equity capital. Furthermore, nationalization has helped difficult industrial restructurings in some cases. Elie Cohen is therefore right to point out that the temporary passage under state ownership somewhat created the necessary conditions for the ensuing liberalization of the French economy. Nationalization policy as a 'good example for capitalism': this is one of the obvious paradoxes of the Mitterrand experiment in economics.[21]

As for privatization, it helped to end excessive state intervention which had proved to be harmful for economic modernization and international competitiveness. It gave companies the necessary freedom to develop their industrial strategies. They were able to expand their international activities from the mid–1980s onwards, in the context of the emerging single market and of increased international competition. Nevertheless, the expectation that privatization in itself would help to resolve the economic problems of the country has proved to be an illusion. At the end of the Mitterrand years, it has become clear that the real problem of French business is not public or private ownership, but their capacity to adapt to new markets and to keep up with international competition. Two problems remain on the agenda. First, the precarious capital structure of many companies, described as 'capitalism without capital' (resulting from a lack of financially powerful institutional shareholders), is a handicap for French groups in comparison to their main competitors. Second, the problematic internal structures of French business (power structure and management, decision-making procedures; shareholders' role and control, etc.) are open to criticism. They hinder necessary strategies designed to enhance competitiveness through quality and worker participation,[22] and they reduce companies' attractiveness for international capital shareholders.[23]

THE END OF THE FRENCH MODEL

The overall economic performance of the Mitterrand era is remarkable. In 1980, the French economy, hit by the two oil shocks of 1974 and 1979, was in a critical state. Serious qualitative problems of competitiveness, together with high inflation, produced an unstable trade and payments balance, the franc suffered repeated devaluations.

Private business lacked confidence, profits and capital, which had engendered serious under-investment for years. France was hesitant about internationalization, seen as a threat rather than an opportunity.

Fourteen years later, the French economy enjoyed a stable macroeconomic setting. Inflation had been mastered, competitiveness regained, the parity of the franc within the EMS was reasonably solid. Moreover, French business, benefiting from a more favourable general legal and fiscal framework, has become profitable again and is able to invest and to form international strategic alliances. The formerly 'parochial', Franco-centric horizon of French business and society has been widened to meet European and global challenges.[24]

But economic renewal was achieved at high social cost. Left- and right-wing governments were unable to combine economic performance with social coherence; on the contrary, the new liberal economic dynamic seems to be founded on unstable labour conditions, mass unemployment, social deprivation and poverty. Thus Mitterrand largely succeeded in modernizing and liberalizing French capitalism, but he failed to reconcile the new economic logic with social needs, thus threatening France's social cohesion.

If France shares this problem with her European neighbours, nevertheless this performance has proved extremely damaging for the French Socialists and the left in general. Not only did the 1981 promise of an alternative, non-capitalist way out of crisis prove to be an illusion; it is difficult to find a specific (and convincing) socialist way of dealing with economic liberalization and deregulation. Thus, ironically, the two periods of Socialist government in the Mitterrand era succeeded in convincing OECD commissions and international capital markets but did little to satisfy the demands of ordinary people.[25]

Going beyond these arguments about political performance, and trying to place the Mitterrand presidency in the larger context of post-war economic development, the Mitterrand era can be seen as a transition period. Mitterrand came into power when the post-war period of rapid economic growth – the 'thirty glorious years', as Jean Fourastié put it – had come to an end. The global setting of economic policy had changed radically. The 'Fordist' growth pattern of the Western world, characterized by Keynesian macroeconomic regulation, the development of the welfare state and regular wage increases, which had produced a positive feedback between social progress and economic growth, no longer worked because its central internal and external conditions had disintegrated.[26] Since the left's economic strategy in 1981, especially its redistributive Keynesianism, was founded on 'Fordist' mechanisms, it inevitably faced severe problems. After 1983, governments attempted to adapt the French economy to the changed framework, trying to find a path towards a 'post-Fordist' pattern of sustainable economic and social development. This search for a new socio-economic model is still ongoing, in France as elsewhere; ultimately the Mitterrand era could not avoid being destructive, tearing down the foundations of the old model but proving unable to create a new model of development.[27] A specifically French socio-economic model prevailed in the post-war period, which Mitterrand helped to end. Summarized by several '-isms' (etatism, Colbertism, centralism, productivism), its main features can be seen as the rapid, and largely efficient, modernization of the French economy and society after 1945, initiated and steered by the state.[28] Using the broad arsenal of instruments at its disposal (nationalized companies, planning, control of the financial circuit, regulation, sectoral development plans, *grand projet* high-tech programmes), the state had leapt from economic backwardness to modernism within only three decades. State-managed socio-economic modernization, the specificity of the post-war French model, had worked successfully within the framework of 'Fordist' growth but began to stagger in the 1970s. Faced with economic crisis, rapid internationalization, and the needs of structural adjustment, the French economy proved particularly vulnerable and the French Etatist model dysfunctional.

Following a first timid but unsuccessful attempt to change by Raymond Barre (1976–1981) as prime minister under Giscard, and the failure of the left-wing government to re-establish the French model in 1981–1982, the Mitterrand governments began to deconstruct this model from 1983. The U-turn considerably changed the relationship between state, economy and civil society. The state not only ceded powers to the market (through deregulation and the general shift to a more liberal economy), to private business (privatizations) or to private associations (urban policy; measures tackling exclusion); decentralization, and the increasing role of the European Community, have restricted the regulatory powers of the central state and installed a complex, multi-level system of public intervention.

At the end of the Mitterrand era, this deep transformation of France's economy and society is still unfinished. It has been easier to tear down excessive state intervention than to rebuild a stable pattern of regulation relying more on market forces, local government and civil society. There is currently no such pattern which would be accepted by all political, economic and social forces. The debates on different models of capitalism,[29] as on new, 'global' competitiveness,[30] point the way forward. They call for necessary changes in the behaviour of the state, administration, business, trade unions and society as a whole, touching the core of behaviour patterns and vested interests. The search for a new economy combining competitiveness with social cohesion is still ongoing. The Mitterrand experience has shown to what extent this process is erratic, contradictory and complex, calling for a global approach far beyond economic policy.

NOTES

1. I wish to thank Joana Ardizzone for reading this text and improving my English.
2. This chapter is based on H. Uterwedde, *Die Wirtshaftspolitik der Linken in Frankreich. Programme und Praxis 1974–1986* (Frankfurt: Campus, 1988).
3. See, for example, A. Lipietz, *L'Audace ou l'enlisement* (Paris: La Découverte, 1984).
4. Institut Français des Sciences Administratives (ed.), *Les Déréglementations* (Paris: IFSA, 1988; J. Métais and P. Symczak, *Les Mutations du système financier français* (Paris: La Documentation Française, 1988).
5. E. Balladur, *Vers la liberté. La réforme économique 1986* (Paris: 1987).
6. For en early criticism of 'rigueur', see Lipietz, op. cit., pp. 218 ff.
7. 'La tentation britannique', *Le Monde*, 3 June 1994, compares the Bérégovoy and Balladur policies.
8. P. Bauchard, *Deux ministres trop tranquilles* (Paris: Belfond, 1994).
9. A. Bihr and R. Pfefferkorn, *Déchiffrer les inégalités* (Paris: Syros, 1995).
10. G. Ferréol (ed.), *Intégration et exclusion dans la société française contemporaine* (Lille: Presses Universitaires de Lille, 1995).
11. See the exhaustive evaluations made by the Ministry of Labour and the OFCE Institute.
12. G. Cornilleau et al., 'La gestion sociale du chômage: un bilan', *Futuribles*, September 1990, pp. 37–49.
13. A. Lebaube, 'Aides à l'emploi: un bilan décevant', *Le Monde*, 12 June 1996, supplement 'Initiatives', I.
14. A. Lebaube, *Le Monde*, 27 April 1991, p. 27.
15. E. Cohen, *Le Colbertisme 'high-tech'* (Paris: Hachette, 1992); E. Cohen, *L'Etat brancardier: politiques du déclin industriel* (Paris: Calmann-Levy, 1989).

16. C. Durand (ed.), *De l'économie planifiée à l'économie de marché: l'intervention de l'Etat dans l'industrie* (Paris: Publisud, 1990).

17. H. Uterwedde, 'Compétitivité et politique industrielle: les stratégies allemandes et françaises', in *Agir pour l'Europe: les relations franco-allemandes dans l'après-guerre froide* (Paris: 1995), pp. 199–221.

18. See, for example, J. Gandois, *France: le choix de la performance globale* (Paris: Commissariat général du Plan, préparation du XIe Plan, 1995).

19. Haut Conseil du Secteur Public, *Rapport 1984*, Vol. 1 (Paris: La Documentation Française, 1984), p. 13.

20. N. Chabanas and E. Vergeau, 'Nationalisations et privatisations depuis 50 ans', *INSEE Première*, April 1996, No. 440, pp. 1–4.

21. E. Cohen, 'Nationalisations: une bonne leçon de capitalisme', *Problèmes Economiques*, 30 April 1996, No. 1972, pp. 13–18.

22. Gandois, op. cit.

23. See the recent discussions influenced by the British corporate governance debate, in particular, 'Le gouvernement d'entreprise, *Les Notes bleues de Bercy*, 16–31 January 1996, No. 79, pp. 1–12.

24. F. Hatem and J.-D. Tordjman, *La France face à l'investissement international* (Paris: Economica, 1995).

25. A. Gauron et al., *Changer l'économie* (Paris: Syros, 1992).

26. J.-P. Durand (ed.), *Vers un nouveau modèle productif?* (Paris: Syros/Alternatives, 1993).

27. B. Perret and G. Roustang, *L'Economie contre la société: affronter la crise de l'intégration sociale et culturelle* (Paris: Seuil, 1993).

28. B. de Foucauld, *La Fin du social-colbertisme* (Paris: Belfond, 1988); Cohen, *Le Colbertisme*, op. cit.

29. M. Albert, *Capitalisme contre capitalism* (Paris: Seuil, 1991).

30. Gandois, op. cit.

8 French Business in the Mitterrand Years: The Continuity of Change

Joseph Szarka

The political economy of the Mitterrand years was rich in drama, being marked by a series of shifts from a *dirigiste* to a neo-liberal mode of governance.[1] The 1981–1982 dreams of a *rupture avec le capitalisme* through massive nationalization gave way during 1983–1985 to austerity and the fight against inflation, only to be trumped by the liberal agenda of privatization and deregulation in 1986–1988. In his second term, Mitterrand's electoral pledge of *ni privatization ni nationalization* proved untenable, whilst the redistributive concerns of the RMI and the ISF (*impôt de solidarité sur la fortune*) were overtaken by the imperatives of international competitiveness and European integration. In turn, the hard-won gains of competitive disinflation were undermined by the recession of 1992–1993 and by mass unemployment; these twinned shadows darkened the Mitterrand *fin de règne* in the eyes of the French electorate who, in the parliamentary election of 1993 and the presidential election of 1995, gave the right major victories. Thus it is understandable that the period has been described as one of discontinuity.[2]

Yet though policy-making and the business cycle were marked by sudden lurches in direction, the *underlying* process of transformation (or *modernization*) of French industry and commerce has been surprisingly consistent, since the pace of broad-based change tends to be gradual. This chapter aims to report on those broader trends within French business, to evaluate their significance and, where possible, to correlate them with policy-making. Whilst discontinuities can be discerned in some areas, on balance change has been the product of a long-term, evolutionary process. Further, the occurrence of change is one issue, but the direction of change is another, and the latter can be evaluated as being either positive or negative. Consequently, 'change' will not automatically be equated with 'progress'.

The first half of this chapter considers economic changes, principally in economic structures, internationalization of the economy as well as small firms and regional development. The second half

151

considers social changes, specifically firm ownership, composition of the managerial elite and employment. Overall, the chapter argues that, despite the about-turns of economic and industrial policy-making during the Mitterrand period, the pace of change for French business has been incremental and largely consistent. However, whereas the direction of economic change has been mainly positive, the direction of social change has been problematic.

ECONOMIC CHANGE IN THE MITTERRAND YEARS

In recent years, much discussed structural changes in business have been tertiarization and internationalization, with the balance of trade receiving considerable scrutiny. Other key concerns include the role of small firms and the development of regional economies. What changes can be detected in these areas during the Mitterrand period?

Economic Environment

The period offered a roller-coaster ride in terms of changes in GDP (see Table 8.1). The early 1980s were marked by a sudden reflation, then an abrupt lurch into austerity, followed by moderate economic growth. From 1988, the French economy experienced its strongest period of growth since 1970, followed by recession in 1992 and recovery over 1994–1995. However, the causes of these developments were markedly different. Much of the fluctuation in Mitterrand's first term resulted from policy errors and their correction. In the second term, orthodox economic policy prevailed, but the French economy was buffeted by external fluctuations. These included oil price reductions, deregulation of financial markets, German reunification and the

Table 8.1: Annual GDP Increases (1980–1994)

1980	1.6%	1987	2.4%
1981	1.0%	1988	4.8%
1982	2.4%	1989	4.7%
1983	0.5%	1990	2.3%
1984	1.2%	1991	0.8%
1985	1.9%	1992	1.3%
1986	2.7%	1993	− 1.5%
		1994	2.7%

Sources: Herter; INSEE.

Gulf war. The impact of international factors attests to the openness of the French economy and its integration within the world economy. Thus the difference between the early and the later years was the transition from state-led *volontarisme* to acceptance of international market forces, a transition in which Mitterrand was a key protagonist.

Economic Structures

Change in the overall structure of the economy was slight. As a proportion of GDP, the service sector increased slightly between 1980 and 1992 (from 60 per cent to 61.3 per cent), industry contracted slightly (35.5 per cent to 33.8 per cent), whilst agriculture showed marginal change.[3] However agricultural employment did decline significantly, from roughly 1.5 million *agriculteurs exploitants* in 1983 to 855,000 by 1994, a fall of 43 per cent.[4] Relatively little intersectoral change took place within industry. Activities such as energy, intermediate goods, car manufacture and consumer goods accounted for much the same proportion of total value added in 1994 as in 1984, though the construction industry suffered decline. The largest change was in the commercial services sector, which expanded from 16.4 per cent to 20.9 per cent of total value added.[5] Overall, structural change within the economy continued in the expected directions during the Mitterrand years, but at a slower pace than in previous decades.

Internationalization

What then of the much-vaunted globalization of markets? Did France develop a more open economy? At first sight, the answer seems to be no. As Table 8.2 shows, imports and exports as a percentage of GDP have varied only slightly.

Table 8.2:   France's International Trade in Goods and Services (1970–1992)

| Year | Imports as % of GDP | | Exports as % of GDP | | | Overall openness | |
	Goods	Services	Total	Goods	Services	Total(imports+ exports) as % of GDP	
1970	13.4	1.9	15.2	12.5	3.3	15.8	15.5
1980	20.5	2.2	22.7	17.4	4.1	21.5	22.1
1985	20.7	2.6	23.2	19.2	4.7	23.9	23.6
1990	19.6	3	22.6	18.1	4.6	22.6	22.6
1992			21.3			22.6	22

Source: P. Arnaud-Ameller, 'Le commerce extérieure français (1981–1992)', *Regards sur l'actualité*, No. 191, May 1993, p. 41.

However this is not to say that France maintained a protectionist course. On the contrary, by the end of the 1970s France already had a fairly open economy and that development was confirmed subsequently. Inward direct investment increased almost fivefold during 1981–1992 as compared to 1973–1980 (from $15.7 to $70.8 billion), whilst investment by French firms abroad increased nearly tenfold (from $13 to $124 billion), although comparable increases were witnessed in the UK, Japan and other OECD (Organization for Economic Co-operation and Development) countries.[6] Whilst France had often been hesitant about inward investment, by the 1980s DATAR was actively encouraging foreign investors. Between 1977 and 1992, the proportion of the total stock of publicly quoted French shares held by foreigners increased from 12 per cent to 20 per cent.[7] Interestingly, government analysts discovered that employment in foreign-owned firms in France remained stable over the 1979–1989 period, but fell by some 15 per cent in French manufacturing firms;[8] this called into question the received idea that foreign firms were unreliable social partners. Preferred destinations for outward investment were, in order, the USA, the UK and Germany. Although investments were mainly in OECD countries, French interests in Asia-Pacific have been increasing.[9] Geographical diversification has been slow, however, and France's focus on Europe and Africa has not radically altered.

In the 1980s and 1990s, France maintained her position as the fourth largest international trading nation (after the USA, Germany and Japan), despite early problems. The misjudged Mauroy reflation package of 1981 provoked an initial flight of capital and a record trade deficit in 1982, but the return to economic orthodoxy in 1983 stopped the haemorrhage. In the second half of the 1980s, trade deficits in manufactures caused much anxiety, yet these were largely compensated by surpluses in services – France is the second largest exporter of services, after the USA. In the early 1990s, manufactures staged a comeback (see Table 8.3). Since 1992, the trade balance has been in the black, reaching a record FF100 billion surplus in 1995. The success of French business around the world is not restricted to the products popularly associated with France – luxury items, food and drink – but spans a wide range of sectors. Goods with a high technology content, such as aviation, cars and vehicle components, pharmaceutical products and chemicals have been internationally successful, as have services such as insurance, hostelry and tourism.[10]

Table 8.3: French Trade Balances (1981–1995) (in billions of francs)

1981	−59.4	1988	−32.8
1982	−93.5	1989	−43.9
1983	−43.2	1990	−50.1
1984	−21.0	1991	−29.5
1985	−24.0	1992	31.1
1986	0.3	1993	87.7
1987	−31.6	1994	88.1
		1995	100.0

Source: *Le Parisien*, 22 février 1996, p. 8.

A number of causes explain the highly favourable outcomes of the recent period. First and foremost, the competitiveness of French firms had much improved. Although investment was inadequate in the lean years of the early 1980s,[11] it picked up strongly in the boom at the end of the decade. Price competitiveness was improved by accepting leaner margins and by downward pressure on costs, including salaries. External factors played their part. Oil-price reductions from 1986 onwards eased the *contrainte extérieure*. German reunification provided a one-off opportunity for France to expand trade with her main partner. The recession of 1992–1993 weakened the export drive, but sapped domestic demand even more, so with fewer imports being sucked in, the trade balance remained in surplus. Economic and monetary policy cranked up the performance of the French economy by winning the fight against inflation. This was noticeable not just in low inflation rates (around 2 per cent in 1992–1994) but also in a negative inflation differential with Germany[12] – a major coup given that France usually had much higher inflation rates than Germany. The strong franc reduced the imports bill[13] and encouraged firms to compete on quality and service, rather than rely on the 'easy option' of price-cuts subsequent to devaluation. Mitterrand, as a prime mover in the project of European integration, contributed to trade developments by reaffirming France's membership of the EMS in the watershed period of 1983, by his role in the formulation of the Single European Act, by accepting deregulation of EC financial markets and by his sustained advocacy of the Maastricht Treaty.[14]

Whilst the start of the Single Market in January 1993 proved an anti-climax, with Europe deeply mired in recession, over the previous decade intra-European trade had already picked up significantly. In 1980, around a half of France's international trade in goods and services was within the EC, but by 1991 it was over 63 per cent.[15]

Yet sceptics still harboured suspicions of French tendencies to national or European protectionism, and these seemed to receive support from the acrimonious debate over GATT in 1993.[16] In reality, the Uruguay Round proved contentious for all parties, and thus its protracted resolution cannot be laid solely at France's door. In the event, the Balladur government agreed a compromise between safeguarding national interests (such as cinema) and opening doors abroad for French manufacturing and services.

The Mitterrand years fostered a consensus that economic prosperity depended on globalization. Calls for reversion to protectionism were twice rejected (in 1983 after the failed reflation and in 1993 in the GATT talks). The enhanced international competitiveness of French firms gave confidence in the future. The need to expand domestic employment encouraged favourable attitudes to inward investment. Successful promotion of the internationalisation of French business during the Mitterrand period is one of its key outcomes.

Small Firms and Regional Development

Yet without sound regional economic bases, business cannot thrive. The conviction that the French economy was over-centralized around Paris had animated French regional policy since the 1960s. Yet policy was paradoxical in that the centre decided what was good for the regions, which usually meant transplanting subsidiaries of large manufacturing firms to the provinces, taking relatively low-skilled jobs with them. At the start of the 1980s, three new developments occurred to alter this perspective. Firstly, the *loi Defferre* implemented the political decentralization that had been discussed for over a decade. The new frame of reference for regional policy-making raised hopes of economic renewal. Secondly, although French industrial policy had favoured giant firms since the post-war period, the crisis years of the 1970s and early 1980s had exposed the limitations of these 'national champions'. Meanwhile small firms had fared relatively better than large firms in terms of employment, turnover and profits.[17] Consequently, during the 1980s the pendulum swung back in the favour of small firms. Thirdly, these two developments were combined in the hypothesis that the rejuvenation of regional economies depended on the small firm sector. Decentralization provided – in principle – the opportunity to implement local and regional economic policies which stressed endogenous development by the promotion of small firms. Great expectations were aroused by these developments.

Although those expectations were sometimes overblown, small and medium-sized enterprises (SMEs, here defined as firms having between 10 and 499 employees) have played an important role. In 1993, SMEs in France represented 59 per cent of employment, 51 per cent of value added and 45 per cent of total turnover. Employment in SMEs rose by 5.7 per cent over the 1983–1993 period but fell by 29.6 per cent in large private firms. Though this is encouraging, two caveats should be added. Firstly, employment creation was of the modest order of 438,000. Secondly, restructuring in the 1980s often involved employment transfers: the jobs 'created' by small firms were sometimes those 'lost' by large firms though 'externalisation'. Undoubtedly, the small firm vogue resulted in record numbers of start-ups, with numbers peaking at 308,000 in the boom year of 1989, free-falling to 273,000 in 1993 in the depths of the recession, but climbing back to 294,000 in 1994; running in parallel, small firm failures numbered 41,747 in 1989, rising to 60,139 in 1993.[18] In response to these fluctuations, the Mitterrand years were punctuated by calls for greater support for SMEs, leading to the establishment of some 1,500 different types of public help, mostly fostering company start-ups. Latterly, the realization dawned that SME survival and growth are as important as firm creation, with France being perceived as deficient in relation to neighbours with respect to numbers of established medium-sized firms. Gordon advanced the figure of 8,200 for Germany, 6,000 for the UK but only 5,000 for France.[19] However, surveys have revealed that around half of SME owners have no strong desire to grow their firms.[20] Subsequent to the death or retirement of the entrepreneur, identifying a successor and meeting the tax burden are large hurdles in France. Overall, despite the ups and downs of the economic cycle, small firm revival has been real and ongoing, but it has been more modest and less capable of employment generation than sometimes proclaimed.[21]

Policy-makers at national and regional levels have struggled to respond to the diversity of the small firm phenomenon. National government tended to be remote, whilst regional authorities had to learn new skills quickly. Initially, the latter were hesitant in relation to choice of policy (direct subsidies or indirect support? if the first, to which firms? if the second, delivered how?) and in relation to criteria for evaluation of policy.[22] As Ganne noted, the effectiveness of policy has been undermined by competition between regions and localities for 'star' firms.[23] The regions are also chronically under-resourced. Morvan calculated that economic interventions by the regions increased from FF4.4 billion in 1984 to FF10.8 billion in 1989, but this only represented the equivalent of ten per cent of state aids; moreover as a proportion of the regional budget they actually fell from around 15–20 per cent to 5–10 per cent.[24] The assessment of this situation offered by Le Galès was scathing: 'French regional economic policies are, with few exceptions, poorly developed and insignificant'.[25] Yet this harsh judgement underestimates the time required for successful endogenous development of business, where the appropriate scale is decades rather than years. Decentralization, with its potential for renewed regional economic development, together with the recognition of the importance of small firms, remain significant policy initiatives of the Mitterrand years.

SOCIAL CHANGE AND FRENCH BUSINESS

If economic trends proved frequently positive, social changes related to business were sometimes limited or even negative, as a review of patterns of firm ownership, composition of the managerial elite and rising unemployment will reveal.

Ownership

Family ownership is not only the norm in SMEs; it still plays a major role in large firms. Morin found that of the 200 largest privately-owned French enterprises in 1987, 57 per cent had as majority shareholder a single individual or family.[26] Yet if family capitalism in France is alive and well in large and small firms alike, the consequences of this stability are limited promotion hopes for non-family members and fewer opportunities to develop the stock-market and 'popular capitalism'.

The other main forms of ownership are by the state, by financial institutions and dispersed shareholding by the general public. Public policy in the Mitterrand years provoked developments in all these areas. Industrial policy of the period was dominated by the see-saw between nationalization (1981–1982) and privatization (1986–1988 and 1993 onwards). Given the extensive literature on these subjects,[27] only the key themes related to state ownership will be stressed here. Firstly, one notes the massive nature of state intervention in many of the largest French firms at a series of junctures: initial take-over, subsequent restructuring and re-capitalization, and preparation for privatization. Secondly, the legitimating rhetoric surrounding both nationalization and privatization was based on the notion of an essential modernization of the economy. Thirdly, both major phases of industrial policy maintained and developed a distinctly French system of state-market linkages: blatantly in the case of nationalization, subtly in the case of privatization.

In 1982, the combination of 'old' and 'new' nationalized firms produced state capitalism on a scale unprecedented outside the Communist bloc. To describe this model, the term *économie mixte* was preferred, by which was understood not just the coexistence of private and public firms, but the interpenetration of state and market. The liberal governments of the two periods of *cohabitation* (1986–1988 and 1993–1995) rushed to undo this model by major privatization programmes. Once again industrial policy was conducted on a uniquely gigantic scale. By 1995, Balladur and Chirac had almost completely dismantled the Socialists' 'mixed economy'.

The result resembles the *status quo ante*, but with new twists. At this juncture, it is worth stressing what French capitalism is *not*. Firstly, shareholdings by financial institutions (specialising in pension funds, unit trusts, etc.) are underdeveloped in France and remained proportionately unchanged over the period (seven per cent of all quoted shares in both 1977 and 1992). Secondly, the proportion of quoted shares held by households actually fell (from 41 per cent in 1977 to 34 per cent in 1992), despite the surge in the numbers of individual shareholders during the 1986–1988 wave of privatization. Indeed, 80 per cent of French shares are not even publicly quoted.[28] Thus French capitalism does not follow the Anglo-American model of broad-based institutional investment, nor can it be likened to a speculative, casinolike operation as the left was once wont to do; nor does it live up the image of *capitalisme populaire* espoused by right-wing ideologues in the 1980s. Rather, a distinctively French model of large-scale capitalism pertains. Whereas in the 1970s two financial 'empires' existed (structured around Paribas and Suez), Morin discerned three 'poles' in the new financial and industrial landscape. These were, in order of size: first, Paribas–AGF–Crédit Lyonnais; second, Suez–BNP–UAP; and third, Société Générale–Alcatel Alsthom.[29] However, in 1994 serious losses at Crédit Lyonnais led to a reduction in its influence and to a *recomposition* of the first pole, with Société Générale and Alcatel Alsthom replacing Crédit Lyonnais.[30] Once again, two major empires have emerged, each of them organized around a generalist bank, a major investment bank, plus other interests, but the reach of their operations is even greater than in the 1970s, with France aiming to approximate the German system of tight bank-industry links.

Further, as the formation of these poles is partly a result of the formation of *noyaux durs* (a 'hard-core' of controlling interests) in the privatization process, state-sponsored cross-shareholding set the relations between privatized firms in concrete. The chairmen of privatized firms have had the opportunity to 'choose' their key shareholders, whilst the Minister of the Economy chooses the chairmen. The *noyaux durs* have the advantage of stabilizing the companies concerned and protecting them from take-over bids (particularly from abroad, a frequent preoccupation of French industrial policy). The ensuing cascade of interdependency produces the latest variant of French capitalism in which the state apparently disengages from the market, abstains from intervention and encourages competition, yet decision-makers in the main industries and in government still form a closed circle and continue to collaborate. Privatization has reduced the financial linkages between the state and 'national champions', but not the networks of influence that link them in the search for mutual advantage.

Managerial Elites

The underpinning of the French model of capitalism is provided by the interpenetration of state and business elites. As Suleiman noted, although Socialists affirmed their intention to *changer la société*, the institutions and practices of elitism in the recruitment and promotion of top managers emerged unscathed under Mitterrand's presidency.[31] Appointments to top posts in nationalized firms have consistently been made on the criteria of political affinity, graduation from a *grande école* (the most prestigious are the Ecole Nationale d'Administration and the Ecole Polytechnique) and membership of a *grand corps*, the pinnacle of France's elitist system.[32] Bauer noted that in 1981 the new left-wing government replaced 29 of the chairmen of the 36 largest public-sector firms in the competitive sector,[33] yet the patterns of recruitment conformed to previous practice under Giscard, with the majority of nominees being members of a *grand corps* and having previously led a politico-administrative career rather than one in industry or commerce. In 1992, the contracts of 45 chairmen of public-sector firms were due to expire. Whilst Edith Cresson was prime minister, major innovations were expected as her aversion to the *grands corps* was well-known, but she was replaced in mid-stream by Bérégovoy who, preferring to maintain continuity, renewed the contracts of most of those concerned.[34] In the second cohabitation, Balladur continued the practice of appointing friends to high office when three of his closest advisors – Pébereau, Jaffré and Friedmann – were appointed respectively as the chairmen of BNP, Elf and UAP. It is no coincidence that these strategically important companies are among the *pièces maîtresses* of the landscape of French capitalism described in the previous section. These appointments assured a complementarity of views between government and business leaders, irrespective of changed shareholdings.

The French system of elite recruitment has been premised on the tight coupling between state and firms. The various phases of France's interventionist industrial policy – post-war national planning, the concentration process of the 1960s and the 1970s, Mitterrand's nationalizations, Balladur's privatizations – all involved the state in intensive exchange relationships with public and private firms, whether in terms of financial subsidies, research grants, procurement of goods and services, shareholding or, last but by no means least, personnel transfer. Movement between the top echelons of the civil service (often via *cabinets ministériels* – ministers' private offices) and high managerial positions is frequent. The incidence of this practice, known as *pantouflage*, has steadily increased for ENA alumni since the 1970s.[35] More extraordinary still is that many graduates of top business schools, such as HEC and ESSEC, enter state service because they see *pantouflage* as the quick route to the top: 30 per cent of entrants into the Inspection des Finances between 1985 and 1989 came from management schools.[36] Neither nationalization nor privatization modified recruitment practices. Indeed, privatization constitutes the acme of *pantouflage*: when public sector firms are privatized, top *fonctionnaires* are spared the burden of finding posts in the private sector. Overall, the system of elite recruitment and promotion set harder in the Mitterrand years.

But as the means and justification for industrial policy weakened over the 1980s, so deficiencies in the system of elite recruitment appeared, going beyond the traditional criticism of its narrow social base. The stress on educational attainment at an early age within the *grandes écoles* system and acquisition of membership of the *grands corps* (itself dependent on educational attainment) is looking increasingly incongruous when compared to competitor nations. The general pattern for recruitment and promotion procedures in the business world is to stress business experience gained over the long term, with demonstrable and quantified proof of success in relevant domains. In France, directly relevant business experience is not always a prerequisite for high-level appointments, since politico-administrative connections are so highly valued. Indeed, the prevalence of *pantouflage* presents a barrier to the promotion hopes of able in-house candidates.[37] The decline of industrial policy and the removal of the protective arm of the state have exposed the competence of the state-bred elite to greater scrutiny. The variable performance of former nationalized firms (loss-makers in 1995 included Alcatel Alsthom and Suez), which often kept the same managers on after privatization, has raised questions about the merits of the French elite system. In some cases, heads have rolled – for example, at Crédit Lyonnais after huge losses caused by misguided investment strategies and at Air France after failed restructuring. The elite is no longer considered invulnerable. Its members rarely have experience of working abroad, unlike the Americans, the British or the Germans.[38] With the increase in inward direct investment and foreign shareholding already noted, instances of imported patterns of management can only increase. As Moreau Defarges points out, the process of integration within the EU raises questions about French elite recruitment practices, even within the public sector, with the privileges previously enjoyed by the SNCF, Air France, France Télécom et al. receiving increasing attention from Brussels.[39] When viewed from these angles, the traditional pattern of elite recruitment now resembles a vestige from the *franco-français* protectionist era.

Employment

Meanwhile, between 1981 and 1991 the working population increased by over a million, from 23,529,600 to 24,604,900.[40] The French economy created around half a million new jobs, but this was not enough to compensate for job losses and satisfy the demand for work. Headline unemployment levels rose steadily from 7.4 per cent in 1981 to 10.5 per cent in 1987, dropping to 8.9 per cent in 1990, but climbing back to 12.4 per cent in 1994, with over 3.1 million unemployed.[41] But it is not just the absolute numbers of unemployed which give cause for concern but also the structural features of unemployment.

The average period of unemployment lengthened from 11.7 months in 1981 to 13.9 months in 1991. Levels of unemployment have been consistently higher amongst women than among men, but the rate of increase in unemployment was more marked with men. In 1981, the unemployment rate for women was 10.6 per cent, rising to 14.5 per cent in 1994, whereas for men it was 5.3 per cent in 1981 rising to 10.8 per cent in 1994.[42] The large growth in unemployment among the young has given cause for grave concern. In the 15–24 age-group, 15 per cent were unemployed in 1980, rising to 17.5 per cent in 1990 and to 24.7 per cent in 1994.[43] The occupational groups most affected by labour shedding were agricultural and factory workers, with members of ethnic minorities being especially hard hit since so many of their number have depended on manual work. Even the best placed category of employees, the *cadres*, have seen a near-doubling of their unemployment rate from 3.7 per cent in 1989 to 6.1 per cent in 1993.[44] With so many social groups prone to joblessness, resentment and anxiety have multiplied across French society.

Patterns of employment and unemployment are inextricably linked. Employees on short-term contracts increased in France from 3.3 per cent of the workforce in 1983 to 10.2 per cent in 1991; similar proportions of around 10 per cent were found in Germany and Japan throughout the period, although the proportion was lower in the UK at around five per cent.[45] In 1994, 1.4 million French people were in various forms of short-term employment.[46] Moreover, whereas in 1980 14 per cent of unemployment was occasioned by the expiry of a short-term contract, by 1992 the proportion grew to 33 per cent.[47] Employment is now both hard to find and difficult to keep.

The financial circumstances of those in work have added to the ambient gloom. Although the early 1990s brought record lows in inflation, with an increase in prices of approximately two per cent per year, salaries have stagnated, with average annual increases of just 0.3 per cent in 1992, 1993 and 1994.[48] Further, salaries calculated as a percentage of value-added fell from 68.3 per cent in 1980 to 60.7 per cent in 1992; meanwhile, gross profit margins increased from 25.8 per cent to 32.3 per cent.[49] These developments demonstrate that the policy of competitive disinflation delivered lower inflation and higher competitiveness, but the employment gains expected from wage moderation proved too limited to contain – let alone reduce – unemployment.[50]

In summary, the French economy has grown increasingly capital-intensive, displaying on the one hand a marked concentration of financial and industrial power brokered by a narrow elite and, on the other, less need for salaried employees and a heightened tendency to rely on short-term contracts to adjust to rapidly changing market conditions. French business has often been lampooned as *capitalisme sans capital*, but in the 1990s it showed signs of becoming a *capitalisme sans travail*. The French business world reflects a divided society in which insidious dissatisfaction is mounting. These outcomes reflected badly on the Mitterrand period, and gave Jacques Chirac the opportunity in the 1995 presidential campaign to claim squatters' rights on the usually left-wing theme of the *fracture sociale*.

CONCLUSION

France benefits from a mature economy and a highly developed business community which can ride out the vagaries of the business cycle, as well as the stops, starts and about-turns of economic policy. The fourteen years of the Mitterrand presidency did not produce a paradigm change, being characterized by incremental but substantive adjustment. Thus, this chapter has stressed the continuity of change, rather than posit change as the alternative to continuity. Expressed differently, under Mitterrand the promised revolution did not take place, but French capitalism did evolve markedly.

French business presents a distinctive model which has developed in response to internal factors and external trends, though largely on its own terms. Its persistent feature is the intertwining of the state and the market. However, the institutional, social and political arrangements through which the linkages are manifested and enacted, tightened or loosened have been subject to a range of reforms, indicating a capacity to adapt to changing national and global demands. Although the international trend to deregulation and privatization resulted in a revision of the French 'mixed economy', with the public sector shrinking in size, the density of the exchange networks that link large firms to the state still allows the exercise of *mutual* influence.

Public policy-making towards business changed significantly over the period along three dimensions: first, a political and ideological swing from *dirigisme* to liberalism (but without turning to an *ultra-libéral* laissez-faire); second, a victory for technocratic modernizers over the conservatism of the French administration (evident in the discarding of interventionist instruments such as price controls, credit controls and exchange controls); and third, a partial but significant swing from the politics of sovereignty to a stress on European ambitions, centred on market and monetary integration as the means for political union. Governments of both the right and the left found common ground in these orientations and, in equally bullish mood, France's business classes increasingly favoured the outward-looking strategies of liberalization, Europeanization and internationalization. Mitterrand's enthusiasm for European integration pushed him into accepting its inbuilt free-market agenda.

Turning to performance, French business viewed from an economic perspective faltered in the initial Mitterrand years but prospered in the 1986–1991 period; it traversed the recession of 1992–1993 tolerably well in comparison to its neighbours and has grown steadily more competitive over the last decade. In the early 1990s, inflation was running at historic lows, profitability and investment recovered and exports increased to give a record surplus of the balance of trade. If the regional distribution of production shifted only slightly, the importance of small firms to economic well-being was recognized.

But viewed from the social perspective, the outcomes are less encouraging, with change being either too slow or in the wrong direction. French patterns of ownership and elite recruitment remained true to type. The division between a powerful minority and the masses is nothing new, but the accentuation of that gap in contemporary France is striking, with at one extreme a talented, well-educated but closed elite controlling almost all key functions of both the state *and* large firms, whilst at the other extreme, the disenfranchisement of the greater number is embodied in the twin armies of unemployed and short-term workers. Even though Western nations grew inured to unemployment in the 1980s, the features of the French case, namely a persistent creep to ever higher levels (as compared to a pattern of rise and fall in the UK, for example), with high proportions of young and long-term unemployed, constitute a specific and worrying configuration which blots the record of business and president in the Mitterrand era.

The key irony of the period was undoubtedly the requirement that it be a left-wing president who reconciled a France traditionally chary of competition with the rigours of the market. Moreover, in a country often taxed with the stereotype of protectionism, this conversion was enacted less through domestic economic and industrial policy-making *per se* than through the enthusiasm of Mitterrand, and of much of France's political and business elite, for the project of European integration. Yet in the task of putting the country back to work, the Socialists – and Mitterrand foremost among them – signally failed. It would constitute a most welcome counterbalancing irony of history if the Chirac presidency succeeded in curing these socio-economic ills.

But the president, government and business leaders will need to demonstrate extraordinary inventiveness and courage to achieve economic development, low unemployment and European monetary union.

NOTES

1. See J. Szarka, *Business in France* (London: Pitman, 1992); V. Schmidt, *From State to Market? The Transformation of French Business and Government* (Cambridge: CUP, 1996).
2. R.F. Kuisel, 'The France we have lost: social, economic and cultural discontinuities', in G. Flynn (ed.), *Remaking the Hexagon: the New France in the New Europe* (Boulder: Westview Press, 1995), pp. 31–48.
3. J. Généreux, *Chiffres clés de l'économie française* (Paris: Seuil, 1993), p. 29.
4. INSEE, *L'Economie française. Rapport sur les comptes de la nation de 1994* (Paris: Librairie Générale Française, 1995), p. 71.
5. Ibid, p. 123.
6. *Problèmes Economiques*, Nos. 2368–2369, p.71.
7. A. Babeau, 'Qui possède les entreprises françaises?', *Le Monde*, 11 October 1994.
8. C. Lévi, 'Les investissements étrangers', *Le Monde*, 6 April 1993, p. 31.
9. J.-L. Bricout, 'La présence des entreprises françaises dans le monde', *Problèmes Economiques*, No. 2428, 14 June 1995, pp. 1–4.
10. Conseil Economique et Social, 'L'image des entreprises et des produits français à l'étranger', *Problèmes Economiques*, No. 2338, 25 August 1993, pp. 9–18.
11. P. Artus and E. Bleuze, 'Déficit du commerce industriel de la France et capacités de production: un examen sectoriel', *Economie et Statistique*, No. 228, January 1990, pp. 19–28.
12. INSEE, 1995, op. cit., p. 225.
13. J.E. Le Cacheux, 'The franc fort strategy and the EMU', in Flynn, op. cit.
14. European integration became the key theme of the second *septennat*.
15. Arnaud-Ameller, op. cit., p. 45.
16. S. Berger, 'Trade and identity: the coming protectionism?', in Flynn, op. cit., pp. 195–210.
17. M. Devilliers, 'Performances et comportements comparés des petites et grandes entreprises depuis le second choc pétrolier', *Problèmes Economiques*, No. 2031, 1 July 1987, pp. 6–11; M. Amar, 'Dans l'industrie, les PME résistent miuex que les grandes entreprises', *Economie et Statistique*, No. 197, 1987, pp. 3–11.
18. B. Duchéneaut, *Enquête sur les PME françaises. Identité, contextes, chiffres* (Paris: Maxima, 1995).

19. C. Gordon, *The Business Culture in France* (Oxford: Butterworth Heinemann, 1996), p. 147.
20. Duchéneaut, op. cit., p. 526.
21. A. Bull, M. Pitt and J. Szarka, *Entrepreneurial Textiles Communities. A Comparative Study of Small Textile and Clothing Firms* (London: Chapman & Hall, 1993); C. Lane, *Industry and Society in Europe. Stability and Change in Britian, Germany and France* (Aldershot: Edward Elgar, 1995).
22. J. Szarka, 'Regional economic development in France since 1982: theories, policies and realities', in M. Kelly and R. Böck (eds), *France: Nation and Regions* (Southampton: University of Southampton, 1993), pp. 111–120.
23. B. Ganne, 'France: behind small and medium-sized enterprises lies the State', in A. Bagnasco and C. Sabel, *Small and Medium-Sized Enterprises* (London: Pinter, 1995), p. 130.
24. Y. Morvan, 'Dix ans d'interventions économiques des régions: un essai de bilan', *Cahiers économiques de Bretagne*, No. 2, pp. 1–9.
25. P. Le Galès, 'Regional economic policies: an alternative to French economic *dirigisme?*', in J. Loughlin and S. Mazey (eds), *The End of the French Unitary State? Ten Years of Regionalisation in France (1982–1992)* (London: Frank Cass, 1995), p. 72.
26. F. Morin, 'Qui possède les 200 premières entreprises françaises?, *Science et Vie: Economie*, No. 52, August 1989, pp. 51–74. Annual variation since has been small.
27. More recent discussions of nationalization and privatization include F. Dion, *Les Privatisations en France, en Allemagne, en Grande-Bretagne et en Italie,* (Paris: Documentation Française, 1995); M. Maclean, 'Privatisation in France 1993–1994: new departures or a case of *plus ça change?*', *West European Politics*, Vol. 18, No. 2, April 1995, pp. 273–290.
28. Babeau, op. cit.
29. F. Morin, 'Les trois pôles du pouvoir économique', *Le Monde*, 8 March 1994.
30. F. Morin, 'La recomposition du coeur financier français', *Alternatives Economiques*, No. 128, 1995, pp. 26–28.
31. E. Suleiman, 'Change and stability in French elites', in Flynn, op. cit., pp. 161–179.
32. Key examples are the Corps des Mines, the Corps des Ponts et Chaussées and Inspection des Finances. Many CEOs of France's major firms are members of a *grands corps*: Rodier at Péchiney, Beffa at Saint-Gobain, Mer at Usinor, Collomb at Lafarge are all *X-Mines*, whilst Pébereau at BNP and Friedmann at UAP are Inspecteurs de Finances.
33. M. Bauer, 'La gauche au pouvoir et le grand patronat: sous les pavés...des mouvements de classe dirigeante', in P. Birnbaum (ed.), *Les Elites socialistes au pouvoir, 1981–1985* (Paris: PUF, 1985), pp. 263–306.
34. E. Leser and C. Monnot, 'Quarente-cinq patrons sur la sellette', *Le Monde*, 6 April 1992, p. 32.

35. A. Reverchon, 'Grandes écoles françaises: la fin des rentes de situation', *Problèmes Economiques*, No. 2460, 1996, p. 5.
36. Suleiman, op. cit., p. 169.
37. M. Bauer and B. Bertin-Mourot, 'Une caste dirigeante', *Alternatives Economiques*, No. 128, 1995, pp. 29–32.
38. G. Moatti, 'La France contre ses élites', *L'Expansion*, 7–20 December 1995, pp. 94–108; Reverchon, op. cit.
39. P. Moreau Defarges, 'La France, province de l'Union Européenne?', *Politique Etrangère*, Spring 1996, p. 44.
40. Généreux, op. cit., p. 90.
41. INSEE, op. cit.
42. Généreux, op. cit., p. 95; INSEE, op. cit., p. 207.
43. INSEE, *L'Economie française. Edition 1994. Rapport sur les comptes de la nation de 1993* (Paris: Librairie Générale Française, 1994), p. 189.
44. Gordon, op. cit., p. 79.
45. *Problèmes Economiques*, Nos. 2368–2369, p. 37.
46. INSEE, 1995, op. cit.
47. Généreux, op. cit., p. 98.
48. INSEE, 1995, op. cit., p. 227.
49. *Problèmes Economiques*, Nos. 2368–2369, p. 37.
50. J.-P. Fitoussi *et al., Competitive Disinflation. The Mark and Budgetary Politics in Europe* (Oxford: OUP, 1993), p. 18.

9 Industrial Relations in France: Towards a New Social Pact?

Susan Milner

In his last New Year's message to the nation, President Mitterrand called for a 'new social contract' to combat unemployment: rather late in the day, one might think, and something of an acknowledgement of the failure of the Mitterrand presidency to create the conditions for meaningful social dialogue in a country so proud of its 'social model'. Industrial relations reform is not conspicuously one of the great successes of the Mitterrand era, and it did not take long after the arrival of the first Socialist government for the strained relations between state, employers and trade to become evident. It could even be argued that the French industrial relations system has been destabilized by the policies and economic trends of the Mitterrand era, with no alternative structures to replace it. Trade unions, already in 1981 weaker than many of their European counterparts, have been further marginalized in the Mitterrand years: from over 25 per cent in 1981, trade union membership has fallen to only seven per cent of the workforce today (and a tiny five per cent in the private sector):[1] hardly a sign of healthy industrial relations.

But the trade union movement is far from dead. In the winter of 1995–1996, France's economy and daily life in Paris and some other large cities were paralysed by the biggest strike movement since May 1968. How should we interpret this new militancy? As the sign of a renewal of trade unionism which could help to redress the balance of power, currently hopelessly weighted in favour of employers, and thereby boost social dialogue? Or as yet another sign of the weakness of civil society in French political life, the latest symptom of France's chronic inability to carry through peaceful reform? The argument, dating back to Tocqueville, goes that the all-powerful, centralized French state snuffs out intermediate associations and weakens civil society, individualizing social relations and destabilising political life. A different argument, close to Crozier's analysis of 'La société bloquée', sees the culprit not as the absence of intermediate associations but as the presence of narrow, corporatistic bodies competing with each other and determined to block reform. Both analyses point to a perceived backwardness of French social relations.

The notion of 'backwardness' implicit in calls for renewal and modernization is of course inspired by comparisons with industrial relations systems in other countries. In the 1960s and 1970s, debates on industrial relations were largely inspired by the 'industrial democracy' discussions in Britain. According to Moss, the French 'modernists' looked to the British and American experience in particular.[2] They advocated the establishment of consultation and bargaining bodies, especially within the workplace. This was the thinking behind the 1963 Bloch-Lainé recommendations and the Sudreau report in 1975. The 1981–1982 Auroux laws also placed emphasis on negotiation within the firm. More recently, the model for France – not unnaturally, given their close trade relations – has been Germany. What is attractive in German industrial relations, from the French perspective, is the high level of trust between employers and workers' representatives: employers benefit from returns to their investments in human capital through increased productivity and high-quality production. The state provides some legislative underpinning (through provisions on works councils or worker representation on supervisory boards in certain industries) but the key to the system is the autonomy of social partners in free collective bargaining. Bargaining takes place primarily at sectoral level, so the German model is less company-based than the British or US model, but there is a high degree of articulation between the two levels, thanks largely to the dual representation of workers through works councils (many of whose members are trade unionist delegates) and trade unions. In recent years, however, the company level has become more important as employers seek to free themselves from the perceived rigidities of the annual sectoral bargaining round. Despite this recent trend towards decentralization of bargaining in Germany, the organizing capacities of employers' organisations and trade unions remain strong.[3]

The 'German model' functions less as a coherent set of solutions for solving France's perceived weaknesses than as a vague, desirable 'other' against which France is measured and found wanting. French politicians of right and left, employers' representatives and 'modernist' trade union leaders all use the German model in this way.

Recent analysis of the task facing trade unions in Europe has used the concept of modernization developed by Hans van der Loo and Willem van Reijen, based on four processes: differentiation, individualization, rationalization and participation.[4] According to this analysis, Western societies have entered a second phase of modernity (rather than post-modernity) in which certain features of modernity are radicalized. Trade union practices, particularly the narrow professional base of traditional trade union activity, are called into question. If they are to survive, trade unions must adapt to take account of changes in the labour force and their deployment by companies (differentiation and individualization); for example, problems in organizing white-collar workers and young workers are well known. Rationalization concerns the slow death of old industries, the reorganization of trade union structures, and the decline of utopian (notably communist) ideologies. Finally, new ways of integrating a wide range of workers and new themes (such as ecology) into trade union life must be addressed (participation).

In general terms, then, modernization means greater involvement of employees in management decisions at the level of the workplace, more mechanisms for collective bargaining at all levels but particularly in the workplace, trade union strategies for adapting to labour market changes and dealing with unemployment, new ways of organizing trade union activity and a new relationship between the organization and its potential members, and employer recognition of trade unions and willingness to bargain. It also requires state legislation to establish bargaining structures, but the absence of the state from bargaining procedures and outcomes. In the next section, we look briefly at the traditional characteristics of the French industrial relations system, before going on to assess how far these have changed during the Mitterrand era. Finally, this chapter examines current trends and possible future directions for industrial relations in France.

CHARACTERISTICS OF THE FRENCH INDUSTRIAL RELATIONS SYSTEM

By industrial relations system, we mean in general terms that 'the interplay of actors, through their conflicts and negotiations – which are two sides of the same system of relations – sets the rules concerning employment, wages, everything which governs work, which is not determined by the market but by a system of rules which are socially agreed'.[5] In recent years, industrial relations systems in industrialized countries have been seen to be under threat, as individualized contractual relations between employers and employees (sometimes under the banner of 'human resource management') increasingly take the place of centrally bargained deals between collective actors; in other words, the market is being freed from socially agreed rules.[6] Some would argue that industrial relations systems as we know them are in crisis and no longer have a place in post-industrial society.[7] Others point to differences between countries and chart shifts within systems rather than a general crisis.[8]

The French industrial relations system is undoubtedly in crisis. A conference organised in 1993 by the Confédération Française Démocratique du Travail (CFDT, then second largest but since 1995 recognized as the largest union confederation) concluded that 'the French industrial relations system as it was set up in the 1930s–1950s and consolidated during the "thirty glorious years" is being dismantled, and no new coherent system has yet been established'.[9] This rather dramatic conclusion needs to be qualified, however. Not all changes taking place in industrial relations in France are negative, nor is there a total absence of new structures to replace the old.

Traditionally, French employers have mistrusted trade unions and sought to keep them out of the company. This has not, however, led them to seek national-level agreements, and the central employers' organisation (CNPF) has low levels of coverage and co-ordination. Furthermore, a deep division exists between large companies and the very small companies which make up the economic fabric of France. This partly explains the relative importance of industry-level bargaining (but it is still weakly institutionalized at this level in comparison with other countries) rather than national or company level. Traditionally, certain key companies have taken the lead in bargaining; often these have been public-sector companies such as Renault. The state's ability to extend agreements throughout a sector or geographical region has not sufficed to alleviate these imbalances in bargaining coverage. Employers' mistrust of trade unions has also limited the scope of bargaining. As Amadieu notes: 'Employers consider organizational change to be one of their prerogatives. Three-quarters of the labour force works in firms with fewer than 50 employees, which are generally family-owned, and where management is reluctant to cede any of its right to manage and looks upon trade unions with a jaundiced eye'.[10]

Trade unions have developed in response to these conditions, as agents of contestation rather than negotiation. Workers are weakly organized at company level. On the other hand, the trade union audience has traditionally extended beyond the narrow circle of members and activists, both informally and formally through the election of enterprise committee members and workers' delegates. Labbé reminds us that the French model of trade unionism, at its apogee in the long period from the 1930s to the 1970s, depended on a network of activists working closely with colleagues in the workplace, with a strong company-based culture.[11] This company-based trade unionism (associated especially with the CGT) was situated in key companies and industries (notably metals), reflecting the lead taken by certain companies in the industrial relations system. At national level, trade unions looked increasingly to the state throughout the twentieth century, despite the early rejection of the repressive state in the form of revolutionary syndicalism. This was true especially after the 1936 Matignon reforms, seen as an important workers' victory over management. National-level strategy after the Popular Front sought to replicate this victory by preparing the way for a left victory which would provide legislation to compensate for the relative weakness of trade unions vis-à-vis employers. However, this strategy proved deeply unpopular with employees, who bitterly criticised the 'politicization' of trade union activity.

The role of the state was crucial in shaping the industrial relations system, but it has been an ambiguous one. Moss notes that in the post-war period, the state had little success in establishing bargaining structures and it was not until the left government arrived in 1981 that a series of measures aimed at reinforcing worker representation and encouraging industry- and company-level bargaining was put into place.[12] However, the right-wing government in the early 1970s did have some success in boosting sectoral-level legislation through its 'politique contractuelle' (associated with Jacques Chaban-Delmas and Jacques Delors, the would-be modernizers of the industrial relations system). It is interesting to note that this early phase of modernization reinforced the existing system of sectoral negotiation rather than company-level bargaining (despite the 1971 amendment to the 1950 collective bargaining act), and also depended to a large extent on the pioneering role of certain large companies. In terms of labour legislation, then, the role of the state was fairly ad hoc and piecemeal, but the political activities of the trade union confederations created an expectation that the state would intervene. In other words, there was a gap in the system that could only be filled by state intervention, since it was not being filled by free collective bargaining. On the other hand, the state shaped the industrial relations system by creating a network of welfare institutions to be jointly administered by trade unions and employers, notably the social security funds and family allowance funds. This left trade unions in an awkward position, because it diverted resources away from company-level activities and also weakened their legitimacy at company and industry level (with employers) and with workers during the later period when membership started to fall, widening the gap between the leadership and the grassroots.[13]

Finally, the importance of the public sector in shaping industrial relations must be mentioned. The state retains a central role in the system through its pay awards in the public sector. The trade union movement depends to a large extent on public-sector members, who enjoy job security and are therefore free from fears of dismissal associated with joining a union or taking part in industrial action. This tends to reinforce the weak presence of trade unions in the private sector, particularly in small firms, as national trade union activity focuses overwhelmingly on 'days of action' stopping public services, and also strongly influences the image of trade unions in public opinion. The divide between public- and private-sector trade unionism may well hinder modernization (in the sense of differentiation and individualization) simply because it is easier for national confederations to organize public-sector days of action than to spend time and limited resources on the slow and painful work of building links with new categories of worker in small, private companies.

On the whole, then, France's industrial relations system (driven by employers and the state) appears ill-suited to the kind of high-trust, consensual relations desired by modernizers. Given the traditional weakness of trade unions and of collective bargaining in France, did the Mitterrand years improve things or make matters worse? We might expect that the poorly cemented structure of industrial relations would have difficulty withstanding the wave of neoliberal deregulation sweeping industrialized countries in the 1980s. Yet we might also expect a left-wing president and successive governments to reinforce the structure through legislation.

THE MITTERRAND YEARS

The major achievement of the Mitterrand years was the Auroux legislation passed in 1981–1982, designed to strengthen the ailing industrial relations system by giving workers new rights to have their say in issues affecting their companies and their work, strengthening existing consultation mechanisms by awarding them competence in specific areas (such as technological change) and obliging employers to engage in collective bargaining, thus also pointing trade unions towards a more participatory role within the company.

The effects of this legislation have been most visible as regards collective bargaining in the workplace. As Caire states, collective bargaining ('the process by which the social partners, acting together, define a set of rules which will govern the form and substance of their relationships') is the cornerstone of any industrial relations system.[14] In 1981, a large number of employees were not covered by any kind of collective agreement: three million workers in companies of more than ten employees. Have the Auroux laws succeeded in creating a bargaining culture in France? The November 1982 law obliging companies to negotiate annually on effective wage rates, working hours and the organization of working time resulted in a steady increase in bargaining coverage, although owing to the weakness of sectoral bargaining coverage remains very patchy. The number of workers not covered by collective agreements dropped from three million to one million in ten years. But this global figure hides considerable disparities at subnational level, both geographically and between sectors or companies. Nationally, the number of agreements increased from 420 to 526 between 1982 and 1990. But at departmental level, the increase was only slight: from 479 to 491, and at regional level the number of agreements actually dropped from 300 to 271.[15] Improved coverage also hides the fact that sectoral bargaining is increasingly limited in scope (fixing minimum pay levels, with considerable leeway for companies to set their own wage levels), although some would argue that this has been compensated by the rise of company bargaining.[16]

The number of company agreements rose immediately from 1,477 in 1981 to 5,165 in 1985, and 6,750 in 1991.[17] The decentralizing trend towards company-level bargaining intensified in the late 1980s and early 1990s: 7,450 agreements were signed in 1994, an increase of 14 per cent on the previous year.[18] The Auroux laws were only partly responsible for encouraging this decentralization of bargaining. A series of laws on the organization of working time, notably the 1987 Séguin law, backed up the thrust of the Auroux laws by encouraging companies to negotiate derogations from legislative limits, thus inciting employers to move from their traditional reluctance to bargain on non-pay issues. Since 1984, it is obligatory for negotiations to take place on the aims and methods of training at either industry or company level. The level of the company is often better suited than the sectoral level to discuss issues such as technological innovation, job content, work organisation, skills and training: thus, for example, working hours ranked only eighth in the priorities of sectoral bargaining in 1994, but was the most important single issue in company bargaining.[19]

However, the rise in the number of company agreements hides considerable disparities between companies, with certain large companies leading the way. The goal of encouraging bargaining in medium-sized companies was achieved only to a limited degree,[20] and small companies remain largely untouched by legislative spurs to bargaining. We may see the rise in company-level bargaining, then, as a partial restructuring of the industrial relations system in which a fraction of French companies use bargaining as a tool to accomplish changes in work organization: '[some companies] have tried to establish new forms of mutual collaboration in order to share the higher cost of innovation'.[21] But the majority of companies prefer to bypass institutional actors and act unilaterally, using the new freedoms which governments have given them, most notoriously the 1986 suppression of the notification requirement for mass lay-offs. Even those exceptional agreements held up as models, such as the 1989 Renault 'Accord à vivre' singled out for praise by Coffineau,[22] ran into problems. The agreement (which the CGT refused to sign) stressed the need to train workers to adapt them to technological change (25,000 workers to be trained over five years), with the creation of autonomous teams and the introduction of new working hours (a daily increase of half an hour in exchange for longer holidays and a pay bonus). Workers tended to notice the disadvantages rather than the advantages of the new working hours, and trade unions felt uncomfortable in their new role, expecting more support from management.[23] Above all, pioneering agreements in large companies have been undermined by the steady and sometimes spectacular reduction of the workforce.

As regards the 'droit d'expression des salariés' (4 August 1982 law), the official evaluation of the impact of the Auroux laws (by Coffineau) claimed considerable success in changing the climate of workplace relations: 25 per cent of companies (subject to the law, that is, with more than ten employees) surveyed in 1991 by the employment ministry had organised expression meetings in 1990. In a SOFRES survey carried out in December 1992, 28 per cent of employees felt that relations between workers and management were very good, and 56 per cent quite good; 30 per cent stated that they had improved over the last few years. But again, it was very large companies which tended to comply with the new rules on worker expression. Moreover, it is now generally known that expression groups tend to be run by management rather than employees themselves, and trade unions find it particularly difficult to use the new fora of expression to raise grievances. Whether expression groups have given rise to a new culture of 'participatory management' has been hotly debated, but it does seem to be the case that they reinforce paternalistic practices instead of democratizing life in the workplace, where the major decisions are taken far away at headquarters.

What of the institutional mechanisms for, on one side, expressing grievances and, on the other, informing and consulting workers? French politicians in the 1980s made much of the 'European social model' of workplace information and consultation to which France subscribed. In the mid–1980s, large companies set up 'comités de groupe', and often these same companies (notably BSN, l'Oréal, Rhône-Poulenc, Péchiney) were at the forefront of initiatives to create European works councils. Again, institutionalized consultation procedures in the large companies hid the reality of extremely patchy coverage in medium-sized companies, not to mention their virtual absence from smaller companies. The October 1982 law was designed to improve the functioning of representative institutions in the workplace (*comités d'entreprise, délégués du personnel* and *délégués syndicaux*): it gave the committees greater say in a wider range of issues affecting work organization and allowed workers in smaller companies to group together to gain access to representation. But a 1991 study found considerable overlap between different institutions, patchy coverage between firms, lack of appropriate training for delegates called upon to express opinions on financial or technical matters, and above all a dwindling pool of people willing to take on responsibility for these tasks.[24] These findings echo comparative European studies, which attribute the relative weakness of the French bodies to the ineffectiveness or absence of trade unions. Without a strong network of activists able to call on collective resources, workplace institutions find their capacity to intervene severely constrained.

The trends which have been identified towards company bargaining and creation of participative culture in some companies may be an encouraging sign of modernization, but they are very limited in scale. Despite the Auroux laws, the balance of power shifted further in management's favour during the Mitterrand years as successive governments yielded to employers' demands for deregulation of labour markets (under the banner of flexibility) and a lightening of the tax and welfare contributions burden on companies. Labour market flexibility came about in three main ways. First, external flexibility (freedom to hire and fire) was boosted by the 1986 removal of the requirement to notify the labour inspectorate of planned mass redundancies, but even more by laws allowing employers to make greater use of fixed-term contracts and temporary work. Thus, 70 per cent of jobs filled in 1989 were fixed-term appointments, and this trend has continued. Second, a series of laws on working time enhanced temporal flexibility by allowing companies to negotiate working hours to suit business needs, within certain limits. Third, youth training schemes and other initiatives for specific categories of unemployed workers gave employers financial incentives to take on cheaper and more disposable labour.

Labour market deregulation reflected the new economic climate. The main impetus for change in the industrial relations system in the 1980s and 1990s was the unrelenting battle for international market share and the emergence of new, low-labour-cost competitors in the south and east. Even as company profits soared, these same companies looked to invest overseas and cut investment (and therefore jobs): the case of GEC-Alsthom is emblematic. Since the creation of the Franco-British joint venture in 1989, rationalization has resulted in regular plant closures. In late 1994, one of the largest private-sector strike movements for years spread through the company's plants in response to planned lay-offs and a pay offer of two per cent at a time when company profits soared and the managing director's annual salary was revealed by journalists to reach around FF15 million. Even Danone (formerly BSN), long known as an employee-friendly (and trade-union-friendly) company, not just in France but throughout Europe, besmirched its image in 1996 with the announcement of mass redundancies. Perhaps the most telling statistic for any study of industrial relations in the Mitterrand years is the number of unemployed: 1.9 million in 1981, 3.3 million and rising in 1994, representing 7.3 per cent and 12.7 per cent of the workforce respectively.

In these circumstances, collective bargaining has barely made inroads into traditionally resistant sectors, and even in favourable sectors its nature has changed. Yvon Chotard (an experienced CNPF negotiator, representing the Catholic, 'social' wing of the organized employers' lobby and therefore ideologically and professionally attached to collective bargaining) summarizes this employer-driven change:

There can be no question of doing away altogether with collective agreements: quite apart from any ideological attachment we might have to them, they can play a regulatory role for companies as well as for employees. But the content of such agreements needs to be changed, pared down, so as to allow companies to define their own wages policy, particularly in successfully rewarding merit and taking account of individual and collective performance.[25]

Attempts to apply a similar logic in the public sector have created a confrontational situation in which the defence of categorial interests remains paramount,[26] culminating in the spectacular strike movement of autumn-winter 1995.

WHITHER INDUSTRIAL RELATIONS?

The post-Mitterrand era was ushered in by a wave of unrest such as France had not seen for decades. The strikes in the autumn of 1995 highlighted the explosive situation in the public sector. They involved mainly public-sector workers (public transport, post office, education, social security, health, financial administration).[27] Conflicts in the public sector look likely to continue, with heavy job losses announced in autumn 1996 in ship-building and telecommunications. Although the government has fought shy in the 1997 budget of a blanket pay freeze in the public sector, its intention to reduce public debt levels to comply with the Maastricht convergence criteria will in the longer term result in drastic change. 'Normalization' of France's public sector may well only be possible through steady privatization, along similar lines (but less brutal, since phased over a longer period) as in Britain.

The autumn 1995 strike movement had been preceded by a series of strikes throughout the previous years involving private-sector workers (as at GEC-Alsthom). These private-sector strikes suggest a trend towards more conflictual relations in the large companies which once constituted the flagships of the French industrial relations system. At the same time, the gradual retreat of the state from its regulatory role, encapsulated in Mitterrand's explicit preference for bargained solutions rather than a reintroduction of legal and administrative procedures, as in the case of the notification procedure for lay-offs abandoned in 1986, tends towards inertia within the system: the flagship companies which used to pull industrial relations along (whether indirectly or directly, through state extension of company agreements) are no longer to fulfil this function.

A new impetus for collective bargaining is sorely needed if the industrial relations system is not to collapse entirely. Any prospect of change is likely to come from the employers rather than the state. It may possibly come from the CNPF's new leadership and the bargaining process it initiated in January 1995. The CNPF seems to be aware of the negative public image of companies at a time of high unemployment. In a television interview in April 1996, the CNPF president, Jean Gandois stated that he was no longer seeking reductions in employers' social contributions, as the costs were merely transferred to taxes. Gandois also raised a good many eyebrows with his admission, in tune with growing academic and political opinion, that the prevailing unemployment policy of wage subsidies to employers (of which Chirac's much-touted Contrat Initiative-Emploi was the latest example) was costly and of dubious efficacy.

On becoming CNPF president late in 1994, Gandois immediately opened up talks with the trade union confederations. The CNPF had become alarmed at the weakness of trade unions and some feared that they might lose their interlocutors altogether. In response, some employers envisaged drastic solutions: Claude Bébéar, at AXA insurance company, had already instituted a 'chèque syndical' giving employees a money voucher to enrol with the trade union of their choice. The scheme, viewed with suspicion by employers and trade unions, remains limited to a handful of companies, mainly in the insurance sector, but it does reveal the extent of the trade union crisis and its effects on the bargaining system. In January 1996, the CNPF discussed a confidential note on trade unionism drawn up by the veteran negotiator Pierre Guillen. Guillen's analysis, which appears to be widely shared within the CNPF,[28] is based on deep anxiety about the consequences of the extremely low membership rate of unions (given France's increasingly volatile social climate). He recommends a continuing strategy of conducting intersectoral talks and encouraging the formation of a 'reformist pole' (essentially CFDT, with CFE–CGC and CFTC).

This strategy would appear to be the only viable one for the CNPF, although by itself it is unlikely to pay dividends. Previous attempts between CFDT, FEN and CFTC (with or without FO) to form a 'reformist pole' quickly came apart. The CFDT is badly divided, as Secretary-General Nicole Notat's poor reception at the 1995 congress, and subsequent expulsions and splits from the confederation, showed.

Nonetheless, if the bargaining process produces some real *grain à moudre*, those unions involved will gain real legitimacy and public approval. Thus, for example, the Renault *Accord à vivre* agreement resulted in the short term in a marginalization of the CGT, which had not signed up.[29] However, as disillusionment with the results of the agreement grew, the CGT's share of workplace election results increased again later. During the 1992 negotiations on working time at Hewlett-Packard, the CFDT (which had been heavily involved in the negotiations) won out in workplace elections over the CGT, which had maintained a firm opposition. The CNPF could gain considerable goodwill points and give a major boost to the CFDT by showing more flexibility on the issue of working time reduction, which to date it has refused to countenance except in terms of annualization of working hours.[30] If the CNPF does not make substantial concessions to the CFDT leadership's priorities of reduction of working time and youth employment over the next couple of years, it will be seen to be guilty of bad faith in its pronouncements about the sorry state of French trade unionism. Guillen's report, which praises the German model of industrial relations whilst acknowledging German employers' fears about loss of competitiveness, appears rather unclear about its real wishes for the future of industrial relations in France: what do French employers really want?

The CNPF can certainly count on continuing trade union division, although this is not necessarily in itself a sign that the trade unions will not adapt to new roles in the medium to long term. Cultural shifts take decades, and the process of change for trade unions is underway, but it would be unrealistic to expect such fundamental cultural change to take place without the persistence and even exacerbation of earlier traits which are under threat (such as categorial demands, or the refusal to sign agreements which remove existing protection). Trade union division is likely to continue to exist in France because of structural inertia, but also because of the important role trade unions play in the polity as providers of ideas. What is more worrying in the long term is the failure to reach out to new types of worker, women and young workers. Recent evidence from Britain suggests that assumptions about the 'unorganizable' nature of women and white-collar workers are erroneous, as trade unions which offer a diverse range of services have made considerable inroads into greenfield sites. There are also signs in France that a new generation of activists may be emerging to voice grievances and aspirations of younger and a more diverse professional range of workers.[31]

At workplace level, some pioneering agreements in major companies also provide a pointer to cultural shifts in French industrial relations. Indeed, France currently leads the way in Europe in bargaining on working time. The vast majority of these agreements are defensive rather than offensive, in the sense that they seek to preserve existing jobs (often in exchange for wage cuts); effectively, trade unions are forced into acceptance of management wishes under the threat of job losses, and it is hard to see how they can modernize or adapt in such conditions.[32] Examples of innovative 'offensive' agreements include the 1992 Hewlett-Packard (Isle d'Abeau) agreement on working time, which allows longer opening hours but exchanges temporal flexibility for reductions in working time. The 31 October 1995 agreement opens the way for such agreements to become more widespread in companies, and also sets out a new articulation between sectoral and company level (although the CGT and FO refused to sign this section). Within this framework, sectoral level does not set minima but lays down themes and general principles for workplace bargaining. According to employers, 'The content of bargaining has been enriched. Its traditional, rule-setting role is now complemented by one of innovation, experimentation and monitoring'.[33]

There is a chance that agreements such as that at Hewlett Packard could become the scaffolding for a new system of workplace regulations, but if they merely become rubber stamps for employers to dispose of employees' working hours as they see fit there is little point in having a regulatory system at all. Today, there is little doubt that employers are in the driving seat. The fact that they appear reluctant to discard bargaining altogether and deregulate the markets completely – or perhaps that they feel constrained by societal pressures – suggests that the industrial relations system will not collapse entirely. But there is as yet little sign of a renewal of industrial relations, or a new social pact.

NOTES

1. UIMM, 'Situation sociale: épreuve de force et de vérité', *Actualité*, No. 143, 1995, pp. 24–31.
2. B. Moss, 'La réforme de la législation du travail sous la Ve République: un triomphe du modernisme?', *Le Mouvement social*, No. 148, July–September 1989, pp. 63–91.

3. F. Traxler, 'Farewell to labour market associations? Organized versus disorganized decentralization as a map for industrial relations', in C. Crouch and F. Traxler (eds), *Organized Industrial Relations in Europe: What Future?* (Aldershot: Avebury, 1995).
4. R. Zoll, 'La modernisation qui reste à faire', *CFDT aujourd'hui*, No. 109, 1993, pp. 85–95.
5. Jean Saglio, in CFDT, 'Nouvelles relations sociales: le défi (actes du colloque)', *CFDT aujourd'hui*, No. 109, 1993, p. 24.
6. S. Milner, 'Comparative industrial relations: towards new paradigms?', *Journal of Area Studies*, No. 5, 1994, pp. 19–33.
7. A. Touraine, 'La crise du système des relations professionelles', in J.-D. Reynaud et al. (eds), *Les Systèmes de relations professionnelles*, (Paris: CNRS, 1990).
8. Crouch and Traxler, op. cit.
9. CFDT, op. cit.
10. J.-F. Amadieu, 'Labour-management co-operation and work organisation change: deficits in the French industrial relations system', in OECD, *New Directions in Work Organisation: the Industrial Relations Response*, (Paris: OECD, 1992), p. 72.
11. D. Labbé, 'La crise du syndicalisme français', *Revue de l'IRES*, No. 16, 1994, pp. 75–101.
12. Moss, op. cit.
13. G. Adam, *Le Pouvoir syndical* (Paris: Dunod, 1983); R. Soubie, 'Cause du déclin syndical', *Droit social*, No. 1, 1992, pp. 11–15.
14. G. Caire, 'Négotiations collectives en France: évolution avant et après les lois Auroux', *Revue de l'Economie Sociale*, 1992, p. 407.
15. M. Coffineau, *Les Lois Auroux, dix ans après* (Paris: La Documentation Française, 1993), p. 48.
16. Ibid.; see also R. Huiskamp, 'Collective bargaining in transition', in J. Van Ruysseveldt et al., *Comparative Industrial and Employment Relations* (London: Sage, 1995).
17. Coffineau, op. cit., p. 41.
18. J.Y. Boulin, 'Trade union modernisation in France: is there still time?', *Transfer*, No. 1, 1996, p. 139.
19. Ibid, p. 140.
20. Huiscamp, op. cit.
21. W. Sengenberger, 'Les relations professionnelles sous la pression de la concurrence et des restructurations', *Revue Internationale du Travail*, No. 131–2, 1992, p. 164.
22. Coffineau, op. cit., p. 45.
23. D. Ferrat, 'L'accord à vivre... au ralenti', *Liaisons Sociales*, No. 74, 1992, pp. 20–22.
24. A. Le Maître and R. Tchobanian, *Les Institutions représentatives du personnel dans l'entreprise: pratiques et évolutions* (Paris: La Documentation Française, 1991).
25. Y. Chotard, *Les Patrons et le patronat* (Paris: Calmann-Lévy, 1986).
26. L. Hoang-Ngoc, 'Le système néo-corporatiste français de relations professionnelles et son secteur public', *Revue de l'Economie Sociale*, 1992, pp. 459–473.

27.	R. Mouriaux and F. Subileau, 'Les grèves françaises de l'automne 1995: défense des acquis ou mouvement social?', *Modern and Contemporary France*, NS4, No. 3, 1996, pp. 307–319.
28.	EIRR, 'Employers' body debates strategy towards unions', *European Industrial Relations Review*, No. 266, 1996, pp. 5–6.
29.	Ferrat, op. cit.
30.	S. Milner, 'French trade unions and the work-sharing debate', *Contemporary Political Studies*, Vol.3, 1996, pp. 1384–1397.
31.	P.-M. Deschamps, 'La France syndicale en 1995: ni Marx, ni maître', *L'Expansion*, No. 510, 1995, pp. 154–164.
32.	Milner, 1996, op. cit.
33.	C. Lot, 'Négotiations interprofessionelles: "l'imagination au pouvoir"', *Actualité*, No. 143, 1995, pp. 44–48.

10 Women and Political Representation during the Mitterrand Presidency – or the Family Romance of the Fifth Republic

Siân Reynolds

The Fifth Republic has often been described as paternalist, with particular reference to its first president. To describe it as patriarchal suggests a different order of power relations. This paper uses the idea of 'the family romance', as applied by Lynn Hunt to the French Revolution, to re-examine the successes and failures of women politicians before, after, but especially during the Mitterrand years. Its argument is that their story reveals something of the contradictions under the surface of the left's acceptance of the Fifth Republic.

François Mitterrand, like his predecessor Valéry Giscard d'Estaing, positively went out of his way to promote women as ministers, although the percentage of women in parliament scarcely changed during either presidency. To explore this much-observed paradox, while avoiding going over too-familiar ground,[1] I would like to try reading French Republican culture in our time as an odd mixture of patriarchy and fraternity. From Hunt, I shall borrow the suggestion that 'the French [have] a kind of collective political consciousness that [is] structured by narratives of family relations'. There are obvious risks here, but the reader is invited to consider whether an essentially metaphorical approach can help reformulate some old questions. The hypothesis, as couched in family romance terms, is that the Republican ideal of fraternity – the band of brothers resisting a tyrannical father (or uncle) or a manipulative (step)-mother – creates a symbolic order in which sisters may find it particularly hard to take their place, and that this has been exposed by some aspects of the Fifth Republic.

WOMEN AS DEPUTIES[2] AND MINISTERS: THE STORY
SINCE 1945

If one were to take a long view of the situation of women in post-war
France, all the evidence would point to remarkable incremental
change. In education and the workplace, equal opportunities have
become far more available than in the past. And if 'French public
life' is broadly defined, to cover the personnel of the civil service, local
government administration, the judiciary, the welfare state and the
educational system, women seem, by and large, to be well represented
there today, as a result of gradual change. In the more narrowly
political arena, however, this pattern of steady change is not well
established.

To take a much-quoted figure, women members of the National
Assembly at the Liberation represented just 5.63 per cent of the total.
Since women had only just voted for the first time in 1945, one might

Table 10.1 Women parliamentarians as a percentage of the National
Assembly in France (actual numbers in brackets):

Fourth Republic		
October 1945	5.6	(33 of 586)
June 1946	5.1	(30 of 586)
November 1946	6.8	(42 of 618)
June 1951	3.5	(22 of 627)
January 1956	3.2	(19 of 596)
Fifth Republic		
November 1958	1.5	(9 of 586)
November 1962	1.6	(8 of 482)
March 1967	2.0	(10 of 487)
June 1968	1.8	(9 of 487)
March 1973	1.6	(8 of 490)
March 1978	3.7	(18 of 491)
June 1981	5.3	(26 of 491)
March 1986	5.9	(34 of 577)
June 1988	5.7	(33 of 577)
March 1993	6.0	(35 of 577)*

*The current percentage was the joint lowest in the European Union,
alongside Greece, in 1996 (other examples: Germany 26.6 percent; UK 9.2 per
cent)
Figures for the French Senate are lower (4.3 per cent in 1992)
(Source: J. Jenson and M. Sineau, *Mitterrand et les Françaises, un rendezvous
manqué*, Annexe 8, p. 369 and 9, p. 371.)

have expected numbers of women deputies to rise thereafter. On the contrary, if anything they fell, and in the present Assembly, elected in 1993, they still stand at a mere 6 per cent, the lowest percentage in the EU except for Greece. Instead of a rising graph, one finds a dead flat line (see Table 10.1).

The number of women ministers in government, by contrast, has made more erratic progress. There had been very few precedents, when, in the mid-1970s, Giscard appointed several women to government, notably putting Simone Veil in charge of the Health ministry. Thereafter, their number regularly hovered between about four and six during the Giscard and Mitterrand years, rising to a sudden peak of 12 (25 per cent of all ministers) in Alain Juppé's first cabinet of 1995, under Jacques Chirac's presidency, before falling back again to four (see Table 10.2).

Whatever we have here, neither pattern shows the model of gradual incremental change which one might reasonably have expected, given the social context. Politicians of the right and left may have very different kinds of rhetoric when they approach gender issues, but there has been little variation in the figures, whether right or left has been in power.

To take parliamentary representation first, the usual explanations for this are multi-factor, and will probably be familiar to the reader. They fall broadly into two groups: first, it is often argued that some form of discrimination has taken place, whether by party machines or the political milieu in general, perhaps reinforced by utterances from the press and public opinion polls: 'politics doesn't accept women'. Secondly, it is sometimes said that women have been unfamiliar with or hostile to the political arena as presently constituted, and have themselves been reluctant to enter it: 'women don't want to go into politics'. Neither of these is easy to verify or falsify, and in the absence of clear data, it has in recent years been suggested that some formal mechanism would be the only way to bring about any change (assuming such change to be desirable). The response to attempts to introduce such a mechanism have, however, been, revealing.

Pressure from parliamentary feminists was high during the early years of the Mitterrand era, and the most favoured mechanism then was a fixed percentage quota of women candidates for all elections. The Socialist majority in the Assembly passed a bill in 1982 providing for no more than 75 per cent of candidates in municipal elections to be of one sex, but the Constitutional Council (a sort of Appeal Court on legislation) vetoed it, on grounds which may be found significant. The Council found that the proposal for a quota infringed the principle of:

Table 10.2   Women ministers in France since 1936
[for this table, 'ministres' or 'ministres déléguées' have been counted as senior ministers, 'secrétaires d'état' as junior ministers]

Year	Cabinet	Number of women ministers
1936	Blum	3 junior
1946	Bidault	1 junior
1946	Blum	1 junior
1947	Schumann	1 senior
1957	Bourgès-Manoury	1 junior
1959	Debré	1 junior
1968	Pompidou	1 junior*
1968	Couve de Murville	1 junior*
1969	Chaban Delmas	1 junior*
1972	Messmer	1 junior*
1974	Messmer	1 junior*
1974	Chirac	1 senior, 5 junior
1976	Barre	1 senior, 3 junior
1977	Barre	1 senior, 5 junior
1978	Barre	2 senior, 3 junior
1981	Mauroy	4 senior, 2 junior
1983	Mauroy	3 senior, 3 junior
1984	Fabius	4 senior, 4 junior
1986	Chirac	1 senior, 3 junior
1988	Rocard	3 senior, 3 junior
1991	Rocard	3 senior, 3 junior
1991	Cresson	5 senior, 1 junior (+ prime minister)
1992	Bérégovoy	5 senior, 2 junior
1993	Balladur	3 senior
1995	Juppé	4 senior, 8 junior
1995	Juppé	1 senior, 3 junior

* = the same individual
(*Source*: J. Pascal, *Les Femmes députés de 1945 à 1988*, (Paris: chez l'auteur, 1990; Jenson and Sineau (1995) Annexe 3.)

the equality of citizens before the law, by virtue of Article 3 of the [1958] Constitution and of Article 6 of the Declaration of the Rights of Man and of the Citizen [1789]. These principles are opposed to any kind of division by category of the voters and those eligible for election.[3]

Despite a favourable vote by the people's representatives, then, the measure was opposed in the name of revolutionary universalism of 1789, a point to which we will need to return.

In the short term, while Mitterrand was president, the matter was left to political parties to apply quotas or not as they saw fit.[4] For elections held by proportional representation, there was a slightly greater tendency than in the past to promote women's candidatures, thus avoiding lists of single-sex names, but when parliamentary elections were held under the single-member system, little change took place. It was not until November 1993, with Mitterrand still in the Elysée but with the Gaullist RPR in government, that a new initiative emerged from the grass roots. This time, the campaign went beyond quotas to call for parity of representation between the sexes. A petition in *Le Monde* was signed by 288 men and 289 women (the total being 577, the same number as there are seats in the Assembly), mostly intellectuals, academics and politicians. Their argument was that men could not represent women, that attempts to leave the matter to chance, or even quotas, would always fail, and that complete parity was the only response.[5] Various mechanisms have been proposed to enable parity to be enacted: double-member constituencies; alternate candidates on lists and so forth.[6]

The parity campaign caused some stir, attracting both support and hostility, as one might expect. Perhaps on balance more signatories were on the left than the right, but in the event neither left nor right-wing parties have officially embraced the cause. It is true that Michel Rocard's list for the 1994 European elections contained equal numbers of men and women, and the issue was raised briefly during Jacques Chirac's 1995 presidential campaign (but referring back to quotas). But neither left nor right either came out strongly against parity or unequivocally for it, despite a certain amount of lip-service. Meanwhile, as before, 94 per cent of deputies in the National Assembly were men. Readiness for affirmative action was, in other words, perpetually on hold.

On the question of women ministers, the situation is very different. Visible change has taken place. Once more, though, it is not easy to analyse in partisan terms: both right and left have promoted women. Giscard d'Estaing was certainly a path-breaker in this respect, but had Mitterrand won the presidency in 1974, he would probably have done much the same, and we should now be viewing the policy historically as one introduced by the left. The new move to affirmative action is confirmed by a very brief survey of the history of women as government ministers. The first step of all was taken by the Socialist Léon Blum in 1936. The three junior ministers he appointed had no successors before the war, however, and during the period 1945–1974 there was no more than one woman in a government post, junior or senior, whoever was in power. Giscard was therefore innovating when during his seven-year presidency (1974–1981), he appointed several women, including well-known figures like Françoise Giroud. There were between four and six in office at any one time. After the 1981 elections, the Socialists sought visibly to pursue the same tactic, while increasing the proportion of senior to junior ministers: the total number hovered around six. In 1986, when the incoming prime minister Chirac failed to appoint any women in the first instance, there was an outcry, upon which he belatedly named Michèle Barzach Minister of Health, with three other women in junior posts. The return of the left after 1988 saw the number of women ministers return to about six, under Rocard and his successors. When Chirac became president in 1995, his prime minister, Juppé, caused a sensation by appointing no fewer than 12 women to government posts, mostly junior. Many of them were comparative newcomers, and when in the autumn of that year the government was cut in size, eight of the women were casualties of the reshuffle.

What this catalogue shows is that there has been a sort of muffled competition here not to seem sexist. In policy matters, the left unquestionably accomplished more progress on women's rights. But with some wobbles, the right too was concerned to show that, in matters of appointment at least, it favoured affirmative action.

What concerns us here is not policy but the mechanism by which women were made ministers, a mechanism built into the Fifth Republic from the start. De Gaulle's wish that ministerial office be separated from taking one's seat in the National Assembly was certainly not devised with women in mind. It was intended to prevent parliamentary and ministerial irresponsibility on the Fourth Republic pattern. But in practice it has enabled prime ministers, with or without prompting from the Elysée, to promote individuals with no parliamentary – and in some cases no political – background. Several prime ministers have themselves been promoted by the same mechanism (for example, Georges Pompidou, Raymond Barre). Technocrats, lawyers, outsiders in the political game, many male ministers under the Fifth Republic, have entered parliament by this high road, taking seats on their ministerial benches without (or before) being elected. The same has been true of almost all women ministers. The key point here is that not only may parliament be by-passed, so may the claims of political parties, both repositories of Republican legitimacy.

The 'king's good will and pleasure' has thus been a formidable source of patronage since 1958. The individuals concerned may or may not turn out to be competent in practice. But their appointment has in principle perturbed the normal processes of Republican democracy. In the kind of case that concerns us, affirmative action in favour of women, the model could charitably be described as promoting individuals 'pour encourager les autres', to provide role models, so to speak. But it has the disadvantage of looking illegitimate, unofficial, un-Republican. It might enable presidents to score public relations successes (the appointment of Edith Cresson in 1991) or it might backfire (Cresson again). Either way, the role-model theory does not seem over-persuasive, since it has had no impact on the number of women politicians in the Assemblies. The French example thus seems to have reached some kind of impasse, despite what have almost certainly been 'good' intentions.

THE FAMILY ROMANCE AND FRENCH REPUBLICAN THEORY

Lynn Hunt's starting point in her influential if controversial book was that the family romance (a Freudian term, but here used more loosely) conditioned cultural representations of revolutionary politics. Her chapters are headed 'The rise and fall of the good father', 'The band of brothers', 'The bad mother', etc. She depicted the revolutionaries, and in particular the regicides, as a band of brothers, killing their father, the king, for being tyrannical and – literally – patriarchal. To replace the patriarchy, a fraternity was the preferred model at first, and this subsists in the liberal theory of citizenship. The French citizen was always male, defined by blood-brotherhood in battle. Sparta and Rome provided the models, Jacques-Louis David the illustrations. Hunt's book and those by other historians of the Revolution have pointed out that the thinking of the Jacobins in particular did not so much marginalize women as provide a set of instructions for their proper role in public life. In this scenario, they were to be good wives and supportive sisters, visible non-participants, instead of the 'bad' mothers or mistresses, ruling from the alcove, of the *ancien régime*.

The family romance helps shed light on the question of promoting women ministers. In the early days, the *Canard Enchaîné* drew parallels between the Fifth Republic and the *ancien régime*, and we are all familiar with criticism of de Gaulle's régime as 'an elective monarchy'. Yet over the years, most commentators have come round to agreeing that, despite its origins, it is a widely acceptable régime to both right and left.[7] However contradictions open up when instead of looking at the legislative process and relations between president, government and parliament, one considers appointments. The scope for patronage is immense, the president in particular dispensing posts at many levels. The most exposed form of patronage is appointment of the prime minister. Murmurs of disapproval have greeted certain male appointments to the premiership over the years. But they are as nothing compared to the reactions to the appointment of Edith Cresson as France's first woman premier.

To describe this appointment in *ancien régime* terms, the revolutionary brothers regarded patriarchal tyranny as one thing, but occult and illegitimate power exercised in the boudoir as another, whether the woman behind the throne was the wedded queen or a royal favourite. The Salic Law, whereby women could not inherit the throne, was no doubt a salient factor. The absence of such a rule in Britain meant that historical examples of strong, war-waging, or long-lived queens in their own right, such as Mary, Elizabeth I, Victoria and Elizabeth II, could be part of the mental furniture of politics. But the connection in France between arms and the citizen was from the start one between arms and the man.

When Cresson was appointed, then, despite surveys indicating that she was a popular choice, political comment was couched in terms of favouritism. Although, unlike some of her predecessors, Cresson had quite wide ministerial experience, the suggestion was that she benefited from personal links to the president. The term 'la Pompadour' was actually printed in the press. A better historical parallel might be Marie Antoinette. As Lynn Hunt has pointed out, the radical press campaigned tirelessly against Louis XVI's queen in sometimes pornographic terms, to back up a more serious agenda: attacks on her political influence over the king. When, in November 1793, she was executed, one of the charges against her brought by the *Moniteur* was that she had been a 'bad mother' who overstepped the line.

As Pierre Bourdieu put it, women might be thought to 'owe to intrigue or sexual complaisance, which provide them with male protection, advantages so obviously undeserved that they inevitably appear to have been acquired by the wrong means'.[8] Much of the opposition to Cresson came from within the Socialist Party. From

Mitterrand's point of view, one of her advantages was that she was *not* a faction leader. But this was what cost her with her parliamentary colleagues. The fraternity of the brothers in the PS had indeed become fratricidal, as in 1793, but they could momentarily unite against an attempt by the father (Dieu) to impose his law, using a frail vessel to do so. Henri Emmanuelli is reported as saying to Cresson, 'You will never be legitimate'. From the opposition benches, Charles Pasqua remarked: 'She cannot succeed and her failure will discredit women for a long time' – an extraordinary remark on the face of it. A man who failed would not discredit all men. The explanation is that her method of coming to power was seen as deeply illegitimate. By the same token, the promotion, outside normal channels, of any woman was in truth similarly judged. The bad mother or manipulative mistress ran the risk of being symbolically lynched (in practice dismissed), 'pour décourager les autres'.[9]

This crack in the system enables us to see that all such appointments are really resisted by Republican tradition, even if in other cases the opposition has been muffled, perhaps because the new incumbent posed no threat (Simone Veil?) or was a 'safe pair of hands in a crisis' (Barre, Bérégovoy?). The Cresson incident ('booby-trapped' from the start, as one commentator calls it) exposed some nerve ends in the Fifth Republic.[10] There always has been and still is an allergy to the president's paternalism in the Republican tradition. When the president is a Gaullist, Republican unease may be confined to the opposition, since Gaullists accept presidential prerogatives as a matter of principle. Thus when Chirac unaccountably decided to promote as many as twelve women in 1995, murmurings were kept low: real hostility emerged only after most of the women had been dropped in a reshuffle. But when as in the test-case of Cresson, a left-wing president appointed a woman, the reaction came from his own side. What this episode tells us is that reaction to patronage in the Fifth Republic may be over-determined in some cases, but that it is potentially ready to be exposed in all its clarity when the appointee is a woman, without any reassuring features, as Cresson found to her cost. It is of course arguable that there was some straightforward old-fashioned misogyny abroad, and as we know, Cresson did herself no favours by her actions. But it was primarily the manner of promotion that irked her enemies. The patriarchy, in other words, was at its most naked and provocative in this example.

If we accept that the unease over Cresson was a symptom of wider unease over ministerial appointments, it is clear why affirmative action at the level of women parliamentarians has also been hard to accept in a Republican framework. We find a modern reworking of Republican theory in Pierre Rosanvallon's book, *Le Sacre du citoyen*. This study of universal suffrage, one of the few written in France to pay serious attention to the exclusion of women, makes the point that for citizenship to have value, there had to be a group of the excluded, without citizenship. When other exclusions fell away, that of women persisted until 1944. We may read this not too fancifully, given the importance of military service, as the brothers excluding sisters from their games: no gun, no penis, no vote.

Where Rosanvallon seems to me to begin sharing the views he sets out to analyse is, significantly, over the coming of truly universal suffrage, that is in 1944–1945. He spends no time on this event, yet his book opens with the words 'one man [sic], one vote' and goes on to state that 'if women have only been able to vote for half a century, *that seems ancient history to us now*, extraordinarily distant from us... a sort of prehistorical age, difficult to understand. Universal suffrage is now the cornerstone of any political system'.[11] This appeal for collective amnesia is telling. It proclaims that women are on the same footing as men, that they have been honorary (though over-looked) brothers all along, and certainly need no special treatment now.

There is no room here for any theory of separate representation, i.e. parity, which would counter the existing model of Republican uni-versality; indeed, Rosanvallon goes to some pains to condemn any notion of separatism. All citizens, whatever their gender, are equival-ent in Republican theory. It is therefore impossible to envisage sepa-rate histories. Yet what is the history of France before 1945 (and since, to a large extent) if not the separate history of men and women on almost every level one cares to think of? Republican individualism does not encompass the possibility that men and women may have certain rights and interests in common, as human beings, while as groups in history they may have conflicting or at any rate different interests. This is the key to the response of the Consti-tutional Council to the question of quotas.

We can agree with Rosanvallon that the Republic in France had a particular mental map of politics, but that map has been and remains incomplete – not just because it excluded women, as he recognizes, but also, as he does not recognize, because the Republic embodied the particular interests of men. As Anne Phillips points out, 'the idea that citizens must leave their bodies – hence their selves – behind when they enter the public arena has been challenged by feminists who argue that there is no gender-neutral individual'.[12] The problem with Republican theory is not just that it does not recognize the separate interests of women, but that it has for so long assumed that the interests of men were universally applicable. The citizen was constructed as male the first time round and gender-neutral the second – or, to put it in family romance terms, the band of brothers admitted their sisters in the end, but only if they were prepared to wear shorts and not cry when they fell over – like George in the Famous Five. The question was deemed resolved once and for all in 1945, leaving the period before that as unreal, 'distant'. There was no call for quotas, since at a stroke girls had become boys.

CONCLUSION

This paper might seem to be about women, but it is in part about a wider issue. It has argued that the Republican theory inherited from the Revolution is basically incompatible with certain aspects of the Fifth Republic, a regime with (as we all know) a strongly Bonapartist flavour. Bonapartism is perfectly compatible with the promotion of favoured individuals (even women) provided that some claim for merit can be made. Republicanism prefers the electoral principle. The interest of the case of the women ministers is that a mechanism devised by de Gaulle and his advisers to by-pass parliament was turned to 'politically correct' uses by more than one of his successors, inspiring some muffled opposition. Mitterrand was the 'left-wing', 'Republican' president, the one who had most fiercely rejected the Fifth Republic at its start, so it is a fitting paradox that he was most violently criticized by his own side over the Cresson appointment, in other words over his adoption of Gaullist (read Bonapartist, read patriarchal) practices. It had happened before, over Laurent Fabius, but in a far more muted manner. The outcry over Cresson can indeed be seen as a return of the repressed. It was particularly illegitimate to promote her, because she seemed to embody both the image of the occult power of the woman over the ageing patriarch – and his manipulation of her to achieve his ends.

All this being so, it is not hard to explain the reaction to quotas from the Constitutional Council, and the later reluctance to go far down this road. The Council (and many parliamentarians of left and right) opposed affirmative action to increase the numbers of women in

Parliament because the admission of women to voting rights in 1945 was deemed simply to have wiped out the past, allowing sisters to become brothers under universal starting orders. Any special treatment would be suspect and illegitimate.

We may conclude as follows. Promoting individual women can be seen as the wrong answer to the right question, opening up all kinds of reflexes repressed within the cultural representation French people have of the Republic. On the other hand, it may be legitimate to expose Republican theory to the questioning which Rosanvallon and others do not wish to consider: namely that citizenship may indeed have a gendered content; that the interests of men and women may not always be identical, and that the rules, ideas, culture and imagery of the Republic have always been those of its male citizens. What has been absent from the discussion (apart from in feminist circles, where this is commonly debated, of course) is the maleness rather than limpid neutrality of the 'universalism' of the French Republic. It is significant that the matters under discussion in this paper are very frequently evoked under the heading 'women', but are not generally mentioned in numerous post-mortems on 'the Mitterrand presidency'.

NOTES

1. There is now a large literature on the subject. See J. Jenson and M. Sineau, *Mitterrand et les Françaises, un rendez-vous manqué* (Paris: Sciences Po, 1995); E. Viennot (ed)., *La Démocratie 'à la française' ou les femmes indésirables* (Paris: CEDREF, 1996); special issue of *Modern and Contemporary France*, Vol. NS3, No. 2, 1995, which all contain bibliographies. For the original application of the expression, see Lynn Hunt, *The Family Romance of the French Revolution* (London: Routledge, 1992).
2. Members of the National Assembly are known as *députés/députées*. The anglicized form will be used here.
3. Dates added. See D. Loschak, 'Les hommes politiques, les "sages" et les femmes', *Droit Social*, No. 2, 1983, p. 131, and Jenson and Sineau, op. cit., pp. 306–311.
4. In the latest development, the Socialist Party has decided to observe a quota of one-third for the 1998 parliamentary elections (8 February 1997), while the RPR and UDF are reported to be considering it, *Le Point*, 8 March 1997.

5. The petition was signed by (among others) Pierre Bourdieu, Lucie Aubrac, Michel Piccoli, Marina Vlady, Dominique Voynet, etc.
6. The arguments for parity were outlined in F. Gaspard et al., *Au pouvoir, citoyennes: Liberté, Egalité, Parité* (Paris: Seuil, 1992).
7. See S. Berstein and O. Rudelle (eds), *Le Modèle républicain* (Paris: PUF, 1992).
8. Quoted in Jenson and Sineau, op. cit., p. 334.
9. The Cresson case is fully discussed by Mariette Sineau in her article 'Edith Cresson à Matignon', *Actes du colloque: L'engagement politique* (CEVIPOF, 1994), and also in Jenson and Sineau, op. cit., pp. 331 ff.
10. E. Schemla, *Edith Cresson, la femme piégée* (Paris: Flammarion, 1993).
11. P. Rosanvallon, *Le Sacre du citoyen: histoire du suffrage universel en France* (Paris: Gallilmard, 1992) p. 9.
12. A. Phillips, *Engendering Democracy* (Cambridge: Polity, 1991), Conclusion.

11 The Failure of Anti-Racist Movements in France, 1981–1995

Peter Fysh

At the start of Mitterrand's first septennate, anti-Jewish and anti-Arab racism were rife, with four dead in the street in front of the synagogue in the Rue Copernic the previous October and the outgoing government's dogged attempts to force the return 'home' of up to half a million Algerians.[1] But there was also a vibrant anti-racism, involving sit-ins and hunger-strikes to gain residence and work permits and the right to family reunion, hostel rent strikes and industrial strikes to win better wages and conditions. These forms of struggle characteristic of a 'first generation' of unskilled single male workers[2] would persist during the 1980s and 1990s with the carworkers' strikes of 1982–1984 and the arrival of new waves of unskilled workers from countries which hitherto had not exported labour to France in great numbers. Practical support for such campaigns was available from members of the host community, grouped in organizations like the Ligue des Droits de l'Homme, which offered legal advice and representation, lobbied national and local government in support of individual cases or to seek changes in the law or administrative practice, exposed and prosecuted racist crimes, pursued and publicized the activities of Nazi sects. But these endeavours generally occurred at local level without affecting the national political climate. When such struggles did acquire political overtones, the foreign workers immediately exposed themselves to deportation, a fate which befell hundreds of hostel-dwellers on rent strike during 1975–1980.

The turn of the decade witnessed also, however, the blossoming of a new range of cultural and community organizations in the densely populated urban peripheries, covering sport, leisure, educational and cultural activities as well as attempts to gain a voice for minorities in the media.[3] The founders of these assocations, largely of Maghrebi origin, largely born in France, were with varying degrees of awareness the potential leaders of a generation of young immigrant-origin

French citizens – the *beurs* – whose indignation at the police racism and relative social deprivation of which they were victims[4] stimulated repeated attempts from 1983 to 1990 to form a unified national movement which could put the issues that concerned them on to the national political agenda. During the first half of the decade, marked by marches, anti-racist concerts, campaigns in schools and a successful battle against reform of the nationality code, this new anti-racism appeared confident and politically on the offensive. From 1988, however, anti-racists were driven back on to the defensive, abandoning national for local arenas, capitulating to assimilationist discourse around the headscarf issue (see below), forced to accept reform of the nationality code and a bundle of new restrictions on freedom of movement and rights of entry and residence. The right to vote for foreigners, even at local level, was never won.

Clearly, these defeats are partly explained by the parallel rise of the Front National and its pushing the centre of gravity of French politics to the right.[5] But what also needs to be explained is the mirror image of that process: the failure of anti-racists in the Mitterrand era to build a movement which could effectively challenge the FN's progress, or indeed any kind of anti-FN movement, until 1992. In this chapter it will be argued that this failure was three-fold: failure of the '*beur* generation' to produce an autonomous national anti-racist movement; the fact that *beur* and mainstream French left forces frequently neutralized rather than co-ordinated their efforts; and their joint failure to impose a clear, unambiguous anti-racist defence of the right to be different.

THE FAILURE OF BEUR UNITY

Between Mitterrand and the *beurs* there was no honeymoon; at best an uneasy courtship. *Beur* protests at a wave of deportations of juvenile delinquents were put on the national agenda right in the middle of the presidential election, when Christian Delorme's cleverly organised three-man hunger-strike in his native Lyons harrassed Prime Minister Barre into agreeing to suspend expulsions for three months, a moratorium subsequently made permanent by the incoming government.[6] But another violent conflict between *beurs* and police broke out in Lyons in July-August 1981, even before the Socialists had had time to ease family reunions, suspend aided repatriation, permit foreigners to form their own associations and organize an amnesty which eventually covered 130,000 undeclared foreign workers. By 1983 the favourable reception given to these measures was neutralized by government leaders' groundless claims that Islamic militants were fomenting strikes in the motor industry,[7] another crisis between police and youths in Lyons and a new rash of racist attacks all over France.[8] Adding insult to injury, the bombastic tones of Le Pen began to be heard over the airwaves for the first time, following his party's successes in that year's local government elections.

In these circumstances, the autumn 'March for Equality and against Racism' was a success of enormous symbolic importance. The ten young Maghrebis who set off from Marseilles in October were greeted in Paris in December by a solidarity demonstration of 60–100,000 people and an audience with the President of the Republic – a moving contrast to the unbridled onslaught on men, women and children demonstrating for Algerian independence which disfigured Paris in 1961. Nevertheless, Mitterrand did not keep his promise to the marchers to introduce a law punishing racial violence more severely, and the single tangible result of the interview, the later introduction of a ten-year joint work and residency permit, was of little relevance to the *beurs*, most of whom had French nationality.[9]

Furthermore, the planning and execution of the march had revealed serious differences concerning its strategic orientation. Was it against the FN? Did it concern the specific grievances of the *beurs* regarding the police and the justice system? Or should it be the beginning of a social movement for equal rights carried on by the mainstream left, not just the Maghreb community? Linked to this was the question of autonomy. If mainstream associations or parties – in this case Christians and pacifists – were allowed to join the march and the support committees, was there not a danger that they would attempt to take over, imposing their own slogans, and taking credit for whatever the march managed to achieve?[10] Papered over during the march, these differences were hotly debated at a fractious national convention of *beur*-led community associations held in Lyons in June 1984. Those who warned against the manipulative and self-interested tendencies of the French left were accused of proposing a purely 'ethnic' strategy, with little resonance for the thousands of *beurs* whose cultural references were mostly French, condemning the 'community' to continued marginality and discrimination. On the other hand, those who argued that the *beurs* should take their place in a broader social movement were caricatured as yielding to the assimilationist Republican tradition which rejects ethnic communities as illegitimate.[11] With the Parisian delegates taking a broadly multiculturalist approach and the Lyons organizers defending beur autonomy, others admitted ruefully that the divisions ran through 'each collective, each association, even each person present'.[12] The conference's dispersal without result was later seen by two very different participants as a missed opportunity: the movement was not mature or self-confident enough to adopt a strategy of alliance with the left, of which *beur* autonomy could have been the precondition, not the negation.

In this unpromising context a new national initiative, Convergences '84, had five columns of youngsters of diverse origins, representative of the African, Asian, Caribbean, Portuguese and French communities, converge on Paris by moped from five different cities. They were met in December by a solidarity march and a carnival with a multicultural theme, challenging both assimilationist French orthodoxy and the 'isolationist' temptation of the minority communities. The event was attended by some 30,000 people – fewer than in 1983, but still an important achievement in the year in which the FN sent ten deputies to the European Parliament. Once again, however, behind the scenes there had been discord. The idea of Convergences was that *all* communities should come together to tackle issues of inequality and discrimination. Yet some of the mopedders were highly critical of the European, middle-class, left-dominated reception committees which in many towns were unwilling to examine their own shortcomings and had failed to make contact with peripheral working-class Arab youth, who were either absent from the receptions or reduced to the role of silent spectators. Although the Convergences initiator, Farida Belghoul, vented her spleen on this issue in front of the crowd at the Place de la République, some of the mopedders who had visited other towns hastened to publicize their disagreements with Belghoul's 'autonomist' position.[14]

Despite two dress rehearsals attracting a sizeable audience, a unified and autonomous *beur* movement open to working with the mainstream left had failed to appear on cue. Efforts to repair the damage would continue, but there were to be few second chances, since at national level centre-stage would be occupied for the next few years by two new organizations, each in different ways hostile to the autonomous project.

One of these, France Plus, symbolized in its own discourse and activities the schizophrenia of *beur* political mobilization, for it made real contributions to community affirmation and mobilization while insisting at the same time that the best way to defend oneself against racism was to avoid behaviour drawing attention to differences from the French 'norm'. It marched for equality of rights in 1985 and campaigned on nationality law and for voter registration in 1986–1987, trying hard to bring together the descendants of the mutually hostile camps of Algerians who took opposite sides in the war of liberation.[15] But France Plus more or less ignored the FN, concentrating instead on persuading foreigners to apply for naturalization and the *beurs* to vote and run for election. In the 1989 city council elections, with opinion polls in hand, it persuaded local politicians of left and right to offer young Maghrebis places on their lists of candidates in order to improve their appeal to sizeable local immigrant-origin electorates.[16]

Critics of France Plus have not focused on the electoral strategy as such, for those favouring a more radical autonomous *beur* self-affirmation have also long urged electoral registration and full use of civic rights,[17] but rather on its hypocritical use as a tool of upward social mobility by middle-class Maghrebis insisting that 'communities don't exist' (as France Plus leader Arezki Dahmani told *Le Monde*)[18] while getting themselves elected on the basis of an 'ethnic vote' and an ethnic mobilization strategy.[19] Worse still, France Plus was not accepted as a truly autonomous vehicle of community concerns, of whatever social class, since it was widely assumed to be in origin a tool of the Socialist Party[20] – even, according to some, a tool of one faction of Socialists in their battle with another credited with using SOS Racisme for the same purpose.[21] The association's audience in the suburbs was so narrow[22] that its 500 or so candidates, once elected, were often no more than captive tokens of the political correctness of their patrons, with no power to influence policy.[23] These weaknesses likewise limit the association's capacity to fulfil what would seem to be its real vocation – to act as a partner for state and local governments in their variously defined battles to manage social conflict and 'integrate' rebellious suburban youth.[24] Nonetheless, the political patrons of France Plus have ensured that the association has a handsome income comprised almost entirely of public subsidies, as well as good media attention at crucial moments such as during the 1985 march, the 1986–1987 nationality campaign and again during the headscarf 'debate' in 1989, when the more radical *beur* associations were trying desperately to get an audience.

THE FAILURE OF INTER-COMMUNITY CO-ORDINATION: SOS RACISME AND THE BLOCKING OF *BEUR* AUTONOMY

Founded in 1984–1985, SOS Racisme has been variously represented as the mass moral outrage of a multiracial generation at the unfair treatment reserved for black and Arab 'pals', as a stage in the personal career strategy of its behind-the-scenes leader Julien Dray, and as the machination of a group of backroom staff at the Elysée.[25] All of these versions are consistent with SOS's development until 1988, although its character changed somewhat thereafter. At first, like Convergences '84, it was the vehicle of a multiculturalist vision of France as a melting-pot, symbolized by the ubiquitous badge with its catchy message, 'Hands off my pal', and realized in a series of great multicultural rock concerts; strategy was based on the belief that the most effective way of convincing someone that an idea is just is for a famous celebrity to endorse it on television. For a programme the association appeared to have no more than the urgent desire to record and publicize all racist attacks. The vaguely defined target audience, 'people, not big-wigs, the schools, the campuses, young people ...' responded in their thousands to the obvious sincerity and simple eloquence of the telegenic SOS president, Harlem Désir, whose regular debates with 16–19 year-old school children in *lycées* were conveniently facilitated by Socialist officials.[26] In short, SOS was a mass organization of a new type, unthinkable before the audio-visual age, whose members were urged to organize locally but only as transmission belts for the latest national initiative. Dray's disillusionment with a decade of activism in Trotskyist and student politics had led him to conceive a structure sufficiently loose to obviate the eternal battles to 'take over the apparatus' by rival sects, and in which communication with the membership by television was ideal, for it allowed everyone to 'participate' without having to go to meetings![27] Lavishly financed by the Ministry of Culture and Socialist-controlled trade unions, SOS fitted perfectly the needs of Mitterrand's campaign for re-election, its themes and slogans massaged by his communications experts to create a climate which the president adroitly exploited during the 1986–1988 'cohabitation' to pose as the friendly uncle, protector of youth and minorities. The association came to play a critical role in the massive mobilization of school students against the 1986 Devaquet bill to extend selectivism in higher education. This episode was in turn one of the keys to the Mitterrand era, helping to ruin Chirac's chances in the 1988 presidential election.

Dray failed, however, in his attempt to persuade *beur* associations to join a kind of federation under SOS hegemony,[28] for they mistrusted what they regarded as a vehicle of the mainstream left created by inexperienced people who had little contact with or knowledge of the existing *beur* movement.[29] Those few *beurs* who did join the association in the early days soon left, unable to accept either the prominence of the Union of Jewish students, which they regarded as Zionist, or Dray's peremptory manner of dealing with critical voices in the 'fake' national bureau.[30] They were especially infuriated by SOS's habit of responding to racial violence by 'parachuting' locally unknown activists into localities for photo-opportunities, which gave an exaggerated impression of SOS implantation.[31] The disruptive impact of SOS on the anti-racist movement and its lionization by the media were amply demonstrated at the end of 1985, when it unilaterally announced the 'third march against racism', this time on scooters, from Bordeaux to Paris. *Beur* anger at this attempted takeover was so intense that a rival march was set up by a collective of *beur* associations which in turn split into rival factions after only four days, when the recently formed France Plus was accused of trying to impose its own assimilationist vision by reducing the march to a simple campaign of electoral registration. The majority continued the march, baptised Divergence '85, on a radical autonomist platform more or less ignored by the media. The polemics arising from this double split necessarily undermined the efforts of the support committees, both *en route* and on the separate arrival dates in Paris, when neither contingent attracted many more more than 10,000 supporters.[32]

The SOS media bulldozer had thus contributed to blocking the emergence of a radical but tentative and divided national *beur* movement. Nor was it particularly useful in developing a serious campaign against the FN. The media strategy required anodyne activities with the potential to mobilize more or less unthinking assent among the passive television audience. A call to demonstrate against an FN meeting or an attempt to dispute territory on the streets with its paper sellers obviously did not fit this prescription; a campaign against *apartheid* was much more acceptable, though hardly urgent since this theme had been well worked over for many years by the Communist Party and the MRAP (Mouvement contre le Racisme et pour l'Amitié entre les Peuples). The association produced a book which, instead of stressing themes of racial and social exclusion, recounted in upbeat style its collaboration with members of the

Socialist business elite in developing job and entrepreneurial opportunities for the occasional black or *beur* success story.[33] In an hour-long television interview in August 1987, Désir told his audience that if they really wanted to fight racism it was no use just shouting 'Le Pen, Le Pen!', but much better to set about repairing the lifts in the seedy tower blocks which were its breeding grounds.[34] Slowly but surely the association and its claimed 17,000 active members were evolving from an 'anti-racist force' into what *Le Monde* called a 'movement for equality and integration'.[35] The 1988 conference adopted a programme of six demands covering nationality, rights of entry, the right to vote, an independent police authority, housing and schools and simply submitted them to the government, rather than contemplate a militant campaign for their implementation. Explaining that they were increasingly being asked to give legal advice, find housing, organise children's holidays, Désir commented with satisfaction on the association's role at local level as 'mediator' between the people and the authorities.[36] Paradoxically, SOS Racisme had evolved into a decentralized network of community associations sucked into a role of conflict management paralleling that played by many *beur* associations, which had been among its sharpest critics.

Meanwhile, among the *beur* associations which had stood apart from both SOS and France Plus, the desire to create an autonomous national immigrant-based movement was still alive but carried by activists with different strategies – *Texture*, of Lille, favouring a movement open to all immigrant-origin communities, while the JALB (Young Arabs of Lyons and its Suburbs) favoured a more restrictive 'Young Arab' self-identification. After four planning meetings during 1986–1987, a new convention took place in May 1988, attended by delegates from 130 associations from all parts of the country and by representatives of the older generation of activists as well as the *beur* generation. Debates were less passionate and more consensual than in 1984, and agreement was reached on the creation of a new national peak organization: 'Fertile Memory action for a new citizenship'. The title expressed a protest at what many saw as the artificial, media-created barrier between a troublesome 'first generation' of immigrants, good only for kicking out once industry no longer needed them, and an 'assimilable' second generation which had grown up in France.[37] The concept of a new citizenship referred to the movement's demand that political rights should not be restricted only to those able (or willing) to take on French nationality. After the founding conference voted overwhelmingly in favour of addressing the national political arena, the Spring 1989 local elections revealed divergent strategies at work, affiliated associations in some areas willing to negotiate lists of candidates with the left and the Greens, while elsewhere a more strictly autonomous strategy was adopted: commenting from the sidelines or organizing meetings at which all the main candidates were invited to answer questions about their attitude to immigration-related issues. Fertile Memory never managed to develop into a structure able to carry a nationally agreed discourse or strategy independently of the sum of its parts, a failing partly attributed to the leadership's neglect of mundane organizational and financial matters in favour of the intense debates of the period 1989–1990 around issues such as the headscarf affair, the bicentenary of the French Revolution and French participation in the war to liberate the Kuwaiti oilfields, during which it gradually disintegrated.[38]

THE LEFT, TRYING TO REPAIR THE DAMAGE...

The Socialist leaders' moves to the right on immigration questions during the 1980s resulted in a gradual rupture with SOS Racisme, for which Mitterrand had no further use after his re-election in 1988 in the light of a new strategy of building a coalition on his right.[39] When he said on television in December 1989 that the number of immigrants in France had now passed the infamous 'threshold of tolerance', many SOS members were said to be 'traumatized'.[40] But the 1988 presidential elections were a watershed in another sense. Le Pen's 14 per cent score alerted many grassroots leftists to the feeble impact of the moralistic anti-racism propounded by SOS and to the realization that FN successes in 1983–1986 represented more than just a mood of frustrated protest around which no solid organization could be built. This new context gave initiatives by two small Trotskyist currents a growing audience.[41] The first was developed by a tiny faction called Convergence Socialiste, led by a former student leader, Jean-Christophe Cambadélis, which had recently broken away from the Parti Communiste Internationaliste to join the PS. In June 1987, Cambadélis launched the 'Manifesto of the 122' which called for the left to mount an anti-racist campaign targeted at the FN in a way which SOS never was. After a period spent seeking endorsement from a range of political and media personalities during 1987–1988, the group launched an appeal to French mayors in June 1990, calling on them to use all possible means to deny Le Pen and the FN the use of municipal halls for meetings, a practice which soon became quite widespread. A 'National Convention of the Manifesto' brought together 200 delegates in June 1991, followed in the autumn by a well-organized media re-launch of the Manifesto itself and a 3,000-strong meeting at the Mutualité on 27 November. At a weekend conference ten days later, a wide range of associations met to share anti-FN ideas and strategies and endorse the Manifesto group's plan for a permanent co-ordinating structure. Autumn 1991 also saw the parallel launch of a separate text, the 'Appeal of the 250', the brain-child of the Ligue Communiste Révolutionnaire but piloted on the intellectual and showbiz circuit by the radical freelance writer close to the Ligue, Gilles Perrault. Both initiatives played important roles in bringing several tens of thousands of demonstrators on to the Paris streets against the extreme right on 25 January 1992, a feat which would be repeated on a smaller scale in February 1993, after a year during which the 'Appeal' transformed itself into a permanent structure, Ras l'Front, ('Fed up with the Front') with a monthly paper of the same name. As well as providing a national focus, the new structures brought local strategies and successes to the attention of a wider audience. These were at their height during the regional election campaign in early 1992, when prospective FN councillors were targeted and asked to explain themselves, while FN meetings in the provinces were systematically opposed with counter-demonstrations or even pickets, which frequently drew larger numbers than those addressed by Le Pen himself.[42] But this first real mobilization of anti-FN forces since its breakthrough in 1983 (according to *Le Monde*) was constrained by weaknesses which help to explain why Le Pen's forward march through French institutions was at best delayed but certainly not halted. First, there was the limited spread of the two umbrella organizations. Cambadélis claimed that the 'co-ordination' arising from the Manifesto's 1991 conference covered only 95 associations (some of which were parallel national organizations like the MRAP and the LICRA, the Ligue Internationale contre le Racisme et l'Antisémitisme), concentrated, according to the Manifesto's own report, in a mere 30 departments.[43] For its part, *Ras l'Front* for the first three months of 1993 gives contact addresses for 35 local groups, nearly half of them in the Paris region. Even added together, the two structures look feeble compared to the strength of the FN itself. Second, the existence of two different anti-FN structures is evidence of a certain organizational rivalry, even if they avoid criticizing each other and prefer to speak of their cumulative impact as a source of strength. The Manifesto in particular has from the beginning linked the fight against the FN to the task of asserting its own leadership on the left fringe of the PS. From 1987 to the second half of 1991, Manifesto messages were circulated in the *Lettre Hebdo*, the weekly information bulletin of Convergence Socialiste, under the masthead, 'Strengthen the left in the Socialist Party', reflecting the founders' conviction that the only way to be rid of the FN was through the ballot-box and that this in turn required the 'renovation' of the PS, a process for which the Manifesto had its own particular recipes. Thirdly, the founders and inner leaderships of the two anti-FN 'fronts' operate with distinct theoretical and ideological references which appeal to different 'sensibilities' within the French left, the Manifesto backing the government's war on Iraq, for example, and endorsing the Maastricht Treaty, while *Ras l'Front* and its audience took the respective opposite views. More significantly, *Ras l'Front*'s prominent features on issues like the Holocaust or the Nazi attitude to women and the family explicitly stress the link between the FN and the fascism of the 1930s, while the Manifesto downplays it, in obedience to its philosophical mentor, Pierre-André Taguieff, who has attacked this 'commemorative' anti-racism as hindering a proper analysis of the Le Pen phenomenon.[44] Manifesto leaders have linked Taguieff's preferred description of the FN as 'national populist' to re-emergent nationalism in central and eastern Europe, frequently lacing their analyses of the French FN with references to Jaruzelsky, Zhirinovsky or the Balkan imbroglio; however impeccably internationalist, this is a strategy in which the general obscures the particular and immediate, necessarily limiting the Manifesto audience among the *beurs*, for whom the theatres of 'ethnic cleansing' are Vénissieux and Sartrouville as much as they are Vukovar or Sarajevo.

...BUT SURRENDERING THE BATTLE OF IDEAS

While on one level the failure of anti-racism in the Mitterrand era can be accounted for by fractured organization or opportunist manipulation of the resources needed to oppose the FN or exert pressure on the levers of power, on another level the failure has been ideological. On several occasions during the Mitterrand era when populations of Maghreb origin or Islamic religion were isolated and stigmatized, anti-racist organizations retreated from their previous defence of the stigmatized groups, the inadequacy of their theoretical foundations resulting in a collapse of militancy as the political environment became more hostile. Despite the tentative assertion of community identity carried by the *beur* associations and the marches of 1983–1984, there has been no explicit break with the lay Republican tradition which claims that France has successfully integrated generations of immigrants by denying community attachments, treating citizens only as interchangeable individuals.

In 1986–1987, France Plus campaigned against government plans to abolish automatic citizenship at eighteen for French-born Maghrebis, a reform it saw as carrying 'enormous dangers of marginalization for foreign youth',[45] but in 1993, having taken on the role of pressure-group for the integration of 'good' immigrants, it accepted both nationality reform and increased police surveillance powers on the grounds that only potential wrongdoers could object to constant identity checks.[46] In autumn 1989, three schoolgirls wearing the traditional Muslim headscarf were stigmatized as enemies of French identity in a vast media campaign, joined by France Plus as well as by the Communist *Humanité* and the middle-class left *Nouvel Observateur*, but denounced by MRAP and SOS Racisme.[47] In 1994, when the headscarf was again made an object of suspicion and rejection on the instructions of the Education Minister, SOS joined the anti-scarf coalition, demanding that it be banned along with other religious signs like the crucifix and yarmulka because of the growth of Islamic fundamentalism in the suburbs.[48] In truth, both positions were compatible with SOS's vague melting-pot vision of the non-racist society in which all cultures are equally valid but the melting-pot eventually succeeds in obliterating differences. Nor did the Ligue Communiste, inspirers of Ras l'Front, see the headscarf affair as an occasion for springing to the defence of a stigmatized minority, their rather one-dimensional Marxism leading them to avoid seeming to endorse a 'communitarian' practice, itself a potential brake on class mobilization.

In the winter of 1990–1991, constant press speculation about the likely terrorist activity of Maghreb-origin residents in France during the war against Iraq sparked off a run on gun-shops in various southern cities. Even the socio-professional elite among French citizens of Arab origin had a new sense of community thrust upon them as the true depth of their 'integration' was systematically called into question,[49] while there were massive panic departures of Tunisian building and agricultural workers from the South-East and Corsica.[50] With many *beur* associations choosing resigned silence rather than appear to support Saddam Hussein, butcher of the Kurds, France Plus and the Manifesto applauded the war effort. SOS's timid oposition to the war on humanitarian grounds triggered resignations and public condemnations by members of the Parisian intellectual set who had been among its first sponsors in 1985.[51]

But it is the Manifesto against the FN which provides the most striking example of the hazardousness of attempting to run an anti-racist movement on the abstract basis of equality of all citizens before the law; asked whether 'community' associations had been systematically invited to its 1991 co-ordinating conference, the group's spokesman justified the fact that no such initiative had been taken by a lengthy statement of the orthodox Republican rejection of communities. The Manifesto is influenced by the FN's pretence that it is *cultural*, not racial difference which makes it impossible to assimilate Maghreb-origin immigrants into French society; FN ideologues try to deflect accusations of racism by defending the equal validity of all cultures and even the need to protect and nurture them by guarding against unnecessary mixing and dilution. The Manifesto leaders are far from taken in by this 'non-racist' justification of repatriation and the FN doctrine of 'national preference', treating it for what it is: a smokescreen which hides the authentically racist intentions of the FN. But, following their mentor, Taguieff, they conclude that, since the FN defends (however hypocritically) the right to be different, it would be a mistake for anti-racists to do the same, since this would strengthen the FN's position. This looks like a rather specious justification for a rejection of difference rooted in left-Republican discourse since long before Le Pen came on the scene. This opinion can be advanced all the more confidently in view of the fact that Taguieff has taken a diametrically opposed position on a different theme, arguing that anti-racists should *not* 'abandon' to Le Pen the defence of national sentiment and the national community.

Structural division and personal rivalries in the French anti-racist movement are serious enough; in addition, its lamentable theoretical confusion is displayed by the plethora of conflicting communication strategies: rejection of difference, because Muslim fundamentalists support it; rejection of difference, because Le Pen supports it; defence of the nation, also because Le Pen supports it. Until the mainstream left and the *beurs* can sink their differences and unite around a simple commitment to defend communites under attack, we can expect anti-racism in France to go from defeat to defeat.

NOTES

1. P. Weil, *La France et ses étrangers* (Paris: Gallimard-Folio, 1995), pp. 180–181; 206–209.
2. M. Miller, *Foreign Workers in Western Europe, an Emerging Political Force* (New York: Praeger, 1981).
3. F. Gaspard and C. Servan-Schreiber, *La Fin des immigrés* (Paris: Seuil, 1985), pp. 192–197; R. David, 'Nouvelles Cultures, nouveaux droits', *Informations Sociales*, No. 14, October – November 1991, pp. 68–77; J. Cesari, 'Les leaders associatifs issus de l'immigration maghrébine: intermédiaires ou clientle?', *Horizons maghrébins*, Nos. 20–21, 1993, pp. 80–95.
4. D. Lapeyronnie, 'Assimilation, mobilisation et action collective chez les jeunes de la seconde génération de l'immigration maghrébine', *Revue Française de Sociologie*, No. 28, 1987, pp. 287–318.
5. P. Fysh, 'Government Policy and the Challenge of the National Front: the first twelve months', *Modern and Contemporary France*, No. 31, October 1987, pp. 9–19; C. T. Husbands, 'The mainstream right and the politics of immigration in France: major developments in the 1980s', *Ethnic and Racial Studies*, Vol. 14, No. 2, April 1991, pp. 170–198.
6. C. Delorme, *Par Amour et par colère*, (Paris: Le Centurion, 1985), pp. 71–86; Weil, op. cit, pp. 207–209.
7. R. Mouriaux and C. Wihtol de Wenden, 'Syndicalisme français et islam', in R. Leveau and G. Kepel (eds), *Les Musulmans dans la société française* (Paris: FNSP, 1988) pp. 39–64.
8. S. Bouamama, *Dix ans de marche des beurs, chronique d'un mouvement avorté*, (Paris: Epi-Desclée de Brouwer, 1994).
9. Bouamama, op. cit., p. 67; Weil, op. cit., pp. 278–280.
10. Bouamama, op. cit., pp. 56–61; A. Jazouli, *Les Années banlieues* (Paris: Seuil, 1992), pp. 56–59.
11. Bouamama, op. cit., p. 96; Jazouli, op. cit., pp. 85–87.
12. Jazouli, op. cit., p. 87.
13. Jazouli, op. cit., pp. 80–81; Bouamama, op. cit., p. 96.
14. Bouamama, op. cit., pp. 98–111; Jazouli, op. cit., pp. 88–94.
15. *Le Monde*, 25 May 1987.
16. M. Poinsot, 'Competition for political legitimacy at local and national level among young North Africans in France', *New Community*, Nos. 20–21, October 1993, pp. 79–92.
17. Jazouli, op. cit., p. 48; Bouamama, op. cit., p. 206; Poinsot, op. cit., p. 86.
18. *Le Monde*, 8 February 1991.
19. Bouamama, op. cit., p. 127; V. Geisser, 'Les élites politiques issues de l'immigration maghrébine: l'impossible médiation', *Migrations Société*, Vol. 4, Nos. 22–23, 1992, pp. 128–138.
20. Jazouli, op. cit., p. 106.
21. Bouamama, op. cit, p. 126; Poinsot, op. cit., p. 88.
22. Jazouli, op. cit., p. 107.

23. Geisser, op. cit., p. 135; Bouamama, op. cit., p. 208.
24. J. Cesari, 'Les leaders associatifs issus de l'immigration maghrébine: intermédiaires ou clientèle?', *Horizons maghrébins*, Nos. 20–21, 1993, pp. 80–95; O. Roy, 'Islam in France: Religion, Ethnic Community or Social Ghetto?', in B. Lewis and D. Schnapper (eds), *Muslims in Europe* (London: Pinter, 1994), pp. 54–66; R. Leveau, 'Les Associations Ethniques en France', in B. Falga et al., *Au Miroir de l'Autre, de l'immigration à l'intégration en France et en Allemagne* (Paris: Cerf, 1994), pp. 291–300.
25. H. Désir, *Touche pas à mon pote* (Paris: Grasset, 1985); S. Malik, *Histoire Secrète de SOS Racisme* (Paris: Albin Michel, 1990); Poinsot, op. cit, p. 88.
26. Désir, op. cit., pp. 26–30.
27. J. Dray, *SOS génération*, (Paris: Ramsay, 1987), p. 205.
28. Malik, op. cit., p. 30.
29. Désir, op. cit., p. 27.
30. Malik, op. cit., p. 58; pp. 71–72; Bouamama, op. cit., p. 120; Jazouli, op. cit., pp. 103–104.
31. Malik, op. cit., pp. 68–69, 84; Poinsot, op. cit., p. 83.
32. Bouamama, op. cit., pp. 130–143.
33. Désir, op. cit.
34. *Le Monde*, 18 June 1988.
35. *Le Monde*, 5 April 1988.
36. *Le Monde*, 18 June 1988.
37. Bouamama, op. cit., pp. 83–85.
38. Bouamama, op. cit., pp. 212–219; Poinsot, op. cit., p. 86.
39. A. Hargreaves, *Immigration, 'Race' and Ethnicity in Contemporary France* (London: Routledge, 1995), p. 184; J.E. Vichniac, 'French Socialists and *Droit à la Différence*, a changing dynamic', in *French Politics and Society*, Vol. 9, No. 1, Winter 1991. pp 40–56.
40. *Le Monde*, 9 January 1990.
41. This account of the Manifesto is based on interviews conducted in April 1996 with Eric Osmond, the Manifesto's spokesperson. The account of Ras l'Front draws on an April 1996 interview with Christian Picquet of the Ligue Communiste Révolutionnaire. I am grateful to Véronique Lambert of SOS Racisme and Arezki Dahmani of France Plus for interviews conducted in April 1995. Jim Wolfreys of King's College, London, participated in the conversations; I am grateful to him for tape-recordings covering 15 and 17 April 1996, when I was unable to attend.
42. *Le Monde*, 25 January 1992.
43. *Le Figaro*, 21 January 1992.
44. P.-A. Taguieff, 'Les métamorphoses idéologiques du racisme et la crise de l'antiracisme', in P.-A. Taguieff (ed.), *Face au racisme* (Vol. 2) (Paris: La Découverte, 1991), p. 20.
45. S. Wayland, 'Mobilising to defend nationality law in France', *New Community*, Vol. 20, No. 1, October 1993, p. 96.

The Failure of Anti-Racist Movements in France, 1981–1995 213

46. J. Costa-Lascoux, 'Les lois "Pasqua": une nouvelle politique de l'immigration?', *Regards sur l'Actualité*, March 1994, pp. 19–43; interview with A. Dahmani, 20 April 1995.
47. Hargreaves, op. cit., pp. 125–131.
48. *Le Monde*, 27 October 1994.
49. N. Rachedi, 'Elites of maghreb extraction in France', in B. Lewis and D. Schnapper (eds), *Muslims in Europe* (London: Pinter, 1994), pp. 67–78.
50. *Le Monde*, 22 January 1991; 26 January 1991.
51. *Le Monde*, 19 January 1991.

Part 4
History and Biography

12 François Mitterrand between Vichy and the Resistance
Eric Duhamel

On 12 September 1994, the French gathered around their television sets to watch a rather pathetic spectacle.[1] Their president, looking elderly, weak and ill and appearing to have trouble with his memory, was replying falteringly and in a feeble voice to questions on his past being put by a journalist with a poor grasp of historical reality. This interview, which the Elysée itself had requested, was aimed at putting an end to the debate surrounding Mitterrand's past under the Vichy regime.

As is now well known, the whole scandal or affair or controversy or psychodrama – all terms used at the time – began with the publication of a book by Pierre Péan, *Une Jeunesse française, François Mitterrand 1934–1947*, featuring a shocking picture on its front cover. This depicted Pétain meeting Mitterrand on 15 October 1942 at an audience for those in charge of the Centre d'Entr'aide aux Prisonniers de Guerre of the Allier region. The book was presented and read by both the press and the public as containing 'revelations' on three periods in Mitterrand's life. The first of these was the period before the Second World War, when Mitterrand was a student in Paris. The book also referred, second, to the Occupation when, before joining the Commissariat des Prisonniers de Guerre in Vichy, Mitterrand is alleged to have been part, in January 1942, of the Légion Française des Combattants and then, a year later, to have joined the active Resistance but without severing his links with Vichy. The final period under scrutiny in the book is the post-war period, particularly the links Mitterrand kept right up to the 1980s with some of the Vichy partisans. Denis[2] recounts how, by Mitterrand's own admission, his 'friendship' from 1942 onwards with René Bousquet was crucial to Mitterrand from 1949 up to 1986. It should be borne in mind in this context that Bousquet's activities as Secretary General of the Police under Vichy became public knowledge from the late 1970s and that he was formally accused in 1989 of crimes against humanity.

217

By coincidence, a French publishing house was at precisely that time bringing out a book which would have shed more light on Péan's book and the mechanisms of the whole controversy.[3] It is interesting to chart Mitterrand's activities during the Occupation, but more interesting to assess the level of feeling these 'revelations' aroused in France[4] and to consider what this recovered memory and this voluntary dredging-up of the past tell us about the end of the Mitterrand era.[5]

THE FACTS

Most of Péan's revelations were already in the public domain. The value of his book lies less in what it reveals – if indeed it reveals anything – than in the way he brings together things that were already known but seldom considered as historical truth.

Mitterrand's biographers have depicted him during the 1930s as keenly interested in political debate and willing to follow changes in trends but never committing himself to one side or the other. The press has frequently published articles, most of them originating in the far right, that present Mitterrand as being close to Action Française or even to the so-called Cagoule,[6] although it has never offered any formal proof for these allegations. Péan confirms that Mitterrand was a Catholic young man, with right-wing leanings, but that he was not a member of Action Française and there is no evidence of his ever having been part of the Cagoule. Indeed, one of the things the book does reveal is that Mitterrand has admitted being a 'Volontaire National' – that is a member of a young socialists' organization under Lieutenant Colonel de la Rocque, and that he took part in demonstrations in Paris against 'the invasion of immigrants'.[7] This was very shocking in 1990s France: the president had spearheaded the fight against xenophobia, and had on several occasions proposed giving immigrants voting rights. This revelation therefore called his sincerity into question.

Mitterrand was called up in 1939 and taken prisoner in 1940, when he experienced the Stalags. After two unsuccessful escape attempts, he finally escaped from a transit camp at Boulay en Moselle, some 30 kilometres from Metz, on 10 December 1941.[8] Péan recounts that once back in France, he took part in January 1942 in the activities of the Légion Française de Combattants,[9] one of whose roles was to disseminate the arguments for national revolution. Mitterrand challenges this point in *Mémoires interrompus*, acknowledging that he worked for Jacques Favre de Thierrens's documentation service but denying that he was paid by the Légion.[10] However, Mitterrand did not explain what the role of the organization was that carried out intelligence work for the counter-espionage section of the Armistice Army headed by Captain Paillole.[11]

Mitterrand, who was unemployed, then went on to a job he has described as that of 'subaltern'[12] to the Commissariat Général aux Prisonniers de Guerre in Vichy, heading its information service. He was a contract worker and did not swear an oath to Pétain, nor to the regime.[13] The role of the Commissariat was to aid repatriated or escaped prisoners of war and their families in settling down to 'normal' life again. It is well known that POWs were a particular target for Vichy propaganda; to an extent, the Commissariat was thus helping to disseminate national revolution propaganda among them. During the Occupation, but also afterwards, Mitterrand was to rely on the POW community to build his Resistance movement and then his political audience. It should also be borne in mind that POW centres were set up in all French *départements*, financed directly by the Commissariat and run by volunteers at local level in Centres d'Entr'aide aux PG (known as CEAs). His first Commissaire Général, Maurice Pinot, was considered anti-German and opposed to Pierre Laval's policies. Under his responsibility, the Commissariat restricted its role to social and moral action out of the deepest possible respect for the person of Pétain and what he embodied. However, some members of the Commissariat, including Mitterrand in the Allier region, set up escape networks and departments for counterfeiting papers. The aim was to help their comrade POWs and not to oppose Vichy policies. Gradually, Mitterrand and his friends moved on from helping POWs to acts of resistance proper.

'Once back in France, I became a Resistance fighter without any agonising'[14] is a rather audacious summary of a longer, more complex process.[15] Pinot left the Commissariat on 14 January 1943 at the instigation of Laval, who accused him of not making the organization available for carrying out Laval's policies, and was replaced by André Masson, a notorious collaborator. This prompted Pinot's closest colleagues to resign, including Mitterrand along with Jean Védrine, Pierre Chigot, André Magne and Pierre Havez.[16] On 2 February 1943, at Chez Livet in the Creuse region, the 'Candlemas meeting' was held at Chigot's home, which was some time later to lead to the creation of the Fédération Autonome des Centres d'Entr'aide

(FACEA) whose role was to pursue non-Resistance social action under Védrine. Also set up was another body, the Rassemblement National des Prisonniers de Guerre or RNPG, also known as 'Pin-Mitt' after Pinot and Mitterrand, its two main leaders.[17] In April 1943, the meeting at Crépieu-la-Pape, near Lyons, effectively got the RNPG up and running with the support first of ORA (Organisation de la Résistance de l'Armée, made up of those from the Armistice Army) and then of Combats. Finally, in November, the decision was taken to launch a secret newspaper, *L'Homme libre*, and to work to get the very special nature of POW Resistance acknowledged by the United Resistance Movements (MUR), the CNR and de Gaulle. Mitterrand was less politically marked than Pinot but also more ambitious and more political, so it was he who took charge of this work.

Mitterrand left for London on 15 November 1943. The meeting with de Gaulle in Algiers went badly: de Gaulle demanded the merger of the RNPG with the Communist CNPG (Centre National des Prisonniers de Guerre) and the MRPGD (Mouvement de Résistance des Prisonniers de Guerre et Déportés) headed by his nephew, Michel Cailliau.[20] Mitterrand accepted the idea of a merger but would not accept Cailliau's leadership and, indeed, rejected the idea of the whole Resistance being under the general's control. On 18 June, he accused de Gaulle of denying the quality of 'patriot' to those who refused his authority, and of confusing France with his own person. He fundamentally refused to consider 18 June as a date whose events created a new legitimacy. For the Gaullists, everything derived from the rejection of the Armistice as being contrary to the national interest and national honour. Mitterrand was at the time representative of the 'Giraudist' Resistance fighters who accepted the Armistice and the Vichy government and who then, from 1942 or 1943 in many cases, moved over to the Resistance.

Finally, on 12 March 1944, the MRPGD, the RNPG and the CNPG merged under the leadership of Antoine Avinin, a CNR representative, to form the Mouvement National des Prisonniers de Guerre et Déportés or MNPGD; this body also included, for the first time, deportees.[21] At the time of the Liberation, Mitterrand was appointed Secretary General for Prisoners of War and Deportees,[22] until the arrival of Minister Henri Frenay. This appointment demonstrated that his acts of resistance had been acknowledged by de Gaulle, and Mitterrand was to argue on many occasions thereafter (although rather twisting the meaning of the words) that he had been a member of de Gaulle's first government in the metropolis after the Liberation.

In November 1944, Mitterrand continued to work to widen the base of his movement by merging the MNPGD and the CEAs. This was a very important step, for in bringing together POW Resistance fighters (of whom, by definition, there were very few, as in other sections of the Resistance) and the CEA POWs (most of whom preferred a 'wait and see' policy or were Pétainist and only too happy to be part of a movement with a strong Resistance colouring in late 1944), Mitterrand was laying the foundations for his future sphere of influence.[23] It was during the Occupation and around, if not in, Vichy that he built up his resources and the basis of his political wealth under the Fourth Republic by relying on POWs,[24] most of whom had great respect for Pétain's memory.

By merging non-Resistance POWs – some of them Pétain supporters and most of them supporters of his policies – and Resistance POWs, and building himself up as a spokesmen for both groups, Mitterrand was in fact constructing a kind of time-bomb. In 1994, the spotlight of attention focused on the first group but left the second in the shadows.

WHAT WAS, OR WAS NOT, ALREADY KNOWN

Mitterrand's successful escape, his (albeit modest) role in the Vichy government, his support for Pétain and his gradual integration into the Resistance without having first broken his links with Vichy were all common knowledge. These episodes in Mitterrand's life were often written about on the basis of Mitterrand's own accounts of them, such as the Marigny lecture,[25] in his 1969 book *Ma Part de vérité* or in *La Paille et le grain*.[26] Historians also had access to the less frequently read account of his activities during the Occupation recorded by Védrine and countersigned by Mitterrand himself in *Dossier PG – rapatriés 1940–1945* in 1981. This contained all the 'revelations' of Péan's book. It was a two-volume publication bringing together explanations on POWs' lives, organization and Resistance activities as well as eighty first-hand accounts. This typewritten collection of papers, collated by Védrine in the 1970s, was aimed at giving an account of POW resistance so as to entrench the idea of the MNPGD as a combat unity. What it actually did was to give an account of the Resistance action of elements that for the most part had originated in the Commissariat Général aux Prisonniers de Guerre under Vichy. For the founders of the MNPGD, seeking its legitimation was both symbolic and an important act of remembrance; the key issue was no more and no less than acknowledging the resistance activity of Pétainists or even the Pétainist Resistance.[28] As a result, the Communist Pierre Bugeaud, the national head of the CNPG, refused to give a first-hand account for the collection on the grounds that he did not want to contribute to what seemed to him to be an attempt to rehabilitate Pinot. Although Védrine's papers need to be approached with caution, reading the personal accounts does shed considerable light on POW resistance. For example, the departure of Mitterrand and his comrades from the Commissariat did not mean that they had severed their links with Pétain or his regime, and Chigot was to rejoin his entourage. Péan was viewed as revealing the fact that Mitterrand was a Pétainist, but this was well known; Védrine presented January 1943 as the point of breaking with Laval and the policy of non-collaboration with Pétain.[29] Péan tells us, however, that Laval's return to power a few months earlier, in April 1942, had been no problem at all for Mitterrand.[30]

When I began working on the Union Démocratique et Socialiste de la Résistance (UDSR), the only political grouping to have come exclusively out of the Resistance and one that Mitterrand headed between 1953 and 1965, I was interested in Mitterand's past, with the exception of the 1930s. Although it was no surprise that he had Pétainist leanings, I was struck by the fact that his support for Pétain was so long-lasting. I had read the first-hand account, also used by Péan, of Eugène Claudius-Petit, one of the leaders of the Franc-Tireur movement and a Companion of the Liberation. He had been entrusted in early 1943 by the MURs with making contact with the POW Resistance movement and was very suspicious of a movement that had come into being within the Vichy regime. He gave Mitterrand clearly to understand that his comrades were fighting as much against the Nazis as against Vichy, and was surprised and shocked to learn that Mitterrand, the supplicant in that situation, sprang to the defence of some aspects of the national revolution, particularly corporatism. This account is particularly interesting, since Claudius-Petit was behind Mitterrand's joining the USDR in 1947 and his first ministerial post in 1947, in the Ramadier government.

In other words, the founders of the UDSR, Resistance fighters and for the most part thoroughgoing Gaullists (his parliamentary group had the highest concentration of Companions of the Liberation), were aware of Mitterrand's past but did not condemn him because his unquestionable role in the Resistance outweighed all other considerations. Moreover, their sensitivity to Vichy was entirely different from that of the French people in the 1990s. The Armistice had been a key factor in support for de Gaulle and the Gaullists, and Mitterrand was part of the Resistance that did not consider the Armistice as dishonourable or the Vichy regime as illegitimate or illegal. The Resistance fighters for whom rejection of the Armistice was the beginning of their resistance banned access to the UDSR to all those with blood on their hands or who had been collaborators, while for others, all that mattered was Resistance action or the need to forget. Of course, within the UDSR there was a symbolic hierarchy, ranging from the Free French who were Companions of the Liberation to former POWs, not all of whom had fought in the Resistance, including also the Résistants de l'Intérieur, and this sometimes meant struggle over the symbolic capital and its role in securing acknowledgement of the specific nature of the POW Resistance, a struggle that continued well into the 1980s and left its mark on the 1994 controversy.

In 1994, Péan and others seeking to chronicle Mitterrand's past took as their starting-point Vichy, not the Resistance, an angle that reflected the central role Vichy plays in historical accounts of France during the Second World War.

The televised interview with Elkabbach made it very clear that the specific role of the POWs had been forgotten in the controversy over Mitterrand's past. POWs were, of course, prisoners and excluded from their national community. They did not live through the Armistice or assess its implications or comment on the Vichy government in the same way as the French populace at home. It is astonishing that under Elkabbach's questioning, Mitterrand did not develop this point more. The experience many POWs had of the reality of 1940 and 1941 was what Vichy propaganda told them. When the Liberation came, the POWs were wiped out of history; to have been a prisoner aroused compassion but not glory, and centre-stage was occupied by the Resistance fighters as a mass. The Resistance activity of some of the Vichy government was also forgotten because not much was known about it. There was a lack of academic studies that persists to the present day (very little is known about the ORA and the Armistice army) but above all, it was, and remains, difficult to explain how an individual could be both a Pétainist and a Resistance fighter. The myth of France as a nation of Resistance fighters, perpetuated by de Gaulle and the Communists, is insufficient explanation, as too is the presentation during the 1970s of France as a predominantly Pétainist nation.[31]

RECOVERED MEMORY AND EMOTION

Péan's book made few revelations, therefore, yet stirred up considerable furore. Mitterrand was most surprised of all at the emotion the book's publication aroused.[32] He answered Péan's questions which were more about confirmation than revelation, and did not, strictly speaking, make any confessions. Of course, it has been asked why Mitterrand should have 'collaborated' with Péan's investigations. Did he want to give the French people a last history lesson and juxtapose the complexity of his political development with the simplistic vision of de Gaulle? Did he want to take the wind out of the sails of other books? Whatever his reasons, the help he gave Péan and his subsequent comments along the lines of 'I have nothing to be ashamed of' appeared provocative,[33] especially as the debate centred less on his youth and the 1930s and more on his long friendship with Bousquet.

As Andrieu writes, 'the debate has been not about the past of one man but about the way in which he had combined his past with his role as president of France. It is the relationship between a recovered past and a present-day role that creates a formidable political and intellectual short-circuit' – and, hence, the whole controversy. While the debate was around the past of a remarkable man, the real issue was how it was possible to support Pétain and fight for the Resistance at the same time. Some historians have come up with some answers.[34] While the debate was around the articulation between the actual and claimed past of a remarkable man who went on to become president of France, the real issue was how that man could be both the first Socialist president to be elected by direct universal suffrage and a diehard supporter of Pétain. This, albeit implicit, question is what gave the controversy its enormous scale.

Péan's book has a teleological vision; the author wants to give an account of Mitterrand's past in terms of what we already know of his subsequent career – hence the concentration on the pivotal years 1942–1944. In other words, Péan's book came at the confluence of two different types of interest or curiosity: interest in Mitterrand's life and in how he kept his identity throughout his different or successive roles, and interest in his involvement in Vichy, and in particular in the Shoah.

Once a Head of State talks of his past, what he says becomes not only a personal historical account but also a political message. The historical importance of Mitterrand also explains the scale of the controversy. In France, the Head of State *is* the nation. Mitterrand gave an account of his personal political development when what the French people were expecting, and wanted, to hear was an account of France's history. However, I differ from Andrieu in challenging the argument that the complexity cited by Mitterrand in his defence (which incidentally answers the first question but not the second) 'could tend to wipe out the distinction between the Resistance and collaboration', even though some of those nostalgic for Vichy took advantage of the occasion to try to rehabilitate the regime on the pretext that some Resistance fighters were part of it.[35] I do not believe the argument, if only because the French know enough of their own history, the experience of their elders, the tradition of families and the recent findings of historical research not to believe it. This is probably one of the reasons why the French as a whole took relatively little part in the controversy. However, I do agree with Andrieu when she comments that historical research 'progresses in an increasingly complex environment' and that 'political discourse requires a certain level of simplification'.

Yet far from simplifying, Mitterrand made everything complex and confused, making the present-day French witnesses of the obscurity of a period in history when what was expected of him was a clear and unmistakable condemnation of Vichy. Mitterrand replied, particularly on 12 September, at a personal level when people were listening to him as Head of State. He presented the French people with an account of the complexity of Vichy that he portrayed as 'bedlam'.

The intense emotion, echoed in large sections of the foreign press, is part of a very specific context. Mitterrand was a few months off the end of his second term of office. Part of the French press was quick to feed the controversy because there was very little risk of reprisals from the Elysée.[36] In the middle of a period of political 'cohabitation', a sick president was also politically weakened.

Not all Mitterrand's accusers were motivated by the same factors, and indeed, some of the motivating factors were either unconscious or subconscious. Besides the 'professional' accusers, those representing the Resistance in its purest and simplest form, there were left-wingers who accused Mitterrand of betraying the left and its identity and who condemned his preoccupation with business and money; they saw the

explanation in his past as a man who had remained a Pétain supporter, who had been corrupted and perverted as a result of his trip
through the looking-glass. This was the interpretation of Edwy Plenel,
a journalist, who accused Mitterrand of having betrayed the ideals of
the left.[37] This was, however, at odds with the fact that he presented
Mitterrand as an opportunist, for how is it possible for someone to
betray ideals in which they do not believe?

Mitterrand's ambiguous replies to Elkabbach's questioning in the
interview added to the confusion. Mitterrand threw his state of health
into the pot along with his past, perhaps in an attempt to ride on a
wave of sympathy from the French for his only recently revealed
illness or even to gain absolution, and refused to condemn Vichy in
so many words.

Mitterrand has been accused of lying; that is, however, an excessive
charge. It is true that he did not tell the whole truth, but it needs to be
asked why certain questions were not put much earlier. Once they
were, Mitterrand's whole past was re-examined in the light of the 1994
controversy; there was discussion about the hidden meanings in some
of his writings, his escape from prison camp and so on.

Some commentators used Vichy's complicity with the Nazi policy
of exterminating the Jews as a matrix for judging Mitterrand's past,
succumbing to the anachronistic temptation to evaluate his past from
current memory. The Bousquet, Touvier and Papon affairs, each very
different from the others, nevertheless had an impact on the controversy surrounding Mitterrand and created a climate of suspicion.
Mitterrand's friendship with Bousquet, organiser of the Vel d'Hiv
raid, and the fact that Mitterrand claimed to know nothing of Vichy's
exclusion policy towards the Jews caused deep shock. As president, he
had created the feeling that at that time the fate of the Jews was as
meaningless to him as to many others or, at the very least, of only
secondary concern. Some commentators asked whether Mitterrand
was anti-Semitic, although there is no evidence of this. Yet how
could an alleged friend of Israel refuse to condemn Pétain? Mongin
notes that in claiming the duty to recover memory, his questioners
shifted the focus from the scrutiny of one individual to suspicion of
the whole nation.[39] It was, he argued, not possible to claim that
France still supported Pétain because the Head of State was one of
his supporters. This gradual drift fuelled the myth of the taboo existing in France around Vichy. By attacking Mitterrand, some commentators also sought to secure condemnation for Vichy, to bring it into
the dock, forgetting that de Gaulle had already said all there was to

say on the matter. The debate was enlivened and also made more complex still by the fact that historians had little relish for a media-dominated presentation of the whole controversy, driven by investigative journalists rather than scholars. Many of those involved in the controversy also sinned by anachronism. Mitterrand was of interest because he was president, but the conclusions drawn were often over-audacious. France was being accused of being a Vichyist nation, and the notion that there was a taboo surrounding this period in French history, despite the fact that large numbers of historians were studying it, made good copy for the press. The president was accused of seeking to rehabilitate the Vichy regime simply by his own presence. It was absurd, as absurd as accusing de Gaulle of trying to rehabilitate the Third Republic simply because he had been Under-Secretary of State in Reynaud's cabinet.[40]

All in all, Mitterrand's political development is not particularly exciting. He embodies the complexity and diversity of the situation during the Occupation. The 1994 controversy was, for France, a confrontation with its own past and its memory of that past. What did being French between 1940 and 1944 mean? The French were not all supporters of Pétain or de Gaulle. Being French was to find a place on the spectrum accommodating all shades between ideological collaboration with the Nazis and Resistance born of rejection of the Armistice,[41] but things were often more complex than that. The complexity of the situation does not mean that everyone should be banded together. As far as the Resistance is concerned, the 1994 controversy had the advantage of highlighting the fact that Resistance fighters included those who were *maréchaliste* and those who were not, those who were Pétainist, non-Gaullist and even those who moved from being *maréchaliste* to Giraudism and then Gaullism.

Mitterrand represented a part of the French elite that believed in national revolution before joining the Resistance. Mitterrand swayed most in his political allegiance in 1943, the year of real support for the Resistance, of the unification of the various Resistance movements, of real awareness and a turn-around in the economy. A number of other former POWs followed a similar path: *maréchaliste*, a job at the POWs' Commissariat, Resistance fighter and then a leader of the FNCPG.

Mitterrand's reaction to his own past is also unsurprising. Immediately after the Liberation, no one spoke of it. Those Resistance fighters who had learned from the diversity of the movement preferred to present a united front rather than air their different realities in public.

The least that can be said is that the Resistance was a river with multiple tributaries.

The interest of the Mitterrand affair lies less in the fact that he was president than in the fact that he embodied all the ambiguities and complexities of the period. Until the end, he remained loyal to his past and to himself, denying nothing. Kiejamn notes that Mitterrand had been a man of many pasts, but that there was a hierarchy to his pasts.[42] As far as my own view is concerned, I prefer to focus on the unity of a man and a past in which one key concept is anti-Gaullism. The legitimation of his own political identity and development, based on denunciation of the incarnation of France in the person of de Gaulle, was as live an issue in 1994 as fifty years previously. Some commentators have claimed that the 1981 victory was a posthumous defeat for de Gaulle. The predominant interpretation of Mitterrand as Resistance fighter was then used to stress and give new significance to the internal Resistance obscured by de Gaulle. In 1994, on the palimpsest of his own past, the Vichy episode overshadowed Mitterrand's role in the Resistance. The controversy was due also to the mismatch between Mitterrand's self-constructed image and identity, and reality. In 1994, Mitterrand's loyalty to his own past, in its entirety, appeared more shocking because 'the dominant obsession with Vichy was reaching its paroxysm'.[43] For example, there had been much criticism of Mitterrand's laying a wreath on Pétain's tomb, or his refusal to meet the demands of some Jewish organizations that he make a political gesture at the commemoration of the Vel d'Hiv raid that would acknowledge the role of 'the French state'.

Mitterrand's loyalty to his own past and to that of his comrades who, like him, believed in Pétain at one point in French history thus fuelled the debate, although it was a debate restricted to a small circle of journalists and intellectuals; the broad mass of the French people took no part in it. All the evidence points to the fact that the French as a whole were less inclined to condemn Mitterrand than were those with access to the media. Opinion polls conducted in September and October 1994 indicate that the controversy had no effect on the way public opinion in France judged Mitterrand.[44] The political parties remained discreet and although, within the Socialist Party, some activists were upset, very few actually left the party.[45] The barons of Gaullism who were implicated, some of whom had served Vichy as senior officials,[46] remained silent. It should be borne in mind that the controversy was relatively short-lived, lasting a few weeks at most, and that it was over by early 1995. The presidential election campaign then took up people's attention and energy, in which the left needed to build a post-Mitterrand future itself. The new French President, Jacques Chirac, turned the page and made a speech at the ceremony to commemorate the Vel d'Hiv raid in which he said what was expected of him about the French state's collaboration in the Nazi extermination policy.[47] The attempts by the newspaper *Le Monde* to keep the controversy going met with failure.[48] The death of Mitterrand aroused national emotion that simply precluded a historical stocktaking. Mitterrand's *Mémoires interrompus*, in which he comments on some aspects of the controversy, was not a success and sold considerably fewer copies than his *De l 'Allemagne, de la France* (1996) which was a defence of his foreign policy. On 10 January 1996, in a short article in *Le Monde*,[49] Gérard Courtois recalled Mitterrand's past and wrote 'none of this detracts from the courage of François Mitterrand and his gradual swing to an authentic and combative resistance'. This marked a considerable shift in tone.

The 1994 controversy was probably the apogee of this crisis of memory, this psychodrama which has served neither citizens' duty to recall memories nor the need that historians have of knowledge. Its only merit was to make even more necessary the writing of a history of France that takes account simultaneously and in an integrated way, although not at the same level, of free France, internal Resistance and Vichy.

NOTES

1. Interview broadcast on France 2 between President Mitterrand and Jean-Pierre Elkabbach.
2. According to Denis, Mitterrand is alleged to have met Bousquet in 1942 in Vichy through contacts with Jean-Paul Martin, Head of the Office of the Director-General of Police (*Paris Match*, 22 September 1994 and *Le Monde*, 24 September 1994).
3. E. Conan and H. Rousso, *Vichy, un passé qui ne passe pas*, (Paris: Fayard, 1994 (1st edition); Gallimard-Folio, 1996 (2nd edition)).
4. It would be interesting to study the reactions of other countries. Stress has been laid on Mitterrand's participation in xenophobic demonstrations in the 1930s in Italy or his support for the Vichy regime, associated with the deportation of the Jews, in Germany.
5. *French Politics and Society*, Vol. 13, No. 1, Winter 1995.

6. The Cagoule was a secret far-right organization in existence during the 1930s whose aim was to overthrow the Republic.
7. P. Péan, *Une Jeunesse française, François Mitterrand 1934–1947*, (Paris: Fayard, 1994).
8. F. Mitterrand, *Mémoires interrompus*, (Paris: Odile Jacob), pp. 51ff.
9. P. Péan, op. cit., p. 175.
10. F. Mitterrand, op. cit., p. 70 .
11. P. Péan, op. cit., p. 176. See also P. Paillole, *L'Homme des services secrets*, interviews with Alain-Gilles Minella, with a preface by Admiral Pierre Lacoste (Paris: Julliard, 1995).
12. F. Mitterrand, op. cit., p. 72.
13. Ibid.
14. F. Mitterrand, *Ma part de vérité*, (Paris: Fayard, 1969), p. 1.
15. The complexity is also due to the difficulty of defining what 'resisting' means. Beside the Free French in London after 1940 or the secret resistance after the Occupation started, there are many other situations and this means that it is often difficult to categorize behaviour.
16. They were all, with the exception of Védrine, in the UDSR with Mitterrand.
17. On the history of POWs and POW Resistance movements, see, in particular, Y. Durand, *La Captivité, histoire des prisonniers de guerre français* (Paris: FNCPGCATM, 1980).
18. Paillole acknowledges that 'in early 1943, [Mitterrand's] Resistance activity had developed under the sphere of influence of our secret military organizations', especially the ORA (op. cit., p. 200).
19. The Crépieu-la-Pape meeting brought together around Pinot the first POW Resistance fighters from the Commissariat Général, the chairmen of the CEAs and some Companions of Honour and former students at the Ecole d'Uriage: cf. J. Benet, *Historique de la création et des activités du Rassemblement National des Prisonniers de Guerre* (Paris: Benet, 1983), p. 23.
20. In *Dossier PG – rapatriés*, Védrine writes that the MRPGD was 'an active group of some 12 members'. This figure is considerably lower than was actually the case.
21. Pinot was the first Commissaire Général of POWs at Vichy and was to give way to François Mitterrand.
22. A prestigious post for a young man with no training.
23. The merger between POWs from the former Maisons du Prisonnier and the CEAs also served to isolate Communist Resistance fighters.
24. E. Duhamel, *L'Union démocratique et socialiste de la Résistance, 1945–1965*, doctoral thesis in history at the University of Paris IV-Sorbonne, 1993.
25. Lecture given at the Marigny Theatre under the auspices of the Conference of Ambassadors, 16 May 1947.
26. These texts sought to build an image and shape the identity of a politician rather than to serve the cause of historical knowlege; there are therefore omissions and telescoping of the time-frame. C. Andrieu, 'Managing Memory: National and Personal Identity', *French Politics and Society*, Vol. 14, No. 2, Spring 1996.

27. Under a decree from the Minister of Defence on 5 March 1986, the MNPGD was assimilated with a combat unit between 22 March 1944 and the Liberation (cf. Conan and Rousso, op. cit., p. 256). Under a decree of 9 July 1948, the MNPGD were recognized as a 'movement of French internal resistance' (ibid. p. 258). See also Duhamel, op. cit.
28. It was no coincidence that just as the French were discovering, in 1994, that some Pétain supporters had been Resistance fighters, historians became interested in the definition of the term.
29. The Védrine papers implicitly take up the myth of Pétain as the 'good guy' and Laval as the 'bad guy'.
30. P. Péan, op. cit, pp. 187–188.
31. H. Rousso, *Le Syndrome de Vichy* (Paris: Seuil, 1987).
32. Laure Adler echoes this in *L'Année des adieux* (Paris: Flammarion, 1995). She indicates that arguments had been prepared to respond to questioning of the president's collaborators.
33. Essentially a non-conformist, Mitterrand had always presented himself as a free man, at liberty to spurn what he saw as prejudice or malice towards him.
34. The issue was virtually taboo during the 1980s.
35. D. Venner, *Histoire critique de la Résistance* (Paris: Pygmalion/Gérard Watelet, 1995).
36. Adler, op. cit., notes that no one would have dared to this only a few years earlier.
37. After the interview, the cable channel LCI brought together a number of journalists to comment on Mitterrand's performance. Plenel used the occasion to argue his case, interspersed with sobbing; the journalist clearly had an enormous personal and emotional investment in the case.
38. See the controversy around the article written by Claire Andrieu in *Le Monde* of 15 September 1994 on Mitterrand's own article, 'Pélerinage en Thuringe', published in *France, revue de l'Etat nouveau* in December 1942.
39. *Esprit*, November 1994, p. 93.
40. Cf. articles in *Le Monde*. In *Le Nouvel Observateur* of 15 September 1994, J. Julliard demanded the president's resignation (cited in Conan and Rousso, op. cit., p. 435).
41. Philippe Burrin uses the concept of 'accommodation' in his book *La France à l'heure allemande* (Paris: Seuil, 1995).
42. Comment made by Kiejman at the Round Table on the Mitterrand Years, University of Paris X-Nanterre, 16 November 1996.
43. Conan and Rousso, op. cit., p. 308.
44. The 24 September 1994 edition of *Figaro-Magazine* indicated that the number of those polled by SOFRES who were 'fairly' or 'very' sympathetic towards Mitterrand remained unchanged between January and September at 49 per cent. However, 67 per cent of all those surveyed were shocked at the relationship with Bousquet.
45. Only one of the Paris federation's staff resigned over the issue.
46. For example, Maurice Couve de Murville, former prime minister under de Gaulle.

47. The term *Etat français* has two meanings, the Vichy regime and the machinery of the state.
48. See the February 1995 articles on the past of André Bettencourt, a friend of Mitterrand's. A former minister under the Fourth and Fifth Republics, Bettencourt had written anti-Semitic articles during the Occupation.
49. The article bore the title 'The Vichy confession', misleading readers to understand that in 1994, Mitterrand confessed to his role in the Vichy government, whereas he had never sought to conceal it.

13 The Making of a President: Political Culture and Collective Memory in the Morvan

Marion Demossier

In its edition of 11 January 1996, *L'Express* quoted Mitterrand's description of the central role of a personal fief in his career: 'I have remained in political life for nearly fifty years because first the *Nivernais* then the French decided so in electing me'. Like many other politicians in the aftermath of the Second World War, Mitterrand built his career upon local foundations consolidated over a period of many years. Throughout his career, the Nièvre, and specifically the region of the Morvan, served as the canvas for a wide variety of his official speeches, political writings and image-making. His 1981 presidential campaign, under the slogan of 'La Force Tranquille', had a striking poster of the candidate set against the background of the small town of Sermanges in the Morvan. The Morvan is a classical example of a rural world that has been gradually disappearing since the 1960s,[1] with an ageing population rapidly depleted by successive waves of emigration, especially to Paris. A poor, lightly populated and little known region of lakes, forests and mountains, the Morvan would occupy a key position in the story of Mitterrand.

The inspiration behind this research[2] came from a meeting several years ago with a local politician, the mayor of a small village of 200 inhabitants and self-proclaimed 'friend' of the president. He drew my attention to the photographic portrait of François Mitterrand strategically positioned above the fireplace, where one would normally expect to see family photographs. He then delivered a speech in praise of the president, describing their regular correspondence. In fact, more than 150 postcards had been sent to our informer by the president since 1965. Subsequent interviews in the region confirmed this attachment to Mitterrand and caused more serious reflection about his relationship to his fief. What were the ties between

233

Mitterrand and his voters in the Morvan or the Nièvre? How had he established himself in the region, and what role did it play in his electoral strategies, both locally and nationally? Finally, and more widely, how has the relationship between the man and his constituency been shaped by events and by the political system itself? In short, what is the legacy of Mitterrand for the Morvan?

These questions have been approached from an anthropological perspective, which places emphasis on what Marc Abélès has called 'the interweaving of politics and other forms of social behaviour'.[3] A variety of sources have been used, including interviews conducted at regular intervals and over a lengthy period around the theme of political culture in the Morvan. Although those interviewed were predominantly local politicians, principally but not exclusively sympathetic to the Socialist Party, there has been an attempt to integrate the impressions and opinions of ordinary electors. Current political leaders were contacted (some refusing to participate in the survey). The analysis of the interviews was complemented by research in both national and departmental archives,[4] and amongst the many issues raised for discussion two are highlighted here. The first involves an examination of Mitterrand's relationship to his supporters, while the second concentrates upon the interaction between the president and the identity and politics of the Morvan.

A PARACHUTIST PUTS DOWN HIS ROOTS

Marc Abélès has coined the term 'anchorage' to describe the complex process by which an individual imposes his authority on a given region, acquiring a political legitimacy that may subsequently become significant nationally. All of those interviewed were unanimous in arguing that in the Morvan, Mitterrand had put down roots over a long period by carefully nursing his constituency until at least his election to the Regional Council of the Nièvre in 1964. The following year, he stood as a candidate for the presidency.

In order to understand his success, it is helpful to begin with the original 'parachute drop' of Mitterrand into the Nièvre in 1946, which today has acquired great symbolic importance.[5] According to Mitterrand, Henri Queuille, minister during the Fourth Republic, suggested that he stand for election in either the Vienne or Nièvre, because in these two departments the Rassemblement des Gauches Républicaines[6] had not been represented. Mitterrand initially ignored this advice, standing unsuccessfully for the RGR in the Second Constituent Assembly elections of Neuilly-Puteaux (Seine) in June 1946. However, Queuille's suggestion had not been forgotten, and in November 1946 Mitterrand decided to put himself forward as the moderate right-wing candidate of Action et Unité Républicaine in Nevers, a canton close to the holiday home he rented in the village of Tannay. It was an inspired choice and his list came second with 25.4 per cent of votes, cast ahead of the Socialists and the Mouvement de Rassemblement Populaire and only marginally behind the Parti Communiste (33.7 per cent). His performance was particularly noteworthy because he had been parachuted into the election only two weeks before under the patronage of Marquis de Roualle, head of the food packaging firm Olida. As Catherine Nay[7] has noted, Mitterrand was, in later years, reluctant to recognize the many local patrons from whom he benefited. A particularly striking example of such aid came from Edmond Barrachin, who had presented the young Mitterrand to the Marquis de Roualle with the request that he find a suitable constituency for 'this ambitious young man who wants to hunt on my land'. With this socially distinguished backing, Mitterrand's campaign in 1946 was not surprisingly anti-Communist, denouncing industrial nationalization and inflationary economic policies, whilst preaching the virtues of law and order with sufficient fervour to attract the approbation of the clergy of Nevers.

Once elected as deputy, Mitterrand was careful to consolidate his position by seeking further local legitimacy through his election to the Conseil Municipal of Nevers in 1947 and to the Conseil Régional of the Nièvre for the canton of Montsauche in 1949. Despite these efforts, the legislative elections of 17 June 1951 saw a decline of seven per cent in the vote for Mitterrand's party list. The cause was the presence of two new political groupings, the Rassemblement du Peuple Français (RPF) and an independent right-wing list which had been encouraged to stand by the modifications to the electoral law of 4 May 1951. It was, therefore, thanks to the system of proportional representation that he held his seat, albeit in third place behind a Communist and the new RPF deputy. In the legislative elections of 1956, he headed the list of Union Démocratique et de Défense Républicaine which was endorsed by the Radicals, but not the local Socialists. The elections of 23 and 30 November 1958, using a new electoral system following the establishment of the Fifth Republic, cost Mitterrand his seat because the Nivernais preferred Jean Faulquier, who lost no opportunity to remind the voters that Mitterrand had been an implacable opponent of de Gaulle and the new regime. As the Nièvre had voted by 94,808 votes to 31,997 in favour of the Fifth Republic, Mitterrand's position was cruelly exposed and defeat predictable. He was not long out of favour, and in 1959 he was elected senator and Mayor of Château-Chinon. His opposition to de Gaulle bore fruit in the elections of November 1962, because the left-wing parties were prepared to bury their earlier differences and support him successfully in the second round against the Union pour la Nouvelle République. During the 1960s, he would crown his career at the local level by being elected President of the Regional Council of the Nièvre in 1964. To these achievements should be added his participation in the presidential campaigns of 1965, 1971 and 1974 which increasingly added lustre to his name, thus consolidating further an already powerful influence on the local political scene.

One of the most striking features of Mitterrand's career in the Nièvre was the parallel drift of both the region and its deputy to the left, climaxing in his election as president in 1981. In the legislative elections of March 1973 all three deputies elected in the Nièvre were from the Socialist Party, and in the first round of the presidential elections of May 1974 the department was well in the lead of those voting for Mitterrand with no less than 57 per cent of the electorate in his favour. In the opinion of Jean-Bernard Charrier,[8] this was more than just a sign of enthusiasm for a 'local candidate' as it represented the evolution of an older Republican radical tradition. Jean Pataut, in his *Sociologie électorale de la Nièvre au XXe siècle (1902–1951)*, had already identified certain historical factors which he believed were favourable to what he called the 'party of movement'. He stressed the long absenteeism of the local nobility, who had not succeeded in constituting a political force; the large number of retired people who had been exposed to the ideas of the capital; the strong tradition of trade unionism amongst local forestry workers, particularly in the early twentieth century and, finally, the presence of heavy industry and its workers in the North of the Nièvre. After the Second World War, the status of the region as a foyer of the Resistance, the left-wing sympathies of the principal regional newspaper and the arrival of Mitterrand all gave additional impetus to the swing to the left. Yet, for Charrier, it was a left-wing movement characterized by the strong presence of the local notability and rural bourgeoisie.[9]

These factors, taken together, make it clear why the Nièvre offered fertile soil for a politician of Mitterrand's background and intellectual disposition. From his first election as deputy in 1946, he worked assiduously at his 'anchorage' in the Nièvre through his personal presence and an active involvement in reconstruction and development. In the immediate post-war period, the ease of access of a deputy to the central government administration was vital to the success of reconstruction projects and offered a closely observed gauge of the effectiveness of a politician. In this respect, Mitterrand displayed great talent which would enable him to broaden the networks of his local clientele. The example of the electrification of the scattered communes of the Nièvre between 1949 and 1956 remains a major landmark in the lives of contemporaries. His knowledge of the central administration and the legislative situation smoothed the way to the necessary financial assistance, not just for electrification but also with the Ministry of Agriculture or other public institutions such as the Crédit Agricole, or the Caisse des Dépôts et Consignations. Amongst the more important development projects were the provision of domestic water supplies and public telephones in the more isolated villages, as well as the improvement of the road network. These were expensive undertakings for the region and between 1944 and 1950,[10] the communities in the canton of Montsauche spent FF46 million on water supplies alone. The same canton borrowed no less than FF150 million for electrification between 1953 and 1955. In 1956, Mitterrand, in the capacity of President of the Syndicat Intercommunal of Montsauche, personally organized a loan of FF10 million from the Caisse des Dépôts et Consignations of Nevers to complete these various schemes. There is little doubt that his involvement in these projects would facilitate his election as President of the Regional Council in 1956 and as a Senator in 1959.

Mitterrand thus succeeded in bonding himself to the Morvan through the accumulation of elective offices, the pursuit of local development projects and a firm defence of its interests at the national level. That he should have taken such care with these comparatively mundane affairs makes it clear that despite his high national profile, he could not take his provincial base for granted. Mitterrand was nevertheless able to use his national position to good effect. When he 'parachuted in' for the campaign of 1946, he was presented by the region's press as 'one of the first companions of de Gaulle...who has occupied himself with the problems of the *Anciens Combattants*'.[11] This was, of course, a reference to Mitterrand's occupation of the office of *secrétaire des prisonniers de guerre* in 1944, and in 1947 he was appointed to the Ministry of Ex-Service Men, both especially significant portfolios in the context of the Nièvre, whose hills and forests had been a centre of the Resistance during the war. Mitterrand was quick to reveal his sensibility on this point by inaugurating the complete reconstruction of the 'martyred villages' of the Morvan and by arranging in 1954 for the Croix de Guerre to be given to the communities of Nevers, Planchez and Montsauche. It was at this time that he chose Dun-les-Place as the site of an annual pilgrimage to honour the memory of those who perished in the Resistance. A few years later, Mitterrand revealed the excellent state of his contacts with the networks of the former Resistance by borrowing from the Mutuelle des Anciens Combattants, the Caisse Autonome des Anciens Combattants and the Mutuelle Générale Française at attractive interest rates in order to finance his policies in Château-Chinon. As late as 1985, the president took the decision to site the national pensions office of ex-service men in Château-Chinon, facing the *Mairie* in the square recently named in his honour. Finally, the president created a Museum of the Resistance in the Parc Régional of the Morvan.

Such careful cultivation of a powerful and symbolic lobby was matched by his concern for the interests of the doctors, veterinary surgeons and pharmacists who formed the bourgeois elite of the small towns of rural France. Richard Vinen[12] draws our attention to the importance of the Société Syndicale des Pharmaciens de la Nièvre, which recognized the goodwill that Mitterrand showed to its interests. In a note dated January 1955, Godinoux, President of the Federation du Parti Républicain et Socialiste de la Nièvre and spokesman for pharmacists asked his 'friend' to intervene in the National Assembly against a series of measures which threatened the profession. Mitterrand, in conjunction with Edgard Faure and Pierre Mendès-France, responded vigorously. Nor was the relationship between Mitterrand and these liberal professionals purely that of deputy and lobby groups. It was from amongst doctors and veterinary surgeons such as Dr Barrault of Lormes and Dr Roclore of Saulieu that Mitterrand found some of his most active political supporters in the Nièvre. Both men accompanied the candidate on his tour of the constituency during his early campaigns, and it is Dr Signé who currently holds many of the elective offices once held by Mitterrand. Given the respect and the large clientele enjoyed by these professions in the post-war period, it seems reasonable to assume that their close association with the deputy further extended his roots into local society.[13] At a time when the media presence in electoral campaigns was hardly felt, personal contacts, however slight, could be vital and individuals with large professional clienteles, like doctors or vets, could exert great influence.

From this discussion, it is possible to identify a number of key factors in Mitterrand's political conquest of the Morvan. After an initial opportunistic campaign for deputy in 1946, he was careful to seek local respectability through additional elective mandates. His success was due to his active participation in the administrative and development projects of the region, and to effective use of his position as a politician of national status to advance the interests of major constituencies such as the *Anciens Combattants*. Moreover, despite his national commitments as a deputy and even a minister in Paris, he was conscious of the need to maximize his time in the Morvan.

'FRIENDSHIP' OR THE BOND OF SOCIAL PROXIMITY

As Marc Abelès has recently argued, in the French countryside the model of notability defined by family wealth tradition and social ties remains strong.[14] The Morvan is a good example of this type of structure. In the relationship between Mitterrand and the Morvan, 'friendship', which can be defined as a bond of social proximity, plays a fundamental role. For Abelès the political right defines itself in terms such as 'the family' or 'affinity', while the parties of the left speak of a 'current of opinion' or a 'friendship'.[15] After Mitterrand's death, the national press missed no opportunity to underline the fact that the former president possessed many loyal 'friends' in the Morvan: 'Of course, Mitterrand visited the Morvan less often after his ascent to the Elysée, but he did not forget his friends'.[16] In the exhibition on Mitterrand on display at Château-Chinon, attention is drawn to the loyalty of the man in respect to his 'friends' and 'supporters'. For example, '1959: Clamecy is managed by one of his friends, Dr Barbier, who was ready to offer him his place at Château-Chinon'. Françoise Plet has described this system very neatly as 'a collection of individuals primarily attached to François Mitterrand'.[17] Indeed, it is this same circle of 'friends' who recently formed the Association François Mitterrand, dedicated to the preservation of the president's memory. The question that needs addressing is: why this continual reference to 'friendship'? What is the political function of these bonds of proximity?

It is well known that Mitterrand used his own personality and authority as a vital instrument in his political behaviour, and when creating a provincial powerbase he benefited from (and in turn constructed) a system of notability with himself at the apex. The vast majority of those interviewed were conscious of the consequences of this system, referring to the absence of a political culture or perhaps more specifically of debate. As one former 'friend' declared: 'I do not want to be too critical but...François Mitterrand, he was something of an idol in the period that I knew him [after 1965]...there was François Mitterrand, and that removed the need for personal political thought'.[18]

Further investigation reveals a hermetic political system or what our interviewees describe as a 'Mitterrandien' system. His name has been transformed into several adjectives, including 'Mitterrandolâtrie', used with suitable devotion during interviews.[19] What gave the system sense and consistency were the bonds of social proximity: 'He was a very loyal person, reliable to those with whom he had ties... He was certainly very loyal in his friendship'.[20] Around the figure of the president a tapestry has been woven in which every participant has a place defined in terms of the relationship with Mitterrand. The political system was highly personalized, and the strategy of the prince was thus to control the political arena from above using the inevitable competition and divisions to reign undisturbed. For the courtiers such opacity bred insecurity: 'For 14 years, everybody was trying to interpret his thoughts which he himself did not express. Everybody recommended themselves, or rather insisted upon their knowledge of the wishes and opinions of the president, that was the local game'.[21]

In the career of Mitterrand, the concept of 'friendship' hid the reality of political struggle in which the ties of proximity amongst individuals and between those same individuals and the prince were fundamental, and where a network of favours, alliances, strategies and obligations assured the functioning of the machine. It was these factors that would assure the reproduction of a closed system which continued during the presidency of Mitterrand and is now being fought out between the self-proclaimed 'friends' of the president and their opponents. Both sides are aware of the acts and symbols involved: 'since his death, there is the case of the mayor of P., Mitterrand's lake is in his commune, he will try to present himself at the next cantonal [elections] as the heir'.[22] Mitterrand's political system consisted of networks of sympathizers or 'friends', which, whether real or imagined, carried a symbolic weight capable of assuring the survival and the continuation of his authority. As one mayor explained matters: 'It's from friendship. We can support the mayor of M. in the cantonals because he backed B., who, without him, would never have been elected'.[23] By leaning upon a network of notables and by personalizing their social and political ties, Mitterrand created a structure of patron-client relations typical of the Fourth Republic: 'He said himself that he cultivated distance, because that allowed him to retreat, to watch, to act, to see the others act ... but I was never part of the circle of close friends'.[24] An expression used locally to 'present oneself under friendly pressure' would thus appear to reveal a peculiarity of politics in the Nièvre. At a time when academics are examining the professionalization of politicians, the idea of democracy itself deserves reconsideration. It is perhaps not by chance that in its founding charter the Association François Mitterrand places last on its list of objectives the development of 'local democracy in the Nièvre'.

The value accorded to the social bonds linking a provincial notability to the person of the president was thus fundamental to a form of politics characterized by clientelism and an absence of genuine political debate. Mitterrand's choice of notables was determined by his own political status and by the peculiar nature of the social hierarchy in the Nièvre. To this culture of notability, it is also necessary to take into account the interaction between a poor and isolated region and a man destined to assume the highest office in the land.

MITTERRAND AND THE MORVAN: THE VALUING OF IDENTITY

In *régions* isolated by their geographical position, or touched by economic crisis, the deputy represents a symbol of hope and expectation for development and renewal. Many regions could be categorized in this way, such as the Aveyron or the Corrèze. The Morvan is a particularly pertinent example of this tendency, with an ageing population and a largely agricultural economy shedding labour and accelerating an already advanced process of depopulation. In this context, it is understandable that the arrival of a dynamic politician with a national reputation stimulated fresh hopes. As one local dignitary observed: 'his presence in a canton like ours ... brought a sense of dignity to people.'[25] The relationship between such a politician and his region is nevertheless reciprocal. The locality benefits from the image of its representative and the national functions he exercises: 'there was an ingrained sense of pessimism in the region and, in a way, he gave us a sense of self-worth...people no longer saw themselves as before because Mitterrand was elected here'.[26] His presence was thus a source of local pride and identity: 'He was nevertheless our President, people said it is to some extent thanks to us because we supported him locally'.[27] The politician also benefits from a firmly entrenched local powerbase: not only can he count upon the electoral loyalty of the fief, but it also offers the opportunity to recharge his batteries during moments of crisis.

By the simple fact of his presence in the Morvan, Mitterrand had ensured that the region would henceforth occupy a small, but important place in French history. Throughout his public career and especially after 1981, the Morvan and the Nièvre have been cited countless times in connection with his name. To give only one modest, yet symbolic example, in 1981 the national television network changed its weather map in order to inform France of its forecast for Château-Chinon and the Nièvre rather than the neighbouring Côte d'Or. It is through such details that a region can, in part, become the emblem of a presidency. Mitterrand was undoubtedly conscious of the symbolic importance of his tie to the Morvan and he was careful to integrate regular visits into his political calendar. The national meetings of the Convention des Institutions Républicaines (CIR) of 7–8 November 1970 were held in the Nièvre. In 1972, he celebrated 25 years as a deputy in the Morvan, and for every presidential election he was sure to be present at Château-Chinon in order to vote.

Yet if we examine the effect of the projects supported by Mitterrand after 1965 or 1981, it is more the image than the economic infrastructure of the Nièvre that benefited from his influence. Such was his reputation, however, that criticism was muted, even if not all could say, 'Mitterrand, he's my God even if I don't agree with everything he's done'.[28] The verdict of Laurent Pieuchot[29] says much about the effect on Château-Chinon: 'it possesses an infrastructure worthy of a town of 5,000 inhabitants [it has 2,952]. Employment has grown with an active tertiary sector. However...the development of the town has not been achieved to the advantage of the surrounding area. The canton, and more generally the Morvan, is in an advanced state of desertification'. A small town with a famous name, Château-Chinon was perhaps the only community to enjoy a serious development policy. It was there that the president inaugurated the Musée du Septennat, and for the town that he provided the patronage for the siting of the monumental fountain of the artists Jean Tinguely and Niki de Saint Phalle. To this list can be added the European

Archaeological Centre of Mont Beuvray, a child of the president's *politique des grands travaux*, which represents a veritable folly of marble beneath the mythical granite mountain. Finally, the Parc Régional du Morvan created as an association by Mitterrand and Dr Roclore in 1967 completes an impressive collection. It was described by its authors in grandiloquent terms as the permanent constitutional centre for the management of the countryside in Burgundy. Yet despite these boasts, it has singularly failed to win the enthusiasm or recognition of the local population. Controversy has instead been the result, the most recent concerning the sale of a plot of land on the archaeological site of Mont Beuvray to Danièle Mitterrand for the token price of one franc. The intention was for the former president, already dying of cancer, to be buried there, but such was the outcry that he opted instead for his town of birth, Jarnac. Not surprisingly, Mitterrand used the park's Conseil d'Administration to place his clients and the current president is his 'friend', Dr Signé, Mayor of Château-Chinon, and a senator. The Academy of the Morvan, largely composed of the local notables, also plays a major role in the administration of the park which is frequently isolated from the economic problems and aspirations of the local population.

The relationship between Mitterrand and the Morvan has therefore been conducted at a cultural and symbolic level rather than through more practical measures such as the construction of roads or the encouragement of industry. What Mitterrand achieved by patronizing various cultural projects of a national (even international) standing was the promotion of the image of the Morvan. These projects have often been misconstrued by the local people and only the Musée du Septennat has acquired the status of a place 'where one takes the family to visit'. Many of the other schemes are perceived as an attempt to impose the cultural values of an alien Parisian elite upon a region suffering a profound economic crisis. Although somewhat incongruous in a poor rural setting, these cultural monuments remain the most visible traces of Mitterrand and offer a testimony of his attachment to the region. If his policies were not always understood, the underlying sentiment was nevertheless reciprocated, finding form in the local expression 'Mitterrand is the Morvan'. Since his death, the Association François Mitterrand, largely composed of mayors and other elected officers of the canton and even some national politicians, has been busy naming and renaming squares, roads and public buildings after the late president. At the time of writing at least ten such baptisms have occurred since February 1996. Taken as a whole, it is undoubtedly true that the elections of 10 May 1981, which saw the election of its representative to the office of president of the Republic, added lustre to the Morvan. The *morvandelle* identity is now a source of pride and the region is no longer easily dismissed as that from which comes 'neither good winds, nor people'.

CONCLUSION

The example of François Mitterrand and the Morvan helps to broaden our knowledge of the strategies employed in the construction and maintenance of a political fief. The social and economic characteristics of the Morvan undoubtedly affected the decisions and conduct of Mitterrand. He was initially supported by members of the local notability and it was on their shoulders that he created his political machine. What he offered in return was an understanding of, and access to, the levers of national power, which he turned to the advantage of key constituencies in the region. His networks of support were sufficiently broad and well chosen as to constitute a system that continues to function even after his death. In the Morvan, Mitterrand relatively quickly acquired the status of a public figure with great local credibility, resulting from his passing the initiation tests for a 'parachuted' deputy, while gaining recognition as a statesman of national stature. He revealed a capacity to forge his own destiny in conjunction with that of his adopted region and to mark its public space with his own imprint. Seeking above all not to be forgotten, he created through his cultural patronage the stage for his future commemoration. For today there are: 'Thousands of traces left behind him which haunt the spirits of the orphaned Morvandiaux'.[30] The only question which remains is, for how long will the legend he created endure?

NOTES

1. M. Vigreux, *Paysans et notables du Morvan au XIX siècle* (Château-Chinon: Académie du Morvan, 1987); J. Bonnamour, *Le Morvan, la terre et les hommes, essai de géographie agricole* (Paris: PUF, CNRS, 1966).
2. I would like to thank Marc Abélès and Richard Vinen for their helpful comments.

3. M. Abélès, *Anthropologie de l'Etat* (Paris: Armand Colin, 1990), p. 7.
4. I wish to thank Richard Vinen for drawing my attention the archives of the UDSR (AP 412) and to the Fondation Nationale des Sciences Politiques for allowing me to consult them.
5. Nearly all my interviewees cited this episode as proof of his political success.
6. Mitterrand had early associations with the Radical Party that operated best at local level and was also influenced by the RGR, who taught him to build coalitions.
7. C. Nay, *Le Noir et le rouge ou l'histoire d'une ambition* (Paris: Grasset, 1984), p. 147.
8. J.-B. Charrier, *Géographie de la Nièvre* (CRDP, Académie de Dijon, 1976).
9. Charrier, op.cit.
10. Archives Nationales, AP 412 65, 66.
11. *Journal du Centre*, 4 November 1946, p. 2.
12. R. Vinen, *Bourgeois Politics in France 1945–1951* (Cambridge: CUP, 1994), pp. 35–36.
13. J. Ferré, *Parole d'élus. Le travail politique au quotidien* (Erès, 1996), p. 67. Ferré has emphasized the importance of these professions in providing rural political leadership.
14. Abélès, *Anthropologie*, op.cit., p. 108.
15. Ibid., p. 145.
16. 'Le regret de Château-Chinon', *France Dimanche*, 14 January 1996.
17. F. Plet, 'La Bourgogne', in Y. Lacoste (ed.), *Géopolitiques des régions françaises*, (Paris: Fayard, 1986), Vol. 3, p. 414.
18. M.B., PS and CGT activist of the Nièvre, and a retired headmaster.
19. Amongst his 'friends', some have started to collect postcards and letters written by the 'president', as well as other more commercial souvenirs, including cigarette lighters and tee-shirts which form part of a post-humous personality cult.
20. M.B., see note 18.
21. M.J., Conseiller général.
22. M.J., Conseiller général.
23. M.M., former mayor.
24. M.J., Conseiller général.
25. M.J., Conseiller général.
26. M.J., Conseiller général.
27. M.J., Conseiller général.
28. M.M., former mayor.
29. L. Pieuchot, *Le Développement d'un centre urbano-rural: Château-Chinon* (Les Annales du Pays Nivernais, La Camosine, 1991), No. 66, p. 3.
30. *France Dimanche*, 14 janvier 1996.

14 The Political Leader and his Heritage

Alistair Cole

An attempt will be made in this chapter to appraise the personal contribution of François Mitterrand to French politics, with special reference to the period 1981–1995. The objective of this chapter is not merely to appraise Mitterrand's personal and policy contribution to the Fifth Republic, however, but also to address the issue of whether Mitterrand left a legacy, and, if so, how best to understand that legacy.

EVALUATING THE MITTERRAND HERITAGE: PRELIMINARY REMARKS

When considering Mitterrand's legacy, and the lessons to be drawn from it, several preliminary remarks are essential. First, as a seasoned politician whose career spanned over fifty years, Mitterrand performed a variety of distinct leadership roles at different stages of his career, and these required varied skills and responses. The search for consistency in any politician's beliefs or activity over a long period is bound to be problematic. The attributes essential at given periods varied in accordance with changing historical circumstances. To take one example, the mobilizing qualities required by the Republican opponent to de Gaulle in the 1960s, or as leader of the left-wing alliance in the 1970s, were not the same as the visionary qualities required as a European statesperson in the 1980s or 1990s. Thus, talk of the Mitterrand legacy in the singular can be misleading.

Taking this into consideration, there are two rather different manners of appreciating the Mitterrand heritage: first, in terms of Mitterrand's personal contribution to the evolution of the French polity; second, in terms of the policy legacy left by the double Mitterrand *septennat*. To separate these is a rather artificial and subjective exercise, but one that imposes itself in any attempt at evaluation.

Any attempt to evaluate the personal legacy left by a particular political leader is faced with the difficulty of how to measure his or her impact. There are important methodological issues involved here. Classical biographies may suffer from an over-familiarity with the subject, leading actions to be judged disproportionately in the light of personal claims by the political leader to explain his or her behaviour. This is especially valid when a politician's memoirs, interviews or official personal archives are relied upon as a guide to his or her beliefs, attitudes, ideas or behaviour. As a general comment, classical political biographies tend to exaggerate the free will possessed by political leaders, as well as the extent to which they can mould their environment to their image. National political leaderships have limited margins of manoeuvre in an increasingly interdependent and global age.

Nonetheless, attempts to evaluate personal and political legacies assume that individuals do make a difference. Individual political leaders exploit opportunities created by particular sets of circumstances, make choices from a number of different available options, and exercise such unfathomable personal characteristics as political skill, courage and intelligence. It is a reasonable supposition that individual leaders attempt to maximize their influence wherever possible. Mitterrand was no exception in this respect.

In measuring the legacy of any individual political leader, attention will be drawn to features such as political style, beliefs, attitudes, goals and policy achievements. While none of these is satisfactory on its own, consideration of these facilitates a fuller appreciation of the multifaceted aspects of an individual political persona. A broader understanding of political leadership also requires a comprehension of the dialectical quality of the interaction between the individual leader, and the cultural and contextual environment within which this leadership is exercised.

MITTERRAND'S PERSONAL AND POLICY HERITAGE

Personal Qualities, Resources and Beliefs: a Political Florentine?

Rarely has an individual peacetime politician sparked such interest as François Mitterrand. The *fin de règne* was accompanied by an explosion of books on various aspects of Mitterrand's life and political career, many of a critical nature: in its obituary issue *L'Express* listed over one hundred books published on Mitterrand since 1981.

The prevailing journalistic image of Mitterrand stressed his talent for political manoeuvring. The prevailing assumption is that

Mitterrand was a tough political operator and a survivor rather than a man of high principle. Biographers frequently depict Mitterrand as a political animal adept at cunning and deviousness, and with an unerring survival-like instinct, portraying him as an old fox. Closely related is the characterization of Mitterrand as a sphinx-like figure, mysterious, obscure and ancient. Most biographers converge to discern in Mitterrand a Machiavellian prince. Underpinning this image was the view that Mitterrand was an unprincipled political leader, ready to compromise beliefs in the interests of self-promotion: in short, a political opportunist and a skilled political manoeuvrer.

The portrayal of Mitterrand as the Machiavellian prince is probably necessary, but certainly insufficient. It might be objected that the consistency with which Mitterrand held to his strategic objectives after 1958, throughout difficult political circumstances, contrasted strongly with the portrait sometimes painted of him of a political dilettante. However rich in political manoeuvres and manipulations, there was a definite sense to Mitterrand's political activity at each of the major stages of his career. His long career was permeated by a relatively small number of guiding themes, which slowly changed as circumstances evolved, but which gave a sense to his political activity: these related to Africa and colonial reform in the 1950s, Republican opposition to de Gaulle in the 1960s, the union of the left in the 1970s, and the building of Europe for most of the 1980s and 1990s.

Within Mitterrand's political persona, there was a curious combination of pragmatic and idealistic political traits. Throughout his presidency, there was ample evidence of principled political activity, notably in relation to European integration, which became a crucial mission from the mid–1980s onwards. But it is clear that Mitterrand's beliefs were neither rigid, nor impermeable. Mitterrand's political persona recalled the classical traditions of Radical Republicanism of the Third Republic, transposed to the political conditions of the Fifth. The apparent paradoxes and contradictions of his beliefs were themselves typical of a particular type of Republican tradition. In accordance with the Radical tradition, there were two faces to Mitterrand. A firm belief in values such as the Republic, the nation, social justice or the rule of law coexisted alongside a highly developed sense of politics as an autonomous activity (or game), with its own rules and rites which occasionally conflicted with the former.

Mitterrand will be remembered not only as one of the key statesmen of his century, but also as a gritty and determined political survivor. His ability to survive repeated political and personal setbacks – as in

1958, 1968 and 1978 – was well established before his election as president in 1981. Mitterrand survived at the helm for 14 years, longer than any other French political leader in the twentieth century. His status as a survivor is highlighted by most biographers. Survival testified in part to his political skill and determination; in part to fortuitous circumstances; in part to the strategic mastery over the resources available to him, especially as president.

In this respect, Mitterrand's position was far stronger during his first presidential term than his second. In 1981, Mitterrand exercised a degree of mastery over key resources rare even for a French president. These included: a direct elective mandate; a seven-year term-in-office; an established constitutional precedent in favour of a strong presidency; a principle of presidential initiative in policy formulation and personnel selection; a strong presidential bargaining position in relation to other key institutions (bureaucracy, government, parliament, parties, interest groups); an absolute majority for the president's supporters in parliament, and a sympathetic public opinion. Mitterrand's early political credit was rapidly dissipated: within one year, public opinion had become wary of *la vie en rose*, and the full force of constraints facing the new government had become apparent. The loss of a sympathetic parliamentary majority to support him in 1986 accentuated a process of presidential withdrawal from domestic politics which had been gathering pace since 1983. The arbitral interpretation of the presidency (forcibly) espoused by Mitterrand during the 1986–1988 'cohabitation' was carried over in a modified form to his second presidential term after 1988, when the Socialists disposed only of a relative majority within the National Assembly. The Socialists' shattering defeat in the legislative elections of 1993 removed Mitterrand's last remaining source of political legitimacy and virtually reduced the president to observer status. Mitterrand's presidency was thus subject to a law of diminishing returns of power that had characterized previous French presidential terms.

Mitterrand's personal resources also varied throughout his career. However difficult it is to gauge elusive concepts such as political skill, intelligence, or capacity for mobilization, most observers concur that Mitterrand displayed consummate political skill, resolute physical and political courage, and demonstrated a vivid intelligence, all features associated with successful political leadership. But these personal qualities were not consistently demonstrated. Mitterrand also revealed a capacity for miscalculation, as well as a diminishing tendency for astute political judgement throughout the course of his second presidential term. It was painfully obvious from 1992 onwards that the physical decline caused by his prostate cancer was having a detrimental effect on his ability to provide effective political leadership.

Ambiguous Goals and Unintended Achievements

Blondel has urged that the concept of leadership goals should be adopted as the basis for appraising achievements, comprising attitudes, strategy, and expectations of behaviour.[1] Mitterrand's overriding goals of the 1970s, avowed or otherwise, were to reduce the dominant position of the Communist Party amongst the left-wing electorate, to rebuild a great Socialist Party, to mould the Socialists as a presidential rally behind his leadership and a powerful vehicle for the capture of the presidency. With the benefit of hindsight, Mitterrand appeared remarkably successful in pursuing these goals, although such an impression did not always prevail at the time. The restoration of Socialist fortunes and the decline of the PCF stemmed from far more immutable structural factors than Mitterrand's personality, however effective his leadership.

In most respects Mitterrand's key achievements as president were in those spheres where his action had been least expected. He promoted European integration beyond the limits observed by former French presidents; he contributed under pressure towards the modernization of French industry and financial capitalism; he de-ideologized the left and reconciled it to the market economy. These real achievements bore only a tenuous relationship to the *110 propositions*, his presidential platform of 1981, which comprised: an economic reflation via a relaunch in popular consumption; the priority objective of combating unemployment; the erection of the state as an instrument of industrial policy via nationalizations, and as a dispenser of social justice through welfare reforms. None of these goals were successful, at least not in the sense originally envisaged. Mitterrand came to office as a champion of the people of the left. In the French context this meant alliance with the Communist Party, Keynesian reflationist economic policies, nationalization, and support for traditional industrial sectors. By 1984, a complete reversal had taken place: a definite abandonment of Keynesian reflation in March 1983 for the strong franc policy; a drastic industrial modernization programme, which virtually shut down the coal and shipbuilding industries; the beginnings of a partial privatization programme, and the expulsion of the PCF from government.

Mitterrand's achievements were unintended ones. The failed economic relaunch of 1981–1982, for instance, forced a 'learning process' on the Socialist government which transformed the French government into one of the faithful exponents of economic monetarism in Europe. This had not been one of the original goals but it was, arguably, one of the major achievements. Similar conclusions might be drawn, *inter alia*, in relation to industrial policy and foreign policy: the achievements of the Mitterrand presidency were real in both of these spheres, but they were not those originally anticipated. Mitterrand's goals varied throughout the course of his presidency. From an early preoccupation with domestic affairs, Mitterrand later immersed himself in European affairs and foreign policy: not for the first time, a political leader sought solace in the more glamorous, less controversial sphere of external relations, after expending vital political capital on contentious domestic issues.

I have argued elsewhere that we might understand Mitterrand's personal contribution to the development of French politics in the Fifth Republic in terms of four criteria: first as a catalyst for the expression of various social and political movements in the 1970s and early 1980s; second, as a legitimator of new policy directions, notably after the economic U-turn of March 1983; third, as an imperfect consensus-builder, notably over European integration and foreign policy; and fourth, as a reluctant modernizer of capitalism.[2] By his active support as president for policies he had previously eschewed or underplayed, Mitterrand helped to legitimize new policy directions. This role was especially important in relation to economic policy, European integration, and in his acceptance of key aspects of the Gaullist legacy in foreign policy. Mitterrand's leadership was most effective as a legitimator of new directions, rather than in a directive sense.

Mitterrand was also responsible – at least symbolically – for the democratic maturing of the Fifth Republic. The political institutions of the Fifth Republic experienced a double evolution during the 1980s under Mitterrand's aegis: the first alternation in power between right and left in 1981; the first 'cohabitation' between left and right in 1986. The transfer of power from right to left in 1981 legitimized the Fifth Republic in two key senses. It proved that the regime could withstand the democratic alternation in power, the key measurement of any liberal democracy; it represented the final rallying of the left to the presidential institutions created by de Gaulle. The advent of 'cohabitation' in 1986 was equally significant, since the regime did not collapse under the pressure of competing political forces controlling the presidency and the National Assembly. Instead, for the first time, the 1958 constitution was actually applied as it was written: the president presided, but the government governed.

As personally representative of *le changement* in 1981, Mitterrand symbolized the arrival of a new political order, and was involved in many of the important policy decisions of the early period in office. It was Mitterrand himself, for example, who insisted that the government maintain its electoral commitments with respect to the nationalization programme of 1982 rather than moderate its provisions. Presidential interventionism was particularly marked during the early reformist years of the Mauroy premiership (1981–1984), but gradually Mitterrand intervened less frequently in matters of domestic politics. His most critical arbitration occurred in March 1983, when he opted that the franc should remain within the European Monetary System, at the expense of the Socialist government's Keynesian attempt to reflate the French economy. Mitterrand's subsequent interiorization of this policy reversal should not obscure that fact that for the most part he was forced to address agendas he had not selected, and to react to events he had not predicted.

Mitterrand's Leadership Style

However constrained the policy-making environment, there was a Mitterrand style which was recognizably different from that of other French presidents and European political leaders. Certain facets of this were imposed by the presidential office itself, notably Mitterrand's aloofness and monarchical posture, which Mitterrand adopted far more ostentatiously than his successor Chirac, the citizen president. Other features of Mitterrand's style include an individual manner of operating within the political arena – embracing a patient reflection and a refusal to be rushed into decision-taking; the cultivation of plural sources of information and rival policy advisers; a taste for secrecy; an antipathy towards collective forms of decision-making; a sharp awareness of the balance of power in any given situation; and a proclivity for the counter-attack. These positional and personal attributes translated into a political leadership style which combined adaptability to changing circumstances with the pursuit of a limited number of precise policy objectives.

Mitterrand's style of reactive, adaptable leadership had both positive and negative aspects. At best, his flexible style of political leadership facilitated the pursuit of a series of difficult policy choices and necessary reversals with a degree of credibility, as in the spheres of economic policy, industrial policy and foreign affairs. In many areas of policy, especially economic policy, major changes in direction were imposed upon Mitterrand by complex forces outside his control. Mitterrand usually accompanied unforeseen policy changes, occasionally resisting but more often facilitating developments, as in European integration. The secret of Mitterrand's leadership lay in his ability to accommodate constraints and transform them into opportunities. The pursuit of limited but precise objectives was the counterpart to a generally facilitating style. This was illustrated in the sphere of European integration from the mid–1980s onwards, especially in relation to Economic and Monetary Union, an issue that Mitterrand pursued with determination from 1988 onwards.

Flexibility was a practical virtue of Mitterrand's political leadership, almost a price for survival, as with other social-democratic leaderships elsewhere, forced to come to terms with the constraints represented by society and the external economic and international environment. While occasionally giving the impression of reacting to events and of drift, Mitterrand's style of adaptable leadership might be contrasted with a more innovative and voluntaristic brand of affirmative leadership, of the type associated with Margaret Thatcher (who appeared unable to assume the consequences of unpalatable but unavoidable decisions, notably the Single European Act of 1986) and – possibly – Jacques Chirac.

It is irrefutable that Mitterrand's personal characteristics had an impact upon his manner of operating within the political system, especially via his cultivation of leader-follower ties, his distrust of party and his building of personal networks upon which to base his authority. Most observers discerned powerful negative features of Mitterrand's leadership style, including cynicism, a weakness of long-term perspectives, and an excessive taste for personal *règlements de comptes*. The proliferation of corruption scandals throughout the course of his second presidential term led to a pervasive mistrust of Mitterrand's entourage. The belief was widespread that the president was too bound by ties of personal loyalty to apprehend the corrupt practices of those around him. This rebounded against Mitterrand, as did his feeble attempts to mitigate the gravity of corrupt practices.

The Machiavellian manouevrer was only one face of Mitterrand, but it would be futile to deny that it formed a powerful part of the public's impression of him. Widespread cyncism in relation to politics was aggravated by Mitterrand's rather cynical political style, notably his obvious 'divide and rule' tactics which appeared to many to lie beneath the dignity of a statesman. On occasion, this was unfortunate for Mitterrand himself, since it fuelled suspicions that he was engaged in base political manoeuvres even when his motives were noble. As a political leader, even of the PS in opposition, Mitterrand favoured a system based on the cultivation of personal networks in all walks of life, and amongst all types of politician. This might have been appropriate – inevitable? – for a presidential system, but it left him an isolated, lonely figure at the end of his presidency. The manner in which Mitterrand set leading PS tenors (Fabius and Jospin) against each other proved highly damaging to the Socialist Party, the vehicle for his conquest of power in 1981. By undermining his own prime ministers (especially Rocard, 1988–1991), he ultimately weakened his own political powerbase.

Towards the end of his presidency, the appearance of Mitterrand as a manoeuvrer came more starkly to the fore, since his ideological and policy achievements lay in the past. The fixation with leaving his name in history became increasingly obsessive. The curious alchemy of courage and duplicity coexisted within Mitterrand until his final hours. The belief that Mitterrand stage-managed his death (by voluntarily ceasing his treatment against cancer) provided the final political curtain. Evidence emerging shortly after his death that the former president had suffered from prostate cancer since late 1981 produced mixed emotions. Of admiration for the embattled fighter; of anger over Mitterrand's duplicity in hiding evidence of his cancer from public opinion, in spite of the publication of six-monthly health bulletins. The manner of his death confirmed the pervasive image of Mitterrand as 'prince of the equivocal'.

THE FUTURE OF THE MITTERRAND HERITAGE: A MYTH TO BE ACCEPTED OR REJECTED?

Whether Mitterrand left a legacy, and, if so, how best this should be understood is a matter of some contention. Mitterrand's heritage can be understood on at least three levels: his personal legacy, his party legacy and his policy-political legacy.

The Personal Legacy

Any judgement of Mitterrand's personal legacy, as appraised above, must be mitigated. An astute comprehension of the changed rules of political competition of the Fifth Republic, of the importance of presidentialism as a political and organisational principle, and of the need to embrace the Communists made Mitterrand a shrewd leader for the conquest of power preceding 1981. Mitterrand's political style was carried over into the exercise of power after 1981. His personal system of governing ultimately inspired mistrust, even amongst traditional supporters. This is a legacy that his successor Jospin is attempting to reject rather than accept.

The Party Legacy?

The question of Mitterrand's political inheritance is one that deeply divides the French left – not just predictably Socialists and Communists, but also within the Socialist movement itself. The ambivalent status of the Mitterrand legacy can best be illustrated with respect to the French Socialist Party. The renovation of the PS in the 1970s crystallized around the personality of Mitterrand. However important the underlying structural and social forces explaining the rise of the PS, it was attributed in part by the actors involved to Mitterrand's own personality. Mitterrand displayed great political skill in transforming the old socialist party (SFIO) into a new presidential-style rally, helping to break the hold of the PCF on the left, making the non-Communist left fit for government, and building up the PS as the natural alternative governing party to the parties of the right. While the resurrection of the PS in the 1970s depended ultimately on fundamental changes in French society, Mitterrand's astute political leadership contributed to its success.

The first term presidential mandate (1981–1988) witnessed an unsteady, if generally loyal subordination of party to president and a stout defence of presidential policy. This mechanism has been explored elsewhere.[3] By the end of the second term, however, the reference to the personality of Mitterrand had become embarrassing. By any standards, this was a measure of personal failure on Mitterrand's behalf. After its crushing defeat of 1993 – attributed in part to the exercise of power symbolised ultimately by Mitterrand – the Socialist Party purged itself of its Mitterandist identity, even while Mitterrand remained at the Elysée. The controversy over Mitterrand's

Vichy past occasioned by the publication of Pierre Péan's book, *Une Jeunesse française*, in September 1994 helped accelerate the movement, the intensity of the debate over Mitterrand's past revealing in particular a nation still to come to terms with its Vichy antecedents (see above, Chapter 12). This greatly facilitated the post-Mitterrand period; overt Mitterrandists became rarer after 1993.

Lionel Jospin symbolized this transition. Jospin had been introduced to the PS by Mitterrand in 1973. He had been one of a handful of young pro-Mitterrand PS *cadres* in the 1970s, before taking over as First Secretary of the party (1981–1988). As party leader, Jospin had already begun marking his distance from Mitterrand in the mid–1980s, as the tensions between the presidential and party logics became apparent. Jospin won the Socialist Party's 1995 presidential nomination against most traditional Mitterrandists (notably his arch-rival Fabius). With a certain ambiguity, moreover, Jospin reserved the right to judge the legacy of the Mitterrand years on a case-by-case basis, a clever tactical decision designed to distance himself as far as decently possible from Mitterrand's heritage. As a presidential candidate in 1995, Jospin stoutly resisted moves from Mitterrand loyalists to enrol the incumbent president's assistance in the campaign.

The 1980s and 1990s suggested that there were natural limits to the type of party renovation undertaken by Mitterrand, strongly personalist in character. The exercise of power in the 1980s and early 1990s shattered the optimism upon which the PS had built its former revival. It also revealed the fragility of a party based on factional identities, and which reproduced presidential rivalries within its midst. The PS was racked by instability throughout Mitterrand's second presidential term; four party leaders succeeded each other in quick succession in five years. The new PS leader Jospin – himself invested with presidential stature after his narrow defeat in 1995 – has maintained his distance from Mitterrand's legacy, in spite of being initially a product of Mitterrand's patronage.

Mitterrand's most enduring party legacy was nonetheless to erect the Socialist Party into the cornerstone of the French left. The PS appears as a permanent feature of the French political landscape, as a natural alternative to the parties of the mainstream right. Had Mitterrand not existed, it would have been necessary to invent someone to fulfil the task of modernizing the Socialist Party and reconciling it to the institutions of the Fifth Republic. The fact remains that Mitterrand did exist and performed the role to perfection.

As a party of government from 1981 to 1993, the Socialists were victims of their idealistic but unrealistic pre–1981 discourse and of their early reformist programme of 1981–1982. From a party viewpoint, the real achievements of economic management after 1983 were overshadowed by the fact that the economy tended to exclude any other social or political perspectives. While the Socialists accept the Mitterrand policy heritage – can they do anything else? – they are implicitly critical in relation to the limited manoeuvre this implies. Hence, the party is engaged in attempts to reconstruct an identity at the margins which exceeds its obligation to re-establish its management capacities and to proclaim itself as cleansed after the corruption scandals of the later Mitterrand years.

The problem for the PS is that, until 1981, the party lacked a solid social-democratic tradition upon which to base such claims of managerial competence. Social democracy was a dirty word in the cultural context of the French left, and remains so despite the government experience. Under the influence of Marxism and of political competition from the PCF, the PS had traditionally adopted a radical discourse. This is henceforth excluded on account of changed political and policy circumstances, not least the experience of the Mitterrand years themselves. More precisely, the resurrection of the PS in the 1970s had been based on its role in articulating the demands of new social movements and new social groups, most notably those influenced by the May '68 movement. It is uncertain what can replace this discourse. Jospin is determined to promise only what the PS can deliver, in the context of 'cohabitation' with Chirac. At the level of discourse, Jospin appears committed to transparency and to realism – the reverse, in fact, of Mitterrand. This places the PS in the mainstream of the European left, but the party continues to suffer from its traditional thirst for a utopian vision.

The Policy and Political Legacy

It is a genuine paradox that political change often comes from the least expected source. A Socialist president, Mitterrand helped to reconcile the French with the market economy; since 1995 the Gaullist President Chirac has helped partially to ease France back into NATO. This is in part inherent in the nature of the policy process. In an increasingly interdependent and global age, governments have limited margins of manoeuvre. Difficult political decisions impose themselves on governments of left and right; ideological justifications follow.

Whatever their political hue, governments are anxious to demonstrate legitimacy by governing in the interests of the whole nation, at least symbolically. In practical terms, this explained why Mitterrand's governments appeared most competent when carrying out conservative policies and why only a Gaullist president could begin to supersede the Gaullist foreign policy legacy.

As explored above, the policy record of the Mitterrand presidency was one of unintended achievements. In important respects, the heritage of Mitterrand involved the weakening of the 'French exception', both domestically and on the international stage. In most respects France was a country rather less different from its European neighbours in 1995 than in 1981. The modification of French exceptionalism can be measured in relation to several spheres: the reshaping of the state, notably subsequent to the decentralization reforms of the 1980s; the dilution of the left–right cleavages; a weakening of traditional 'anti-system' movements (albeit tempered by the advent of new ones); a new policy convergence amongst French elites, and the growing impact of European integration on domestic French politics. The French model – based on centralism, state intervention in economic management, high inflation, and growth – has been modified by a German model, with its insistence on low inflation, high productivity, central bank independence and a strong currency. French economic policy has been driven since 1983 by a determined effort to match Germany in terms of economic performance, a precondition for preserving French rank as a pre-eminent European power.

The policy legacy of the Mitterrand presidency was far too imposing to be ignored by any serious party, either of the left or of the right. This is notably the case in relation to European policy, where the fundamental policy choices undertaken by Mitterrand – especially in relation to the Single European Act and EMU – have in all probability bound themselves upon his successors.

Mitterrand's principal political heritage has been a blurring of the identity of left and right. The bipolar, partisan political culture of the 1970s, and the mobilizing references to Socialism, or the defence of freedom it induced, appeared archaic in the mid–1990s as France moved towards the twenty-first century: the left–right cleavage is of less significance in French politics in the mid–1990s than it was in the mid–1970s. The general ideological climate has changed, both in France and elsewhere, as have perceptions of the possibilities of governmental action. Despite the plurality within both left and right until (and including) 1981, each political camp was able to mobilize by referring to distinctive sets of values. Whichever side one was on, the sense of identity and of belonging to one camp or another was strong. Since the Socialist experience in office (1981–1986, 1988–1993), the ideological bearings of left and right have become far more confused. Each side has borrowed themes hitherto voiced by others in order to justify its policies. This is a legacy that the French left cannot willingly ignore, however hard it attempts to rediscover its identity.

The crucial political problem faced by the PS is one that confronts social-democratic parties everywhere. Mitterrand's principal achievements were difficult to reconcile with a traditional social-democratic political agenda. Moreover, they were couched in a political discourse borrowed from traditional adversaries of the left (constraints, rigour – the language of Barre during the 1970s). In European policy, the SEA and the Treaty on European Union were major achievements for which Mitterrand could claim some credit. But however fine Mitterrand's discourse evoking a 'social Europe', the Maastricht Treaty imposed a monetarist vision of an ever closer union, a logic which had little in common with Keynesian reflationary policies. The crusading anti-inflation and strong franc policies were likewise references borrowed from traditional adversaries. These new references cannot be abandoned, for they form the real Mitterrand heritage, with which the PS leadership remains indelibly associated.

CONCLUSION

In practice, it is difficult to distinguish a personal Mitterrand heritage from the more general lessons of fourteen years of French history. For all the popular enthusiasm sparked by his presidential victory on 10 May 1981, the Mitterrand legacy is not specifically a left-wing one. Its salient characteristic revolves around a necessary but painful abandoning of traditional left-wing mythology that appears henceforth irreversible. Its impact has been most obvious on the left. Indeed, in order to avoid engaging in an incrementalist type of public policy, the new Socialist government under Jospin might have to call into question the crucial choices determined during the Mitterrand presidency, notably the particular type of European integration project launched in the 1980s. This appears unlikely. The core of the 1981 policy agenda – nationalizations, reflation, welfare expansion, wealth redistribution – appears off the policy agenda for the foreseeable future. On account of the legitimizing function performed throughout

Mitterrand's presidency, the policy legacy – one of European integration, governmental realism, and economic rigour – imposes itself in equal measure on governments of the centre-right and centre-left.

Of the personal legacy, it is too soon to draw final conclusions. Political scientists will observe with interest the limitations of the personalist type of political movement produced by the Fifth Republic. As Gaullism could not really survive without de Gaulle, neither can Mitterrandism without Mitterrand. Despite renovating the PS on the basis of a presidential rally, Mitterrand distrusted political parties. In time, the Socialist Party learned to distrust Mitterrand. The former president's input was manifestly an important one notably in terms of the pursuit of power, adaptation to the presidential system and conversion to governmental realism. But ultimately it is difficult to point to a specifically Mitterrandist heritage that is reserved for the PS, except arguably for a historic memory of shared victories and a particular type of party organization. The Mitterrand heritage has to be considered as part of a more general one imposing itself on left and right alike. For this reason, it is far from certain that Mitterrand will be treated with the same reverence on the Socialist left as Léon Blum or Jean Jaurès, despite being markedly more successful than either.

NOTES

1.   J. Blondel, *Political Leadership* (London: Sage, 1987).
2.   A. Cole, *François Mitterrand: a Study in Political Leadership* (London: Routledge, 1994).
3.   Ibid.

Part 5
Culture

15 Mitterrand's *Grands Projets*: Monuments to a Man or Monuments to an Age?
Eric Cahm

According to the distinguished architectural critic François Chaslin, President Mitterrand displayed 'the somewhat exhibitionistic desire to live on in stone',[1] and French public opinion thought likewise from the moment several major new cultural facilities were announced early in his first term of office: the Grand Louvre with its corollary, the removal of the Finance Ministry to a new building at Bercy, the Institute of the Arab World, the Bastille Opera House, and the Centre for Music, together with the projects inherited from President Giscard d'Estaing: the Orsay Museum, the Tête Défense buildings, and the park of La Villette. These were immediately dubbed 'the president's major projects' and they soon became 'the president's major building works'.

Mitterrand naturally disclaimed any personal ambition in respect of this vast programme: 'My ambition,' he told a journalist in 1984, 'is not for me but for France'.[2] In October 1981, after the announcement of the initial decisions, he declared in cabinet that 'there could be no policy of greatness for France without great architecture'.[3] Indeed, architecture, great architecture, was for him the preferred medium for reaffirming French greatness. France had fallen behind, he asserted; it was time to try to catch up.[4] He declared in 1984 that he was launching 'a political initiative aimed at restoring to France the means to her greatness, and more particularly her inspiration towards greatness – and the more she is under threat the more she must be great; the more she tends towards the universal, the more she remains herself – architecture is the best means to express this ambition'.[5] Here was a new version of the Gaullist call to French greatness, but it was based no longer on the grand diplomatic gesture or on defence policy, but on the grand architectural gesture. Mitterrand planned to restore France's reputation in the world through buildings.

In architecture, he said, grand gestures had been made abroad rather than in France since the First World War[6] – and it was true that under the Fifth Republic Pompidou had given his name to only one building, and Giscard only had three incomplete projects to his credit. A period of poor architecture, Mitterrand claimed, had corresponded to a period of weakness for France.[7] But now, at long last, socialism was settling into the long-term exercise of power, which fulfilled the essential precondition for major architectural achievement: 'Nothing new and forceful can be built within the time scale imposed by promoters and speculators'.[8] The Socialists could surely do better than their predecessors: 'Can we really not show ourselves capable, in the situation we are now in, of signalling our choice in the future and our confidence in the country by putting this great enterprise into effect ?'[9] A period of weakness, marked by poor architecture, could now be succeeded by a period of strength.

There would be no question, however, of Socialist architecture. Could indeed there be such a thing? Roger Quilliot, in an interview in *Le Monde*, rejected the idea in the name of the president : 'Architecture cannot be the result of government wishes: Stalinist pomposity is only another form of academicism.' He insisted on the 'necessary freedom of the creative artist'.[10] The relations between Socialism and architecture had always been difficult to define. For Mitterrand and his ministers, the state clearly had its part to play. According to Quilliot, it both inspired and commissioned architecture. And one may add, Socialism had always given architecture the social objective of creating rational, healthy and perhaps beautiful collective housing for the people. In the current connection, it would be a matter of building an opera house for the people, and Mitterrand would later claim that the new National Library would make the whole of knowledge available to all.

However, in the aesthetic sphere, as Jack Lang put it in *L'Architecture d'aujourdhui*, the Socialists had 'no preordained model... French society today is pluralistic, and sensibilities, aspirations and tastes are different and often contradictory. The architecture of a Socialist regime must therefore reflect this pluralism. It must not institute a single style, but the cohabitation of forms of architecture which express themselves differently'.[11]

When asked directly before he was elected whether there would be a Mitterrand style, the future president replied evasively, 'You must wait till the end of my term of office';[12] fourteen years later, when interviewed by Bernard Pivot, he had made up his mind: 'There is no Mitterrand style'.[13]

Did this mean that there was, in regard to the Mitterrand projects, no issue of style at stake? Things were not as simple as they might appear from the official statements just quoted. It is clear that Mitterrand and his ministers actually had a definite preference for the modernist school, so that the relationship between this preference and the actual buildings which were constructed demands some examination.

The signs are not difficult to read. Ieoh Ming Pei, directly commissioned by Mitterrand without a competition for the transformation of the Louvre, explicitly placed himself in the modernist tradition of Mies van der Rohe and Le Corbusier.[14] And Mitterrand actually gave a few revealing hints himself about his personal tastes in architecture in his interview in *Le Nouvel Observateur*. 'In the end I believe my tastes are fairly classical and that I am attracted by pure geometrical forms.' He added: 'I rather tend to fight shy of excess, overloading and embellishment'.[15] Pure geometrical forms, simplicity, and lack of decoration: were not these among the most classical characteristics of modernist architecture?

In any case, the president had let the cat out of the bag even more when he remarked that Paris had not given a sufficient place to modern architecture.[16] He naturally rejected any notion that he had imposed his own views on the competition juries. 'I have been guided by the juries, because everywhere, except in the case of the Grand Louvre, there was a competition. However, within the limits set by the competitions, my taste did express itself'.[17]

The conformity between these tastes of Mitterrand's, implicitly and to an extent explicitly favourable to modernism, and the architectural choices finally made does raise the question as to whether this was simply a matter of coincidence. The evidence suggests it was not, and the stylistic disclaimers, followed by the construction under Mitterrand of a number of large projects predominantly modernist in style, demands some explanation in the light of the links between socialism and modernism, the historical and architectural context, and the actual workings of the competition system.

The founding fathers of modernism certainly had socialist sympathies. But it has often been noted that modernism has since come to serve regimes of all kinds, not only socialist, but also capitalist. A socialist regime could not openly associate itself with a school which no doubt had stronger capitalist than socialist connotations in 1981.

But it certainly reacted against the architectural and planning climate which had set in under Giscard. There had been in the 1970s a massive public backlash against tower blocks and much of what modernist architecture had produced in France since the Second World War. Tower blocks had become anathema, and when the postmodern wave appeared in the United States in 1975, just after Giscard d'Estaing's election, architects in France were also beginning to look, in a similar spirit, towards the past and towards regionalism. Ricardo Bofill was producing a new version of Versailles 'for the people' at Saint-Quentin-en-Yvelines, and numerous old buildings and quarters were being restored or reshaped for new uses. Responding to this climate, President Giscard began to extol the virtues of so-called 'architecture in the French style', an architecture 'based on moderation and harmony', 'a reasonable architecture', which, he said, 'turned its back on models from across the Atlantic, cold, impersonal and deliberately imposing', and which would be 'a natural architecture... strongly linked to the environment and to geographical diversity'.[18]

Giscard's planning decisions followed from this clear return to classical values, with a touch of postmodern regionalism and contextualism: the Left Bank expressway and the Apogée tower at the Place d'Italie were cancelled, and a limit was set on the height of tower blocks. The International Trade Centre planned for Les Halles would be replaced by a garden. The central theme here was a repudiation of modernism and its excesses. The return to the past and to classicism was manifested in the plan for the Orsay railway station to be turned into a Museum of the Nineteenth Century, to balance the modernism of Beaubourg; in the plan for a large classical park at La Villette; and in that for two buildings with mirror façades to be constructed at the head of La Défense, so as not to affront the historical perspective of the Arc de Triomphe.

When François Mitterrand was elected in May 1981, a battle among architects between the moderns and the postmoderns was reaching its height in France, with the exhibition 'Presence of History' presented at the Festival d'Automne the same year, followed, in November 1982 by the modernist counterblast, another exhibition entitled 'Modernity, an unfinished project.' It was in this context then that Mitterrand's preference for the moderns was clearly exhibited in his choice of Pei to renovate the Louvre. Pei actually quoted the theme of the modernist exhibition in an interview: 'The modern movement has hardly begun. It has not yet fully exploited all the possibilities of technology'.[19] There were other infallible signs: left-wing architects consistently rejected Giscard's traditionalism; they considered all postmodernism a form of neo-conservatism. There was thus an unambiguous and practically explicit choice by Mitterrand of modernist architecture for the new Louvre.

Finally, there was at least a conformity between the president's expressed tastes and the decisions of the competition juries on the other projects. Though Mitterrand did not directly intervene, except at the margin, in the aesthetics of the remaining projects, the very mechanism of the competition juries worked in such a way as to produce results in keeping with his tastes. The juries were composed of architects selected by Mitterrand's men; in any case they played safe in their choices and chose established architectural figures who would tend to be modernists rather than the newer postmoderns: both this, and their inevitable tendency to keep to simple, clearly defined projects, all worked towards a harmony with the president's wishes without his actually imposing his own views.

The result was a reassertion of modernism through these large state commissions. The public debate between moderns and postmoderns was stifled in the 1980s by the monopolizing of public attention by the *grands projets*, and so Mitterrand actually did, by these indirect means, reorient French architecture in the early 1980s in a definite stylistic direction.

A detailed examination of the *grands projets* will make clear in each case the extent of the modernist stylistic dominance. The postmodern influence most strongly characterized, inevitably, the projects inherited from Giscard, and most notably the Orsay Museum project which was at a fairly advanced stage when Mitterrand came to power. According to the architects originally selected, the aim was to 'bring up to date an architectural work which could give rise to a reinterpretation and to a geometrical recomposition on the basis of a pre-existing outline'.[20] This rehabilitation of a former railway station, involving a dialectic between past and present, was entirely consistent with the postmodern spirit. The choice of an Italian woman architect, Gae Aulenti, for the internal architecture also pointed in the same direction. Her coming disrupted the execution of the project: instead of taking second place to Laloux's architecture, she set out to develop a second rival scheme of architecture for the interior, visibly based on ancient Egyptian forms; the final juxtaposition of two rival and conflicting styles, and the introduction of colours and details considered to be postmodern, intensified the impression of postmodernism. The museum was attacked by out-and-out modernists, said François Chaslin: 'They readily identified Giscardism with the rediscovery of the nineteenth century and the bourgeois *pompier* style',[21] and if the museum gained immediate public favour, it did not convince French professionals, while across the Channel Peter Buchanan, in the *Architectural Review*, found the whole 'like a stage set for a Cecil B. de Mille production of Aïda' and 'hopelessly jumbled in design and concept'.[22]

To an extent, too, the park at La Villette still reflects the postmodern climate. Adrien Fainsilber had proposed under Giscard an extremely sober and classical park 'in the French style', with regularly planted lines of tall trees. Once Mitterrand took over, everything changed. Fainsilber lost his park, and a radically new scheme was envisaged, neither Classical nor Romantic, and certainly not eclectic or postmodern: an urban park, whatever that was, a left-wing park, a park of the future.

In practice the futuristic park did not entirely materialize. Bernard Tschumi, the winner of the new competition, created a park which was modern, certainly, by its resolutely urban character. There was precious little greensward, and the rationalism of the regular geometrical chequering of the site, with red Follies at each intersection of the squares, manifestly aping Russian constructivism, was unambiguous: Tschumi naturally upset all the upholders of traditional park architecture. At the same time, he talked of breaks, conflicts and hiatuses, which was the very language of postmodernism. In any case, the La Villette park was also the site of a major rehabilitation project, the Grande Halle of 1867, while the Lions Fountain and several other nineteenth-century structures were also integrated into the scheme. And if Fainsilber's reworking of the unfinished saleroom on the site as a Science and Technology Museum appeared classical to some by virtue of its overall structural form, its interior is festooned with high-tech, and punctuated with busts of philosophers – another provocative stylistic juxtaposition.

It must finally be noted that the commission for the Conservatoire and the Centre for Music at La Villette went to Christian de Portzamparc, whose name was directly linked for some with the postmodern school, though he personally rejected the label. He has certainly been strongly influenced by Le Corbusier, whom he quotes directly, but he does set himself apart from the most abstract forms of modernism by his return to the symbolic function in architecture, by his poetics of form and space, and by the account he takes of the city as it exists cheek-by-jowl with the park. By the force of his imagination, by his use of the play of light and colour, de Portzamparc seems to have made remarkable use of his limited resources at the Centre for Music – the Bastille Opera seems positively opulent in comparison – and his work at La Villette must count among the best of the architectural achievements among the Mitterrand projects.

All in all, the balance sheet of La Villette is a varied one: it has retained a considerable number of postmodern features, despite the introduction of the modernist park, and the Conservatoire and the Centre for Music are a world away from the most austere forms of modernism: Mitterrand kept clear of the musical project, as he did not feel competent to intervene, and left it to the professionals.

His influence on the projects for the Tête Défense however, decisively orientated the site away from Giscardian ideas. The more or less backward-looking projects, on which the previous regime was still hesitating when he was elected, were immediately dropped, and a new competition was organized, won by a Dane unknown in France, Otto von Spreckelsen. His Grand Arch was originally intended by the Mitterrand regime to become a Crossroads of Communications, a meeting place for all the peoples of the earth. The immense hollow cube of white marble was planned by the architect as 'a modern "Arc de Triomphe" celebrating the triumph of mankind'. Von Spreckelsen also foresaw 'protected areas covered with sheets of glass, which, like drifting clouds, would seem to move about gently above the heads of people and their activities. And there, amidst real plants and small fountains, they will be able to relax, have a coffee, walk about and take a look at many things'.[23]

The Grand Arch he constructed, though modernist in its huge scale, its simple geometrical form and the purity of its expanses of white marble, at the same time also marks a return to symbolism, the strong symbolism, obviously, of the triumphal arch and of a window into the future, as well as that of the 'clouds' and 'hills' (the sides of the cube) and that of technology – the outer surface being intended to symbolise the microchip, 'the greatest invention of genius due to modern technology'.[23] This mixture of the modern and of a symbolism ranging from the most classical to the most futuristic, transcended, for the professionals, the stylistic quarrels of the day and won unanimous praise. It was now clear, declared Roland Castro, what Mitterrand was looking for: 'self-evidence and simplicity, both formal and political, a consensus, in fact'.[24] So here was modernism, modulated by a variety of symbols.

At the same time, it must be added that the abandonment of the Communication Crossroads in April 1986, and the turning over of the building to commercial offices, detracted greatly from its initial impact – and as for the disappearance of Spreckelsen's friendly garden, with its plants and fountains, and its replacement by a open windswept terrace, this made the Arch's approaches less than welcoming. Only in 1997 were the gardens of the Arch, extending westward, to soften its environment.

When one turns to the projects initiated by Mitterrand, modernism becomes almost wholly dominant. First, the Bastille Opera House, the unloved project, the one over which Mitterrand said he had hesitated the most before accepting the jury's verdict.[25] It has also been widely condemned by the professionals as an unconvincing assemblage of neo-modernist elements.

The Institute of the Arab World, by Jean Nouvel, has, on the other hand, been generally hailed as a fine example of new French architecture, and one of the best of the Mitterrand projects. Its modernism expresses itself through the regular geometry of the façades and by the high-tech effects, notably the famous moucharabiehs which allow the modulation of light to the interior by the use of aluminium diaphragms. The modernity of this 'architecture of light' is attenuated by the references to Arab history and culture and to the Parisian context.

The explicit modernism of the architecture of the Grand Louvre has already been noted: it was of course only confirmed by the initial outcry against the pyramid by the self-appointed guardians of tradition in the conservative press. However, for Ieoh Ming Pei, the pyramid, being in glass not stone, was far from symbolising any pharaoh-like ambition in Mitterrand; it was in itself a classical form, characteristic of all periods; with the little pyramidions, the pools and fountains, it was intended, through the use of modern technology, to provide a neutral foil to the Cour Napoléon, with some additional reference to the gardens of Le Nôtre. The pyramid soon gained general approval and today, after the cleaning of Lefuel's façades, it forms a fine modernist tribute to one of the most prestigious sites in Paris. As for the Hall Napoléon below, it is certainly too noisy, but it has great monumental elegance. The treatment of the materials and the colour produce the sumptuous and warm effect of a palace for the people which is nevertheless in no way intimidating. The Richelieu wing, when it opened, won unanimous praise. Pei's architecture succeeds in being timeless, and must be counted one of the great successes, if not the greatest, among the Mitterrand projects.

The Finance Ministry at Bercy is a stupendous exercise in brutalism, the work of Chemetov and Huidobro, selected by a purely French competition. This is basically the largest office building in Europe, and it proclaims its modernity out loud; it takes the form of a long viaduct stretching from the Gare de Lyon to the Seine, at right angles to the river, into which it dips its feet. It is intended to mark in the East the entrance to Paris, as the Eiffel Tower does in the West. Its immense length is measured out in huge rectangular arches: every element throughout is rectangular, repetitive and ultra-severe, as befits the function of tax-collecting; there is virtually no colour in this black-and-white composition, even in the interior, and hardly a single curve (Mitterrand insisted on a rotunda at the end of one lateral wing). The austerity and grandiose proportions of the building aptly figure the authority of the state, but critics were mistaken in talking of neo-Stalinism or neo-Fascism: the citizen and taxpayer is not dwarfed and crushed by enormous heights as in Mussolini's neo-Caesarist buildings. Such criticism stems from the political prejudice which colours discussion of architecture and of so much else in France; although it is true that Chemetov had once demonstrated some enthusiasm for the Stalinist style.

And there is after all some slight relief, with patches of vegetation in the line of internal courtyards and in the 'French-style garden' alongside the building with its moats and classical statues, which remind us of the older architecture of the French state, and of the links between the rationalism of the Ancien Régime in France and the rationalism of the modernists.

At Bercy, Mitterrand's interventions in the detail are worth noting: he insisted on the slimming-down of the columns with 'their feet in the water', and on a toning-down of the brutalism of the concrete façades, henceforth to be faced with stone. The modernism of the Finance Ministry is thus clear-cut and, apart from the odd touch, uncompromising.

The final link in the modernist chain is the new national library or Library of France. Its huge dimensions, as at Bercy, cannot fail to impress, but the main bulk of the monument, composed of four wings arranged round a rectangular courtyard, is, as it were, buried, largely below ground level, to emerge only as a low, sloping mound, covered by roof treated as public terraces, with, at each corner, the four glazed bookstack towers in the shape of open books facing inward. The garden of tall evergreens, which fills the vast inner courtyard, is invisible from outside and can only be looked at from the roof terraces and from the inward-facing reading rooms. The avowed aim of the architect, Dominique Perrault, was to avoid building a huge mastodon which would overwhelm the new Seine Left Bank quarter, of which the library will become the heart. Perrault's modernism is again rectangular and rational, but above all abstract, innocent of any image apart from that of the book: 'I am not an image-maker.' He sees himself as a minimalist.[25] To build a great library on time and within budget, a building well integrated into the surrounding quarter and above all effectively fulfilling its functions in regard to its readers, while simultaneously reducing the rôle of architecture to a minimum and with no idea of a manifesto: these aims, together with a certain desire for timelessness, sum up the architect's approach. 'The building ought to appear as belonging to the end of the twentieth century rather than to the 80s or 90s.' This modernism seems closer to its origins than that of the other projects. The only concession to any specificity is in the taking into account of the links with the new quarter, but as this did not antedate the libary, the architecture could remain entirely abstract.

The interior is very discreet, and, with its use of wood and of acres of red-brown carpet underfoot, it speaks of a certain comfort, and a certain visual warmth, as well as of a contemplative silence, aided by the views of the internal garden which no member of the public will be allowed to defile. The garden will remain a 'living fresco', to be looked at but not entered. The minimal metal fittings and the remaining concrete walls do not obtrude themselves on the observer. All this is a far cry from the coldness of some modernist interiors, but there remains a lingering suspicion that the building's huge scale, the high ceilings and endless vistas down the corridors may somewhat intimidate the users. In the end, it certainly demands to be judged in use, Perrault holding firm to the modernist belief that form follows function.

There is thus no doubt that Mitterrand's *grands projets*, despite some postmodern touches – notably at La Villette, and at the Orsay Museum, whose form was largely fixed before 1981 – represent, through the direct and indirect intervention of the state in the person of the president, and notably through his choice of Pei for the Louvre, a distinct reaffirmation of modernism. They include some work of very high quality which has certainly added distinction to a Parisian landscape dominated since the early 1970s by the Tour Maine-Montparnasse, and so they do meet with Mitterrand's wish to see in Paris more grand gestures and more representation for modern architecture. But whether they include examples of great architecture which could restore France's reputation in the world is more doubtful. It is at any rate clear that, as developments of basically existent forms, they do not mark a new moment in French architecture: there has even been some talk of academicism.

The questions in the title of this chapter still remain: if no one could deny such huge buildings the status of monuments in one sense of the word, can they at all be seen as monuments to Mitterrand, or are they merely monuments to the present age? Of course, if they were all undoubtedly pieces of great architecture, it would be easier for them to be linked in the public memory with Mitterrand. As things stand, this will not be easy. The most likely candidates as monuments to Mitterrand are the Louvre, where the president chose the architect, and the Grand Arch. But the Louvre, after all, had been the work of many princes before François Mitterrand, and the Grand Arch has lost some of its original meaning. And there is another fundamental reason why the *grands projets* cannot, by their very nature, easily fill the bill as monuments to the Socialist president: the limited capacity of any basically modernist building to serve as a monument to an individual, or indeed to anything else. There has been from the beginning a reluctance, on the part of modernism, to convey particular messages of any kind, or at least messages which are not those of universal reason; this is quite apart from the *parti pris* against the past and all its works which has obviously also militated against the celebration of men of the past. The 1996 Paris exhibition entitled 'Monument et Modernité'[26] has been a timely reminder of the long-standing refusal of the celebratory monument by modernism: the surrealists went so far as to desecrate existing monuments, at least in words. Breton's project in 1933 was to blow up the Arc de Triomphe after burying it in a pile of dung; today's modernist artists still set out at least to desacralise Parisian monuments. So that if Mitterrand actually did hope to live on in stone, his predilection for modernism was actually a severe handicap. He himself declared that he thought that each era expressed itself through its architecture. And this is in the end a more promising approach to the interpretation of the *grands projets*: were they not rather an expression of the present era? The difficulty here is one pointed to by Jack Lang, who declared in *L'Architecture d'aujourd'hui* that 'architecture is the expression not of a society but of the public authorities in that society'.[27]

So we have to ask in fact whether the *grands projets* are a monument to the age or to the Socialist regime. It is clear from the foregoing that Mitterrand and his ministers did place their mark on the period through their encouragement of a reaffirmation of modernism, so that the conclusion must be that the *grands projets* reflect their period, but that they reflect it imperfectly, or by default, since the postmodern only survived within the projects as a result of decisions made before 1981. Finally, as to the *grands projets* as a memorial to Mitterrand, the solution began to emerge as soon as he died: calls were immediately heard for his name to be given to the new National Library. As has clearly emerged from the above, the *grands projets* could not commemorate the late president as architecture. And so, just as the Centre Beaubourg, an earlier modernist construction with no obvious visual reference to its progenitor, had to be dubbed Centre Georges Pompidou, the National Library, with its minimalist architecture, could only be made to reall the late president by being given his name. Logically enough, it was announced on the eve of its first opening in December 1996, that President Chirac had so decided. Some protests were raised in *Le Figaro*, mainly on the right, but Mitterrand now had his first memorial. No doubt he will have to wait a little longer for his statue. It is interesting to recall that after the reaction against statue-mania set in in Paris before the First World War, modernism for decades intensified the opposition to putting up statues to great men. It was only under Mitterrand, in fact, that public commissions for such statues began again: as is suggested by the above, they had perforce to return to a decent degree of figuration. Only time will tell whether Mitterrand is to join Jean Moulin, Pierre Mendès France and Georges Pompidou. The first anniversary of his death was commemorated with a certain coolness in view of the controversies surrounding his early life and his state of health as president. Nonetheless, a number of streets and squares had already been named after him in left-wing towns; at his birthplace Jarnac, two busts were unveiled on 11 January 1997 and plans for statues were in hand in the Morvan and at Lille.[28]

NOTES

1. F. Chaslin, *Les Paris de François Mitterrand* (Paris: Gallimard, 1995), p. 18.
2. F. Mitterrand, 'Parce que je suis amoureux de Paris', *Le Nouvel Observateur*, 14 December 1984, p. 69. (Referred to as Mitterrand.)

3. Chaslin, op. cit., p. 21.
4. Mitterrand, op. cit., p. 69.
5. Ibid.
6. Ibid.
7. Ibid.
8. F. Mitterrand, Interview in *Le Matin*, 23 April 1981.
9. Chaslin, op. cit., p. 21.
10. R. Quilliot, 'Architecture et nation', *Le Monde*, 8 October 1982.
11. Chaslin, op. cit., p. 33.
12. Ibid., p. 12.
13. Television interview with Bernard Pivot (April 1995).
14. *Paris 1979–1989* (New York: Rizzoli, 1988), p. 42.
15. Mitterrand, op. cit., p. 66.
16. Ibid.
17. Ibid.
18. Chaslin, op. cit., p. 33.
19. *Paris 1979–1989*, p. 42.
20. Ibid, p. 59.
21. Cf. Chaslin, p. 33.
22. P. Buchanan, 'From toot-toot to Tutankhamun', *The Architectural Review*, Vol. 186, No. 1110, 1989, pp. 48–53.
23. *Paris 1979–1989*, op. cit., p. 19.
24. Chaslin, op. cit., p. 172.
25. D. Perrault, '…où le vide importe autant que les pleins', *Télérama*, 29 March 1995.
26. *Monument et modernité à Paris: art, espace public et enjeux de mémoire 1891–1996* (Paris: Paris-Musées, 1996).
27. Chaslin, op. cit., p. 19.
28. The author owes the information about the Morvan to Marion Demossier.

16 Socialist Film Policy and the Heritage Film

Guy Austin

A POPULAR BUT CULTURAL CINEMA

In his recent study of French cultural policy, David Looseley has written that 'the tradition of state support for French film, steadily strengthened since 1981[...], has allowed France alone among European countries to maintain a respectable production rate of some 140 films annually', and that, rightly or wrongly, Jack Lang, the high-profile Socialist Minister of Culture from 1981 to 1986 and from 1988 to 1993, 'is commonly hailed as the saviour of the industry'.[1] Lang certainly included cinema in his cultural policy from the first: in his budget of November 1981, state spending on cinema and the audiovisual climbed from FF35 million to FF120 million.[2] He had also commissioned the Bredin Report into French cinema, submitted to him in November 1981 and revealed to the press on April Fool's Day 1982. Presenting the report, Lang declared that cinema should become what it had once been in the 1940s and 1950s, a cultural pursuit for the masses.[3] He aimed to foster a consensual form of cinema that would be at once popular and cultural, to win back the audience lost during the 1970s and to end the schism between the commercial and artistic sectors which had widened during that decade.[4] The first of the six objectives of the report was defined as to 'encourage the renewal of creativity and production and [to] preserve regional, national and European cultural identities'.[5] French cinema was seen as facing a threefold danger, from Hollywood, from television, and from the new satellite, cable and video technologies.[6] But what genre(s) did Socialist film policy equip to face this danger? What exactly was the nature of this popular yet cultural cinema that Lang envisaged as competing with Hollywood?

EUROPEAN ART CINEMA VERSUS HOLLYWOOD

By the 1980s, the long-standing French perception of their national culture as struggling against rampant Americanization was felt especially keenly in the realm of the cinema, with falling audiences and a rising American share of the market stirring fears that had dogged the industry at least since the Blum-Byrnes agreement of 1946, which had seen American films imported in exchange for the export of French goods. Fears of Americanization ultimately resulted in the hard-won 'cultural exemption' of films from the 1993 GATT agreement. Unsurprisingly, then, Lang's film policy began as explicitly anti-American. In September 1981, he refused to attend the festival of American cinema at Deauville, in protest at the threat of Hollywood to the health of French cinema and television. Competition with Hollywood entailed not only protectionist measures such as quotas for television and cinema screenings but also the production of French films able to out-perform American ones at the box office. Hence Lang's general policy of aiding prestige cinema, European co-productions, and projects with big budgets and high production values. With the French share of their own domestic box office down to 49.5 per cent in 1981 and 44.3 per cent in 1985, the reaction of the first Socialist government was to increase 'overall aid to the film and audiovisual industries sevenfold' from 1981 to 1986.[7] Despite such efforts, the French share continued to fall, reaching a mere 30 per cent in 1991.[8] One of the reasons for this might well be the targeting of prestige vehicles under Lang's film policy. For, as we shall see, he ignored the one genre which has consistently seen off American competition at the box office: the low-budget popular comedy.

For Lang, it was not simply French national cinema, but European cinema with France as its leader, which had to be armed against the American monolith. Hence in *Cahiers du cinéma*'s review of the first five 'Lang years' in 1986, the policy of state aid to European co-productions was cited as a perfect example of Lang's dream of making Paris the centre of a global non-American cinema.[9] According to Steve Neale, European art cinema has in fact always tended to define itself against Hollywood. In Neale's terms, art becomes 'the space in which an indigenous cinema can develop and make its critical and economic mark'. In other words, 'the films produced by a specific national film industry will have [...] to differentiate themselves from those produced by Hollywood. One way of doing so is to turn to the cultural traditions specific to the country involved'.[10] This is the role Jack Lang envisaged for a cultural cinema based on the national treasures of France's cultural heritage. It is, in short, a blueprint for the heritage film.

THE HERITAGE FILM IN FRANCE

The 1980s saw the rise of several new genres in French film, among them the stylised fantasy narratives of the *cinéma du look* and the North African immigrant films known as Beur cinema. Representatives of these, such as Luc Besson's *Subway* and Mehdi Charef's *Le Thé au harem d'Archimède* (both 1985) did receive state funding in the mid–1980s via the system of *avances sur recettes* (see below). But the genre most closely associated with Socialist film policy from 1981 onwards, and funded in direct state aid as well as through the *avances* system, was the heritage film. In France this is a genre closely related to the *tradition de qualité* – the literary adaptations and historical dramas of the 1940s and 1950s – although chronologically its predominance in the 1980s parallels the British trend for nostalgia inaugurated by *Chariots of Fire* in 1981. The heritage genre relies heavily on a cultural legitimacy derived from the arts, and in particular from 'the adaptation of literary and theatrical properties already recognized as classics within the accepted canon'.[11] In France, recent heritage films have celebrated music, sculpture and painting (*Tous les matins du monde, Camille Claudel, Van Gogh*), have adapted theatre (*Cyrano de Bergerac*), but have concentrated above all on reproductions of the novel, from Balzac and Flaubert (*Le Colonel Chabert, Madame Bovary*) to Zola and Proust (*Germinal, Un amour de Swann*). This emphasis on the great French novels of the nineteenth and early twentieth centuries invokes not only 'the familiarity and prestige' of the literary source, but also the 'status of a national intellectual tradition'.[12] The literary basis for many heritage films in France also appears congruent with the aims of Socialist cultural policy in the early 1980s, described by Guy Hocquenghem in July 1981 as a 'dictatorship' of traditional humanist art (in which François Mitterrand personified literature and Jack Lang the theatre) over the modern consumerist practices of the cinema and television.[13]

But this would be to ignore not only genuine concerns on the part of Lang and Mitterrand with the audiovisual media, but more specifically the fact that the heritage film puts literature on the screen, thus submitting high culture to the mass medium of the cinema, one of the 'cultural industries' cherished increasingly by Lang from 1983 onwards under a policy known as '*le tout-culturel*'.[14] Indeed, although 'one of the most disappointing aspects of Lang's [first] period in office was the failure to update heritage policies',[15] one could say that it was through the cinema that Lang tended to preserve the national heritage (on celluloid) and present it to a wide audience. By the same token, the literary heritage of the nation was democratized under the Socialists, not by Mitterrand's troubled *grand projet* of the Bibliothèque de France (see above, Chapter 15) but by big-screen adaptations of great French novels. To this extent the heritage film has also fulfilled the ideal of André Malraux, de Gaulle's influential Minister of Culture and Lang's most illustrious predecessor, namely that 'an untutored public could relate spontaneously to the visual and the powerfully iconographic'.[16] Thus the heritage film actually unites the two strands of Lang's cultural policy: the democratization of high culture (associated most strongly with the early years of the first Socialist government, and also with previous cultural policies like those of Malraux in the 1960s or the Front Populaire in the 1930s) and the rather more controversial celebration of cultural industries and popular forms (from cinema and video to graffiti art) which crystallized between 1983 and 1993.

The breakthrough of the heritage genre in France during the 1980s was prefigured in 1979 by the success of *Tess*, adapted from Thomas Hardy, filmed in France (although in English) by Roman Polanski, and perhaps most significantly, produced by Claude Berri. As both a director (of *Jean de Florette*, *Manon des Sources* and *Germinal*) and a producer (of his own films, of Youssef Chahine's *Adieu Bonaparte* and Patrice Chéreau's *La Reine Margot*), Berri has been involved in numerous heritage projects, but it is particularly through the latter role that he has come to personify the French heritage film. Critics have noted that while the cinema of the 1960s was a *cinéma d'auteur* characterized by the input and personal vision of the director, the cinema of the 1980s, and the heritage genre as a whole, is a *cinéma de producteur*, where the producer is dominant. The 1981 Bredin report had already identified the producer as the key to maintaining a balance between the demands of industry and art within French cinema.[17] The power shift from directors to producers is also reflected in the functioning during the 1980s of the funding system known as the *avances sur recettes*. Established in 1959, this comprises an advance loan made by the French government to film-makers, theoretically to be repaid from subsequent takings at the box office. The advance comes from tax on cinema tickets and other sources, but under the Socialists an increasing contribution also came from the Ministry of Culture, which gave FF10 million out of a total FF46 million in 1982, and FF35 million out of a total FF80 million in 1984.[18] Under Lang, *avances* were given to established film-makers, to young directors like Luc Besson and Jean-Jacques Beineix, and, often controversially, to major heritage projects such as Berri's *Jean de Florette* and *Manon des Sources*. The system was also refined in several ways, including in the early 1980s the targeting of production and screen-writing, Lang's aim being to encourage film-makers to use established producers and writers. On the one hand, this measure reasserted the importance of writing for the screen, and thus marked another shift away from the *cinéma d'auteur* of the 1960s and towards the more rigid practices of the post-war *tradition de qualité*. (Some heritage directors even turned to screenwriters from the latter period, as did Bertrand Tavernier when choosing to bring to the screen, as *Un Dimanche la campagne*, a novel by Pierre Bost.) On the other, it also meant that by the mid–1980s the *avance* was no longer an incentive to negotiating production for an embryonic project, but a supplementary source of funding once production for a film had already been secured. Even before film-producer Adolphe Viezzi's presidency of the *avances* commission in 1984 (notorious for the targeting of commercial films rather than art films), awards were being made to directors in name only, the deciding factor being the combination of production and scenario.[19]

In addition to the *avances sur recettes*, Lang as Minister of Culture began to grant direct funding to individual projects, including films passed over in the awarding of advances (Agnès Varda's *Sans toit ni loi* and Robert Bresson's *L'Argent*), and prestigious European co-productions of the kind encouraged in the Bredin report: Volker Schlöndorff's *Un Amour de Swann*, Youssef Chahine's *Adieu Bonaparte*, and Andrzej Wajda's *Danton*. In the latter case, however, Lang found that a film co-produced by his own Ministry ended up by being read as a Gaullist critique of socialism.

THE DANTON AFFAIR

Two mythical periods for the French left, the Revolution of 1789 and the Front Populaire of the 1930s, had came together in Jean Renoir's film *La Marseillaise* (1938), an evocation of the Revolution made under the auspices of the Popular Front. A similar attempt to relate Republican history to the society of the day resulted, soon after the election victories of Mitterrand in May 1981 and the Socialists in June, in the making of Wajda's Franco-Polish co-production *Danton*. The political circumstances in Poland, however, ensured that the film would be received as much more than an official history authorized by Mitterrand and the government. In December 1981 the military *coup* led by Jaruzelski and the outlawing of Solidarity broke the 'state of grace' that existed between the new Socialist government and the French intelligentsia (see below, Chapter 18): 'In the space of a few weeks, French intellectuals saw their worst fears of leftist-statist behaviour confirmed. The Socialists reacted weakly and hesitantly to the Jaruzeslki coup'.[20] When Wajda's film was released a year later, the charismatic Danton was immediately identified with Lech Walçsa and the hardline Robespierre with General Jaruzelski. Interpretation of *Danton* in relation to French politics also concentrated on the portrayal of the two protagonists. Historically associated with the victory of 'republican France against the combined forces of feudal Europe', and hence with the birth and identity of the modern state, Robespierre remained an iconic figure for the French left.[21] Hence the delight of the Gaullist opposition and the dismay of both Mitterrand and Lang at the characterization of Robespierre as a tyrant and Danton as a sympathetic pragmatist: 'The persona of Danton created by the immensely popular Gérard Depardieu [...] elicited a conservative bourgeois image in France, was even labelled Gaullist'.[22] Moreover, memories of the initial reaction of the Socialists to the Polish *coup* only intensified the association between Robespierre-Jaruzelski (played by the Polish actor Wojciech Pszoniak, dubbed into French) and Mitterrand-the Socialists, who thus fell foul of an official version of Republican history which they had in effect financed themselves, but whose interpretation they had been unable to control.

THE 'CULTURAL TOURISM' OF THE LATE 1980s

After Viezzi's unexpectedly populist funding round in 1984, Lang chose the publisher Christian Bourgois as president of the commission on *avances sur recettes* for the next year, with a brief to target 'culture'.[23] The result was not without controversy, however, when Claude Berri was granted two awards, each of FF2.5 million, for a project that would eventually cost an unprecedented FF110 million.[24] Berri's avowed ambition in filming two Pagnol adaptations, *Jean de Florette* and *Manon des Sources*, was to make a French *Gone With the Wind* and launch a mythical 'cinéma populaire',[25] and thus coincided exactly with Jack Lang's vision of the medium. With the help of the *avances*, he shot both films simultaneously on location, over a period of nine months.[26] Subsequently in 1986 more than six million spectators saw *Jean de Florette* and more than four million *Manon des Sources*. So potent was the vogue for Pagnol launched in this manner that four years later Yves Robert's far inferior, sentimental diptych based on Pagnol's memoirs, *La Gloire de mon père* and *Le Château de ma mère*, cashed in with a cinema audience of 5.8 million and 3.4 million respectively.[27]

Robert's Pagnol adaptations demonstrate explicitly a quality implicit in those of Berri, and in the heritage genre generally, which one might term 'cultural tourism'. These films combine the exoticism of the Provence region with a nostalgia for the early years of the century. The model of the heritage spectator as a temporal and spatial day-tripper is presented – without a hint of irony – in the narrative of Robert's diptych. If in *La Gloire de mon père* a Marseille family stay in a country villa for the school holidays, in *Le Château de ma mère* they visit a Provençal château every Sunday. A similar cultural tourism had also begun to develop in France at this point, with a boom in public demand for heritage sites: 'it had become clear by the late 1980s that monuments, stately homes and museums were increasingly in demand [...]. Hence the new buzzword "cultural tourism", [...] in which France's historic past played the major role'.[28] Part of this phenomenon was a marked rise in the popularity of the heritage film, which became increasingly successful at the box office as the 1980s drew to a close. After the success of Berri's Pagnol adaptations, Bruno Nuytten's *Camille Claudel* attracted three million spectators in 1988–1989, while in 1990 Robert's diptych was complemented by Jean-Paul Rappeneau's *Cyrano de Bergerac*, with an audience of close to four million.[29] There remained, however, two obstacles in the way of the heritage genre's dominance at the French box office. One was Hollywood, the other the perenially popular French comedy. In 1985, Coline Serreau's *Trois Hommes et un couffin* was watched by more than ten million people, as many as saw Berri's two Pagnol adaptations put together, and in 1988–1989 Etienne Chatiliez's *La Vie est un long fleuve tranquille* proved more successful than *Camille Claudel*.[30] But the most dramatic clash between the heritage genre and the comedy, and the final reckoning for Socialist film policy, came in 1993, the year of the Socialists' electoral defeat and of Jack Lang's exit as Minister of Culture.

THE FINAL RECKONING: LES VISITEURS VERSUS
GERMINAL

When in the late 1980s the Socialists were briefly out of power, Lang's successor at the Ministry of Culture, François Léotard, pointedly suppressed aid for 'artistic' films, but on his return to office Lang continued as before, and introduced a supplementary form of direct aid for ten to fifteen 'high quality' films per year. The films to benefit were again ambitious projects with big budgets, since Lang had been impressed by the success of recent blockbusters such as Jean-Jacques Annaud's *L'Ours* and Luc Besson's *Le Grand Bleu*, and of the heritage films *Jean de Florette* and *Camille Claudel*. It has been observed that the blockbuster model struck Lang as a safer bet than the unpredictable genre of the popular comedy, which had thrown up the surprise hits *Trois Hommes et un couffin* and *La Vie est un long fleuve tranquille*.[31] This assumption was perhaps shaken by the case of Maurice Pialat's enormously ambitious and costly *Van Gogh*, a film granted direct aid by Lang but spurned by the public when released in 1991. Nonetheless, in Lang's last months of office before the elections of March 1993, the Ministry of Culture co-produced another vast heritage project, Claude Berri's *Germinal*. By a telling coincidence, the last heritage film authorized by Lang had to compete directly with Hollywood (in the form of Steven Speilberg's all-devouring *Jurassic Park*) and with French popular comedy (in the form of Jean-Marie Poiré's irrepressible *Les Visiteurs*). The performance of *Germinal* therefore became the litmus test for Lang's film policy: could the official French heritage film beat a Hollywood giant? Could it at least beat a low-budget French comedy? The answer in both cases was no.

Based on a novel by Emile Zola, *Germinal* follows the organization and the brutal suppression of a miners' strike in northern France. The film was interpreted in *Cahiers du cinéma*, however, as a closing-down of the miners' struggle in much the same way that the Socialist government had closed down the mines, and as relegating both Zola's novel and the memory of the coalmines to the realm of the historical theme-park.[32] Meanwhile the male lead, the singer Renaud, criticised Berri in the press, comparing him to Saddam Hussein, the Terminator and, most cogently, to the moguls of Hollywood.[33] In many ways Berri was in fact trying to emulate the success of the movie-moguls of Hollywood's classical age, notably David O. Selznick, whose *Gone With the Wind* remained a model of the popular-cultural blockbuster Berri and Lang both cherished. But the criticism that too much money had been thrown at a lavish and ultimately empty project was reiterated in the film press. At the time of release, *Germinal* was the most expensive French film ever made, having cost FF165 million. *Télérama* asked pointedly if it was worth spending this much money to remind the poor that they would always be trodden on by the rich.[34]

The film performed adequately at the box office, attracting 5.8 million spectators. It was third, however, behind *Les Visiteurs* with 13.6 million and *Jurassic Park* with 6.3 million.[35] The French cinema sensation of 1993 was not *Germinal* but *Les Visiteurs*, the only film in Europe to prove more popular than *Jurassic Park*, and this by a margin of two to one. This fact led *Cahiers du cinéma* to establish a distinction between the genuinely popular cinema of *Les Visiteurs* and the worthy, government-sponsored *Germinal*. In an editorial entitled 'Vous avez dit populaire?', Thierry Jousse credited *Les Visiteurs* with a carnivalesque power, while attacking *Germinal* for vulgarizing and fossilizing literature.[36] This critique was elaborated by Andréa Scala, who remarked that the marketing of *Germinal* as an exemplar of national culture merely converted a cultural object into a commodity in a vain attempt to persuade the public to consume *Germinal* as avidly as they did *Les Visiteurs*.[37] Indeed, Lang had in fact peddled the film as a form of national education by sending free videotapes to schools.[38] While such tactics neatly epitomize Lang's championing of the heritage film, they also reflect a general tendency of Socialist cultural policy in the 1980s and 1990s: the foisting of official, state-sponsored culture on a mass audience whose own popular tastes are ignored. In this regard, Lang's film policy ends up sounding not unlike the mission of Jean Vilar, the founder of the Avignon festival and a prime mover in the democratization of high culture in the 1950s and 1960s, who sought to 'impose on the public what they desire deep down'.[39]

In an interview for *Cahiers du cinéma* in March 1993, director Jean-Marie Poiré pointed out that the making of *Les Visiteurs* had proved difficult, since both actors and producers were only interested in 'useless so-called cultural films'.[40] As his co-writer and star Christian Clavier explained, it was easier to put a small amount of money into a cultural film – which might be funded by grants, the Ministry of Culture, the National Cinema Centre, and by sales abroad generated by its cultural appeal – than to invest in comedy.[41] Moreover, this privileging of cultural over popular cinema was blamed on the previous decade – that is to say, more or less Mitterrand's period of office as president and Lang's as Minister of Culture. Ironically, then, it would seem that by 1993 the popular and cultural, far from being brought together in French cinema as the Bredin report had envisaged, were as far apart as ever, and perhaps had been polarized further by Lang's targeting of the heritage film at the expense of culturally 'low' genres such as comedy. Clavier's rather ominous conclusion was that only the success of popular cinema had allowed a French art cinema to exist at the margins, but that now the former was under threat from a subsidized and essentially unpopular version of the latter. Two years later this point was reiterated by Josiane Balasko: 'There is no future for French cinema – or art cinema – without popular cinema. [...] Luckily there is still a home audience for popular French cinema'.[42] But the fact that Balasko's own comedy *Gazon maudit* out-performed Rappeneau's heritage blockbuster *Le Hussard sur le toit*, and was second only to Clavier and Poiré's *Les Anges gardiens* at the French box office in 1995, suggests that, for all Jack Lang's efforts between 1981 and 1993, the heritage film is still not the dominant genre in French cinema.

NOTES

All translations are by the author unless otherwise stated.
1. D. Looseley, *The Politics of Fun: Cultural Policy and Debate in Contemporary France* (Oxford: Berg, 1995), p. 235.
2. Ibid., p. 81.
3. G-P. Sainderichen, 'La Rupture', *Cahiers du cinéma*, No. 336, p. 18.
4. S. Le Peron, 'L'Affiche douze ou le retour du grand public', *Cahiers du cinéma*, No. 336, pp. 19–20.
5. J.-D. Le Bredin, *The Bredin Report on the Future of the French Cinema* (London: BFI, 1992).
6. Ibid., p. 7.
7. Looseley, op. cit., p. 198.
8. Ibid.
9. S. Toubiana et al., 'L'image a bougé: Abécédaire du cinéma français', *Cahiers du cinéma*, No. 381, p. 19.
10. S. Neale, 'Art Cinema as Institution', *Screen*, Vol. 22, No. 1, p. 15.
11. A. Higson, 'Re-presenting the National Past: Nostalgia and Pastiche in the Heritage Film', in L. Friedman (ed.), *British Cinema and Thatcherism: Fires were started* (London: UCL Press, 1993), p. 114.
12. Ibid, p. 115.

13. Looseley, op. cit., p. 94.
14. Ibid., p. 87.
15. J. Forbes, 'Cultural Policy: the Soul of Man under Socialism', in S. Mazey and M. Newman (eds), *Mitterrand's France* (London: Croom Helm, 1987), p. 148.
16. Looseley, op. cit., p. 217.
17. Bredin, op. cit., p. 10.
18. H. Le Roux, 'La Commission de l'an III', *Le Journal du Cahiers du cinéma*, 45, xiv.
19. Ibid.
20. D. Pinto, 'The Left, the Intellectuals and Culture', in G. Ross, S. Hoffmann and S. Malzacher (eds), *The Mitterrand Experiment: Continuity and Change in Modern France* (Cambridge: Polity Press, 1987), p. 221.
21. R. Darnton, 'Danton and Double-Entendre', *New York Review of Books*, 16 February 1984, p. 20.
22. R. M. Pauly, *The Transparent Illusion: Image and Ideology in French Text and Film* (New York: Peter Lang, 1993), p. 94.
23. R. Prédal, *Le Cinéma français depuis 1945* (Paris: Nathan, 1991), p. 384.
24. Toubiana, op. cit., p. 21.
25. V. Ostria, 'Les Saisons et les jours', *Cahiers du cinéma*, No. 380, p. 62.
26. Ibid, p. 63.
27. Prédal, op. cit., p. 403.
28. Looseley, op. cit., p. 180.
29. Prédal, op. cit., p. 403.
30. Ibid.
31. Ibid, p. 388.
32. A. Scala, 'Le 18 Brumaire de Claude Berri', *Cahiers du cinéma*, No. 374, p. 32.
33. F. Pascaud, 'Le chanteur laminé', *Télérama*, No. 2281, p. 32.
34. P. Murat, 'Germinal', *Télérama*, No. 2281, p. 35.
35. D. Robinson, *The Chronicle of Cinema 1985–1995* (London: BFI, 1995), p. 127.
36. T. Jousse, 'Vous avez dit populaire?', *Cahiers du cinéma*, No. 473, p. 5.
37. Scala, op. cit., p. 24.
38. Ibid.
39. Looseley, op. cit., p. 244.
40. C. Nevers and F. Strauss, 'Entretien avec Jean-Marie Poiré et Christian Clavier', *Cahiers du cinéma*, No. 465, p. 86.
41. Ibid.
42. G. Vincendeau, 'Twist and Farce', *Sight and Sound*, Vol. 6, No. 4, p. 26.

17 The State and the Broadcasting Media: All Change?

Raymond Kuhn

During the Mitterrand presidency the relationship between the state and the broadcasting media underwent significant change. The state relinquished its monopoly of ownership and established new high-profile regulatory authorities in a withdrawal from its previous omni-competent role. Liberalization, deregulation and privatization were the fashionable concepts which informed a new official discourse in media policy-making, as radio and television became increasingly subject to market pressures rather than state controls.

Yet this picture of radical change needs to be qualified. Not only did the state manage the transition from a monopoly to a mixed system of private and public ownership through its control of the policy-making process. More fundamentally, even at the end of the Mitterrand presidency, the state retained important functions as a regulator of the broadcasting media and primary definer of their news agenda. At the same time, however, it was clear that the broadcasting sector had become a more complex field for state management than in the past, with politicians and state officials facing numerous problems in trying to achieve their policy goals in a turbulent and fast-moving audiovisual environment.

ECONOMIC AND POLITICAL LIBERALIZATION OF BROADCASTING

When Mitterrand was first elected President of the Republic in 1981, he inherited a state monopoly broadcasting system consisting of three television channels (TF1, Antenne 2 and FR3) and one radio company (Radio France). Until the Giscardian reform of 1974 these organizationally separate entities had been an integral part of the large, unitary public corporation, the Organisation de Radiodiffusion-Télévision Française (ORTF).[1] The state monopoly suffered from a problem of legitimacy in France because of its association with political control by the government of the day.[2] The ORTF, for example, had become a symbol of Gaullist authoritarianism in the 1960s and this was one factor in the decision of President Giscard d'Estaing to dismantle it.

At a more practical level, the monopoly had become increasingly difficult to enforce, having come under attack in the late 1970s from an assortment of pirate radio stations, including one established by Mitterrand's Socialist Party. With technological change undermining one of the traditional defences of the monopoly – the finite nature of the frequency spectrum – the new Socialist government abolished it in 1982 (*la loi Fillioud*) and embarked on a process of controlled liberalization.

During the next few years the audiovisual landscape changed beyond recognition, as both Socialist and conservative governments opened up the broadcasting system to market entry from private-sector players. In the early 1980s a large number of radio stations took advantage of the new dispensation, offering an impressive variety of programme content to local communities, sectional interests and minority groups across France. In 1984 Europe's first terrestrially transmitted pay-television channel, Canal Plus, began transmissions under the management of the state-controlled multimedia company Havas. In 1986 two commercial channels, La Cinq and TV6, were launched at the personal instigation of President Mitterrand.

The right's 1986 statute on freedom of communication (*la loi Léotard*) pushed commercialization even further, reducing public ownership in broadcasting through the privatization of the main national television channel – TF1 – whose franchise was awarded to a consortium dominated by the Bouygues construction company. The franchises for Channels Five and Six were reallocated to new consortia, whose owners, including the right-wing press baron Robert Hersant, were generally regarded as more sympathetic to the conservative government. At the same time a liberal policy on cable opened up this sector to commercial players after the Socialists' state-driven initiative had begun to flounder. Havas was transferred into the private sector in 1987, joining the ranks of other privatized media companies, including Radio Europe 1. In sum, by the time Mitterrand left office in 1995, much of local and national radio, a large slice of terrestrial television and the majority of cable networks were in private ownership, while the previously all-encompassing public sector had been reduced to a secondary role.

The entry of new private players into the broadcasting market was accompanied by moves towards political liberalization. Successive regulatory bodies were established to act as buffers between the political executive and professional broadcasters. The first of these, the Haute Autorité de la Communication Audiovisuelle (1982–1986), marked a break with the post-war tradition whereby the executive was directly involved in the appointment of key managerial and editorial staff in public-sector broadcasting. Responsibility for such appointments now fell to the regulatory authority, which was also given the tasks of awarding local private radio licences and ensuring impartiality in news and current affairs output.

The High Authority's two successors, the Commission Nationale de la Communication et des Libertés (CNCL) (1986–1989) and the Conseil Supérieur de l'Audiovisuel (CSA) (1989–), were also supposed to symbolize a more hands-off relationship between the political executive and broadcasting. Following the conservative victory in the 1986 parliamentary elections, the CNCL was empowered to award the franchise for the privatized TF1 and to reallocate those of Channels Five and Six. With a new Socialist government back in power after Mitterrand's second presidential victory in 1988, the CNCL was abolished and replaced by the CSA. In an attempt to reinforce the legitimacy and political independence of the new authority, Mitterrand proposed that its role be enshrined in the Constitution of the Fifth Republic. Though this was not carried out, the success of the CSA may be gauged by the fact that it was retained by the conservative government of Edouard Balladur after 1993.

THE STATE IN RETREAT?

Economic and political liberalization of the broadcasting sector may appear to be powerful evidence of a state in retreat. This, however, would be too simple a judgement. In part this is because the French state continued to play a central role during the transition from a monopoly to a mixed system of ownership. The liberalization and privatization policies followed by Socialist and conservative governments did not usher in a process of savage deregulation. This was in sharp contrast to the Italian experience where a regulatory vacuum had been created by the decision of the Constitutional Court to remove the monopoly of the public broadcaster, the Radiotelevisione Italiana (RAI), in the late 1970s.[3] The impotence of the Italian state in the face of the resultant anarchy of the airwaves served as a warning to French policy-makers. Instead the French state sought to control the process of change in a top-down manner.

More important than the state's role in the transitional process, however, was its continued involvement in key aspects of broadcasting throughout the whole of the Mitterrand presidency. In particular, the relinquishing of a large ownership stake in broadcasting was offset by increased emphasis on the state's regulatory function.[4] Paradoxically, therefore, while the concept of deregulation underpinned much government policy-making under Mitterrand, the state introduced waves of detailed regulation in an attempt to manage competition in an increasingly diverse media system.[5]

The Mitterrand presidency witnessed the growth of the regulatory state in the broadcasting sector, with rules applied to market entry, ownership and content. Regulations on market entry were implemented to promote diversity, but also control access to a frequency spectrum which remained a scarce resource. Legislation on monomedia and cross-media ownership was introduced in 1986. This set limits to the market share held by a single company in and across the media sectors of press, radio, television and cable or satellite.[6] Though generous in its maximum ceilings, the legislation recognized that the state continued to have a role in balancing the needs of pluralism and diversity on the one hand with the pressures of economic rationalization, cross-media synergy and the internationalization of audiovisual markets on the other. Content regulations were imposed for political, economic and cultural reasons. These included mandatory quotas on television programmes of French and European origin, rules covering television advertising and provisions regarding news output. In the television sector different regulatory regimes on programme content were applied to the various classes of operator, ranging from the very prescriptive in the case of the public-sector channels to the more liberal in the case of Canal Plus and cable stations.

The state also laid down the composition and method of appointment of the members of the broadcasting regulatory authorities. The composition of the CSA, for instance, was modelled on that of the Constitutional Council, with three members being appointed by each of the president of the Republic, the president of the Senate and the president of the National Assembly. Furthermore, there was evidence that political criteria frequently influenced appointments, as the executive sought to ensure the compliance of the regulatory body. On occasions the executive even imposed its will on the regulators to secure its favoured candidate for top broadcasting posts in the public sector, as in the appointment of Jean-Claude Héberlé as head of Antenne 2 in 1984.[7]

Meanwhile the state under Mitterrand continued to be a primary definer for the media, using its legitimacy, power and resources to influence the construction of their news agenda.[8] When Mitterrand acceded to the presidency, one of the first tasks of the Socialist government was the removal of the Giscardian 'old guard' in top managerial and editorial posts in the state broadcasting companies and their replacement with persons supportive of the new administration. The crude forms of political intervention of the de Gaulle presidency were no longer appropriate in a multi-channel, mixed-ownership broadcasting system. Instead, the president, government and state officials adapted to a mediatized political environment and a more critical audience by seeking to get their message across with greater sophistication than in the past, negotiating with and co-opting rather than controlling and censoring the media. The president and his advisers ('the Elysée'), the prime minister and his staff ('Matignon') and government ministries helped to structure the terms of the debate and the parameters of issue coverage on major domestic and foreign policy issues, from the fight against unemployment to the war in the Gulf. Other primary definers at state level included top civil servants, officials with specialist technical knowledge and the upper echelons of the military and the police. A range of support staff, including public relations personnel and media advisers, presidential and governmental spokespersons, press offices and governmental information agencies, were routinely mobilized to try to ensure that the official version of events dominated broadcast media coverage. As in other West European democracies, special events were staged for media attention, including presidential press conferences, interviews with journalists and television appearances by the president and his ministers. Image projection, photo opportunites and sound bites were also routinely used to gain media attention.[9]

A CONFUSED STATE

The profound changes in the French broadcasting system during the Mitterrand presidency did not result in the marginalization of the state by the entry of new market forces. None the less, the transition from an ownership to a regulatory state was accompanied by and contributed to greater complexity in this media policy sector than under any of Mitterrand's presidential predecessors. The result was less an impotent than a confused state which frequently found it difficult to reconcile the myriad tensions and contradictions of policy formulation and implementation.

For example, the technocratic logic underpinning the state's policy on the new media of cable and satellite was beset with conflict. Both technologies were supported by the state largely for their assumed industrial and economic benefits. The huge potential of fibre-optic and switched-star networks for the provision of a wide range of interactive services persuaded the Socialist government to invest in an ambitious national cable project at the beginning of the 1980s. Simultaneously, the state also provided public resources for the construction and launch of a direct broadcasting satellite, Télédiffusion de France 1 (TDF1), to ensure that France would not be left out of what was hoped would be a lucrative high-tech market for satellite hardware. Unable to establish whether the two technologies were competitive or complementary, the state poured resources into both during the first Socialist government (1981–1986).

At the same time these two technologies were being championed by separate groups of technocrats at the heart of the policy-making process on the new media. On the one hand, the broadcasting engineers of Télédiffusion de France, with apparently limited room for maneuvre in the crowded field of terrestrial transmission, supported satellite as the next step forward in programme delivery systems. On the other hand, the telecommunications technocrats of the Direction Générale des Télécommunications, fresh from the modernization of the telephone network during the Giscard d'Estaing presidency, looked to cable as their next major infrastructural project. Both groups were also aware that technological convergence was undermining the discrete integrity of their separate policy sectors of broadcasting and telecommunications, threatening their specialized expertise.

In the end neither project lived up to the high expectations of the technocrats. The technology was more expensive than anticipated, often unreliable and always open to the possibility of being superseded by technical progress. The state-backed cable plan became a victim of budgetary cuts and was replaced by a more market-driven policy in 1986, while the satellite venture proved to be an embarrassing white elephant. By the end of the Mitterrand presidency, neither cable nor satellite was a major provider of television programming (or indeed of any other information or communication service) to French consumers.

One reason for the failure of the new media to gain an audience was that one of their selling points – the provision of additional television programming – was undercut by the establishment of off-air commercial channels funded by advertising and therefore free to the viewer at the point of reception. This was the second tension in state audiovisual media policy during the Mitterrand presidency: the conflict of technological and electoral logics. In 1985 President Mitterrand, worried about the deep unpopularity of the Socialist government and fearing the arrival of a huge right-wing majority in Parliament after the 1986 legislative elections, decided to set up new off-air commercial television channels. This was an attempt to win easy electoral popularity and reduce the freedom of manoeuvre of an incoming right-wing government in broadcasting policy. The president's desire was quickly translated into policy reality, with the result that two new channels were transmitting by early 1986, just weeks before the elections. Whatever the electoral and political gains for the Socialists in the short term, the new channels undermined the possibility of cable or satellite attracting programme company investment or viewer subscriptions. Nor did they make any contribution to the realization of the technological objectives which supposedly lay at the heart of Socialist media policy.

A third tension in audiovisual media policy under Mitterrand was the result of governmental turnover at the very heart of the state. Executive *alternance* after the parliamentary elections of 1986, 1988 and 1993 transferred responsibility back and forth between Socialist and conservative governments. There were clear elements of continuity in broadcasting media policy despite these changes of government, such as the general thrust towards economic liberalization. But successive governments also introduced policy innovations to differentiate them from their predecessors. Sometimes these changes were ideologically driven, such as the decision by the Chirac government to privatize TF1 – a measure strongly opposed by the left. Others smacked more of political revanchism. For example, the succession of regulatory authorities during the 1980s was a product of the perception on the part of the incoming government that the regulatory body it inherited was politically compromised. The High Authority, for instance, was regarded by the right as too closely associated with the Socialists. In turn, the CNCL was reviled by the left for its alleged pro-right sympathies and publicly denounced by President Mitterrand in 1987.

A fourth tension in broadcasting media policy was that between cultural goals and economic objectives. Concern with the cultural importance of the audiovisual media manifested itself in various ways during the Mitterrand presidency. The Socialist Minister of Culture, Jack Lang, voiced the concerns of many in the media policy community when in the 1980s he inveighed against the threat to the values of French civilization posed by so-called 'Coca Cola' satellite programming. The state used its regulatory power to impose programme quotas and introduced financial aid schemes to protect and promote domestic programme production, particularly in the documentary and fiction genres. During the 1993 GATT negotiations the French government typically fought long and hard to protect its audiovisual and cinema industries from what it regarded as unfair American competition in the proposed international free market of goods and services (see above, Chapter 16). Finally, under Mitterrand the state actively promoted the establishment of a highbrow European cultural channel, initially called la Sept, which was later transformed into a Franco-German joint venture, ARTE. In short, the state clearly regarded the cultural role of the broadcast media as a central policy consideration.

Economic liberalization, however, scarcely facilitated the pursuit of cultural goals. In a very competitive broadcasting environment there was frequently a conflict between the commercial demands of audience maximization and the regulatory imperative of abiding by culturally inspired programming rules. The dilemma for some companies was whether to abide by content regulations and lose audience share or to breach the regulations and risk being sanctioned by the regulatory authority. In the end La Cinq was unable to walk this particular tightrope and the channel went into liquidation in 1992.

A fifth tension was the consequence of the need to accommodate new actors in the policy-making process. These included groups with an ownership stake in commercial television; an increased number of television programme suppliers and production companies; local authorities and utility companies involved in cable television; and local radio associations and private radio networks. Many of the new actors (Bouygues, Lyonnaise des Eaux) entered the media sector from other areas of economic and industrial activity. In some media sectors the state experienced considerable difficulty in maintaining a coalition of interests to support its policy objectives. For instance, the Socialist government of the first Mitterrand term found it hard to reconcile the different interests of the cable companies, local authorities and the state telecommunications agency as tensions emerged on the public–private, centralist–decentralist, hardware–software dimensions of the state-driven cable plan.

Sixth, the opening up of national boundaries in broadcasting posed new problems for the state by introducing a new variable into the media policy-making process. Previously broadcasting had been an overwhelmingly national affair. Technology largely prevented foreign television signals from reaching French audiences (and, of course, vice versa), while the main programme companies were state-owned and domestically oriented in their operations. During the Mitterrand presidency there was growing evidence of the importance of the transnational and supranational dimensions in broadcasting. New technology, notably satellite broadcasting, allowed programmes to be transmitted across national frontiers. The growth of commercial media outlets across Western Europe was accompanied by increasing cross-national operations as strong national champions moved out of their domestic base to acquire a stake in foreign markets. This was a two-way process. Canal Plus, for example, exported its terrestrial pay-television format to other European broadcasting systems (such as Spain and Germany) in which it also acquired a shareholding. In the reverse direction, Berlusconi's Fininvest company used its home market in Italy as a launch pad for the acquisition of an ownership stake in foreign broadcasting systems, including that of France. .

New pan-European programme delivery systems and transnational patterns of media ownership were accompanied by the need to regulate this supranational market. The European Union carved out for itself a regulatory role with the publication of the Television Without Frontiers directive in 1989. Within the EU, the French tended to be more *dirigiste* and less liberal in their attitudes to the free flow of transfrontier television than many other member states, arguing for the need to protect non-Anglophone production. Their Euro-protectionist approach, however, did not generally attract the support of the other major media states in the EU, notably Britain and Germany.

Finally, the French state's capacity to structure the broadcasting media's news agenda became more difficult than heretofore. In part this was due to the huge increase in broadcasting outlets. By the end of the Mitterrand presidency hundreds of radio stations were operating throughout France. The number of terrestrial television channels had more than doubled, and to these have to be added the channels available on cable and satellite. This expansion in outlets facilitated access to the national and sub-national media of other groups trying to influence the agenda-setting process, including the parties of the opposition, pressure groups and new social movements such as the environmentalists.

In addition, the traditionally deferential journalistic culture had also weakened somewhat, even if state legislation in the form of privacy laws protected political elites from media investigation more than their counterparts in Britain. Sometimes the media challenged the official perspective which the state was seeking to propagate. President Mitterrand faced a media credibility problem in dealing with the Rainbow Warrior fiasco. The agenda-setting attempts of various ministers failed to limit critical media exposure of malpractice, negligence and corruption. Two of Mitterrand's prime ministers came in for particularly unfavourable media scrutiny: Laurent Fabius for his handling of the contaminated blood affair and Pierre Bérégovoy for alleged financial irregularities, the public exposure of which contributed to his suicide.

While the state in the Fifth Republic has never been as monolithic as administrative textbooks might lead one to believe, it was even more divided during the Mitterrand presidency and this too had an impact on the state's role as a primary definer of the broadcasting media agenda. Sometimes the conflicts were based on party political divisions within the governing coalition. In the early years of the Mitterrand presidency, for example, the Communist Party became an increasingly sullen and disenchanted participant in government. The most obvious example of conflict at the very heart of the state were the two periods of cohabitation (1986–1988 and 1993–1995) with a head of state and head of government from opposing political camps. During the first cohabitation period, both President Mitterrand and Prime Minister Chirac engaged in a fierce media struggle to impose their respective political agendas and project favourable images in the run-up to the 1988 presidential contest.

CONCLUSION

It is clear that the relationship between the state and the broadcasting media significantly altered during the Mitterrand presidency. A measure of economic liberalization was secured by the abolition of the state broadcasting monopoly, while some political liberalization was attained by the increase in the number of broadcasting outlets and the establishment of regulatory authorities. However, it is too simplistic and ultimately misleading to portray the various changes simply in terms of the liberalization of the broadcasting media after a period of extensive postwar state control. Instead it is more useful to analyse the changes in terms of the transition from an ownership to a regulatory state. This focuses attention on dimensions of state-media relations (notably regulation and agenda setting) where the state continued to play an active role.

The result of the move from an ownership to a regulatory state was a more complex policy-making environment. As a result, the state found it increasingly difficult to achieve its various policy objectives. The goals of the Mitterrand era seemed clear enough. The opening up of the broadcasting system to new private players was designed to prepare France's audiovisual system for the challenges of the twenty-first century. Pluralistic ownership rather than state monopoly would best satisfy the information, cultural and entertainment needs of the French population. The aim of regulation was to ensure that private monopolies did not replace the former public one (ownership restrictions) and that media content respected certain desirable norms regarding information (political balance) and cultural output (production quotas). At the same time the state hoped that France's media industries would be strong enough to compete in an increasingly global marketplace for hardware (technology) and software (programmes).

However, it was never going to be easy to keep all these objectives in harmony. Tensions inevitably arose as policy objectives conflicted. The democratic desire for diverse ownership structures clashed with the economic need for a few powerful French media companies to compete at European and global levels. The state's emphasis on state-of-the-art technology in its cable and satellite projects pushed up the costs of these projects, while the expansion of terrestrial television channels undermined the attraction of the new media in the domestic market. The rapid expansion in television programme output made available to viewers provided new opportunities for domestic production companies, but also guaranteed that much of the televised product would be of non-French origin.

Certainly there were some policy successes. The liberalization of French radio, especially in the early 1980s, allowed a diversity of voices to be heard. Even if many small privately run local stations soon disappeared or were swallowed up by national networks, there was still greater choice of outlets and content at the end of the Mitterrand presidency than at the start. In television, the privatized

TF1 was a huge commercial success. The biggest triumph was Canal Plus, which after early teething problems built up a sufficiently large subscription base to become a major media player at both the national and supranational levels. Canal Plus was not just a domestic pay-television channel: it provided crucial support for the French film industry and had a stake in several production companies. It was also a leading European player in controlled access technology and digital television. Indeed, through a strategy combining vertical integration and internationalization, Canal Plus had in just over a decade become one of the major media enterprises in the EU.

There were, however, unfortunate casualties as well. While the collapse of La Cinq was the most spectacular, the condition of public-sector television was the most worrying. Public-sector television in France seemed to be in a condition of perpetual crisis during the Mitterrand era. This was often presented as a matter of organization and finance. In 1989 the government addressed the problem by placing the two remaining public-sector television companies (later renamed France 2 and 3) under a common management structure. However, there was a more fundamental question regarding the function of public-sector broadcasters in a mixed system dominated by private players. Whereas in the past the legitimacy of public service values in French broadcasting had been compromised by the subordination of state radio and television to political control, during the Mitterrand presidency it was the strength of commercial outlets (such as TF1, Canal Plus and Nouvelle Radio Jeune (NRJ)) which threatened to destabilize what remained of the public sector. The launch of a new educational channel, La Cinquième, in 1994 could not mask the enormous problems public broadcasters in France faced in what had become by the end of Mitterrand's second presidential term a highly competitive broadcasting environment.

NOTES

1. R. Kuhn, *The Media in France* (London: Routledge, 1995).
2. J. Bourdon, *Histoire de la télévision sous de Gaulle* (Paris: Anthropos/ Ina, 1990).
3. D. Sassoon, 'Political and Market Forces in Italian Broadcasting', in R. Kuhn (ed.), *Broadcasting and Politics in Western Europe* (London: Cass, 1995).

4. M. Müller and V. Wright, 'The State in Western Europe: Retreat or Redefinition?', *West European Politics*, Vol.17, No.3, 1994.
5. L. Franceschini, *La Régulation audiovisuelle en France* (Paris: PUF, 1995).
6. R. Kuhn, 'France' in V. MacLeod (ed.), *Media Ownership and Control in the Age of Convergence* (London: International Institute of Communications, 1996), pp. 49–63.
7. M. Cotta, *Les Miroirs de Jupiter* (Paris: Fayard, 1986), pp. 157–191.
8. S. Hall et al., *Policing the Crisis* (London: Macmillan, 1978), pp. 57–60.
9 J. Gerstlé, *La Communication politique* (Paris: PUF, 1992).

18 The Silence of the Left Intellectuals in Mitterrand's France

Martyn Cornick

In July 1983 a series of over thirty articles appeared in the pages of *Le Monde* on what was labelled 'the silence of left intellectuals'. It was remarked at the time that this title seemed odd, and indeed it represents something of a misnomer, because the otherwise thin and arid summer pages of *Le Monde* were filled with chatter from the French intellectual class. If this was a silence, then it was a deafening one.[1] Examined with the luxury of hindsight, this so typically French debate provides an arresting case study, particularly when situated in the context of recent French political history. The articles in question have not escaped attention: Keith Reader refers to them in his book *Intellectuals and the Left in France since 1968*,[2] while George Ross considers the debate as a symptom of decline in the status, if not the very existence, of left-wing intellectuals in France.[3] Rémy Rieffel, in his otherwise comprehensive study of intellectual life under the Fifth Republic, skims lightly over the articles whilst acknowledging their importance.[4] In short, the debate has not yet received detailed scrutiny, and this is the motivation for this chapter. The issues of the contemporary period may not measure up to the upheavals of the Dreyfus Affair, or the fault-lines opened up by fascism and antifascism during the 1930s, but none the less there is much impassioned discussion of the great issues facing France and its role in the world in the 1980s, including globalization, modernity, neo-liberalism and socialism, all of which remain relevant. Because there is evidence to suggest that the debate was part of a more general malaise among the intellectual class, we intend also to shed light on the causes. In short, this study will contextualize how the debate began, examine its major themes, and offer some interpretations along the way.

The debate was launched by Max Gallo on 26 July 1983 in an article entitled 'Intellectuals, politics and modernity'.[5] Gallo, a novelist and historian, was labelled as a 'government spokesman', so what he had to say apparently had the backing of the prime minister's office if not the Elysée. The article reads a call to action on the part of left-wing intellectuals, and is couched in language betraying a nostalgia for the great days of the 1936 Popular Front. As Gallo says, in a country steeped in history, whose politics stemmed directly from historical memory and where intellectuals played such a prominent political role, the appeal was not particularly surprising. The problem was, however, that there were some worrying trends. He demanded: 'Has the Left abandoned the battle for ideas?' 'Where are the Gides, the Malraux, the Alains and Langevins of today?' Right-wing ideas were in the ascendant: cultural counsellors were being sacked, and street names were being switched from the commemoration of left-wing heroes like Jules Vallès to that of right-wingers like Adolphe Thiers. Anticipating the Bicentenary of the Revolution, Gallo found that the ideas of the extreme-right thinker Charles Maurras were back in fashion. He ascribed all this to the fact that despite the Socialists' political victory of May 1981, in the domain of ideas the tide had already turned rightwards. Gallo's fondness for the 1930s and the right-wing ascendancy he registered were both reflected in a distinct lack of enthusiasm among left-wing intellectuals after the so-called 'state of grace' following 10 May 1981. Despite all the rhetoric leading up to the election, all the political theatre of Mitterrand's laying red roses on the tombs of Jean Moulin, Jean Jaurès and Victor Schoelcher in the Panthéon on 21 May 1981, with Jacques Attali despatched to do likewise on Léon Blum's grave in Jouy-en-Josas, left-wing intellectuals remained stolidly unenthusiastic about the new government.[6] Typically, Michel Foucault, whilst welcoming the election victory as the sign of a new relationship between government and governed, insisted that being supportive would in no way prevent his being critical.[7] Jean-Denis Bredin, anticipating the debate to come, analysed the trend toward silence, but strove to put a positive gloss on it.[8]

The lack of enthusiasm to which Gallo alluded had crystallized into an explosion of anger in December 1981 when Claude Cheysson, then foreign minister, made what Favier and Martin-Roland have called a 'monumental gaffe' regarding events in Poland, and which compounded left-wing estrangement from the government. Asked on Europe 1 whether France would react to the 'state of war' and arrest of Solidarity activists in Poland, Cheysson replied: 'Absolutely not. Of course we are going to do nothing'. The official line of Mauroy's government was that this was a purely 'internal affair'; after all, there was no hint of intervention by a foreign power (meaning no intervention by the Soviets in a country in their sphere of influence).[9]

Intellectuals of the non-Communist left could hardly believe that a Socialist government, which had paid so much lip-service to the inheritance of the Republican tradition and the Rights of Man, could be so complacent, revealing a mind-set which, from all appearances at least, remained unchanged since the days of Yalta. In 1990, Cheysson admitted that he regretted having uttered these words;[10] but at the time irreparable damage was done, for the columns of *Le Matin*, *Libération* and *Le Monde* were filled with protests and petitions.[11]

More complex reasons for intellectuals' sense of unease could be identified. Globalization, the spread of Reaganite neo-liberalism, and the symptoms and trends which would later lead Francis Fukuyama to proclaim the 'end of history'[12] had already begun to manifest themselves in 1983. If the intellectual right was in the ascendant, the intellectual left had begun a process of fragmentation. Faith in the great Marxist narrative had already been shaken in the late 1960s and throughout the 1970s (this was 'the crisis of the grand narratives', as philosopher Jean-François Lyotard put it[13]), particularly among those fellow-travelling intellectuals who had lent support to the Communist Party. A number of works attacking totalitarian ideologies and leaders accumulated during the 1970s.[14] The 'Solzhenitsyn effect' (1973–1974), and the Soviet invasion of Afghanistan – the 'Kabul effect' (1979) – threw the PCF into ever deeper discredit. Those who remained politically engaged were considered, according to Gallo, 'naive, ambitious or cynical'. Furthermore, political disillusion within France after May–June 1968 was another deep-seated factor explaining the sense of betrayal among the 'generation of 68'.[15] The end result was this generation's seemingly permanent retirement from the political arena. Hence the political vacuum, and the rise of intellectual stars on the right. Since all this was happening at a crucial moment in the history of France and Europe, the fact that the country was suffering from a 'deficit of modernity' made things worse. In Gallo's view, this deficit was traceable in two historical phases.

The first of these occurred between 1944 and 1970, when France struggled to tear itself away from the past. Although this occurred during a period of rapid economic growth, the problem was that it was carried out at first on weak institutional foundations, and then through the exercise of solitary power. The crisis of 1968 demonstrated only too clearly the clash between the recent past and the needs of modernity. The second phase embraced the decade 1970–1980: under the Giscard presidency, although France seemed to make rapid progress, the experiment soon ran out of steam, leaving the country stranded on the threshold of the twenty-first century (it is noteworthy that already in 1983 unpreparedness for the new millennium was stressed as a major motivation for structural change). Stubborn resistance to change in certain sectors, political and managerial inadequacies, and the lack of real forward planning, all compounded the problem. Then, in 1981, the left won power and had to confront all this.

After two years in government, where were the ideas from the intellectual friends of the regime? The challenge was clear: 'Are we sufficiently well equipped to bring about the sea-change in attitudes which will determine the future of the country?' In a sequence of emotional questions and apostrophes, Gallo threw down the gauntlet:

> What a supreme challenge! This country must again become a place where ideas can ferment because this is not a problem calling for old-style solutions. The circumstances are new. We must invent! How can this be done without intellectuals? In a democratic country it is they who mediate and express the collective consciousness. It is perhaps not an exaggeration to say that the success of the left – and beyond that the destiny of France – will depend in large measure on the flow of new ideas which will enliven people's minds.

There are two fundamental points to make here. First, there is Gallo's view of the intellectuals' role as mediators of the 'collective consciousness'. In 1983, this could only be an outdated view. Gallo displays a nostalgia for the 1930s when intellectuals – such as Gide, Malraux, Benda, but also Maurras and Bainville – enjoyed a high public profile and did indeed lead the 'fermentation of ideas'. One gets a good idea of how Gallo conceived their role from a glance at his 1972 novel *Le Cortège des vainqueurs*, in which a twentieth-century *enfant du siècle*, Marco Naldi, progresses heroically through a historical fresco from 1917 to 1970 in which ideas are inseparable from political action, so much so that ideas figure as protagonistic forces determining the characters' fates.[16]

The second point is underlined by writers such as Régis Debray and commentators like George Ross to explain why intellectuals no longer held sway over the cultural market. Debray, in a celebrated and familiar analysis, traces the decline of the traditional role of the left-leaning intellectual to market changes whereby television and the economic demands of media producers came to determine the direction and production of ideas, rather than intellectuals themselves.

Debray locates the beginning of this phase – 'the media cycle' – in the watershed following 1968.[17] To quote George Ross, 'television, the "massification" of a new middle-strata reading public [...] and the consequent concentration of publishing together reconfigured the cultural products industry'.[18] A number of intellectuals benefited from this, the most prominent being Bernard-Henry Lévy, shining as the brightest sun in what Félix Guattari derisively called a new 'intello star system [sic]'.[19] We can now see that Gallo, in his critique of the 'silence' of the intellectuals, merely proved the point.

After Gallo's opening salvo, and whilst the intellectuals donned their thinking-caps, a two-part survey by Philippe Boggio explored some of the reasons behind the intellectuals' mutism. After May 1981 some had hoped to see a '1936 Mark II', a new golden age in which intellectuals would fully support and participate in government. Due to new socio-economic conditions, they were to be disappointed. Despite Mitterrand's public wooing of writers, whether personally or through Jack Lang's Ministry of Culture, embarrassingly the silence persisted. Indeed, as Boggio himself put it, 'intellectuals themselves talk consciously of a "profound malaise", but offer few explanations for it'.[20] The intellectuals were busy elsewhere, and seemed unwilling to lend any support to the new regime. According to Boggio's researches, in the book world Catherine Clément's *Rêver chacun pour l'autre* 'sailed on an ocean of works opposing the government'. In *Le Monde*, only Jean-Pierre Faye, Jean-Denis Bredin and Max Gallo were identifiable as being 'in wholehearted agreement [with the Socialists]'.[21] On the whole, intellectuals were embarrassed to talk about their relations with the state; Michel Foucault and Simone de Beauvoir even refused to participate in the survey. Gilles Deleuze's view was that there was little to concern intellectuals *qua* intellectuals, little to mobilize them.

Various reasons were given to explain the 'profound malaise': some saw the enthusiasm leading up to the victory on 10 May as having been betrayed; others condemned specific policies such as nationalization and higher education reform; others still pointed to internal wranglings within the PS. Jorge Semprun alluded to the fact that with the left in power, the right now held sway everywhere in the cultural domain and in the domain of ideas: 'the left has lost its cultural monopoly'.[22] It is certain, as Pierre-André Taguieff has shown, that in the decade preceding the electoral victories of the Front National in 1983, the so-called 'Nouvelle Droite' (new right) had successfully taken the battle for ideas into the cultural domain through the Groupe de Recherche et d'Etude pour la Civilisation Européenne (GRECE) and other groupings.[23] Another problem was that the pre-election enthusiasm for the left had partially masked the gravity of a number of deep-seated economic difficulties which the Socialists would have to face. As the philosopher François George put it, the 'state of grace [...] has interfered with the appreciation of a number of economic problems'.[24] But the central point in Boggio's survey regarding the traditional role of the intelligentsia as 'keepers of the Nation's conscience' was made by André Glucksmann; commenting on the Panthéon ceremony (whose style was sneeringly dismissed as 'socialo-poujado-populist'), Glucksmann underscored the main reason for the intellectuals' silence:

> At the Pantheon ceremony, through the writers present François Mitterrand wished to assemble those who would bear witness to suffering humanity. He omitted to invite some of these. I'm thinking in particular of those writers in the Socialist camp who are fighting for their freedom.[25]

This is the crux of the problem: the Cold War had not yet ended, and in the domain of human rights, many left-leaning intellectuals believed the government to be hypocritical and in thrall to Communism; indeed, their reaction to the imposition of martial law in Poland in December 1981 had presented clear enough evidence of this. Government supporters Deleuze and George both agreed: the intelligentsia was silent principally because of its anticommunism: 'as long as the government has to play along with the Communist Party, its actions will not be understood'.

Replies to Gallo's appeal and the survey were not long in coming. A fair number were positive and attempted to explain away the reasons behind the supposed silence. Indeed, Jean-Pierre Bonnel, a secondary-school teacher from St. Avold, suggested that since Mitterrand was an intellectual, the latter camp had now achieved their ambition of gaining power.[26] The Resistance author Vercors wrote to say that socialist supporters like himself might well keep their counsel (in his case, through choice), but that such silence signified approval: 'We are not disappointed: we are patient'.[27] The problem was that the French had expected too much, too soon. The case of Catherine Clément is interesting because she was one of a few intellectuals (like Gallo) who had accepted the offer of a government post. At the time of her article, she was 'deputy-director for artistic and cultural exchanges at the Foreign Affairs ministry'. For her, an important part of the battle for ideas was to be fought precisely in the area in which she had been appointed: culture and its dissemination.[28] This optimistic point of view, however, was vigorously contradicted in the same page by the maverick intellectual Jean-Edern Hallier, who insisted that what Gallo wanted, the improvement of the government's standing in public opinion, and what writers and intellectuals could deliver through their creative capabilities, were now incompatible. In short, socialism, in power, and culture did not mix.[29]

The philosopher Jean-Pierre Faye, though irritated by the artifical way in which the debate had been manufactured, insisted on striking a positive pose. He reported that since October 1981, with the active support of research minister Jean-Pierre Chevènement and the help of Jacques Derrida and Dominique Lecourt, he had been developing plans to launch an international college of philosophy which would be open to any interested audience. The purpose of this undertaking was to provide facilities for and foster research in a whole range of fields (urban planning, the media, historiography, feminist and psychoanalytic theory) whose interdisciplinarity was summarized in the sub-title 'Sciences, Intersciences, Arts'. This, he implied, would be one of the most important ways of sparking ideas and communicating them to the intelligent public: despite the injunctions of such as Hallier, there could be a fruitful relationship between research and creation: 'I was hoping for the creation of a space where the silence of inventive thinking would result in effective communication: seminars and free discussion relating to the present.' The Collège was designed to debate precisely that philosophical distinction between the left and right sides of the Assemblée Constituante which had originated with the French Revolution; and in order to prepare the ground for the 1989 Bicentenary, the meaning of the 'Rights of Man' also needed to be debated.[30] When the Collège opened in April 1984, it met with some success; however, given its perception as a government-backed think-tank, it is difficult to resist quoting Anatole France's aphorism in *La Vie littéraire*: 'It is not with Philosophy that one shores up governments'.[31]

The centre of gravity of the whole debate, however, was located in the theme of modernity. Jean Chesneaux, a history professor at the Sorbonne, intervened in the debate at an apposite moment because he was about to publish his book *De la modernité*.[32] Because society suffered from a 'deficit of modernity', intellectuals had been called upon to provide ideas and advice for a further 'great leap forward' in France. Chesneaux admitted that the debate about 'modernity' was certainly overdue, but that it was necessary also to challenge those of its proponents who subscribed to it as 'irreversible' and 'ineluctable'. Agreeing with Jean Baudrillard that change had now become a way of life, that constant change had to be made for change's sake, Chesneaux wrote:

> [Modernity] may be defined by its dual globality, consisting of the element denounced by Sartre, the complete 'joining-together' of people, conditions and mecanisms; the other, so incautiously predicted by Saint-Simon, the 'wired planet' [*la planète câblée*], meaning the inextricable and all-powerful interdependence of economies and states. In the end, we arrive at the equation ≪modernité = merdonité≫ suggested by Michel Leiris.[33]

'Is it inevitable that we should be subjected to these blind processes?', asked Chesneaux.

There were, moreover, political implications in all this: could the left be reconciled at all with the concept of *modernité*? Was it not usually applauded and promoted by the right, such as those proponents of the 'new American liberalism'?[34] France's passage to modernity meant the adoption of a new ideology, and that ideology would inevitably be of the right:

> For us, modernity means passing from political citizenship to economic citizenship, the Americanization of daily relationships, technological dependence, the suppression of social conflict in favour of 'consensus', the degradation of politics into media manipulation, whether one is talking about the opposition or the government majority.

Modernity clearly meant confronting the issue of economic and technological globalization. Moreover, as was relatively common among left-intellectuals in France, the critique has a distinct anti-American flavour. Most importantly, however, through Chesneaux's critique one may detect the beginnings of a French trend towards an acceptance of neo-liberal dogma, in other words, the encouragement of 'consensus' politics and drift towards the centre, a process which would come to be known in France as 'the Republic of the Centre',[35] and which, for the Socialists, would mean the abandonment of old-style socialism in favour of social democracy. Finally, implicit in Chesneaux's conclusion was the view that if intellectuals still had a role, it would not be found in nostalgia for the Popular Front; rather, their responsibility was to provide 'lucidity', to point out what it would cost the left to accept the 'naive fetishism of modernity'. This critique has a profoundly paradoxical quality. As Alain Touraine has pointed out, ever since the Enlightenment intellectuals advocated change as a positive force for social progress; yet since the watershed of 1968, left intellectuals have tended to become 'anti-modern'.[36] In Chesneaux's case, though, it should be noted that his critique was highly ecology-conscious and anti-nuclear, and carried the debate on to another plane.

Félix Guattari suggested that if Gallo had wanted to mobilize the intellectual class, then he should address other themes and engage a critical debate around a 'wish-list' which gives a good idea of the issues uppermost in left intellectuals' minds at this time: Mitterrand's neo-Gaullist style and his apparent refusal of constitutional reform; the functioning of left-wing political parties; development of a multiracial society which would keep its promises to immigrants; the nature of work, in particular work-sharing; radical approaches to the environment and town-planning; switching resources away from the neutron bomb and nuclear submarines; the need to formulate initiatives to reduce famine and to emancipate the Third World.[37]

For some readers of *Le Monde*, however, such earnest soul-searching – in the holiday month of August! – was all too much. A group of readers complained: 'We're sick and tired of intellectuals! [...]*Le Monde* has had the crazy idea to tan the very brains of its poor readers!' Punning on the newspaper's title, the readers pleaded: 'Let's open the windows and look out at the world, not the newspaper!'[38] Then *Le Monde* announced that it would be closing the debate, meanwhile publishing some more readers' letters representing various kinds of response, from the tongue-in-cheek 'Message de M. de Norpois' (borrowed from Proust's *A l'ombre des jeunes filles en fleurs*) sent in by Jean-Yves Tadié ('these days there are more urgent tasks than arranging words in a pleasing fashion'), to the phlegmatic neo-liberalism of Michel Prigent ('maybe we should seek elsewhere than in socialism if not the model, then at least the outline of a new philosophy of man and of society'). There was a similar message from Yvan Blot, speaking for the new right: 'the world turns, we pass from age to age. Socialism cannot escape this rule. [...] It is for others to play a new tune whilst the 'left-wing' intellectuals turn the page in silence'.[39]

What conclusions may be drawn from the debate? Apart from making the point that debates on these and related topics have continued ever since in the pages of informed periodicals such as

Le Débat, Esprit and *Commentaire*, there are three sets of remarks to
be made. First, in the pages of *Le Monde* itself, on 25 August 1983
Philippe Boggio summarized the main points. His article conveys an
air of surprise at the wide variety and quality of responses. 'What a
noise! What polemics!'[40] Almost every point of view, every style of
expression seemed to be represented. Max Gallo had provoked a
'barrage of fierce criticism', and it was time to put an end to the
debate, at least in the pages of *Le Monde*.[41] But what repercussions
had there been? According to reported rumours, Jack Lang regarded
Gallo's article as ill-timed and ill-conceived, while at the Elysée it met
with considerable disapproval because the president knew only too
well that intellectuals tended to jib when offered advice by politicians.
Gallo had been attacked for his writing style, historical sources and
his selective memory, the implication being that he was an inept
spokesman. The central theme identified by Boggio was precisely
that of the intellectuals' anxiety in the face of the (post-)modern
world. The biggest question, now that faith in the 'grand narratives'
had evaporated, was how could intellectuals account for the contemporary world and what was their relationship to it? Some, however,
were willing to wait and see what would happen in a world dominated
by the one 'narrative' (or ideology) which had not evaporated: neo-
liberalism. If anything, it was in the ascendant. Indeed, Fukuyama
would ascribe the 'end of history' to the victory of neo-liberalism.
As far as the French were concerned, there would not be long to
wait. As Catherine Nay wittily records, in April 1984 Mitterrand
returned from a visit to Silicon Valley in the United States appearing
to have undergone a Pauline conversion to Reaganism, in view of the
sudden and symbolic change of style evident at his press conference:
'Léon Blum had just died for the second time'.[42] Thus in several
important respects, the so-called 'silence of the intellectuals' should
be seen as both symptom and prognosis of the crisis in socialism.
Gallo stood by his actions, arguing later that he had only been
expressing himself freely as a 'committed intellectual' in what was 'a
clear political act as government spokesman', and insisted that he
wanted to continue asking questions about the 'very identity of the
left', its 'values' and its 'theory and practice'.[43]

The second set of remarks refers to what one might call the post-
script of the debate, appearing in the form of contributions from those
two intellectual heavyweights Jean Baudrillard and Jean-François
Lyotard. They merit more detailed comment than is possible
here: suffice it to say that in characteristic fashion Baudrillard, in a

two-part article 'La Gauche divine', turned the debate on its head, arguing that already and stealthily the processes of globalization (and especially the mass-media) had rendered the old goals and ambitions of socialism out-of-date and meaningless. Television represented a prosthetic substitute for thought which, by implication, made intellectuals redundant.[44] A few days later, Lyotard added his own voice in a significant text entitled 'Tomb of the intellectual'.[45] For the anti-authoritarian Lyotard, Gallo's appeal was misplaced and confused. Gallo should have addressed his remarks not to intellectuals but to administrators or experts. The authority intellectuals derived in the past was based on the notion of a 'universal subject' in a culture where universal values were assumed: 'the responsibility of "intellectuals" is inseparable from the (shared) idea of a universal subject. It alone can give Voltaire, Zola, Péguy, Sartre [...] the authority that has been accorded to them'.[46] The difference between experts and intellectuals was that the former did not recognize the universal subject, but strove to maximize performance in terms of 'cost/benefit'. In any case, the notion of a totalizing unity had been devalued since 'at least the middle of the twentieth century'. Thus 'Gallo will not find what he seeks' because 'what he seeks belongs to another age'. Despite appearances to the contrary, Lyotard insisted that in principle his conclusion was optimistic:

> The decline, perhaps the ruin, of the universal idea can free thought and life from totalizing obsessions. The multiplicity of responsibilities, and the independence (their incompatibility), oblige and will oblige those who take on those responsibilities, small or great, to be flexible, tolerant and svelte. These qualities will cease to be the contrary of rigour, honesty and force; they will be their signs. Intelligences do not fall silent, they do not withdraw into their beloved work, they try to live up to this new responsibility, which renders the 'intellectuals' troublesome, impossible: the responsibility to distinguish intelligence from the paranoia that gave rise to 'modernity'.[47]

Thus for Lyotard, the philosopher of the postmodern, only a nostalgist (like Gallo) would be saddened or frightened at the prospect of the 'tomb of the intellectual'.

As though dramatically to underscore the relevance of the debate to France's role in the world, almost immediately after the series ended tension and violence escalated in the Middle East, a region where France had many commercial and defence interests. That contradictions and confusion existed between Socialist government policy and French Republican values was emphasized in searing clarity once again, when it was revealed in the press that earlier that year France had made arrangements to lease a number of Super-Étendard fighters to Iraq: now they had been delivered.[48] Could there ever again be a convergence of interest between Socialism in power and the body of left intellectuals, if the latter would ever emerge again, Lazarus-like, from their tomb?

NOTES

All translations are by the author unless otherwise stated.

1. Jacques Cellard called it 'un silence bavard' in 'Une certaine mauvaise conscience', *Le Monde*, 4 August 1983.
2. K. Reader, *Intellectuals and the Left in France since 1968* (London: Macmillan, 1989), pp. 136–40.
3. See, for example, G. Ross, 'The Decline of the Left Intellectual in Modern France', in A. Gagnon, (ed.), *Intellectuals in Liberal Democracies* (Praeger, 1987), pp. 44–65.
4. R. Rieffel, *La Tribu des clercs. Les intellectuels sous la Ve République* (Paris: Calmann-Lévy/CNRS, 1993).
5. 'Les intellectuels, la politique et la modernité', *Le Monde*, 26 July 1983.
6. See P. Favier and M. Martin-Roland, *La Décennie Mitterrand*, I, *Les ruptures* (Paris: Seuil, 1990), pp. 56–60.
7. M. Foucault, 'Est-il donc important de penser?', interview in *Libération*, 30–31 May 1981, *Dits et écrits 1954–1988*, IV, 1980–1988 (Paris: Gallimard, 1994), text 296.
8. 'Les intellectuels et le pouvoir socialiste', *Le Monde*, 22 December 1981.
9. Favier and Martin-Roland, op. cit., pp. 371–381.
10. Ibid., p. 372.
11. J.-F. Sirinelli, *Intellectuels et passions françaises. Manifestes et pétitions au XXe siècle* (Paris: Fayard, 1990), pp. 297–308.
12. F. Fukuyama, *The End of History and the Last Man* (Harmondsworth: Penguin, 1992).
13. C. Clément, 'Choisir sa propre distance', *Le Monde*, 10 August 1983; see also Lyotard's *La Condition post-moderne* (Paris: Minuit, 1982).
14. A. Glucksmann, *La Cuisinière et le mangeur d'hommes* (Paris: Seuil, 1975); B.-H. Lévy, *La Barbarie à visage humain* (Paris: Grasset, 1977).
15. See H. Hamon and P. Rotman, *Génération I. Les années de rêve; Génération II* (Paris: Seuil, 2 vol., 1987, 1988).
16. M. Gallo, *Le Cortège des vainqueurs* (Paris: Laffont, 1972, reprinted 1982).

17. R. Debray, *Le Pouvoir intellectuel en France* (Ramsay, 1979), pp. 94–112.

18. G. Ross, 'Where have all the Sartres gone?', in J.-F. Hollifield and G. Ross (eds), *In Search of the New France* (London: Routledge, 1991) p. 230.

19. F. Guattari, 'Autant en emporte la crise', *Le Monde*, 18 August 1983.

20. P. Boggio, 'Victoire à contretemps', *Le Monde*, 27 July 1983 and 'Les chemins de traverse', *Le Monde*, 28 July 1983.

21. This drew an objection from Yves Navarre: 'Eh bien, faites votre liste', *Le Monde*, 25 August 1983.

22. *Le Monde*, 27 July 1983.

23. See P.-A. Taguieff, 'La stratégie culturelle de la "Nouvelle Droite" en France (1968–1983)', in R. Badinter, (ed.), *Vous avez dit fascismes?* (Arthaud-Montalba, 1984), pp. 13–152.

24. *Le Monde*, 27 July 1983.

25. Ibid.

26. J-P Bonnel, 'Ils ne se taisent pas: ils sont au pouvoir', Le Monde, 2 August 1983.

27. Vercors, 'Pas déçus, patients', *Le Monde*, 6 August 1983.

28. C. Clément, 'Choisir sa propre distance', *Le Monde*, 10 August 1983.

29. J.-E. Hallier, 'L'avènement du tiers état culturel', ibid.

30. J-P. Faye, 'Musique de la pensée?', *Le Monde*, 6 August 1983.

31. See my note on the Collège in *ASM&CF Review*, no. 1, July 1984, p. 25.

32. J. Chesneaux, *De la modernité* (Paris: La Découverte, 1983).

33. J. Chesneaux, 'Un fétichisme de la modernité?', *Le Monde*, 2 August 1983. See M. Leiris, 'Modernité/merdonité', in *Nouvelle Revue Française*, October 1981. The play-on-words between 'moderne' and 'merde' is lost in translation.

34. Guy Sorman extolled the virtues of Reaganite neo-liberalism on the same page: 'Le nouveau libéralisme est arrivé', *Le Monde*, 2 August 1983.

35. F. Furet and P. Rosanvallon, *La République du centre* (Paris: Calmann-Lévy, 1988).

36. *Critique de la modernité* (Paris: Fayard, 1992).

37. F. Guattari, 'Autant en emporte la crise', *Le Monde*, 18 August 1983.

38. *Le Monde*, 18 August 1983.

39. *Le Monde*, 23 August 1983.

40. P. Boggio, 'Le trouble', *Le Monde*, 25 August 1983.

41. Different periodicals continued the discussion; see subsequent issues of *Esprit*; J. Daniel, 'L'heure des intellectuels', *Le Débat*, no. 27, November 1983, pp. 168–92; 'Idéologies: le grand chambardement', *Le Magazine littéraire*, Nos. 239–240, March 1987. The debate is remembered as marking a downturn in the fortunes of the intellectuals; see P. Billard, P., 'Inventaire avant liquidation', *Le Point*, 18 March 1991, pp. 38–43.

42. C. Nay, *Les Sept Mitterrand, ou les métamorphoses d'un septennat*, (Paris: Grasset, 1988), pp. 115ff.

43. M. Gallo, *Les Idées décident de tout* (Paris: Galilée, 1984), pp. 13–17. This volume reproduces the article 'Les intellectuels, la politique et la modernité'.

44. J. Baudrillard, 'La gauche divine: I. La fin des passions historiques'; II. 'Social: grande illusion', *Le Monde*, 21 and 22 September 1983. See also *La Gauche divine: chronique des années 1977–1984* (Paris: Grasset, 1985).

45. J.-F. Lyotard, 'Tombeau de l'intellectuel', *Le Monde*, 8 October 1983. See also *Le Tombeau de l'intellectuel et autres papiers* (Paris: Galilée, 1984).

46. J.-F. Lyotard, *Political Writings*, translated by B. Readings with K.P. Geiman, (London: UCL Press, 1993), p. 3.

47. Ibid., p. 7.

48. See *Le Matin*, 3 November 1983.

Conclusion: The Mitterrand Legacy and the New Millennium

Mairi Maclean

It is difficult to present definitive conclusions about a subject which, in many ways, is still ongoing. For although we have come to the end of the Mitterrand era *per se*, following the completion of Mitterrand's second presidential term in May 1995 and his death in the ensuing January, many of the projects begun by Mitterrand himself, or under the aegis of Mitterrand as president, have yet to come to fruition. The impact of his legacy on France as it embarks on a new journey into the twenty-first century under Chirac, is, as the chapters in this book demonstrate, profound and wide-ranging. At the same time, Mitterrand's own life story, variegated and multifaceted, and distinct from common experience, adds colour and interest to his legacy. His story is all the more unusual in that, as time was running out, he saw to it that those aspects of his life which might be seen subsequently as potentially suspect and questionable were given a public airing – perhaps in an effort to manipulate and guide public opinion, to 'have the last word' on his life, even after death. These end-of-life 'revelations' on his past (as a student with nationalist sympathies, as a minor official in Vichy and admirer of Pétain, and as a friend of René Bousquet, the Vichy chief of police) and existing life (his second family) were important not for what they revealed about Mitterrand – as Eric Duhamel notes, most of this was known already – but primarily for the way in which they have muddied the waters regarding history's assessment of Mitterrand. In many respects, the jury is still out on the former president; it will be some time before history's judgement of Mitterrand finally crystallizes.

This is as true for Mitterrand's achievements as it is for Mitterrand himself. Indeed, that many remain unfinished contributes to the necessary postponement of our definitive judgement. Subjected to two periods of 'cohabitation' in government with the right (an initial novelty in the Fifth Republic to which the French have since grown accustomed), Mitterrand carved out for himself, and jealously guarded, a 'reserved domain' of foreign affairs and security; but, as Dominique David points out, the debates around the final phase of his foreign and defence policy have not yet ceased. Moreover, although Mitterrand's fourteen years at the helm are often grouped together as a whole, it is important to remember that his two terms in office were not identical. Mitterrand had less room for manoeuvre in his second term than in his first; he was politically and physically weaker. The second term seems also to have contained more errors of judgement than the first: above all, his replacement in 1991 of the popular and successful prime minister Michel Rocard (whom Mitterrand disliked) with Edith Cresson (with whom he was alleged to have had an affair), entailing disastrous electoral consequences; and his decision in 1992 to hold a referendum on the Maastricht Treaty, a careless gamble, the riskiness of which he initially underestimated, and which might easily have undone much of what he had worked so hard to achieve. In retrospect, however, the virtue of holding a referendum is rather more apparent. Other countries, such as Britain, which at the time preferred to duck the issue, may yet have to hold one on the single currency.

Mitterrand's successes in European integration are recognized as being among his greatest achievements. With German reunification, David observes, Mitterrand looked into the breach dramatically opened up by history and saw in it the opportunity to accelerate the progress he had long desired towards European political union. Europe has since embarked on its greatest ever project, the quest for economic and monetary union and a single currency by the start of the new millennium, a course which Mitterrand saw as the only way forward, and which became the key focus of his second *septennat*. 'Never separate the grandeur of France from the construction of Europe', he urged his compatriots in his last New Year's address to the nation, measuring his words, 'It is our new dimension, and our ambition for the next century'.[1] But the follow-through has proved problematic. In attempting to meet the strict fiscal criteria necessary to qualify for EMU in 1999, the Juppé government proposed deep cuts in the social security budget and thereby unleashed a wave of strikes and demonstrations. The limits of the action capacity of the French state are being severely tested by 'people power'. When President Chirac decided to hold early parliamentary elections in May–June 1997 – ten months before they were due – in order to secure a solid mandate in support of the austerity package needed to qualify for EMU in 1999, the electorate resoundingly rejected budget cuts in favour of job creation and a softer euro, advocated by Lionel Jospin. The will of the state may well be done in the end; but while the general perception is that the point of no return has been reached, it is not entirely a foregone conclusion. Mitterrand had always maintained that there could be no monetary union without Germany. As unemployment neared five million in that country in the run-up to the 1999 deadline, it became increasingly clear that qualification for EMU could not be taken for granted there either, shrouding the entire endeavour in a veil of uncertainty. Were the European boat to be missed on this occasion, the construction of Europe – which can go either forwards or backwards, but cannot stand still – would inevitably be put in jeopardy. Helmut Kohl is, after all, as Dyson and Featherstone stress, likely to be the last German Chancellor with whom it may be possible to build Europe, since a future political generation might not share his sense of urgency inspired by experience and memories of war.

The benefit of hindsight is not yet ours. Political will may yet drive the EMU project through to a successful conclusion. But it is likely to prove a more protracted and complex process than that envisaged by Mitterrand. And far from solving the problem of unemployment, as President Chirac would have his countrymen believe – 'Our priority is unemployment. It is in the name of employment that we are putting our public finances in order'[2] – many of France's jobless in the closing years of the twentieth century could point to the convergence criteria as one of the main reasons for their despair.

One of François Mitterrand's finest achievements was, without any doubt, to have united the French left and brought it to power. However, Mitterrand's legacy to the socialist left is similarly problematic, for the experience of government has left it without any identity at all, ideologically empty, its dreams spent. The results of the left's experience with government were profoundly paradoxical, characterized, as Elie Cohen highlights, by failed objectives and unintended achievements. It failed in those areas naturally associated with the left, such as nationalization and centralized economic planning, and succeeded in those areas normally seen as the preserve of the right, foremost among which was the conversion of the French to the market economy. The essence of this paradox, as Berstein explains, was that, in order to preserve the doctrinal purity necessary for the survival of socialism, *the left had actually to stay out of power.* Once in power, it became ensnared in the contradictions of government which inhabit the divide between principle and reality. In the post-Mitterrand era, all that the left can do to save its face, is to hide behind the (useful) rhetoric of a Republican model while (following its return to government in 1997) seeking to manage the country along liberal economic lines. But the Republican model does not represent a genuine political culture and vision of society for the left, such as must be created if the left is to survive and prosper in the world of the twenty-first century as anything other than another party of government.

The economy is another, perhaps *the* success story of the Mitterrand years, as the chapters by Uterwedde and Szarka make clear – oddly enough, given the failed Mitterrand-Mauroy experiment of 1981–1982, and given Mitterrand's rather limited understanding of economic matters. If, in 1981, French business was in a critical state – still reeling from the two oil shocks of the 1970s, seriously uncompetitive, lacking in confidence and capital, and suffering a long-standing dearth of investment – by 1995 competitiveness had been regained, profitability restored, and French business was ready to confront European and, more importantly, global challenges. But these irrefutable economic achievements have come at a high social cost. French society at the end of the twentieth century was not the society which Mitterrand had set out to build in 1981; on the contrary, it was characterized by *la fracture sociale* between the haves and an ever-increasing number of have-nots, estimated at five million in 1995. These social inequalities, moreover, were repeated in other arenas, notably those (with which we are concerned here) of gender and ethnic origin.

The crux of the problem rests on the fact that the old system, erected in the post-war era of economic growth and social progress known as the 'Thirty Glorious Years', proved untenable in the new world order, characterized by globalization and growing uncertainty. But while excessive *dirigisme* by the central state has been dismantled over the Mitterrand years, the new structures adapted to the radically changed socio-economic order of the twenty-first century have yet to be defined. In the 1980s and 1990s, the fight for national competitiveness came to the fore, in France and elsewhere, as nations struggled to keep pace with changing global realities. But in this battle to remain competitive, governments failed to carry society with them. The key to the twenty-first century doubtless lies in part in the balance struck between national competitiveness on the one hand and social cohesion on the other; in part the problem is also one of lead and lag. Put simply, national prosperity can no longer be guaranteed by an all-powerful, centralizing state, which in France has withdrawn the better to serve the former (this is the intention, not necessarily the reality); but it may be some time before administration, business, trade unions and society as a whole, with high expectations fostered during the years of economic growth, are able to adapt to these harsher global realities. The return of the left to government in 1997, with promises of higher wages, new jobs, and a reduced working week, echoing those made in 1981, demonstrates very clearly that the French have little stomach for the much-needed and ultimately inevitable reforms (of the pension system, health system and welfare state) which lie ahead.

It is hoped that the (provisional) analyses contained in this book will contribute, however modestly, to the crystallization of history's final assessment of the man who was the irrefutable successor to de Gaulle, however unlikely that may have seemed in 1981, and of his fourteen years as president of France, years which were dramatic, diverse and paradoxical. They were also culturally rich, albeit often in unpredictable and sometimes unconventional ways. Eric Cahm's question, whether the new additions to the Paris skyline represent monuments to a man or monuments to an era, ultimately escapes a categorical answer for as the chapters in this book demonstrate, the two, Mitterrand the man and his years as president, blend together and to some extent resist being disentangled, engendering a mingled legacy, both aspects of which demand evaluation. When history's evaluation of Mitterrand is finally complete, his impact on French history and experience is likely to be perceived as substantial and wide-ranging. Although Mitterrand's blueprint for society and the economy was swiftly abandoned when put to the test of government, it is no small achievement to have accompanied (and guided) France for fourteen years on a hazardous journey from the former post-war era to the new, and much more frightening world order of the twenty-first century.

NOTES

1.   F. Mitterrand, New Year speech to the nation, 31 December 1994.
2.   J. Chirac, New Year speech to the nation, 31 December 1995.

Index

Abélès, Marc, 234, 239
Action et unité républicaine, 235
Action française, 218
Afghanistan
  Soviet invasion, 302
  war, 113
Africa, Mitterrand's policies, 116–17,
  122–3
agriculture, policies, 56
Air France, losses, 162
Alcatel Alsthom, losses, 162
Algeria
  Mitterrand's visit to, 116
  problems, 123
Algerians, racism against, 198
Alphandéry, Édouard Gerard
  (1943–), finance minister, 108
Amadieu, J.-F., 172
ancien régime, 191–2
Anciens combattants, 237, 238, 239
Andreotti, Giulio (1919–), 99
Andrieu, 224, 225
Andropov, Yuri Vladimirovitch
  (1914–84), 114
Annaud, Jean-Jacques, *L'Ours,* 283
Antenne 2, 287, 291
anti-Arab racism, 198
anti-Jewish racism, 198
anti-racism, in France, 198–213
Arafat, Yasser (1929–), 116
Arche de la Fraternité *see* Grande
  Arche
architecture, Mitterrand's interest in,
  16–17, 263–75
Armées 2000, 124
art, and heritage films, 278
ARTE channel, 294
Association François Mitterrand,
  activities, 243
Atlantic Alliance, 118
  and France, 112–14
  role, 121
Atlantic Council, meetings, 113
Attali, Jacques (1943–), 301

audiovisual industries, protection,
  294
Aulenti, Gae, 267
Auroux laws, 54, 56, 134, 170
  aims, 38
  impact, 174–8
autogestion see self-management
avances sur recettes, 279–80
Avignon, festival, 284
Avinin, Antoine, 220
AXA, collective bargaining, 180

Badinter, Robert (1928–), justice
  policies, 54
Bainville, 303
Balasko, Josiane, *Gazon maudit,* 285
Balladur, Édouard (1929–), 108, 137,
  289
  finance minister, 95
  memorandum on EMS reform,
    105
  and Mitterrand, 8
  privatization policies, 27
banks, crisis, 43
Banque de France, 92, 110
  control, 42–3
  cultural change, 107
  empowerment, 106–8
  independence, 105, 108
Banque nationale de Paris, chairman,
  161
Barbier, Dr., 239
bargaining, models, 170
Barrault, Dr., 238
Barre, Raymond (1924–), 26, 55, 57,
  190, 199
  economic policies, 95, 148
Barzach, Michèle, 190
Bastille Opera House *see* Opéra de la
  Bastille
Baudrillard, Jean (1929–), 307,
  309–10
Beaubourg *see* Centre national d'art
  et de culture Georges-Pompidou